What people are saying about the Keys of the Kingdom Bible...

"You're the modern Tyndale; beautiful, poetical translation, just like God intended."

"By far one of the most important works ever done in the world."

"ABSOLUTELY OUTSTANDING! ... It's as if my heart is being revived."

"So much easier to read and understand."

"This is gold."

"Now that's what I call a Bible!"

"You unscramble Paul very elegantly."

"Your uncompromising stand resonates with me."

"You should be preaching to tens of thousands."

"You should be preaching to millions."

"I'm loving it and understanding so much more than from my KJV."

"Absolutely Divine! Outstanding ~ Genius! Glory To Yahweh!"

"So sweet and wonderful."

"It practically sings to you."

"Thank you."

Published by
Filament Publishing Ltd
14, Croydon Road, Beddington
Croydon, Surrey CR0 4PA

+44(0)20 8688 2598
www.filamentpublishing.com

ISBN 978-1-915465-36-8 Amazon
© 2023 Christopher Sparkes

All rights reserved
No portion of this work may be copied
without the prior written permission
of the publisher.

The right to be identified as the translator of
this work has been asserted by
Christopher Sparkes in accordance with
the Designs and Copyright Act 1988
Section 77.

The Earth-Shaking Truth

Exposing the Greatest Scandal in Literary History
2023 edition

Christopher Sparkes

In companionship with

The Keys of the Kingdom Holy Bible

being made according to grammatical rules
and strict principles of internal harmony
from the true and best texts
of the God-authorized Greek Writings
of the prophets and apostles

Typeset in Garamond
For its Greek font this book uses the Unicode font.
For its Hebrew font it uses, with thanks, the GGTAmos2.ttf font,
available from www.FarAboveAll.com.

The Earth-Shaking Truth was first published in 2015

www.keysofthekingdombible.com

OTHER WORKS BY THE SAME AUTHOR
Biblical
The Eonian Life Bible New Testament, 2021 (Authoritize, 2021)
Keys of the Kingdom Holy Bible (Filament, 2022)

Poetry
Kissing Through Glass (Mighty Conqueror Productions, 1986)
One Word of Truth (Sons of Camus, 2011)
Counter Intelligence (www.secretpoetry.co.uk, 2015)

Academic
So You Want to Be a Writer? (with Ray Sparkes, Packard Publishing, 2004)
Grammar Without Groans (with Ray Sparkes, Packard Publishing, 2004)

I believe the divinely-inspired writings of the prophets and apostles of God and Christ,
from Genesis to Revelation, accurately translated,
from the best divinely-preserved manuscripts,
correctly interpreted, internally,
with impregnable organic Translating Laws and Translating Targets,
without regard for any particular tradition
other than that of the prophets and apostles themselves,
and understood literally where it is intended literally
with no signifier of a figure of speech,
a literal Adam and Eve, a real Garden of Eden,
and understood metaphorically where it is intended metaphorically
a figurative, fictional "Hades" in Luke 16\23;
God the Father, and Jesus His Son, being one in unity,
but not in person; God's faithfulness to the twelve tribes of Israel
now under a new and better Covenant,
and the proper identity of the scattered twelve tribes of the sons of Israel.

The writings of the prophets and apostles are the most important literary work in the world.

The Divine light-switches flicked on and blazed for me with glorious light the day it arose in my heart that I wanted to know the real messages of the prophets and apostles, rather than the orthodoxies I had accepted and that had been repeated for centuries.

In August 1997, with a fire inside me for the single extremely expensive pearl of one truth, and inspired by William Tyndale, also burning in my heart after I'd walked around Holy Island discussing him with a friend, I knew I had to make a translation to recover the buried truths of the prophets and apostles.

Over the 24 years since then, after many tens of thousands of hours labour and research, far more has become apparent than I dreamed of in my lakeside vision of 1997. I have restored much of the deliberate styles of the divinely-inspired oracles, reproducing phrases according to their grammatical forms and structures; internal harmonies of themes are recovered that have been long concealed in English translations; words and phrases are corrected that have never appeared properly in English; the books are arranged in their proper order, wrong works excluded. The effects of all these are illuminating. For the truth of God is "twenty hundred thousand times more joy" (Shakespeare) than the word of man.

Increasingly astounded and kept awake by all that I was discovering, I had to formulate strict translation codes, so that the bright-shining jewels of my findings could be justified, explained, and persuasive. These developed into my ORGANIC Translating Laws of Grammar, Internal Harmony, Logic, Research, Text. These stand as impregnable fortresses. The Research element reveals that much that is in this translation has been noted somewhere before, in lexicons, by expositors, or in works of less well-known translators, so that these recoveries of truth are, in fact, "the paths of old" (Jeremiah 6\16), brought at last together for the road to Zion. Nothing has ever really been lost, just buried by traditions of wayward orthodoxies.

These ORGANIC Translating Laws produce richer soils for life-giving fruits and crops. To my ORGANIC Translating Laws there could be added that of being constantly willing to be corrected, long and arduous labour, courage and patience. For Jesus said, "For who among you, wanting to build a tower, does not, having first sat down, calculate the expense, whether he has the things for completion?" (Luke 14\28).

As Tyndale made complaint of those who *quenched the sparkle of the prophets*, so might we make complaint of those who have doctored the language of angels. That there should be tampering with the silver syllables of the divine books, which millions have paid for with their lives, is the greatest scandal in literary history.

In *Keys of the Kingdom Holy Bible* translation, the paths of old are revived and brought to light once again. It is designed to make Bible reading clear, so that everything is made comprehensible for everybody, and without impediments of archaic language. Subject headings and footnotes and appendices provide guidance and explanations and elucidations, always in mind of giving the witness of God and making everything clear to everybody, especially new students of the word of God.

Keys of the Kingdom Holy Bible reveals the truth of the prophets and apostles which should be the only truth ever to have been broadcast.

Contents

	Page
Preface to the 2015 edition	i-xi
Preface to the 2023 edition	xii-xiv

Chapter
1. How and Why *Keys of the Kingdom Holy Bible* Was Made — 1
2. The Longest Odyssey — 21
3. A Bit of Biograph — 28
4. William Tyndale (poem) — 31
5. The Harmonium: A modern Pilgrim's Progress or Piers Plowman — 34
6. *Keys of the Kingdom Holy Bible* is the most accurate and reliable translation of the Hebrew and Greek Books of the prophets and apostles — 45
7. The Deep Word Archaeology Study Method concerning Acts 2\31 and John 1\3 — 49
8. John 11\26 with Genesis 3\4 — 54
9. Samuel and the Woman of Endor — 56
10. Those Pillars of Antiquity — 60
11. Crows (poem) — 63
12. The exaltation of 'the man of God' compared with post-Babylonian myths — 64
13. Grammatical Bedevilments and Myths in the KJV — 66
14. Why the Bible is True — 87
15. The Septuagint — 93
16. Some fool is saying Jesus didn't exist — 96
17. Ekklesia — 99
18. Elohim — 101
19. Concerning holy spirit and Holy Spirit: the two meanings of πνεῦμα ἅγιον (= *pneuma hagion*) — 103
20. Understanding Isaiah 9\6 — 116
21. The Development of the God-authorized Books Translated into English — 119
22. The Proper Order of the Books — 122
23. The Eons Displayed — 124
24. The True Meanings of αἰών (*aion*) and αἰώνιος (*aionios*) — 125
25. Twelve words mistranslated in the KJV which destroy the narrative of God's promises and faithfulness to the twelve tribes of Israel — 133
26. What are demons? — 152
27. Who or what is satan and the devil? — 161
28. Solomon and Esther — 179
29. Was the King James Bible of 1611 an unnecessary publication? The Catholic Douai-Rheims Bible of 1610 was very slightly better — 186
30. God Is Not Flesh: Concerning 1 Timothy 3\16 — 193

Select Bibliography — 197
Honours and Acknowledgments — 200

And *when* they prayed the place in which they were assembled together was shaken, and they were all filled with *the* holy spirit, and they spoke the word of God with boldness. ~ Acts 4\31

[25] Watch out you do not refuse the one speaking. For if these did not escape, having refused the one divinely instructing on the Earth, how much more ourselves in turning away from the one from *the* heavens, [26] Whose voice then shook the Earth? But now He has promised, saying, 'Yet once more I shake not only the Earth, but the heaven as well.'
[27] Now that 'Yet once more' signifies the removal of those things being shaken, as things having been created, so that those not being shaken might remain.
[28] In that case, receiving an unshakeable Kingdom, we should have merciful goodwill, by which we serve God acceptably, with reverence and godly fear. [29] For our God *is* indeed a consuming fire.
~ Hebrews 12\25-29

Yes, yes, of course – we all know that you can't poke a stick through the walls of a concrete tower, but here's something to think about: what if those walls are only a painted backdrop?
~ Aleksandr Solzhenitsyn, *The Oak and the Calf*, p. 10 (1980)

οὕτως	γὰρ	ἠγάπησεν	ὁ θεὸς	τὸν κόσμον	ὥστε	τὸν	υἱὸν	αὐτοῦ
so much	for	loved	God	the world	that	the	son	of Him

τὸν	μονογενῆ	ἔδωκεν	ἵνα	πᾶς	ὁ	πιστεύων	εἰς	αὐτὸν
the	only	He gave	in order that	everyone	the	believing	in	him

μὴ	ἀπόληται	ἀλλ'	ἔχῃ	ζωὴν	αἰώνιον
not	might suffer destruction	but	might have	life	eonian ~ **John 3\16**

καὶ	πᾶς	ὁ	ζῶν	καὶ	πιστεύων	εἰς	ἐμὲ	οὐ μὴ
and	everyone	the	living	and	believing	in	me	most certainly not

ἀποθάνῃ	εἰς	τὸν	αἰῶνα	πιστεύεις	τοῦτο	
will die	throughout	the	eon	do you believe	this	~ **John 11\26**

Abbreviations used in Keys of the Kingdom and here

Aram.	=	Aramaic
CLV	=	Concordant Literal Version
DSS	=	Dead Sea Scrolls
FAA	=	The Far Above All Bible Translation, Thomason (2020)
Gk.	=	Greek
Heb.	=	Hebrew
KJV	=	King James Version (1611)
KTK	=	Keys of the Kingdom Holy Bible (2023)
LIDT	=	The Literal Idiomatic Translation, Hal Dekker (online)
Lit.	=	Literally
LV	=	Latin Vulgate, a Latin translation
LXX	=	Septuagint, a Greek translation of the Old Testament (its dating debatable)
Ms.	=	Manuscript
MT	=	Masoretic (traditional) Text, a Hebrew text of the Old Testament, compiled between sixth and ninth centuries AD
NBD	=	New Bible Dictionary (1978)
RP	=	Robinson-Pierpont Text (2005), the text behind KTK New Testament
TCB	=	*The Companion Bible*, edited by Dr. EW Bullinger (1922)
TED	=	*The Emphatic Diaglott*, Benjamin Wilson (1864)
TELB	=	*The Eonian Life Bible New Testament*, Sparkes (2021 edition)
TR	=	Textus Receptus Greek Text, the text behind KJV's New Testament
YLT	=	Young's Literal Translation (1862)

✷

Preface to 2015 First Edition

✶

Historical Background
Around the time of the third and fourth centuries AD, bishops and scribes known as Church Fathers began to brew up various writings and creeds of their beliefs, and Jerome published his inaccurate Latin translation of the Bible known as the *Vulgate*. These writings formalized the new religion. They were a mangling of two things: stories and teachings from the Bible, mangled with the mysticism of ancient Babylonian worship. The new religion was used, used not as a declaration of the prophets and apostles, but as an imperial and despotic power, an empire founded on lies and violence. And it worked. And is still working.

In 1380 John Wycliffe, using the *Vulgate* as his source, no Greek text being available to him, published the first complete translation in English of the Bible: "In the beginning God made of nought heaven and earth". Wycliffe was hounded for his troubles. In 1526 William Tyndale, whose flag still flies, published his *Newe Testament*, which was the first complete translation of the New Testament into English made directly from a Greek manuscript. Tyndale, too, was hounded and then assassinated for his troubles. We are all deeply indebted to those two men for their work and courage, yet who even knows their names?

In 1611 King James's translating committee completed the *King James Version* (KJV, their so-called *Authorised Version*), which also was an instrument for imperial power, an eirenicon to try to unite religious factions so, too, an intention of extending kingly power.

Since 1380 there have been around 150 or more English translations, an average of nearly one in every four years. Yet not one of these translations has achieved a true and pure parallel of the Hebrew and Greek which underlie the books we know as the Word of God, or the Bible. Nor then, because of that, have they been able to unveil all the truths of God. On the contrary: even the best of them have unashamedly backed up the doctrines of the creeds of the Church Fathers and the Latin *Vulgate* translation. (Wycliffe and Tyndale have to be wholly excused: they were facing unimaginable hostility and it cost them; Tyndale was being pursued; all Wycliffe had in front of him was the corrupt *Vulgate*.) The guiding star for a translator is that the finished work should translate back into the original language. English Bibles do not do that. Nor does the fourth century Latin *Vulgate*; nor do other European language translations I have looked at. Apparently even earlier translations, in Syriac, Coptic and Latin, also suffered at the hands of poor translators. This failure represents the greatest literary scandal of all time.

Readers and seekers have been cheated. The world has been forked up mixtures, sold strange fires. The world has been held back from the straight facts and the magnificent promises of the one true God.

Other than a few heroic torch-bearers, for century after century, generation after generation, decade after decade, translation after translation has, for the most part, done little more than, in Thomas Hardy's withering phrase, "advance / Sound parish views" (poem, "The Conformers"; the irony of "advance" and "Sound"). The achievement of all this underwhelming heritage has been pulled off by the over-bearing dark wizardry of the wording of creeds whose gravity has impressed the minds of men more than the writings delivered by the Angel of God. If this were not so, bar the heroic torch-bearers, how is it that the blunders of darkness are still among us stronger than ever? This should really be no surprise: this age we are in is described by the apostle Paul as "the present eon of evil" and "this eon of darkness" (Galatians 1\2, Ephesians 6\12), and "*the* day of man" (1 Corinthians 4\3). And "the god of this Eon" has "blinded the minds of those unbelieving, so that the brightness of the radiant gospel of the Christ, who is *the* image of God, might not beam out to them" (2 Corinthians 4\4).

The English Bibles should not be considered as independent literary works, but as works of translation. That is how they must be assessed. It surprises me, as I speak to even highly educated people, how few realize that the Old Testament is written in Hebrew (with small portions of Aramaic) and that the New Testament is in Greek. The analysis of the forms of these Hebrew and Greek words of the prophets and apostles, in their contexts, other uses, and their alignment with wider themes – by means of my fourfold principles of the Science of Deep Grammar, Transcendent Logic, Internal Harmony, and Diamond-Mining Research – led me to discover the scandal that the translations are full of grammatical bedevilments. They twist and falsify nouns and adjectives, verbs and adverbs, and prepositions; punctuation is fidgeted; capitalizations are wrongly inserted; words and passages taken out; words added; words changed; words left untranslated; books shuffled haphazardly; the past eons muddled; and at John 11\26 the translations put the mind and words of the serpent spoken in the Garden of Eden into the mouth of Jesus the Messiah. All these in honour of post-Babylonian Myth and Magik.

Perhaps nothing more symbolizes the post-Babylonian poison mixture than the dubious claim that a mosaic from a third century tomb, found underneath St. Peter's Basilica in Rome, portrays Jesus as the sun-god Sol riding in the heavens on his chariot.[1] This mixture has never gone away: it lingers in translations.

Everyone can excuse blunders. But a thousand blunders, destroying every major doctrine of the prophets and apostles, not even adhering to grammatical forms and structures, in fact altering them, that has to be something else. Do that to a commercial document and you'd be sacked. Do that to a legal document and you'd be sued or even jailed for fraud. Then you would think that with around 150 English translations since 1380 the translations would get better, smoothing out the creases, but the reverse has happened. You wonder if some authors have even looked at the underlying Hebrew and Greek. Some versions I have seen can only be denounced as freaks.

The secret behind the cover-up is this: First, translators have been overshadowed by ghosts of the creeds and the so-called Church Fathers and of the Latin *Vulgate* and of the later articles and confessions. The Council of Trent (1545-1563) stated of the *Vulgate* that "no one is to dare or presume to reject it under any pretext whatever". And second, translators arrive at the Greek or Hebrew text with conscious and hasty expectations, deposits already festering in their minds from what they have read before in other translations. (I was guilty of the same once until, in reading Bullinger, I was drawn to look at the underlying languages.) So real meanings and internal harmony are not investigated with extensive vigour over a long period of time. (Where are their deep and laboured expositions? Who are they even?) Orthodoxy has chewed the cables, like plagues of rats.

Here, beginning with the Church Fathers, is the plot outlining how the truth has been concealed from the people, leaving the world in a dense fog:

<u>Step 1</u>: Mix it all up with Babylonian mythology to allure the people by deceiving them that they will not have to give up their polythiestic worship superstition, their never dying false hope, and their eternal destinies.

---

2. Or Saturnalia. Ishtar (Acts 12\4 in KJV). Dagon fish-god mitres.

Step 2: Institutionalize it into a formal religion with compulsory creeds.
Step 3: Translate it into Latin; paraphrase if necessary; slam in a bit of inkslinging here and there; all in order to retain the Babylonian mythology, and to keep it in the hands of rulers.
Step 4: Impose allegorical interpretation.
Step 5: Ban it from being translated into any contemporary language, and death to anyone who tries.
Step 6: Order that the Latin translation is the official word of God, to keep it safely distanced from the people.
Step 7: After William Tyndale Englished it for the "boy who driveth the plough", relax the law against translating but supersede Tyndale and recover its distance from the people by turning Tyndale's English into official translations with Latinized words and phrases and structures, which the "boy who driveth the plough" would struggle to understand. Retain the Babylonian mythology. Add extra difficulty by breaking up the flow and sense by making each numbered verse into a new paragraph. Appoint it "to be read in churches", that is, not at home privately.
Step 8: Institutionalize it further with more confessions, creeds and articles.
Step 9: Introduce mutilated Greek manuscripts. Trivialize the language. Make even further paraphrase. Retain the Babylonian mythology.
Step 10: Flood the world with multitudinous versions to bring still further confusion, each with a new gimmick. Retain the Babylonian mythology.

John's Gospel has suffered worst at the hands of these scribes and translators.

Plagues and destruction for perverting the truth of God
These processes have to be considered, weighed. Are they conscious, wilful "evil reasonings" (Matthew 15\19), or stubbornness, laziness, hastiness, or ignorance, failings at the job, the inexpressible difficulty of it? We cannot really know. When they translated the Hebrew גי הנם (= *ge hinnom*) correctly as "the Valley of Hinnom", but its Greek counterpart γέεννα (= *gehenna*) horrendously and horrifically as "hell", then you have to wonder: men hung over and deranged with echoes of "fire of this world to save you from the fire of the next"; purposeful threats to dissenters, non-conformists. On the other hand, when they blundered the phrase εἰς τὸν αἰῶνα at 1 Corinthians 8\13 as "while the world standeth", with only the word "the" matching the Greek, and when they blundered the two phrases οὐ μὴ (= *ou me*) and εἰς τὸν αἰῶνα (= *eis ton aiona*) at John 11\26 as only "never" for the five words, and "never" is not even in those two phrases, what can you conclude but that they did not have any idea at all what εἰς τὸν αἰῶνα means? (It means "throughout the eon".) So rather than labour and labour over it for years (not that εἰς τὸν αἰῶνα is that difficult!), they put anything they could think of which fitted with their already-held belief system.

When they translated the phrase ζωὴ αἰώνιος (= *zoe aionios*), "eonian life", as "eternal life", perhaps the ghost of Babylon haunting the *Vulgate*'s faulty "vita aeterna" was hovering over them. When they capitalized "Word" at John 1\1, to make readers think of Jesus, rather than what it is, the word of the gospel, it is at the least bordering suspicion, looking for opportunities to force polytheism. When they put "were made" for ἐγένετο (= *egeneto*) at John 1\3, instead of "arose" when ἐγένετο is not even the word for make or create, smuggling in a plural passive verb for what is a singular active verb, and it gives the silly impression that Jesus was the Creator rather than God, then, in twisting verbs like that, was something purposeful and wrong driving them? And when at 1 Corinthians 10\11 and Hebrews 9\26 they turned αἰώνων (= *aionon*), "eons", plural, into "world", singular, and their general insistence on putting αἰών as "world" found them out (since they could not sensibly write "the end of the worlds"), were they, in perverting the sense like that, making deliberate falsifications, "evil reasonings", because they simply refused to believe that there are "coming eons" (Ephesians 2\7)? One day, if they are "members of the resurrection" (Luke 20\36) – and God only knows – they will have to answer for themselves.

From the moment I began reading the Books of the one true God in 1979 it was with immediate and obsessive fascination. However, I would say, though, that I really began voraciously *studying* them, as opposed to voraciously *reading* them, in 1991. As a friend said to me many years ago, there is a vast difference between *reading* the Bible and *studying* the Bible. Not a day passes in which my studies and writings do not make some advance. Understanding and knowledge are always progressive.

I know the inexpressible difficulty of the work. I know the impossibility of achieving full perfection in making a translation of the vast and varied collection of writings of the prophets and apostles. I know too the many years it takes to come to understand the internal harmonies of the themes, and how this work cannot be done in the space of a single decade. In such loyalties to the God-authorized writings, *The Eonian Life Bible* translation has gone through hundreds and hundreds of revisions and checks and editings, as I have constantly looked to make improvements. And continue to do so. I have already made quite a large number of enhancements and corrections to the first edition. And I do not expect to stop making enhancements any time soon. And if there are corrections to be made, I am confident they will be minor ones. As I repeatedly say, I want a translation fit for the Sanctuary of God. The others are not fit.

I do not know, therefore, how translators have had the nerve to make such mind-bending grammatical twists and falsifications. It stands written at the end of Revelation that plagues and destruction face those who dare to mess around with the holy writings:

I myself make the testimony to everybody hearing the oracles of the prophecy of this Scroll: If anybody should add to them, God will add to him the plagues written in this Scroll. [19] And if anybody should take away from the oracles of the Scroll of this prophecy, may God take away his share from the Tree of Life, and from the Holy City *and* the things written in this Scroll.
~ Revelation 22\18-19

Now that is in the context of the prophecies of Revelation; however, it illustrates the extreme gravity of mangling the words of the prophets and apostles. And Peter, in the context of the day of judgement and the burning of the elements of this Earth, writes of those who twist Paul's letters and the other holy writings:

our richly loved brother Paul also, with the wisdom given to him, wrote to you, [16] as also in all *his* letters, speaking in them about these things, among which there are some things hard to be understood which the untaught and unstable make perversions of, as *they do* also to the other Writings, to their own destruction. ~ 2 Peter 3\15-16

Destruction is the penalty. For, "we are not as the hoi polloi [many], making money by corrupting the oracle of God" (2 Corinthians 2\17).

Despite the bedevilments in our translations, it is true that the light of Jesus has still shone through and people have found salvation and divine knowledge and wisdom unavailable anywhere else. It's not all bad. And many words and phrases in the translations are truly excellent and have helped me with passages where I've struggled to achieve clarity. But that does not change the fact that a dark curtain has been pulled over major themes – and that the truths of God have been concealed.

*

How and Why
Now, though, the blunders of darkness have been corrected and reversed. The full dazzling sunlight of the truth of God and Jesus, as written in the prophets and apostles, is declared to the world. "The people who were sitting in darkness have seen a splendid light, and for those who were sitting in a region and dark shadow of death a light has arisen" (Matthew 4\16).

The discovery of the blunders of ancient Babylonian darkness in the translations, and the consequent exciting re-discovery of the Earth-shaking truths of God and Jesus, now open anew the Earth's vast and greatest treasure, richer and more precious than ten thousand mountains of gold and silver, sapphires and rubies. In the writings delivered by angels and the God-authorized prophets and apostles are found true knowledge and wisdom, a status now in Jesus, and unimaginably wonderful inheritances.

Such a work – re-examining all the themes of the prophets and apostles and of Jesus, and expressing these findings in a translation – has never before been undertaken. That is how the darkness and impurity have been allowed to continue so long. The blunders in the translations are not about inconsequential or minor matters. In fact, the more major the theme, the more the blunders. These include the vision of the eons, the gospel promises, who God is, who Jesus is, who the Holy Spirit is, creation, death, election, man's destiny, and man's structural identity.

Not everything that I have brought to light is new. No destinies of Heaven and Hell; death means death and not migrating souls; the fact of the coming eon; eonian life; the difference between Jesus' ἐπιφάνεια (= *epiphaneia*) and his later παρουσία (= *parousia*) (see chart, Eonian Document 19); these are variously in the works of Bullinger and Sellers, and I learned those initially from them. And no Heaven, no Hell, no migrating souls have been excellently told by many others as well, in an underground struggle against the ancient force of demonic myth.

On the other hand, much else in *The Eonian Life Bible* is new. But all these things together have not appeared in any translation. Nor has any translation buried the diseased bones of the mythology, or unveiled all the magnificent truth. These failures have held the world back.

Now that the writings of the prophets and apostles have been translated and explained in purity and truth, and the gospel promise of "eonian life" and life "throughout the eon" is at last revived and can be unveiled, the eonian gates can swing open, and the promised eon of the kingdom of God can commence.

This book, *The Earth-Shaking Truth*, is published in companionship with *The Eonian Life Bible* translation. In its grammatical purity, *The Eonian Life Bible* unveils the deep truths and visions of the prophets and apostles and of Jesus the Messiah – and the true gospel of God and Jesus: the promises of an incorruptible body, a mind capable of conquering every violation, and life throughout the eons which are coming.

The book in your hands, *The Earth-Shaking Truth*, explains why a pure translation was needed and the details of my working processes. I could not have more laid bare my working method. *How and Why The Eonian Life Bible Translation Was Made*, Eonian Document 76, lays out my working with interlinear versions, grammars, and lexicons. And the method is explained in depth with examples in *The Deep Word Archaeology Study Method*, Chapter 7, the name I call my linguistic approach. The method is not new. I am indebted to men who have gone before me: the compilers of lexicons and concordances (mainly English Victorians) which have been a help beyond measure; to Dr EW Bullinger whose works first alerted me; and to Otis Q Sellers (an American). Bullinger and Sellers were pioneers in the same approach; it leads to conclusions quite different to the broad ways of popular religion.

The other Eonian Documents in this book give some extended examples of translated passages and their wider thematic effects and implications; and a few give some personal history. These were written over a long period of time and so vary in styles and speech mark conventions.

★

John 8\58 as an example
Anybody can obtain the lexical works praised in the first Eonian Document in this book. Anybody can download the Robinson-Pierpont Byzantine Textform 2005, compiled by Maurice A Robinson and William G Pierpont, the Greek text on which my translation is based. I believe it to be the best Greek text so far available to us. (My very minuscule quibbles with it are discussed on pages viii-xii of *The Eonian Life Bible*.) And anybody can check for themselves if the grammatical things I say are true.

Is the verb γενέσθαι (= *genesthai*) at John 8\58 really an infinitive, "to come", "to arise", "to appear", and not a past tense verb "was"? *The Eonian Life Bible* has Jesus say: "Before Abraham is to rise, I Am", his emphasis being, then, on Abraham's resurrection. That could also be: "In advance of Abraham to rise, I Am". This verb γενέσθαι appears many times, for example: "these things have to come to pass" (Matthew 24\6, Mark 13\7, Luke 21\9, Revelation 4\1); "to become fishers of men" (Mark 1\17); "to become eminent" (Mark 10\43); "*when* these things begin to arise" (Luke 21\28); "are these things able to arise?" (John 3\9); "Do you want to become whole?" (John 5\6); "before it is to arise" (John 13\19, 14\29); "to become a Christian" (Acts 26\28); "things which must be soon to arise" (Revelation 1\1, 22\6). Et cetera. All these infinitives have a strong future aspect. Bagster's *Analytical Greek Lexicon* describes γενέσθαι as "aor. 2, infin.". Yes then, infinitive. Robinson's and Pierpont's *Byzantine Parsed Text* describes it as "V-2ADN" (Verb – 2nd Aorist Middle Deponent Infinitive). Yes, infinitive. And DF Hudson's *Teach Yourself New Testament Greek* (English Universities Press Ltd., 1960), says: "The Aorist Infinitive ... does not refer to Past Time" (p. 54). Yes, infinitive.

Why, then, at John 8\58 do the KJV and other translations have γενέσθαι as "was", an imperfect past tense verb? The KJV has Jesus saying: "Before Abraham was, I am". This gives the senseless and terrible delusion that Jesus was around before the days of Abraham, backing up the dark and mystical creeds of polytheism. Lying about Christ. Creating "another Jesus" (2 Corinthians 11\4). Who would have noticed it was a cheat if you had not checked the Greek? You see how it's done. How the ancient mythologies have been perpetuated. A phantasmagoria. A swirl of smoke. There, Post-Babylonian Magik, right in front of your eyes!

The dusty inheritance
Those Alchemists of the words of God ... Changing them into fools' gold. The oracles of God delivered to men by angels authorized from God's presence, alchemized in order to form a religion. Constantine extending his empire by religion, King James his kingdom. Dead men's bones. Political flattery. Propaganda. Setting up world power. "All these things I will give you" (Matthew 4\9, Luke 4\6), the world power temptation offered to Jesus. Mythology, the painted backdrop of worldly kingdoms, founded on violence and lies.

How to create new gods and goddesses. Zeus, Apollo, Posiedon, Hermes, Pallas Athena, Hades, Hephaestus, Jove, Mars, Mercury, Venus, Mary, the Angel of God, Jesus ... Do it by invention and grammar. Nobody will notice.

The Israelites of old turned away from Yahweh Elohim and followed the practices of Baal worship. The prophet Isaiah grieved over the idolatrous serving of "other lords": "Oh Yahweh our Elohim, *other* lords besides You have had dominion over us, *but* by You only will we call on Your name" (Isaiah 26\13).

The God-authorized and God-approved writings of the prophets and apostles are not a collection of religious clichés for hooligan theologians of this eon of evil and darkness to play loose with for the benefits of their formalized religion. The angel Gabriel told the young Maria, "I am Gabriel, who stands in the presence of God, and I was authorized to speak to you and to announce to you the good news of these things" (Luke 1\19). That single moment lights up the sacredness of the 66 books from Genesis to Revelation. And the Angel of God said to the apostle and prophet John, "Write *it* down, for these oracles are true and faithful" (Revelation 21\5). They are from God. "If anybody speaks, let him speak in harmony with *the* oracles of God" (1 Peter 4\11). *The Eonian Life Bible: New Testament* labours to provide an honest and accurate representation of the underlying Greek text of the oracles of God's servants.

Well, someone might ask, has not any good come out of the translations? Yes yes yes, where they have been translated *accurately*, and with intelligent activity, many billion-folds of divinely-activated goodness which no man could ever begin to count! How many men and women and children have found the love and light of God and Christ, the mercy and compassion? How many of William Tyndale's ploughboys have understood more of the Scriptures than his savage murderers in the church? "How sweet the name of Jesus sounds in a believer's ear!" And they have kept the Bible in the public consciousness. But where there have been inaccuracies and "evil reasonings" and bedevilments and the black arts of disinformation, a great deal of harm has been done against the truth. Delusions and idolatries have fogged the world in stupors, the true gospel of Jesus smothered, God blasphemed, the eonian purposes of God delayed. Divisions among believers.

Some lusty and atrabilious upholders of errant, dry and impotent tradition, though, will want to defend the past (jobs, income, reputations ...). But, as I say on page 7, I would first turn such people's attentions to picking at all the other translations' manifold failures. And I would say to them, save your pens and go out and enjoy the sunshine.

The truths of God have been obscured for over 1,600 years by the mangling of two sources, poisoning the sacred river. This work is not to be stirred into the cauldron of popular religion. *The Eonian Life Bible: New Testament* is a departure from those 1,600 years of mixing strange fire. This is a declaration reviving the truth and vision of the prophets and apostles.

Over the last 24 years I have had a mass of untangling to complete, unpicking the locks of the prison-house of the past, tearing down the dark curtain of 1,600 years of misrule.

Anybody with a KJV can deceive you that Jesus was around before Abraham. John 1\3 says that all the things concerning Jesus arose through the direct oracle of God: "Everything <u>arose</u> through it, and apart from it there <u>arose</u> not even one thing which <u>has arisen</u>." Not so the KJV: that so manages to bend this verse as to imply even that Jesus is the Creator God: "All things <u>were made</u> by him; and without him <u>was</u> not any thing <u>made</u> that <u>was made</u>." Apart from the ugly phrasing, never mind that the verb ἐγένετο (= *egeneto*) – represented by the underlined words – is a singular active verb. Well, why not put it as passive, even a plural passive verb, so that it says exactly what the translators want it to say? There, a swirl of smoke and ... Whoosh! Another phantasmagoria of post-Babylonian Magik, right in front of your eyes! So I am left with the business of explaining why that KJV rendering is a trick, falsifying the words of God. And that is one of a thousand things and more. The need for the complexity of some of my grammatical and logical discussions, analyses of the forms of words and themes, are not therefore my fault. It all has to be done, to brush aside the trash, clearing the way for truth.

And, while on the subject of blame, where do the fingers of castigation point? The Church Fathers and the translators. It is they who have mixed the poison and polluted the sacred river. Blind leaders of the blind.

This generation, on the brink of change, on the eve of the Messianic eon, has been left a dust-covered inheritance. Now the dust is blown off, and the truths about God and Jesus, about the Angel of God, about the eons, the resurrections, and the gospel promise of an incorruptible mind and body for life throughout the coming eon, are brought back into the light and are seen in their sparkling brilliance, brighter than mountains of priceless jewels.

Can there really be three called God, three gods, yet who, it is said, are all one? Is that not a senseless oxymoron, foolish? Hebrews 3\2 speaks of Jesus being "faithful to Him Who created him", the word "created" being ποιέω (= *poyeo*). God created Jesus by a miracle, as every schoolchild knows. Father, Son, and Holy Spirit: God, and man, and angel.

Can man's destiny really be in Heaven, in outer space, even though God planted Adam and Eve on the Earth; even though David says, "The heavens, *yes*, the heavens, *belong to* Yahweh, but the Earth He has given to the sons of Adam" (Psalm 11\16); even though Jesus says, "they will inherit the land" (Matthew 5\5)? Does not man in outer space for ever sound a very silly idea? And how would he get there? Anyway, Jesus is coming to the Earth, so what will those spiritual astronauts be doing far away up in outer space, away from Jesus who is our Lord and brother? Never is it written that man's destiny is in Heaven. It's an invention. That's all. Somebody's evil dream. Dreaming – scheming – of a future in Heaven, the temporary hiding-place of God and Jesus, is the same proud dream for which the proud figure, the King of Babylon, is rebuked by the prophet: "And you said in your heart, / 'I will mount up into the heavens; / I will exalt my throne above the stars of El [God], / and I will sit on the mount of the assembly / in the recesses of the north; / I will ascend above the heights of the clouds; / I will be like Elyon [the Most High]' " (Isaiah 14\13-14). How terrible for man's heart to be like his! We who believe the one true God have been entrusted with the divine documents concerning the secrets of inner peace and concerning world regime change on this Earth, now and in the eons to come – but to water it down and pretend instead that we all flutter off to outer space is a weak-liver'd rejection of responsibility. Blame the Church Fathers. It is they who brewed up this staggering and mystifying hooch that has made the world reel and forget that the Earth where our feet are planted is our home. "And I saw ... a new Earth ..." But even before the time of the new Earth, Jesus and the angels are coming down to Earth. When God Himself is in the New Jerusalem on the renewed Earth (Revelation 21\3, 21\7, 21\22, 22\3), then Heaven will be evacuated.

And could there really be a place called "Hell"? Where would it be? Ah, somewhere deeply mystical... And how could anyone be burning in torments for ever? Throw a body in fire and it perishes. Hell is a dirty fiction, maligning the God of love. Who would drive his own son into hot torment, never ever ending? What's the point? The hatred that mysticism has for its opponents and detractors, I suppose. The well-known salvation and warning passages speak not of "Hell" but of the "destruction of ungodly men":

[13] Enter ithrough the narrow gate, for wide *is* the gate and broad the road that leads off into destruction, and those entering in through it are many. [14] How narrow, *though*, *is* the gate and constricted the road leading into life, and those finding it are few. ~ Matthew 7\13-14

[16] For God so much loved the world that He gave His only Son, in order that everyone believing in him might not suffer destruction, but might have eonian life. ~ John 3\16

[7] But the skies and the Earth now are stored up by His oracle, being reserved for fire until *the* day of judgement and destruction of ungodly men. ~ 2 Peter 3\7

And could the body really have an unscrewable ghost thing attached to it, departing at death, to go through the stars to outer space, or down somewhere to a "Hell" of torment? Is this unscrewable ghost thing, called "soul", not a hatred of God's truth that "the wages of violation *are* death" (Romans 6\23), and a hatred of the fact of resurrection? God did not make man so.

And does anybody who believes the oracles of God need to go through rituals to be complete in Christ? The apostle Paul says they are already "having been made complete ... in him who is the fountainhead" (Colossians 2\10), and that "Every passage *is* given by inspiration of God, and *is* profitable for teaching, for conviction, for correction, for discipline in righteousness, in order that the man of God can be complete" (2 Timothy 3\16-17). The rituals, then, are outdated for this eon, of imaginary importance, and they devalue what is written.

And do any of the three gods of popular religion really live inside the fat of men's bellies? Gods inside humans? What a funny idea! Who ever thought to make that notion up? How could they fit? Why would they want to be there? And how could they get into millions of other people at the same time as well? Peter says of Jesus: "Heaven must receive [him] until *the* times of restoration of all things" (Acts 3\21). God and Jesus are in Heaven; they are not distributed bits of ghost things living inside humans, like babies in a womb. What a horrible devaluing of who God and Jesus are.

There is truly nothing in all the oracles of God to back up any of these strange and mystical ideas, all of which would have been curious anathemas to the prophets and apostles.

No, my friends, all those are nothing but a smoking swirl of deluding post-Babylonian Myth and Magik, priestcraft. And they will not endure.

★

The real inheritance: *"incorruptible and undefiled and unfading"*
The purpose of this book – and, of course, of my translation – is to help everybody understand the truths of God and Jesus, and to find "eonian life" which is the true salvation and inheritance in Jesus, deliverance from the penalty of destruction.

If you are "a member of the resurrection" (Luke 20\36) and living or raised at the moment when the new eon opens, you will be "changed". If you believe and you die before the eon, you will go into the grave and be resurrected at its opening, "Christ's firstfruit" (1 Corinthians 15\23), "raised in incorruption" (1 Corinthians 15\42):

> It is sown in corruption:
> it is raised in incorruption;
> [43] it is sown in dishonour:
> it is raised in radiance;
> it is sown in weakness:
> it is raised in power;
> [44] it is sown a natural body:
> it is raised a spiritual body. ~ 1 Corinthians 15\42-44

And, Paul says, whether alive or raised, "we will all be changed":

[50] Now I say this, brothers, that flesh and blood are not able to inherit *the* Sovereign Rulership of God. Nor does corruption inherit incorruption. [51] Hear now, I tell you a mystery: we will not all be put into sleep, but we will all be changed, [52] in an atom-like instant, in a twinkling of an eye, at the last trumpet. For a trumpet will sound, and the dead will be raised as incorruptible, and we will be changed. [53] For this corruption must put on incorruption, and this mortality put on immortality. [54] So when this corruption will have put on incorruption, and this mortality will have put on immortality, then the oracle which has been written will come about:

> Death was swallowed up in victory.
> [55] Where, oh death, *is* your sting?
> Where, oh grave, *is* your victory? ~ 1 Corinthians 15\50-55

And then believers, the Sons and Daughters of God, will inherit life throughout the coming eons. They will "most certainly not die throughout the eon" (John 11\26). This is "eonian life" (John 3\16). This is the "inheritance incorruptible and undefiled and unfading". Peter says, "Exalted *be* the God and Father of our Lord Jesus Christ, Who, in harmony with His abundant mercy, has regenerated us into a vigorous hope through *the* resurrection of Jesus Christ from *the* dead, into an inheritance incorruptible and undefiled and unfading" (1 Peter 1\3-4).

Believe God. Believe Jesus. Believe the prophets and apostles. This book and *The Eonian Life Bible* translation unpicks all the Myth and Magik for you, and bring to light the truth of one God; creation; death; "the man Christ Jesus" (1 Timothy 2\5) who was "born out of a woman" (Galatians 4\4); Jesus' resurrection; the Angel of God who is the Holy Spirit; the coming 490 years; the coming 1,000 years; then the "day of God" and the new Earth; the authority of what's written; the gospel of an incorruptible life throughout the coming eons; the apostles' authorizations (Matthew 28\19-20, Mark 16\15-18); the promised exaltation and destiny; the work of the believer today. All this so that you can be complete in Jesus and inherit full life in the coming Eon.

And through Jesus we can be purified and have a clean conscience. Jesus died and took the punishment for all your violations. In Jesus "we have redemption by means of his blood, the forgiveness of violations, in harmony with the outflowing wealth of [God's] merciful goodwill" (Ephesians 1\7).

I hope that all readers of this book are drawn into the sunlight of truth and lifted with a vigorous hope in Jesus, "the Saviour of the world" (John 4\42, 1 John 4\14, John 3\17). Whoever believes in him "will most certainly not die throughout the eon" (John 11\26). Indestructible! 490 years of living in that eon; then Jesus returns; then 1,000 years of him on the Earth; then the new Earth and the sons of Israel will be with God and Jesus in the New Jerusalem and in that day, "the day of God" (2 Peter 3\12, Revelation 21\12-13), they will see God and reign with Jesus as their first-honoured brother over the other peoples on the new Earth.

Whoever thirsts for "the fountain of the water of life ..." (Revelation 22\17).

"May Your kingdom come ..."

cjs, October 2015
revised slightly May 2019

Preface to the 2023 Edition

✶

The purpose of *The Earth-Shaking Truth* is to display how the messages of the prophets and apostles of God and Christ should be translated properly in the English language; that they have not been this is the greatest scandal in literary history; to demonstrate copious blunders of the King James Bible; that these copious blunders have cast that book's dark shadow over other translations; how they have been corrected; that these corrections can be confidently proclaimed; to lay bare proper methods for translating work; and to declare my vision and campaign for a pure and undefiled translation that is honouring to God and Christ and fit to be taken into the Sanctuary of God.

Never is there a day when this work does not progress.

Intense study of the word of God is not just an academic pursuit. It is a spiritual work and labour towards understanding the fullness of God's revelation, with the purpose of knowing more of God and Christ, so knowing how to live. Spiritually regenerated Christians understand this. Only they discern deep spiritual things (1 Corinthians 2\12-14). They spend their life devoted to studying and obeying the word of God.

So it is with translating the word of God. It is a life's commitment. A commitment to find pure words. The words are loaded with doctrinal implications, multiple in themes, and laced with other themes, divinely internally harmonious. It is a job for men of the spirit, not men of the flesh who think they understand. It is done not for pay – I've spent tens of thousands of pounds and tens of thousands of hours on this project – but for love of the word of God in purity and truth. It is done with the cloak of integrity. The church translations have not been done by the right people. The results are pale. (It must be said that there is a handful of versions which are much better, done by believers, individuals rather than committees, but they failed to reach notoriety.)

In 1997 I embarked on my commitment to translate the Books of God. Over the last 26 years new lights have flooded in – from my own studies; other writers; from friends – dazzling lights, heavens beyond my original vision when I first understood that the English translations are riddled with inaccuracies and textual errors. I remember writing, three years after I'd begun the work, "The Scriptures have fallen into the hands of the false". I did not understand then a fraction of what I understand now. I press on ...

What was behind the King James Bible was James's desire to unite Protestants and Catholics, an impossible and naïve intent. In other words, to extend and stabilise the King's empire: echoes of Emperor Constantine. It failed. The whole purpose of the Reformation was a break. A break between Rome and the newly arisen Protestantism, making division. Did James not understand that? Independent Christians were fleeing from James's translators who were inquisitors, seeing the best Christians tortured and murdered by the state. The best Christians, the hungriest for righteousness, did not want – and do not want – the orthodoxies of Protestantism and Romanism. Hungry Christians no longer want to be trapped in orthodoxy and tradition. They're asking questions. And they want answers.

It is not an exaggeration to say, the King James Bible is flawed in every major doctrine. Why do regenerate Christians accept and even revere the works of such unregenerate men? The body of Christ has been in the captivity of these false translators.

As for the Revised Version (1881) of Wescott and Hort – with its new Greek text – its purpose stated by them was "to rid the church of that vile text", by which they meant the Byzantine Greek Textus Receptus Text underlying the King James Bible's New Testament. Why was the divinely preserved Greek text "vile"? Instead, those unbelieving men imposed mutilated texts of their own concoction, one of them, Sinaiticus, now denounced by some scholars as a tea-strained fraud. I have read the works of those men. They were openly hostile to the truth of Christ. They took the word of God even further away from the truth than the King James Bible translators had done.

Why have Dr EW Bullinger and Otis Q Sellers been the only two men before Sparkes to draw any deep attention to translation accuracy, describing in their writings many necessary corrections and enhancements? It is to their pioneering work that I am indebted.

My intention to discover the truth of the prophets and apostles of God and Christ is not the same drive that was behind the King James Bible and the Revised Version. Their results were PROCESSED food, lab meat. The word of God is ORGANIC food from the gardens of God, fresh every morning, real meat from the pastures of healthy soils and meadows.

Over the quarter of a century of this work I have developed ORGANIC principles of translation. 3 TRANSLATING TARGETS: Accuracy; Clarity; Literariness. And to work towards those targets, 5 TRANSLATING LAWS: Grammar; Internal Harmony; Research; Logic; Text. Then this Deep Word Archaeology, as I call it, is for results of restoring and reflecting 1. THE DIVINE STRUCTURE, the right books in the right order and groupings. 2. THE DIVINE LITERARY BEAUTY, its literary and linguistic devices. 3. THE DIVINE TRUTH. The whole magnificence.

The fullness of the working method is described in Chapter 7. It is explained in much further detail – with many examples – in the preface to *Keys of the Kingdom Holy Bible* (first edition; that preface is also on the website). These ORGANIC principles keep bringing to light the grammatical forms and structures and the literary styles of the prophets and apostles. I want the translation of the word of God written accurately, clearly, and beautifully, bringing to life new flowers of spring, enhancing every valley.

Perfect transmission from one language into another is not a possible concept, because of their differing grammars and idioms. However, recovery of grammatical forms and structures and styles is possible to the extent that they reflect the truth and beauty of the original; to the extent that a translation can translate back into similar parallel styles and the same meanings as in the original language or languages. In doing this, it is possible to retrieve the whole truth of the prophets and apostles of God and Christ: ORGANIC food. This has not been done before in the English language. The intentions have not been to reproduce the grammatical forms and styles of the prophets and apostles. The results have been PROCESSED food. Nor, in the popular church translations, has the drive been to create a work that would translate back into the original languages. Nor, in those translations, has the expressed intention been to recover the deep truths of the prophets and apostles. The results of these work such as the King James Bible and the Revised Version – and their derivatives – have created the greatest scandal in literary history, processing the word of God.

Since the first edition of *The Earth-Shaking Truth* was published eight years ago, the complete translation, *The Keys of the Kingdom Holy Bible* (Filament Publishing, 2022), has been published.

There are numerous revisions to the first edition of this book. The sections are now referred to as "chapters" rather than "documents" (which arose from my own record keeping). There is new material: Chapter 25, describing 12 words whose persistent mistranslations in English versions derail the identity of the sons of the 12 tribes of Israel and God's irrevocable promises to them; Chapters 26 and 27, concerning demons and "satan"; Chapter 28, concerning the Song of Solomon and Esther; Chapter 29, concerning the Protestant King James Bible of 1611 and the Catholic Douai-Rheims Bible of 1610; Chapter 30, concerning 1 Timothy 3\16. I have used throughout a more attractive font for Greek words of the New Testament. Typographical corrections have been made. Some material from the first edition is excised, superceded by new light: eight years is a long time in intense daily study. The section on Daniel 9\20-27 has been removed, as I have now seen those "70 sevens" in a new light. The chapter concerning Samuel and the woman of Endor (now Chapter 9), has been enhanced; the whole event is one of human deception.

Constantly I labour to recover the forms and styles, and restore the truth of the prophets and apostles. As long as God gives me breath I will continue in this work. His law is written by "the finger of Elohim" (Exodus 31\18). This image, this figure of anthropomorphism, reminds us that it is all His truth, and His grammatical forms and structures, and His beauty of language. It is now for us to recover all that has been too long concealed.

I have been labouring since 1997 – although the intense focus began in 1995, when I first came across the works of Dr EW Bullinger – towards making for God and Christ a translation that is pure and undefiled and honouring. It is a small labour in comparison to what they have done for us. We say, as Jesus commanded us to respond, "We are unworthy servants. We have done we had to do" (Luke 17 \10). Every day this work progresses in ways which, at the beginning, I could never have even imagined. To God be the glory.

gjs, July 2023

www.keysofthekingdombible.com

Chapter 1

How and Why
The Keys of the Kingdom Holy Bible
Translation Was Made

*

Salvation and righteousness

Without a reliable translation of the God-authorized Hebrew and Greek writings of the prophets and apostles of God and Christ, nobody is able to have knowledge and understanding of the one true God. Nor is anybody able to have knowledge and understanding of salvation out of death and into life.

There is salvation in only one name, the name of Jesus Christ. The apostle Peter proclaimed to the hostile religious authorities, "And not in any other *name* is there salvation, for neither is there any other name which has been given among men by which to be saved" (Acts 4\12). And accurate knowledge of the one true God and of His Son Jesus Christ is found only in the God-authorized Books of the prophets and apostles.

God has spoken through His prophets and apostles. Their writings have been preserved by God, from the Book of Genesis to the Book of Revelation. We need of a pure translation of those Books into our own language. We need to know the truth of the salvation-bringing message of God. Through believing that Jesus died for our sins, we have the forgiveness of God and His unending care and love. We may then progress into the righteous living required by God. And if we continue and endure with Him, we may not only inherit full life throughout the coming eon – "eonian life" – but might also receive God's exaltation and win the "crown of righteousness" (2 Timothy 4\8) and be seated with God and Jesus in the New Jerusalem (Ephesians 2\6) and reign with Jesus (2 Timothy 2\12).

These things can be known properly only through reliable translations – unless, of course, you are so familiar with the original Hebrew and Greek and your understanding of all the themes is so uninhibited by ancient error that you do not need it translating and explaining, but where is such a man or woman?

The process of translation is a long and arduous task. However, it is not just an academic work with solely literary outcomes. The purpose is to discover God's revelation to mankind, the visions of the prophets, the gospel of Jesus Christ and of the apostle Paul, what salvation is, and how to receive that salvation, to understand the beginning of creation, to understand history, to understand the character and workings of God, to understand the nature of man, the times we are in, and to find out what eons went before and what eons lie ahead.

All this needs a converted mind, having the mind cleansed and constantly renewed and filled with the growing knowledge of God and Jesus, and righteous living in the sight of God. The power of God's salvation-bringing words changes everything in a person's life.

The hammer-blow came in 1997. I had been compiling a list of corrections and improvements to the King James Bible. After walking round a Scottish island with a friend and talking about William Tyndale in the summer of that year, I was back in Hampshire relaxing on a bench by the local lake and thinking about these things, and right there I made the decision that I had to make a correcting translation. I went home with fire in my chest. And so began decades of labour.

If the life and death of Tyndale was one driving inspiration for me, another was a footnote in Dr EW Bullinger's *Companion Bible* which says: "By copying out the A.V., and substituting these amended renderings, the student may make *his own* new Revised Version." The dark errors in the King James Bible were another motivation. I felt a desperate hunger to have a translation with the full truth of the oracles of God. Those words delivered in the language of angels and prophets and apostles, what do they mean?

Historical background and necessity
for Keys of the Kingdom Holy Bible translation
Since the scholars and scribes of the King James Bible of 1611 made such an unholy and untidy mess of translating the Hebrew and Greek Books of God, I set out in 1997 to make a translation which would make corrections of traditional errors and present the word of God in a respectful literary style and form. I did not know then the depth of my undertaking. I was hoping to complete it by 2011. It was going to be *The Believer's Bible*, but I learned years later that somebody already had that title.

King James paid his scholars to create a Bible which might unite the two violently opposed factions of religion who had been burning and persecuting each other. Non-conformists were viciously persecuted by James and his men. What good did those paid scholars' great learning do for them?

In the introduction to his excellent edition of *Tyndale's New Testament* (1995), David Daniell, who recovers the importance of Tyndale, has the following to say concerning the attitude of King James (cited with permission):

When James 1 gave his Bible revisers the huge Bishops' Bible as their foundation, which meant that the Latin Vulgate-based Rheims version would be attractive to them, he ensured that a wash of Latinity would be spread over Tyndale's English. The result, and, we must assume, the intention, was to create a safer distance between the Scriptures and the people. Though in the general working vocabulary there were more Latinate terms in use by 1611, Latin words and constructions have, as they had then, the ring of Establishment authority, which is not the same as the *koiné* (κοινή) Greek that Tyndale was translating for the first time ... [Tyndale's] Greek Testament, Englished, was in the hands of the people. The objection was not narrowly political. Powerful ecclesiastical voices throughout Europe maintained that the Latin Bible was the true word of God and that the moves of humanist scholars to press for the originality of Hebrew and Greek was a blasphemous and seditious conspiracy born of hatred.   ~ Daniell, p. xxiv

Indeed: "to create a safer distance between the Scriptures and the people". The truth was concealed. It still is concealed, by bad translating, bad style, bad texts. King James's men's crimes against humanity are greater even than that. The chairman of his translators and some of thre others were persecutors of the real Christians. They were not the right people. Their translation is not a work of righteousness. "For out of the heart proceed evil reasonings" (Matthew 15\19). As well as creating their own inaccuracies, King James's men were dominated in many places by the Latin Vulgate translation. Both the Vulgate and the King James Bible were made political works. And the King's men – all the King's men – were dominated by the Church Fathers and creeds and articles of faith. My book-length study, *How the KJV Conceals the True Jesus and his Salvation* (2013), explains all these things about various creeds and the Vulgate in microscopic detail. And my book-length study, *What Happens When You Die* (2000), exposes, with numerous citations, the Church Fathers' enamour and delight with Platonism and ancient Paganism.

The following examples demonstrate the King James Bible's and other translations' ineptness, blunders so colossal – in the most important matters: who Jesus and the Holy Spirit are, and the gospel message – they are astonishing:–

   * Their failure to put the Hebrew Books in the right orders (see Chapter 22);

   * Their presentation of every verse being broken into a new paragraph, a spoiling of the

rhythm, an impediment and insulting. Nobody would tolerate it with a Jane Austen or Charles Dickens novel;

* Their lack of sensible paragraphing, and lack of lineation for poetical sections;

* Their incomprehensible jibberish at Exodus 38\4: "he made for the altar a brasen gate of network under the compass thereof beneath unto the midst of it"; and their jibberish at 2 Corinthians 6\11-13: "O ye Corinthians, our mouth is open unto you, our heart is enlarged. Ye are not straitened in us, but ye are straitened in your own bowels. Now for a recompense in the same, (I speak as unto my children,) be ye also enlarged"

* Their presentation of Scripture of God as some document centred on the church system, and so smuggling in ecclesiastical words such as "church", "saint", "ministry", "minister", "bishop", "Easter", even though the international system of man's religion was not born until two or three centuries after Jesus, so by these intrusions creating an anachronism;

* Their failure to deal competently with the basic Hebrew and Greek words עולם (= *olam*) and αἰών (= *aion*), which both mean "age" or "eon". The Hebrew word עולם appears 438 times and the Greek word αἰών appears 128 times in the Textus Receptus (the Greek text on which the King James Bible's New Testament is based; 126 times in the Greek text on which my translation is based). Yet not once did the King James Bible men manage to translate either of them as "eon", but, rather, preferred to mistranslate the noun αἰών as either an adverb, "ever", or as "world", a *space* dimension *concrete* noun, whereas αἰών, "eon", is a *time* dimension *abstract* noun. And they did this even though they would have known only too well that "world" is κόσμος (= *kosmos*), not αἰών. And so by their stubbornness to deal competently with these basic words עולם (= *olam*) and αἰών (= *aion*), their concealing of God's arrangement of the eons past, the present eon, and the eons coming, and spoiling the true gospel message;

* Their failure to deal competently with the Greek adjective αἰώνιος (= *aionios*), meaning "eonian" or "age-enduring", which occurs 71 times, yet not once did they manage to translate it as "eonian", but preferred translating it as "everlasting" or "eternal" or "for ever";

* At 2 Timothy 1\9 and Titus 1\2 the King James Bible says that God's "purpose and grace" and "eternal life" were "given" and "promised" "before the world began". But that last phrase is an incorrect translation; it should read "before / in advance of eonian times" or "before / in advance of the times of the eons / ages". The Greek is πρὸ χρόνων αἰωνίων (= *pro kronon aionion*), which means "in advance of the eonian times". In the Greek of that phrase there is no word "since", no word "the", no word "world", and no word "began"; so that only "before" in the King James Bible matches the underlying Greek. Yet at Romans 16\25 it speaks of "the mystery, which was kept secret since the world began" (which, again, is incorrect translation; it should read "a mystery kept in silence in eonian times", or "... in times of the eons /ages"), clashing with its other statements that the gospel was "promised" and "given" "before the world began"; and it clashes with its own Ephesians 3\5 and 3\9-10 ("as it is now revealed"; "the mystery that has been concealed from the eons by God ... in order that now the manifold wisdom of God might be made known"). How could Paul say it was "given" and "promised" before the world began when there was nobody to give and promise it to? And how could Paul say it was "promised" if it had been "kept secret since the world began"? The King James Bible clashes with itself – all brought about by the refusal to translate αἰώνιος (= *aionios*) as "eonian";

* Their failure to deal competently with the Hebrew adverbial phrase לעולם (= *le olam*), which occurs 162 times and in almost all its occurrences means "throughout the eon", yet not once did they submit to translate it as "throughout the eon";

* Their failure to deal competently with the Greek adverbial phrase εἰς τὸν αἰῶνα (= *eis ton aiona*), which occurs 27 times, and in all but two of its occurrences means "throughout the eon", yet not once did they manage to translate it as "throughout the eon";

* Calling various statutes, such as the Passover, "an ordinance for ever" (Exodus 12\14, 12\24, 40\15, Leviticus 23\14, 23\31, 23\41 et cetera), which they are not; they are suspended for now, and they will be fulfilled in type and abolished in the New Jerusalem;

* At John 8\51, 8\52, 10\28 and 11\26 King James's men translated the two adverbial phrases οὐ μὴ (= *ou me*) and εἰς τὸν αἰῶνα (= *eis ton aiona*), which together mean "most certainly not ... throughout the eon", as "never", so they have Jesus saying at John 10\28 "they shall never perish", but that is untrue as all die; and they have Jesus saying to Martha at John 11\26 that believers never die (Jesus himself died; and I'm sure Martha died), a false message showing that the gospel of the translators is the same as the gospel of "the serpent" character in Eden; the greatest lie ever told;

* Capitalizing "Word" at John 1\1 and 1\14, in the pretence it's about Jesus, rather than the declared word and plan of God;

* Their translating of the verb ἐγένετο (= *egeneto*), singular aorist active intransitive stative, as "were made", plural imperfect passive transitive dynamic, and as "made" (passive), and as "was made" (passive), at John 1\3 and 1\10, to give the false impression that Jesus, not God, is the Creator;

* Their translation of the verb γενέσθαι (= *genesthai*), aorist infinitive, as "was", an imperfect at John 8\58, to have Jesus make the impossible statement that he was around before the time of Abraham, which would have made him over two thousand years old. Yet they were able to get γενέσθαι right as an infinitive at Mark 1\17, Luke 21\28, John 1\12, Acts 26\28, and elsewhere, but had it curiously wrongly as "be made", finite passive, at John 5\6, and "be done", finite passive, at Revelation 22\6);

* Their translation of the passive verb ἐγείρω (= *egeiro*) at Matthew 27\64, 28\6, 28\7, Mark 16\6, 16\14, Luke 24\6, 24\34, which means "he has been raised", here in the passive form, ἠγέρθη (= *heegerthee*), as at Romans 6\4 et cetera. The King James Bible, however, has it as "he is risen", active, allowing the pretence that Jesus somehow raised himself, in which case he could not have died and then there is no salvation. (In this the King James Bible echoes the Vulgate's "*surrexit*".) The King James has it correctly as "has been raised" at Romans 6\4. But the King James also has, wrongly, "she arose" for Peter's mother-in-law at Matthew 8\15, which should say "she was lifted up";

* Their translation of the verb εἶναι (= *einai*), a present infinitive, as "was", imperfect, at John 17\5, in order to make it seem as if Jesus existed before the world;

* Their punctuating of Romans 9\5, makes it read "Christ *came*, who is over all, God", so as to make Jesus seem to be God, rather than who he really is, the Son of God;

* Their indiscriminate and wrong capitalizations "Holy Ghost" (90 times, first at Matthew 1\20) in every occurrence, regardless of context, and of "Spirit", regardless of context, some of these capitalised in places they ought not to be capitalized, and by that they cause the idea that the Spirit of God is in the fat of men's bellies, such as Romans 8\9, and some of these not capitalised when they ought to be capitalised. According to *Young's Analytical Concordance*, it has "Holy Ghost" 90 times; in calling him "the Holy Ghost", for example at Matthew 12\31-32, they imply the Holy Spirit angel is a ghost;

* Their 1 Corinthians 8\13 with "while the world standeth", while it might be a nice phrase, makes no vague match to the Greek εἰς τὸν αἰῶνα (= *eis ton aiona*); it properly reads "throughout the eon" (Paul possibly meant the same phrase idiomatically as at Philemon 15, but possibly not);

* Their imposition of the mythological word "hell" (as they spelled it, lower-case), which is a false translation of one Hebrew word, שאול (= *sheol*), and of three Greek words – γέεννα (= *gehenna*) and ᾅδης (= *hades*) and ταρταρόω (= *tartaroo*) – the concept of "Hell" (place names should be capitalized) obviously having no place in the mind of God. It is particularly strange they translated γέεννα as "hell" since its Hebrew form גיא הנם (= *ge hinnom*) they did translate correctly as "the Valley of Hinnom", which is also the meaning of γέεννα;

* At Ephesians 1\3 they rendered the Greek word ἐπουράνιος (= *epouranios*) as "heavenly *places*", instead of the consistent meaning of its occurrences as "most exalted", referring to believers, in harmony with Exodus 19\5-6, Deuteronomy 7\6, Romans 8\29, 2 Timothy 2\12, and Hebrews 11\40 et cetera. Out of their errant rendering many have concocted strange and extraordinary dreams of a future life somewhere in outer space;

* Their seeming dislike of the word "road", so that it occurs only once in their translation, which is at 1 Samuel 27\10 for the Hebrew word פשט (= *pashat*), but their single occurrence of "road" is wrong and ought to read "raid", as the context makes clear;

* Their inclusion of "the foul comma" at 1 John 5\7-8, words which are an insertion made in order to back up the three gods as one god system;

* At 1 Timothy 3\15-16 they have "the church of the living God, the pillar and ground of the truth", implying that everything depends on their religious system, instead of making a sentence break after "the living God" and then making a new sentence about *"The* pillar and ground of the truth";

* For the numerous Hebrew names and titles of God they often merely have "God" and "Lord", obscuring the richness and variety of God's revealed names and the titles attributed to Him by His prophets, which distinguish Him from the many false gods;

* At Isaiah 45\17 they wrote the words "world without end" for the Hebrew phrase עד עד־עולמי (= *ad ole me ad*), yet neither the words "world" nor "without" nor "end" is in those Hebrew words, which really mean "throughout the eon and its duration";

* At Ephesians 3\21 they wrote the words "world without end" for the Greek phrase τοῦ αἰῶνος τῶν αἰώνων (= *tou aionos ton aionon*), yet neither "world" nor "without" nor "end" is in those Greek words, which really mean "the duration of the eons";

* The translators were at odds with themselves because, while they have "world without end" at Isaiah 45\17 and Ephesians 3\21, they then have such phrases as "at the end of the world" at, for example, Matthew 13\40 and 13\49, which again are also wrong because it should be "at the completion of the eon"; and "world without end" clashes too with their phrase "while the world standeth" at 1 Corinthians 8\13 (which is wrong), and with its own 2 Peter 3\10 ("the earth ... shall be burned up"), and with its own Revelation 21\1 ("a new earth");

* At John 3\13 the translators have Jesus say of himself, "the Son of man which is in heaven", yet Jesus was standing on the Earth talking to Nicodemus;

* At Acts 7\45 they wrote "our fathers that came after brought in with Jesus into the possession of the Gentiles, whom God drave out" (bad English; and "drave"??), but Jesus had not even been born then and it should be "Joshua", not "Jesus";

* At Hebrews 4\8 they wrote "if Jesus had given them rest", implying he did not give them rest, so making Jesus seem a failure, when it should be "if Joshua had given them rest";

* They call the writers of the Gospel Accounts and the letters "Saint Matthew", "Saint Mark", "Saint Luke", "Saint John", "Saint Paul" and "Saint Peter", yet there is nobody known by such names in the oracles of God;

* Their punctuation is erratic, colons and semi-colons all over the place, and no speech marks;

* Its occultic and pagan teachings of the Mysteries religion: ghosts, Lucifer, Satan, the Devil, hell fire, people going to Heaven, immortality of the soul, Easter, ghosts, unicorn, satyrs and the cockatrice, all mythological figures and concepts.

I could go on ...
As Solzhenitsyn said somewhere, I could take no more of this, "even by the teaspoonful".

The King James Bible presents a false God who promises men what the King of Babylon wanted, to ascend to Heaven (Isaiah 14); who threatens the torment of fire for not believing what the post-Babylonian creeds demand; who does not understand Chemistry and says men can burn for ever; a false Jesus who says believers in him will never die; a man who was around before Abraham; who proclaimed a false gospel; writers who could conceal the fact of the coming eons; implications of gods in men's bellies; and the teachings of the post-Babylonian religion. With its insulting presentation and false translating, the only conclusion about the King James Bible is that it's processed, inaccurate, unreliable, insipid, toxic.

John's Gospel was maliciously treated by the King James men. It is with major themes and important words that the King James translators concealed the truth of the God-authorized Hebrew and Greek Books. Modern versions are no better, perhaps worse, because they not only commit many of the falsehoods of the King James Bible, including archaisms they refuse to drop, but they also omit from the Greek text many words, phrases, clauses, sentences and even whole passages, because their New Testament is based on corrupt Alexandrian manuscripts.

The translators of these Bibles have twisted and corrupted nouns; they have fidgeted with nouns; adjectives; verb tenses; verb moods; verb participles; adverbs; adverbial phrases; prepositions; and punctuation; they made false capitalizations; clumsy blunders; inconsistencies; incompetent punctuation; awkward grammar; dung-forked in additional words; dung-forked out words and passages; written meaningless verbiage (such as Exodus 38\4 and 2 Corinthians 6\11-

13 in the King James); created a disrespectful layout; imposed eternity on subjects which are not eternal; jammed it full of anachronistic ecclesiastic words; arranged the Old Testament books in a delirious order; made Jesus agree with the serpent in Eden (Genesis 3\4 with John 11\26); made Jesus and the prophets and apostles agree with Plato and the ancient pagans; and, on top of it all, concealed the gospel promise of eonian life; all this to their advantage, so that the Books of God are made to agree with the Vulgate and creeds and the false gospel of the hybrid religion and so that they seem wrapped in mysteries unintelligible to ordinary people. They present a false Jesus. This is the greatest conspiracy in literary history.

Keys of the Kingdom Holy Bible translation: the working method
It is a wonder and truly beyond imagination that so many centuries have passed and the Books of God have remained in the illegal custody of a worldwide system which has twisted the oracles of angels and prophets and apostles and of Jesus in order to try and make them justify that system.

God wants the oracles of the prophets and apostles and Jesus translated accurately and with purity into the English language and other languages. Chapter 6, entitled "Keys of the Kingdom Holy Bible is the most accurate and reliable translation in the English language", lists some of my reasons for my proclamation that it is indeed the first true English translation of the 64 God-authorized Hebrew and Greek Books of God.

No translation has made so clear its working methods and its intentions as I have done with *Keys of the Kingdom Holy Bible*. I could not have gone to more labour to lay bare how I have gone about translating the oracles of God and angels into English, and how I have strived to achieve the most pure representation of those oracles that I am able. Perfection and purity of truth have been uncompromising targets. To those ends, many sensible suggestions have been welcomed.

Because I have declined to serve the orthodoxy of the religious and political systems of this world, and have made it my business to serve only the Lord God, the Father of our Lord Jesus Christ, I know that sharp arrows will fly from opponents eager to preserve the word of man. William Tyndale, who made his *New Testamente* for the love of the truth, was strangled and burned by the church in 1536, yet it is invariably Thomas More, who persecuted Tyndale, who is honoured.

Before arrows are let fly, I say in advance to the scribes and scholars of this world that their first attentions should be more profitably employed in putting right their own translations which have been forcibly obscured by religion's dark falsehoods. A single version with the Hebrew Books in the right order would be a start.

Magnificent is the English lineage behind *Keys of the Kingdom Holy Bible*. The hearts of John Wycliffe (1320-84), and William Tyndale (?-1536), and John Rogers (c.1505-1555), pounded to see the Books of God translated and made available to the English-speaking people – against the cruel, inhuman mind of the bishops of the ritual-based religious system who violently opposed them. (Why?)

In 1737 Alexander Cruden published his *Complete Concordance to the Holy Scriptures* (apparently he mistakenly omitted the name "Chloe"). Three hundred years after Tyndale, in the Victorian era, against much hostility of inimical men, there began a remarkable outburst of lexicography extremely beneficial to the translation and comprehension of the oracles of God (in date order):

Wigram, George V, *The Englishman's Greek Concordance of the New Testament*, 1839
Gesenius, HWF, *Hebrew and Chaldee Lexicon to the Old Testament Scriptures*, 1847
Davidson, Benjamin, *The Analytical Hebrew and Chaldee Lexicon*, 1848
Bagster, Samuel, *The Analytical Greek Lexicon*, 1870
Burgon, John, *The Last Twelve Verses of the Gospel According to Mark*, 1871
Wigram, George V, *The Englishman's Hebrew Concordance of the Old Testament*, 1874

Bagster, Samuel, *The Englishman's Greek New Testament*, 1877
Scrivener, FH, *Novum Testamentum* (= *New Testament*), 1877
Young, Robert, *Analytical Concordance To The Holy Bible*, 1879
Burgon, John, *The Revision Revised: a Refutation of Westcott and Hort's False Greek Text and Theory*, 1883
Bullinger, EW, *A Critical Lexicon and Concordance of the English and Greek New Testament*, 1887
Liddell and Scott, *An Intermediate Greek-English Lexicon*, 1889
Strong, James, *Exhaustive Concordance of the Bible*, 1890
Berry, George Ricker, *Interlinear Greek-English New Testament*, 1897
Bullinger, EW, *Figures of Speech Used in the Bible Explained and Illustrated*, 1898
Thayer, Joseph H, *Thayer's Greek-English Lexicon of the New Testament*, 1901

James Strong assigned 8,674 numbers to the Hebrew words in God's Hebrew Books and 5,624 numbers to Greek words in God's Greek Books. His numbering system was an idea of genius.

I honour the men of these mighty works and I am sure God in His Heaven has been pleased with these works.

I consult these books daily. Thayer and Wigram are magnificent, both works being arranged with Strong's numbering system (not always in strict numerical order). The accuracy of Thayer's and Wigram's works are remarkable. In those vast works I have found scarcely any typographical errors.

Joseph Thayer was modest enough to write at the end of his preface, on Christmas Day, 1885: "No one can have a keener sense than the editor has of the shortcomings of the present volume. But he is convinced that whatever supersedes it must be the joint product of several laborers, having at their command larger resources than he has enjoyed, and ampler leisure than falls to the lot of the average reader. Meantime, may the present work so approve itself to students of the Sacred Volume as to enlist their co-operation with him in ridding it of every remaining blemish" (p. xv). In a work of 726 pages in a small font, I have found no more than eight typographical errors, which is remarkable.

My bibliography includes the interlinears, lexicons, concordances, grammars, as well as commentaries by Dr. Bullinger and Sellers. The inclusion of some texts is only to indicate they have been consulted, and are not all necessarily admired. This bibliography further lays bare my working method and the extent and variety of my sources.

In 1866 Henry Alford published his Greek Testament in 4 volumes, which was a translation with linguistic-based footnotes, some of them extremely useful and enlightening.

After the Victorian era the remarkable scholar Dr EW Bullinger published two of his best works:

How to Enjoy the Bible, 1907
The Companion Bible, 1909-1922

Both books pay attention to first occurrences, general usages and contexts of Hebrew and Greek words. They contain thousands of corrections and enhancements to traditional renderings, and they correct some principle teachings.

How to Enjoy the Bible was the first work which drew me to look more closely at renderings and to consider what was really being said.

On page ix of *The Companion Bible* Dr. Bullinger says: "All important emendations are given ... where the current renderings are inadequate and open to amendment". And, repeating what I cited earlier, a footnote on that page says: "By copying out the A.V., and substituting these amended renderings, the student may make *his own* new Revised Version." Some of *The Companion Bible*'s thousands of suggestions for renderings have been incorporated or adapted in

Keys of the Kingdom Holy Bible.

That footnote – and the life and death and impact of William Tyndale – helped to put it into my mind to make a proper translation.

Then, later, it was the notes in *The Companion Bible* that suggested to me I also should publish footnotes to the text, explaining translations and interpretations.

My discovery in 1998 of the works of Otis Q Sellers was another astronomical leap. These works were especially helpful and inspiring:

What is the Soul?, 1939
The Body in 1 Corinthians 12, 1940
The Earth, not Heaven, is the Future Home of God's Redeemed, 1955
The Word of Truth, 1955
The Thousand Year Reign of Christ, 1957
The Foundation of the World, c1958
What Does Basileia Mean?, 1958
The Interpretation of Philippians 3:20, 1959
The Challenge Stands, 1960
The Word of Truth, 1960
The Rich Man and Lazarus, 1962
Seed & Bread, Volume 1, c1980
Seed & Bread, Volume 2, 1980

Sellers' studies on the words עולם (= *olam*) and αἰών (= *aion*) and ἐπουράνιος (= *epouranios*) and βασιλεία (= *basileia*) and ἐπιφάνεια (= *epiphaneia*) are works of extreme intelligence and logic, as are many of his assessments and observations.

Dr. Graham Thomason's translation and Greek grammars have been an immense help, particularly his following works:

Far Above All Translation, www.FarAboveAll.com
Greek Prepositions and Conjunctions, www.FarAboveAll.com
Translation Issues in the New Testament, www.FarAboveAll.com

It was Dr Thomason who demonstrated to me that the Robinson-Pierpont Byzantine Textform 2005, compiled by Maurice A Robinson and William G Pierpont, on which my New Testament is based, is the best New Testament Greek text compiled so far.

The two works which have most made my translation possible are the two interlinear translations of JP Green Sr:

Interlinear Bible: Hebrew-Greek-English, 1986
Interlinear Bible: Greek-English, 1996

For those unfamiliar with interlinears, an interlinear has the Hebrew or Greek text with an English translation underneath each line. In addition, Green puts the Strong's number above each word, and gives his own translation in the left-hand margin and, with his New Testament, he gives the King James translation in the right-hand margin. Green's interlinears are not without typographical errors, particularly in his Hebrew interlinear, but those do not diminish the fantastic debt owed to him. His interlinears are great gifts to the true believer in God and Jesus, and to the seeker of translation truth. Because they contain the reproduction of the Hebrew and Greek of the prophets and apostles, I consider them the most important books of the twentieth century.

In order to give readers who are unacquainted with interlinears a visual idea of their form, this is how an interlinear of *Keys of the Kingdom Holy Bible*, if one were made, would appear, for John 3\16 and John 11\26 respectively, with the Strong's numbers (the Greek text does not have punctuation and the word order is different to English):

	3779	1063	25	3558	2316	3588	2889	5620	3588	5207
16.	οὕτως	γὰρ	ἠγάπησεν	ὁ	θεὸς	τὸν	κόσμον	ὥστε	τὸν	υἱὸν
	so much	for	loved		God		the world	that		the son

	846	3588	3439	1325	2443		3956	3588
	αὐτοῦ	τὸν	μονογενῆ	ἔδωκεν	ἵνα		πᾶς	ὁ
	of Him	the	only	He gave	in order that		everyone	the/ who

	4100	1519	846	3361	622		235	2192
	πιστεύων	εἰς	αὐτὸν	μὴ	ἀπόληται		ἀλλ'	ἔχῃ
	believing	in	him	not	might suffer destruction		but	might have

	2222	166
	ζωὴν	αἰώνιον
	life	eonian

~ John 3\16

	2532	3956	3588	2198	2532	4100
26.	καὶ	πᾶς	ὁ	ζῶν	καὶ	πιστεύων
	and	everyone	the/who	living	and	believing

	1519	1691		3756	3361		599
	εἰς	ἐμέ		οὐ	μὴ		
	in	me		most certainly not			will die

	1519	3588	165	4100	5124
	εἰς	τὸν	αἰῶνα	πιστεύεις	τοῦτο
	throughout	the	eon	do you believe	this

~ John 11\26

Green's Hebrew and Greek interlinears follow this form. Lexicons which use Strong's numbers can be easily consulted in Hebrew and Greek lexicons which adopt Strong's numbering systems.

Greek has different case forms for nouns (called "declensions"), similar to Latin's range of forms, which are according to the noun's function in a sentence. We do not see this in English, except in pronouns such as "who" and "whom", "I" and "me", "we" and "us". Greek verbs also have different forms (called "conjugations"), also similar to Latin's range; English also has different forms for verbs, such as "I fish" and "I fished", "I am" and "I was" and "I have been", but there are more forms in Greek verbs than there are in English. The forms of all the New Testament Greek words can be consulted in Bagster's *Analytical Greek Lexicon*, or from Robinson and Pierpont's *Byzantine Parsed Text*, 2000, http://www.byztxt.com/download.

In my translating processes, I have worked both horizontally (word by word from the interlinears) and vertically (specific words, or phrases, or themes). This is a check on the variety of meanings a word or phrase can have in its context. It is also a check on internal harmony.

Nobody begins a translation of God's Books as an expert. Translation is a long process. Exact translation from one language into another – let alone from three quarters of a million words in three languages, Hebrew, Aramaic and Greek – is an impossible concept, because connotations, associations, nuances and language devices such as alliteration are lost; some, too, are probably gained when they ought not to be gained, putting different impressions on words. Nevertheless, I know that the God and Father of our Lord Jesus Christ wants His Books translated for everybody's comprehension. I am confident that *Keys of the Kingdom Holy Bible* is a reliable and enjoyable representation of the divinely-preserved oracles of God. Its accuracy and reliability exceed that of the altered versions. I continue to labor our daily, especially in restoring syntactical devices of the inspired Biblical writers.

Full consciousness of the spirit required arises only from the act and very long experience of doing the work. It is unlike any other translating. In other works some degree of paraphrase is permissible, but with the Books of God you are representing His truths that were delivered by angels and God-authorized prophets and apostles. Although there are places where a degree of paraphrase is necessary for English comprehension (continuous exact grammatical imitation would be hardly readable), there has to be linguistic precision, verbal imitation, honouring the grammatical forms and structures and literary style of the writings of the prophets and apostles.

Presentation
The text of the translation was originally without columns but I use columns because with columns more text fits on a page, which means saving space and so making a lighter volume of fewer pages.

I have continued the one good convention of the King James Bible translators of putting in italics any extra English words which have to be added in order to make good English. I have kept these additions to a bare minimum, probably half the number in the King James, in order to get as close as is reasonable to the original Hebrew and Greek literary forms.

Divine names and titles
In my translation of God's Hebrew Books the names and titles of God are transliterated from the Hebrew. For example, אלהים (= *Elohim*) is translated in English Bibles as "God" but I transliterate it as "Elohim" (Genesis 1\1 et cetera). And יהוה רפאך is transliterated as "Yahweh Ropheka" (Exodus 15\26). This, as far as I have been able to establish, is the first time such a transliterating of God's names and titles has been done. I would be glad to hear of any other. Sometimes *The Companion Bible* draws attention to them in footnotes.

I have listed 160 divine names and titles, some revealed by God Himself and some assigned to Him by prophets. These names (revealed by God to His prophets) and titles (assigned to God by the prophets and apostles) are all significant. They distinguish the true God from the many false gods. The prophets and apostles used these in their speech and writings in order to make a distinction, and they used them in their prayers to attract the attention of God. The simple forms of "Lord" and "God" in other versions obscure the many names and titles and they fail to make distinctions.

The Companion Notes to Keys of the Kingdom Holy Bible
In the text of early editions of my New Testament translation, there were thousands of small superscripted asterisks. These indicated that I had made a note regarding translation or interpretation. However, there became so many of them that it began to look untidy, so I deleted them. There are at present over 13,000 of these Companion Notes, as I like to call them, after *The Companion Bible* which had inspired me. These were the basis for the footnotes. Many have been written into the *Keys of the Kingdom* as footnotes, which, at the time of writing (June 2023), number 5,300.

Subject headings and footnotes
Keys of the Kingdom Holy Bible has italicized subject headings. Often these headings are a short phrase such as "*The law – love*" (at Matthew 5\43), relating to an event or theme. Others are more extensive, giving explanation and setting the passage which follows in the wider context. For example, at Ephesians 1\3 – where ἐπουράνιος (= *epouranios*), a composite of *epi* + *ouranios*, has been mistranslated in every translation I have looked at except Otis Sellers' *Resultant Version* of

Ephesians – the subject heading gives a summary and explanation of the wider contexts:

*Jesus heads up his 'most exalted'. Founding
of God's coming world order. Wisdom
& understanding lavished on people of God*

The footnote concerning that "most exalted" gives information regarding other occurrences of ἐπουράνιος, and make comparison with related words.

In the Gospel Accounts the subject headings are predominantly events because true history is being recorded. In the apostles' letters, the subject headings predominantly describe and bring to light the teachings being given by the prophets and apostles.

I did not include footnotes until the 2019 edition of *The Eonian Life Bible New Testament*. It had always been my intention to include footnotes. I was putting them in when I began work in 1997. However, my word processor was not sophisticated enough to permit more than a few, and the screen kept freezing and I was losing work and having to do it all over again. I had to abandon the idea, and make instead the Companion Notes. Eventually word processors became more sophisticated and I began tentatively putting footnotes back in, hoping the screen would not freeze. To my relief, nothing like that has happened again.

The footnotes indicate sources for citations, give cross-references, and explanations of Greek and Hebrew words.

Footnotes are indicated in the text with a superscripted capital letter in bold. At John 8\58 the footnote for the verb phrase "is to appear" gives the Greek verb, its grammatical form, and its typical aspect in a comprehensive list of other occurrences:

8\58, *is to appear*: **γενέσθαι** (*genesthai*), or 'appearing', or 'comes to be'; aorist infinitive (here following preposition 'before'), with future aspect, eg 3\9, 5\6, 13\19, 14\29, Mat. 24\6, Mark 1\17, 10\43, 10\44, 13\7, Luke 21\9, 21\28, 23\24, Acts 1\22, 4\28, 19\21, 20\16, 22\17, 26\28, 1 Cor. 11\33, Phil. 3\21, Rev. 1\1, 4\1, 22\6. See list of prepositions + infinitives at John 17\5. YLT 'Abraham's coming'. *Teach Yourself New Testament Greek*, DF Hudson, (1960): 'The Aorist Infinitive ... does not refer to Past Time' (p. 54). Strong's g1096. Mitchell 'was to come'

The Notes include in bold type the Hebrew or Aramaic or Greek words (with their transliterations) which are under discussion. Reasons are given for my renderings and conclusions. Consideration is given to context, linguistic form, other uses of a word or phrase, first occurrences, and wider themes. Citations are made from lexical authorities. Hebrew and Greek words in the Notes often include the Strong's reference number. Sometimes alternative renderings are offered, and comparisons are constantly made with other translations, sometimes those being useful and sometimes not. The Notes vary in length, from a single line to several pages.

The following are footnotes to John 11\26:

11\26, *most certainly not*: **οὐ μὴ** (*hou me*). 10\28 et cetera. Strong's g3756/g3361. (Omitted in KJV; replaced with 'never', which would be **οὐδέποτε** (*oudepote*). Strong's g3763, as Mat. 7\23)

11\26, *throughout the eon*: **εἰς τὸν αἰῶνα** (*eis ton aiona*). 6\51, 6\58, 8\35, 8\51, 8\52. Strong's g1519/g3588/g165. (Omitted in KJV.) Full Greek of 11\26 on page following Contents. Ap. 6

The text at Hebrews 3\1-2 reads, "Consequently, brothers set apart, partakers of a most exalted position, consider the apostle and high priest of our declaration, Jesus Christ, [2] faithful to Him having created him, as Moses also *was* in all his house." The footnote regarding "created" gives other occurrences of the verb ποιέω, and other agreeable versions, and references the disagreeable King James Bible:

3\2, *having created*: **ποιέω** (*poyeo*). Strong's g4160, 'create', 'make'. In Hebrews at 1\2, 1\3, 1\7, 3\2, 6\3, 7\27, 8\5, 8\9, 10\7, 10\9, 10\36, 11\28, 12\13, 12\27, 13\6, 13\17, 13\19, 13\21. See eg, Mat. 19\4, 23\3 (3 occs.), Mark 10\6, Acts 4\24, 14\15, 17\24, 17\26, Rev. 14\7 et cetera. Equiv. of Heb. ברא (*bara*), Strong's h1254, 'created', at Gen. 1\1. Thayer here has 'create' (p. 525, column 2). LV 'fecit' (he made), (and for the whole clause, 'qui fidelis est ei qui fecit ilium', 'who is faithful to him who made him'). Tyndale 'made'. Douai-Rheims 'made'. Green 'making'. Bagster's *Interlinear Greek-Engish New Testament* 'making'. Alford 'made'. LIDT 'having made'. CLV 'makes'. KJV 'appointed' (?), but 'appointed' here is **τίθημι** (*titheemi*), Strong's g5087, Heb. 1\2, which has both **ποιέω** and **τίθημι**

This demonstrates that ποιέω is a standard Greek word for "create" or "make". In the King James, though, it's badly translated as "appointed". However, as the footnote says, Paul's word for "appointed" just a page earlier at Hebrews 1\2 is τίθημι, not ποιέω. And the two words actually occur together in that verse: "during these end of days spoke to us by means of *His* Son whom He appointed [τίθημι] heir of all things, on account of whom also He designed [or, framed, made; ποιέω] the eons". So here at Hebrews 3\2 we have the plain statement that Jesus was created by God. This discovery is a heartache to those who believe the three gods as one system. Previous translators have not put "created" because they did not believe that Jesus is a created being: they believed, rather, that he is God the Creator. This correction restores the standard meaning of ποιέω and the divine revelation and internal harmony of who Jesus is. The footnote also gives other translations which have translated the passage correctly.

The Deep Word Archaeology Study Method
In the first edition of this book, *The Earth-Shaking Truth*, I referred to this as "the Aligner Study Method". The Deep Word Archaeology Method is the name I have now assigned to my systematic method of translating and interpreting the God-authorized Hebrew and Greek Books. It is an internal and contextual method. This is described in detail, with an example, in Chapter 7, "The Deep Word Archaeology Study Method". It demonstrates the organic methods of translating and understanding.

Keys of the Kingdom Holy Bible has been made with the foundations of 5 Translating Laws, Grammar, Internal Harmony, Logic, Research, and Text (GIHLRT in my shorthand). The Translating Laws have been done with 3 Translating Targets in mind: Accuracy, Clarity, Literariness (ACL in my shorthand).

The method is to line up all internal evidence of any word or phrase or theme. In order to do this, the method pays first attention to grammar: translation, the language and meaning, determining this from the principle of first mention, the grammatical structure, what is figurative and what is non-figurative, and other uses and their contexts. It considers the writer and audience, and how God was dealing with men at the time of writing, distinguishing between what was written *for* us and what was written *to* us, and it considers the wider themes. It makes use of the best available lexicons and commentaries and it makes use of logic and common sense.

Here is an example of the Deep Word Archaeology Method with Psalm 16\9-10, Acts 2\27, 2\31. In the oracle of the prophet King David he said:

> ... my flesh will rest in hope;
> for You will not abandon my dead body in the grave,
> nor will You allow Your holy one to see corruption.   ~ Psalm 16\9-10

The word "grave" in that passage is represented by the Hebrew word שאול (= *sheol*). The apostle Peter cited from this Psalm in his Pentecost proclamation, and the word שאול (= *sheol*) is represented in the Greek (of Acts 2\27 and 2\31) by the word ᾅδης (= *hades*). Therefore, we can be certain that שאול (= *sheol*) and ᾅδης (= *hades*) in these passages are interchangeable, so mean the same. The first occurrence of שאול (= *sheol*) is at Genesis 37\35 when Jacob says, concerning his son Joseph, "I will go down to the grave, mourning for my son." Jacob thought he was going to die and go down to his grave in sorrow. The context of this gives crystal clear definition to the meaning of שאול (= *sheol*).

The translators of the King James Bible, at Psalm 16\10 and Act 2\31, translated both שאול (= *sheol*) and ᾅδης (= *hades*) as "hell". The words שאול (= *sheol*) and ᾅδης (= *hades*) do not mean "hell". The King James men had שאול right at Genesis 37\35 as "grave", but when they got to Psalm 16\10 they put "hell". No words in the Hebrew or Greek Books of God ever mean "hell". From those blunders men have made up elaborate stories about Jesus going down into some imaginary place of fiery torment and agony – and that elaborate story while Jesus is supposed to be in the grave for three days and three nights! From two blunders have come more blunders. The *King James Version* translators, with blunders like these, are exposed. They should not have been let loose on the Books of God.

The Deep Word Archaeology Study Method with Romans 9\5
Another important example is Romans 9\5. The King James rendering, and the one that the translations follow, is: "Whose *are* the fathers, and of whom as concerning the flesh Jesus *came*, who is over all, God blessed for ever. Amen." Now, the apostle Paul knew that the Lord Jesus Christ is a man divinely created in the virgin Maria, and he is not God. In contrast to the King James, *Keys of the Kingdom Holy Bible* has Romans 9\5 as: "whose *are* the fathers, and from whom *is* the Christ in relation to flesh, he being over everything. God be exalted throughout the eons! Amen." This is a matter not only of translation, but also of interpretation, and the correct rendering is made by the simple matter of inserting a full-stop after "everything". Why has no other version seen this? Jesus has, indeed, been placed "over everything". And Paul exalts God for that: "God be exalted throughout the eons!" Paul makes the same phrase of exultation of God at Romans 1\25 and 2 Corinthians 11\31. It seems that the translations were more concerned with following creeds than with the forms of Hebrew and Greek of the prophets and apostles.

The Deep Word Archaeology Study Method with 2 Timothy 1\9, Titus 1\2
At 2 Timothy 1\9 there is the Greek adverbial phrase πρὸ χρόνων αἰωνίων (= *pro kronon aionion*). Its context is God's "merciful goodwill given to us in Christ Jesus *pro kronon aionion* [πρὸ χρόνων αἰωνίων]". The first word, πρὸ (= *pro*), is a preposition meaning before, in front of, in advance of in time or place or eminence or superiority. Its range of meanings can be found in Thayer's *Greek-English Lexicon of the New Testament*, pp. 536-537. Its number assigned by James Strong is g4253. (All occurrences of any word, except minor particles, can be found in *Wigram's Englishman* Concordances.) The second word, χρόνων (= *kronon*), has the Strong's number g5550. It appears in Thayer as χρόνος (= *kronos*). It means "time" or a duration of time. From this word we get our English word "chronology". The entry for its grammatical form in Bagster is simply "gen. pl.". This means that it is a noun in the genitive form [1] and is plural ("times" plural, not "time" singular). So χρόνος (= *kronon*) means "times". The third word, αἰώνων (= *aionion*), has the Strong's number g166. It appears in Thayer (in its nominative state) as αἰώνιος (= *aionios*). It is an adjective whose meaning is "eonian", the adjectival form of the noun αἰών

---

1. *genitive form*. The function of genitive is 'of' something, usually, though not always, possessive. This word is genitive because the preposition πρὸ (= *pro*) is followed by the genitive case in Greek grammar.

(= *aion*), which means "eon". Our English word "eon" is directly from the Greek word αἰών. And our English word "eonian" is directly from αἰώνιος. And that is just what αἰώνιος means: "eonian" (or "age-enduring"). Its grammatical form here in 2 Timothy 1\9, αἰώνων, genitive plural, so agreeing with the genitive plural of "times". So: we have "before / in advance of eonian times". Or, "in advance of times of the eons".

We have to relate that to context. Paul"s context is "merciful goodwill given to us in Christ Jesus before / in advance of eonian times". Since that merciful goodwill had once been kept hidden (Romans 16\25-26 (Romans 14\22-25 in KTK), 1 Corinthians 2\7), and only just been given to Paul and his readers, we deduct that the "eonian times" are the future eons, "the coming eons" (Ephesians 2\7); "in advance of" would therefore be better than "before". To complete, then, we write in "in advance of eonian times". I have translated grammatically, and there is internal satisfaction, harmony with other passages, such as Romans 14\22-25 (16\25-26 in King James), which says that the gospel was "kept in silence in eonian times" but is "now brought to light through prophetic Scrolls". It is also in harmony with Ephesians 1\4 which says "in advance of *the* foundation of *the* world order, He calls us out *to be* in Himself". Titus 1\2 has the same Greek phrase, πρὸ χρόνων αἰωνίων (= *pro kronon aionion*), and the context is the same, the gospel of "eonian life" promised "in advance of eonian times".

Strange, then, that if we turn to the King James Bible at 2 Timothy 1\9 and, where it should say "in advance of eonian times", we find instead the curious phrase "before the world began". Yet we see from the Greek phrase πρὸ χρόνων αἰωνίων (= *pro kronon aionion*) that there is no word "the", no word "world", no verb "began". In fact, no verb at all. And the only noun is plural, "times", and there is nothing in the Greek phrase that means "world". The King James does not match the Greek; it does not say that the gospel was promised "before the world began"; the "us" whom Paul speaks of were not there "before the world began" to receive any promise. The King James men have either not understood the words and the concept, or deliberately falsified the translation. They have put the promise into the deep past, pre-existing mankind; the King James rendering of this phrase does not translate back into the original Greek; it gives a different story. My translation method insists on the English being able to be translated back into the same original language, and finding the nearest and best equivalent, rather than the naughty paraphrase and invention system popular in modern versions, and which the King James does to some extent. The King James Bible insults the grammar, insults the wider context, and makes no chronological sense. It would not translate back into the same Greek – hence not the same message – that Paul wrote.

Yet stranger still if we turn to other versions and see equally curious inventions for πρὸ χρόνων αἰωνίων (= *pro kronon aionion*). One version has "before eternal times", which implies that there was a time before eternity, and that eternity has "times", different eternities. What is their difficulty? There cannot be a plural of eternities. Eternity is an absolute word like "perfection".

Now, could it be that "in advance of eonian times" refers not to the future, "the coming eons" (Ephesians 2\7), but to a time before the eons of old, for Isaiah 63\16 and Psalm 93\2 speak of "the eons past"? Could that possibly be what Paul is meaning at 2 Timothy 1\9 and Titus 1\2, the promise of the gospel being made to Abraham? Or to Moses? (Incidentally, I do believe the election and the promise to refer to the first Covenant, given on Sinai (Exodus 19ff.).) In translating the Greek words in front of me, without falsifying anything, allows that interpretation. The King James translation has falsified the meaning, and stamped an interpretation on it, an interpretation that would back up the claims of Calvinism. We might also note that the time of God's choosing the sons of Israel was when Moses on Mount Sinai spoke His words that they were to be a special treasure to God and His own possession "above all the nations" (Exodus 19\5-6, echoed by Peter at 1 Peter 2\9-10).

The Deep Word Archaeology Study Method with John 8\58
At John 8\58 is the verb γενέσθαι (= *genesthai*). This is a verb, and is derived from γίνομαι (= *ginomai*), which has a range of meanings, such as to be, to do, to appear, to arise, to seem, to come, to come to pass, to happen, to finish, to perform, to become. Its Strong's Concordance reference number is g1096. Its grammatical form γενέσθαι is given in Bagster as "aor. 2, infin", which means it is a 2nd aorist type verb and an infinitive. An infinitive is the verb form beginning with "to", as in those examples just listed, or to fish, to write, to complete, to err, to dodge, to invent, to cheat, to falsify, to correct. This word γενέσθαι occurs in other places with a strong future aspect, such as at Revelation 1\1, "things which must be soon to arise"; "what things have to come to pass" (Revelation 4\1); "the things which must be soon to arise" (Revelation 22\6). The context in John 8\58 is Jesus" superiority over Abraham, so Jesus says, "Before Abraham is to appear, I Am". The verb γενέσθαι is rendered with that strong future aspect. But why, then, when we look at the King James Bible, do we find this strict infinitive, γενέσθαι, translated as "was", a finite imperfect past tense put for an infinitive? It says, "Before Abraham was, I am". But that gives the impression that Jesus was around before Abraham! Whenever did an infinitive verb become a finite imperfect past tense verb? When we look at other versions we see the same falsification. One version has γενέσθαι as "came into existence". Yet they have it correctly as an infinitive in other places.

These inventions and grammatical violations serve the polytheistic error of making Jesus seem to have been around before Abraham, so turning him into one of Mysticism's gods in its three gods as one god system.

The Deep Word Archaeology Study Method with John 17\5
At John 17\5 there is the common and simple present infinitive verb εἶναι (= *einai*), Strong's Concordance reference number g1511. The King James Bible has that infinitive as the imperfect "was". One version has the verb as a noun, "existence". Such translating makes Jesus seem to have been around before the world came into being. But neither the grammar nor wider context nor common sense allow such a mystical notion of "the man Christ Jesus" (1 Timothy 2\5), and his being "created" by God (Hebrews 3\2). The Greek construction of the verb phrase at John 17\5 is an occasional Greek construction of preposition + article + infinitive. (These occasional constructions are footnoted in KTK at John 8\58.) What we have at John 17\5 is πρὸ (preposition) τοῦ (genitive singular masculine) τὸν (accusative singular masculine) κόσμον (accusative singular masculine) εἶναι (present active infinitive). I have translated this as "in advance of the coming of the world", the verb εἶναι being represented by the participle "coming".

Jesus is asking the Father to magnify him, or glorify him, with "the magnificence that I had alongside You in advance of the coming of the world". That could be said to mean either promised before the creation of the world (even though Jesus was not there), or promised in advance of the coming eon. At least by translating it honestly the interpretation is open. The King James Bible's "was" is an incorrect translation, and it stamps down the interpretation.

Readers will understand from these few examples why I am so insistent on saying that translation should be done according to grammar and logic and internal harmony. There are a thousand examples I could explain.

The Eonian Documents and other works
Out of the translation and the Companion Notes there have proceeded the needs for making extended explanations of words, phrases and themes of God's 64 Books. These works I have enumerated as Eonian Documents. Comprehensive and extensive explanations of many words

and themes are given in the Eonian Documents.[1] These have been all part of the discovery for me. I write thematic studies in order to explore meanings and interpretations and internal harmonies and themes. They are also a good test – and editing process – of my own translations.

Among my Eonian Documents I include a masterly and wonderful study by Dr. Bullinger, which I can include because it is long out of copyright date. This is a document titled "This Is My Body" (c. 1898). Dr. Bullinger explains that the bread of the Passover is not literally the flesh of Jesus. It is truly a masterly study.

Eonian Document 30, *God Is Not Flesh: Concerning 1 Timothy 3\16*, included as Chapter 30 here, explains why θεός (= *theos*), "God", cannot be the correct reading in that verse, whereas ὅς (= *hos*), "he", makes internal agreement grammatically and thematically. This is also in the preface of KTK.

As well as those documents, the translations, and the Companion Notes, I have also written the following book-length studies, to be included, God willing, in time on the website:

Anglosaxraelites (2018)

Did You Know? (2022)

How the KJV Conceals the True Jesus and his Salvation

Keys of the Kingdom Songbook (ongoing)

The Companion Notes to the New Testament (ongoing)

The Companion Notes to the Old Testament (ongoing)

The Eon in the God-authorized Hebrew and Greek Books: Concerning the Future of the World, examining nine Hebrew words, one Chaldee word, and eight Greek words, in their every occurrence, totalling 884 words, in every phrase, in every context, in relation to the Eons (2013)

The Man Christ Jesus: The Hoax of Polytheism Exposed (2014)

The truth about the promises to the twelve tribes of Israel (2019)

What Happens When You Die (2000)

Who is the Counsellor and the Holy Spirit?: The Hoax of Polytheism Exposed (2012)

The Eon in the God-authorized Hebrew and Greek Books examines – as its full title says – every occurrence of Hebrew and Greek words which mean "eon" and "eonian" and "throughout the eon" and similar phrases. It gives the context of every occurrence, the King James rendering, and side by side with it the correct and grammatical rendering. In other Bible translations, such words and phrases as "eternal", "everlasting" and "for ever" are inaccurate. The basis of this is that the Hebrew word עולם (= *olam*) (which occurs 438 times) and the Greek word αἰών (= *aion*) (which occurs 126 times in the Robinson and Pierpoint 2005 Textform) mean "eon" or "age". This affects our knowledge about the past and the future, revealed to us by God and His prophets, and it affects our knowledge of the gospel promise, which is "eonian life" (John 3\15-16), that is, assurance of life "throughout the eon". See also Chapter 24 in this, and it is Appendix 6 in *Keys of the Kingdom Holy Bible*.

---

1. In the 2015 edition of this book I listed the (then) 122 Eonian Document titles. They now number 360 (June 2023).

My book-length study *What Happens When You Die* shows that in death man goes into the grave and has no life until he will be resurrected by God. Every passage which might be brought by tradition to try to justify its "migration of the soul" is examined in detail and such "migration" is shown to be an ancient Pagan blinding hangover.

Besides all these, I have two million words of other studies (from early training days) which in time I have come to reject as the light has grown.

The underlying Greek text of my New Testament
I have been surprised in my many conversations with people how few know that the Old Testament is written in Hebrew (with small portions of Aramaic) and the New Testament in Greek (with a handful of Aramaic words).

There are known to be at least 5,686 (last count I read) pieces of Greek manuscripts of the New Testament of varying provenance and pedigree, dating back to 125 AD. On top of that, there are known to be over 19,000 ancient New Testament manuscripts in the Syriac, Latin, Coptic and Aramaic languages.

The King James Bible was translated from a Greek text known as the Textus Receptus (TR). The TR text is certainly magnificently superior to the massacred texts of modernist versions, published after the *Revised Version* of 1881. However, there are troubles with the TR text, such as its inclusion of the polytheist clauses in 1 John 5 which are without Greek textual basis.

It is highly fortunate in this time in that two most diligent and distinguished textual scholars, Maurice A Robinson and William G Pierpont, laboured for 27 years to compile a Greek text which is probably the best to date, the Robinson-Pierpont Byzantine Textform 2005. This is the textual basis for my New Testament (with written permission).

The Robinson-Pierpont Textform is a major and welcome advancement in textual authority. It has the most impressive early support and agreement from other early versions and other writers over a large geographical area and over a long period of time.

Robinson and Pierpont say of the Textus Receptus: "Certainly the *Textus Receptus* had its problems, not the least of which was its failure to reflect the Byzantine Textform in an accurate manner" (Robinson and Pierpont, p. 533); and: "The overall text of those early printed editions [of TR] differs from the Byzantine Textform in over 1800 instances, generally due to the inclusion of weakly supported non-Byzantine readings" (ibid, p. i).

My renderings should be checked against the Robinson-Pierpont Greek text, not the Textus Receptus. My use of the Robinson-Pierpont text (RP) means several variations to the Textus Receptus (TR) text. The differences, although quite numerous, are minor and affect no themes or narratives, but do enhance some passages.

The variations sometimes mean (in translation) no more than "a" or "the"; "Christ Jesus" instead of "Jesus Christ" (for example 1 Timothy 1\2, making it consistent with Paul's style at 2 Timothy 1\2; Hebrews 3\1); sometimes different words; sometimes the absences of words which the TR has; sometimes the inclusion of words which the TR does not have. The TR text has more internal logic and internal harmony than the RP text in the two Revelation verses. These are discussed in *Conventions* (in TELB), and in *God Is Not Flesh: Concerning 1 Timothy 3\16* (Chapter 30).

There are just 9 places where I differ from the RP text and prefer the Textus Receptus; for doctrinal reasons, they are more likely right: Matthew 19\9, Acts 8\37, Romans 9\3, Ephesians 3\5, 1 Timothy 3\16, Revelation 21\1, 21\6 (two places), 22\18.

This means that not only is *Keys of the Kingdom Holy Bible* made in clear language and according to strict Translating Laws and Translating Targets, but is also based on the most superior Greek text, with the most scholarly research behind it and done with the deepest grammatical integrity. We therefore have at last in English a reliable imitation of the writings of the prophets and apostles, something withheld for centuries because of obsequious curtsying to the Church

Fathers and their creeds.

Conclusion

The labour of *Keys of the Kingdom* translation has not come out of theological colleges. Those are not the birth-places of the understanding of the prophets and apostles. More than 28 years ago I obtained a prospectus for one of them. I visited another. And I did one term of "Biblical Studies" in another. Those were not places for men and women of the spirit. They were birth-places of works of the religious system. The word of God is not chained. Nor is it institutionalised.

The approach of producing popular Bibles for the religious system has been an unimpressive enterprise. They have not been commissioned for the right reason, which should be to recover the truth of the prophets and apostles, yet that has never even once been stated; not that I have read. The translators have not been the right people. The translation methods have been ways of PROCESSING, rather than ORGANIC. Particularly in the New Testament, grammatical forms and structures have been violated. There has not been an attempt to recover the underlying styles. They have been the work of committees, receiving the payment of their employers. Who were on these committees? We do not even know their names. We do not know them as great men and women of God. (The names of Wycliffe, Tyndale, and Rogers, men who worked alone, stand apart.) The popular religious translations have been done too quickly. Nobody who builds their doctrines on these translations will be safe from being deceived and misinformed. There are no exceptions.

It might be reasonably wondered why God has allowed so many centuries to pass before His angels and prophets and apostles were translated accurately, and why the world system has been allowed to flourish. How can God force anybody to make a translation, or how can He make anybody do anything? What has been demonstrated in all these centuries is man's rebellious unwillingness to yield to God's truth, man's unrighteous preference for systems and religious leaders. So also in all this has God's patience been demonstrated. How much longer the errant religious system will flourish I cannot tell. Not long, perhaps, especially now we have so many resources out there has been an awakening, and we can have accurate ORGANIC translating, nothing fidgeted out of place. And the true gospel of "eonian life" and life "throughout the eon", so long been hidden, can be proclaimed in its fulness.

It might be asked, how can so many have been so wrong for so long, and how can Sparkes say he is right? The Lord God did not stop the false shepherds and false teachers in the days of the prophets. In fact, they went on so long God had to warn the house of Jacob, and they refused the warning, and punishments came. It is for reasons of integrity, checking my renderings, and allowing others to check, that I developed the Translating Laws and Translating Targets. By ORGANIC translation principles of Deep Grammar, Transcendent Logic, Internal Harmony, Diamond-mining Research, and Text – those five firm foundations – *Keys of the Kingdom Holy Bible* translation is grammatically responsible and true and honest to the underlying Greek text, according to my deepest principles of integrity. The grammatical facts cannot be disputed. Neither should the logic and harmony. No words have been manipulated. Of course, it is impossible that there will not be words and phrases that could not be improved or corrected – perfect translation is a target, not an achievable notion – and I continually look to make enhancements, so that the translation can be better and stronger. I welcome sensible suggestions, and have received them already.

Keys of the Kingdom Holy Bible is not another contribution to the burning cauldron of debate. It is a restoration of the declarations of the prophets and apostles of God who heard the messages from angels of God and from Jesus Christ. This is the restored proclamation of the prophets and apostles. It is an announcement of God's truths – and of the gospel of a coming eon.

If the result of the King James Bible has created a distance between the truth and the people by means of strange and manifold error, the intention with *Keys of the Kingdom Holy Bible* is the reverse: to close the distance, and to present them in truth and purity to everybody.

To those noble-minded men and women and children who are seekers, I present to them in *Keys of the Kingdom Holy Bible* a far more reliable representation than has been published in English of the divinely-preserved oracles of angels and prophets and apostles as recorded in the God-authorized Hebrew and Greek Books. In *Keys of the Kingdom Holy Bible* truth seekers will find the truth of God's indescribable free offer of "eonian life" and the promise of an incorruptible resurrection mind and body, and of such an exultation in Jesus Christ that nobody can even imagine its wonder and its every spiritually-activated exuberance in the Lord God.

> Thanks to the one true God.
> cjs, 12 January 2014;
> slightly revised March 2015, May 2021, June 2023

Chapter 2

The Longest Odyssey

✴

I remember a church with a green dome I could see from my bedroom window. I remember rummaging around the church's garden and picking up small sweet chestnuts which we took home and Dad roasted in the fire over a small shovel then holding them in his fingers without flinching. And I remember a kindly-looking old priest high up in a wooden pulpit, wobbling his jowls like a bloodhound's. I remember catechism classes, and hearing strange things about places called Purgatory and Hell. I would gaze up at the green dome and imagine myself standing in a congested choir in Heaven. I remember going into the butcher's shop with my brother and asking for pheasant feathers to make our arrows, and the butcher greeting us with "*Pax vobiscum*". Peace be with you.

~ ✴ ~

One lonesome Easter in 1977 I sloped my way like a sad pilgrim into Greatham Church in Hampshire, and I prayed my heart out for delivery from the anguish and depression that had been caused by certain personal events, four thunderbolts.

Hazards had hit me like a freight train screaming, and I feared that, like my then hero John Keats, I was going to die young. And I was convinced I was on my way to Hell. A spirit version of me would be mysteriously unzipped from my corpse, and I would tumble alone, forever, through space, in torment of mind, floating between stars for ever, images I picked up from the religious education of my childhood. Hell was a dark space without gravity, lit by a few stars.

I met this "Hell" once again when I began to read English Bibles. Two years after the Greatham Church prayers, I found myself in a Presbyterian service in Liss Forest and I heard John's Gospel read and I was never the same again. I turned my life to God and Jesus and to the writings of the God-authorized prophets and apostles, and I became far more passionate than I had been in the nominal Christianity of my youth. I was a new man in Jesus Christ. Following some months of reluctant submission, I became confident that not Hell, but another region would be my home after death: Heaven, where Jesus is.

Hell, I heard from preachers, is a fire. Shakespeare alluded to Hell as "the primrose way to the everlasting bonfire" (*Macbeth*). The King James Bible has the phrases "hell fire" (Matthew 5\22); "child of hell" (Matthew 23\15); and "the damnation of hell" (Matthew 23\33). That translation also has Peter saying of some "angels" that God "cast *them* down to hell" (2 Peter 2\4); and it has Moses speaking of a fire which will "burn to the lowest hell" (Deuteronomy 32\22); and David prophesying that "the wicked shall be turned into hell" (Psalm 9\17); and Jesus telling a story of a man who "in hell ... lift up his eyes, being in torment ... And he cried and said ... I am tormented in this flame" and the man could see and speak to Abraham across a gulf (Luke 16\23). Hell was true because it was in the New international Bible and King James Bible.

I was believing now though, that Heaven was going to be my future home. In my death, I would somehow be transported before the throne of God to join the choirs of angels and myriads of others and spend eternity mainly standing up and singing.

In 1984 I was living in the Jericho district of Oxford, along the lower end of Walton Street, from where I would walk out to the meadows and the wide River Isis in which I mainly had an interest for checking for trout, but I saw none. I was scraping something of a living performing in poetry and music shows, supplemented by dish-washing in the steamy underworld of St. Aldgate's café's basement kitchen. Despite my beliefs, the year-and-a-half there was one of the unhappiest epochs of my life. I was under-employed and lonesome. A stranger in a strange land. I lay agape all night in sleepless glooms, somewhat like Nicholas in Chaucer's *Miller's Tale*, except that Nicholas's trance was feigned. If I walked by my own window in the day, I looked up at it and prayed for myself as "that man up there" who was alone and so miserable – like the blind beggars in ancient Jericho calling out to Jesus, "Have mercy on me, Lord, Son of David!" Nevertheless, after "The weariness, the fever, and the fret / Here where men sit and hear each other groan" (Keats) of this withering passage of my life, all, I reckoned, would be well in my after-life in Heaven. My ecstasy in odd moments would overcome all my troubled heart. As the prophet Isaiah said:

> ... an ornament for ashes, the oil of joy for mourning,
> the garment of praise for the heavy spirit,
> so that they might be called trees of righteousness,
> the planting of Yahweh, so that He might be magnified. ~ Isaiah 61\3

I left Jericho, returned South and found some sort of peace. I settled into new work, in the Law, and sat myself down to voracious readings of the Scrolls of God.

At the back of all this I was hearing from preachers and writers and translations that our future is sealed, a blissful dwelling on glassy floors of the courts of Heaven, and that any who knowingly reject Jesus will suffer the Hell I once so feared for myself. This created insufferable questions. What about the nice people who profess uncertainty about Jesus Christ? My parents, the best people in the world? And then the arrogant who profess such certainty? Do some go to Hell because they have not been told about Jesus? How can you burn for ever? I spoke about these matters to whom I could, but got no answers, just platitudes.

Along with my other evangelistic certainties, I pressed on in my conviction that my ultimate destiny would be the mysterious journey through starry space from Earth and to Heaven.

Until, that is, I went to Berwick-on-Tweed, which hovers on the England-Scotland border.

~ * ~

In the library of a Berwick-on-Tweed guest-house, I interrupted a conversation with two elderly gentlemen. I overheard them discussing something about "immortality of the soul", so I went over to them and asked what they were talking about. "Well it's not right, is it?" said one of them, Rowland Wickes, tall and austere like my Grandpa Hughes. "The soul that sinneth, it shall die" (Ezekiel 18\4, 18\20). So the "soul" dies. He gave me a copy of a book he had published, *The Path to Immortality*. It cited Moses in Genesis: "the man Adam became a living soul" (Genesis 2\7). Ah, so the soul is the person, the person dies, and returns to dust (Genesis 3\19). Man does not *have* a soul: he *is* a soul.

So what happens at death? Nothing, said one of my new friends. And Heaven? Hell? No, "the wages of sin is death." Nothing, until the resurrection. Nothing. The next morning during a car-ride out of Berwick, Rowland said to me, "Heaven's empty, apart from Christ and angels," and he pulled a mischievous smile.

I saw the connections all right: if man doesn't have a soul, some element which could be unzipped – by whom? angels? God? how? what? – then in death we quit our being. My inner eye, in seconds, was making its greatest journey: falling through a void of dark air without gravity, then up past stars to rejoicing Heaven, and now down somewhere to a fiery Hell – those heavenly choirs, that floating through starry space, those eternal flames – and back on my feet in the safe green Earth, keeling over into the dust in death. "For you are dust, and you will return to dust." Now I was seeing it: death, nothing, resurrection. This, then, is why Jesus and the apostles proclaimed resurrection. Nowhere is there any passage about "reuniting the soul with the body", or "the migration of the soul", as in ancient Mysticism.

On my broken journey home from Berwick – delayed trains, missed connections, tannoy'd apologies, offered refunds later begrudgingly sent – these ideas burned inside my brain and I yearned to explode them to my wife when I got home to Hampshire.

I had to yield my mind to a new paradigm in all my interpretations and translations of God's Books. With an array of new lexical tools soon joining my library, Hebrew and Greek dictionaries, grammars and concordances, off I set. I felt like William Tyndale, making by candlelight his illegal translations of the *Newe Testament*, and on the run from the despicable Cuthbert Tunstall, Bishop of London, who got him in the end. Tyndale was strangled and burned near Brussels on October the 6th, 1536; within a few years, though, there were Bibles throughout England.

It was the original Hebrew and Greek I must rely on, not any English, Latin or other translation.

Before Berwick, I had begun to wonder about the Greek word γέεννα (= *gehenna*), usually translated "hell" or "Hell" in English Bibles. The passages relied on by Hell preachers are often King James Bible citations of "hell fire". For example, the King James Bible in Matthew's Gospel has Jesus saying that, "it is better for thee to enter into life with one eye, rather than having two eyes to be cast into hell fire" (Matthew 18\9).

Did Jesus really say those things? What does the Greek say? Out of where do those King James Bible translations come? The literal reading and actual syntax of Matthew's Greek in that passage has this: "good for you it is one-eyed into the life to enter, rather than two eyes having to be thrown into the γέεννα τοῦ πυρός", that is, "the gehenna of the fire". (Greek syntax is looser than English.)

What is this γέεννα (= *gehenna*)? Well, it does not take much research to discover that γέεννα is a Greek transliteration of the Hebrew for a place-name in ancient Israel, גיא הנם (= *ge hinnom*). The Greek is γέ [valley] + εννα [Hinnom]. This גיא הנם (= *ge hinnom*) in English is "the Valley of Hinnom". The Hebrew phrase גיא הנם for "the Valley of Hinnom" appears 13 times, and the Greek for it, γέεννα, appears 12 times. So why in the King James Bible is the Hebrew גיא הנם (= *ge hinnom*) rendered correctly as "the Valley of Hinnom", but its Greek equivalent γέεννα (= *gehenna*) rendered as "hell"? Let the translators answer for themselves. For the phrase γέεννα τοῦ πυρός (= *gehenna tou puros*), they wrote "hell fire". They should have written" the fire of the Valley of Hinnom". On the Internet there are contemporary photographs of the Valley of Hinnom.

It much maligns Jesus the Son of God to say that he threatened people with the torture of eternal burning for not believing him.

The 12 occurrences of γέεννα (= *gehenna*) ought to be translated just as the Hebrew is, "the Valley of Hinnom". The words of Jesus cited above ought properly to read, "... having two eyes to be thrown into the fire of the Valley of Hinnom." This aligns Jesus' words with statements by Isaiah and Jeremiah, the prophets of old, that enemies of God will one day, at the close of the future Messianic Eon, at Jesus' coming to the Earth, be destroyed in the Valley of Hinnom. Other names for the site are "Tophet" (Isaiah 30\33, Jeremiah 7\31-32), "the Valley of the Son of Hinnom" (2 Kings 23\10, Jeremiah 7\31-32), and "the Valley of Slaughter" (Jeremiah 7\32).

Not in a single translation have I seen this correctly as "Valley of Hinnom" in the New Testament. They have either "hell", "Hell", or "Gehenna".

The prophet Joshua describes the Valley of Hinnom as being "to the southern side of Jebusite, that is, Jerusalem" (Joshua 15\8). There the wicked king of Israel, Manasseh, "caused his sons to pass through the fire in the Valley of the Son of Hinnom" as sacrifices to the demon-god called Molech (2 Kings 21\6, 2 Chronicles 33\6). The good king Josiah demolished the idols, so those evils were stopped. Eventually the valley became a garbage dump, a perpetual burning fire. The rising smoke and the stench were a reminder to the inhabitants of Jerusalem of past idolatries.

When Jesus asked the Pharisees, "How can you escape from the judgement of the Valley of Hinnom?" (Matthew 23\33), he was implying that they, like the discarded rubbish of Jerusalem, were fit only for destruction by burning.

So those images of my youth, floating through a darkness of eternal solitude, or of underground fires, are not something deep inside our psyche, but they are images taught and learned. And when we know the truth, they are discarded as so much rubbish. The false story about Hell is itself a γέεννα (= *Gehenna*). A burning garbage-tip of an idea.

This γέεννα (= *gehenna*) is not the only word wrongly rendered "hell" in English Bibles. The two gentlemen I met in Berwick pointed out to me that in the King James Bible there is one word in the Old Testament, שאול (= *sheol*), translated three ways ("hell", "grave", "pit"). And there are three words in the New Testament, γέεννα (= *gehenna*), ἅδης (= *hades*), ταρταρόω (= *tartaroo*) – translated one way, "hell". (I wonder why the King James has "heaven" and "hell", specific place names, in lower-case.)

The concept conveyed by the words שאול (= *sheol*) and ἅδης (= *hades*) is different from γέεννα (= *gehenna*). The first occurrence of שאול (= *sheol*) is spoken by the patriarch Jacob. Believing his son Joseph was dead, he groaned, "I will go down to the grave, mourning for my son" (Genesis 37\35). If שאול (= *sheol*) really were some sort of Hell, did Jacob believe that his grief would cause him to go into some fiery Hell, and that his son was already there? Those two patriarchs are listed among God's "great cloud of witnesses" in the letter to the Hebrews. Clearly Jacob meant "death", or "the grave". Not even the sloppy King James has שאול (= *sheol*) as "hell" in that verse.

We can also see in many passages – by the literary device of grammatical parallelism, where an idea might be repeated in different words but in a similar grammatical structure – that שאול represents death, or the grave. David wrote:

> For in death, there is no remembrance of You.
> Who in sheol is going to give You thanks?   ~ Psalm 6\5

Sheol, then, represents a state of death, total unconsciousness. Perhaps nothing so clearly defines שאול as this statement spoken by the prophet Hosea:

> I will redeem them from the power of sheol;
> I will redeem them from death.   ~ Hosea 13\14

The obvious parallelism of "sheol" and "death" suggests synonymous connotations. It does not suggest anything that might be called "Hell". Furthermore, the passage concerns God's redeemed, so שאול (= *sheol*) is not anything to do with some fictitious, mythological place of fiery punishment.

The next word, ἅδης (= *hades*), I need not labour, because it is the exact Greek equivalent of the Hebrew word שאול (= *sheol*). This is seen in Peter's speech on the Day of Pentecost when Peter cited a Psalm of David: "You will not abandon my dead body in the grave" (Acts 2\27, from Psalm 16\10). This equivalence of ἅδης for שאול is seen again at the end of 1 Corinthians 15 when Paul refers to the prophet Hosea:

> Where, oh death, *is* your sting?

> Where, oh grave, *is* your victory?   ~ 1 Corinthians 15\55

In Greek Mythology, the word "Hades" – ᾅδης – came to represent an underworld of tormented souls. "Hades" was the ancient name of the Greek god who ruled the underworld, a son of the Titans, and the god of the dead. He was harsh and ruthless, the opposite of the true God. He was later named as "Pluto" by the Romans. In Mythology, this demon-god Hades had demons and servants such as Charon the ferryman who took souls in his boat across the river Acheron to the kingdom of the dead and they were never allowed to return. Post-Babylonian priests and bishops picked up this mythology and imported it into the religion they were constructing, Peter, for example, perhaps representing Charon.

The Holy Scrolls of God, far from aligning with any demonic mythology, contradict and oppose it.

The one exceptional use of ᾅδης (= *hades*) in the Scrolls of God occurs in Luke, when we read of Jesus brilliantly parodying the Pharisees' amalgamation of mythology and Moses. They had already imported it into their national religion, so it was an easy thing for the post-Babylonians to take up the baton of mythology. So in Jesus' parody of their impossible beliefs, a fictional narrative about a rich man and a beggar, the word ᾅδης does represent a place of fiery torment, but it was only for Jesus' clever purpose of mocking its impossibility.

All that mythology came from the ancient world, and God's view of that world is shown by Peter: God "did not spare the ancient world" (2 Peter 2\5). Evil men, though, wanted to cling onto it and preserve it.

And so to the last word which appears as "hell" in the King James Bible, ταρταρόω (= *tartaroo*). This occurs only once – in Peter's second letter, in the King James: "For if God spared not the angels who sinned, but cast *them* down to hell" (2 Peter 2\4). But there is no Greek word for "hell" here. What appears in the Greek is a transitive verb, here in the form of a participle: ταρταρώσας (= *tartarosas*). This verb is well rendered as "swallowed underground". The reference is to Korah and others whom God punished for their grumbling rebellion: "the ground which *was* underneath them split apart, [32] and the ground opened its mouth and swallowed them up ... all the men of Korah, and all *their* goods" (Numbers 16\31-32). Jude speaks of "the rebellion of Korah" (Jude 11).

It is true what Rowland Wickes told me: there is no Hell in all the pages of God's Books. While there is, indeed, "boiling anger and indignation, tribulation and anguish" in the day of God's anger for those who "obey unrighteousness" (Romans 2\5-9), there is no such thing as any eternal conscious punishment, not anywhere, any time, for anybody. It's an invention, of demonic mindset. Jesus and the apostles warn of the "destruction of ungodly men" (2 Peter 3\7), God-haters – but speak nothing of eternal torments in fire, which is a physical impossibility anyway. Jesus speaks of the wide gate and the broad road "leading off into destruction" (Matthew 7\13). He speaks of believers in himself not suffering destruction (John 3\16). He speaks also of angels separating the evil off from the righteous and throwing them "into the furnace of the fire" (Matthew 13\49-50), a refining fire. But the only time Jesus speaks of the concept of torment in fire is to mock it heavily in his satirical narrative of the rich man and Lazarus (Luke 16\19-31). Destruction is a different matter to some impossible eternal torment in fire.

~ * ~

In the year 2000 I stayed in the Lake District with friends. While walking the hills and around the lakes, I pressed a point. The prophets and apostles speak strongly about Jesus making a visible and permanent return to the Earth. In not many years yet, Jesus will come as lightning flashes, and riding on clouds of angels, down to the Mount of Olives on the East side of Jerusalem, the prophets say, and he will walk a highway to the Temple's East gate (Zechariah 14\4). So what, then, would be the point of anybody going off to Heaven where Jesus had just come from?

I could not and did not let go of this. Once home from the lakes, I began to reconsider the contexts, interpretations and translations of any passages suggesting the heavens. There really only is one passage in the King James Bible which seems to uphold it and this is in Paul's opening to the Ephesians, which reads:

Blessed *be* the God and Father of our Lord Jesus Christ, who hath blessed us with all spiritual blessings in heavenly *places* in Christ. ~ Ephesians 1\3

That King James Bible rendering needed challenging. The Greek word the King James Bible has as "heavenly *places*" is ἐπουράνιος (= *epouranios*, *epi* + *ouranos*), an adjective acting substantively (as a noun).

I began to understand that the prepositional phrase "in heavenly *places*" in Ephesians is linguistically unstable. The King James Bible's italicization of "*places*" gives away the instability of the interpretation. When I wrote out the 20 occurrences of this adjective ἐπουράνιος, I saw that in Philippians 2\10 it acts substantively for "heavenly beings". What ἐπουράνιος means is not "heavenly *places*", but something like "the most exalted", so describing people, not places. Jesus used ἐπουράνιος of the Father. Paul used it of Jesus, angels, demonic-minded world rulers, bodies, describing the noun "realm", and describing the New Jerusalem. (Eonian Document 25, not included here, displays all the occurrences.)

Deep study shows that ἐπουράνιος means anything but "heavenly *places*". There are five occurrences of ἐπουράνιος in Ephesians. The first three of those five refer to believers' exaltation with Jesus. The last two of those five occurrences refer to world rulers and powers with hostile minds (Ephesians 3\10 and 6\12). Unfortunately, at Ephesians 3\10 the King James Bible has ἐπουράνιος as "heavenly *places*" and at 6\12 it has it as "high *places*". Well, if there are hostile demonic-minded powers in those "places" – if, only *if*, hypothetically, that were the correct rendering – how could ἐπουράνιος represent the future place of the redeemed if it's also full of hostile-minded world rulers? The contexts, then, of those two occurrences of ἐπουράνιος demand a corrected rendering: not "in heavenly *places*", but (distinguishing the demonic-minded from the exalted believers) "among the most eminent". Then at 3\10 and 6\12, relating to the hostile people, we understand that the evil world rulers are among "the most eminent [ἐπουράνιος]" of the demonic-minded powers.

The King James rendering of ἐπουράνιος as "heavenly *places*" is impossible. Nobody is going to Heaven. My late friend Errol Palmer gave me two extremely fine studies by Otis Q Sellers who made intricate and indisputable arguments against the rendering "heavenly *places*". Sellers' study concludes with the linguistically consistent, contextually logical and highly satisfactory rendering for ἐπουράνιος at the opening of Ephesians of "the most elevated" or "the most exalted".

I developed this satisfying rendering of Ephesians 1\3:

Praised *be* the God and Father of our Lord Jesus Christ, the one having exalted us with every spiritual exaltation among the most exalted in Christ.

1\3, *most exalted*: **ἐπουράνιος** (*epouranios*). 1\20, 2\6, 3\10, 6\12, Mat. 18\35, John 3\12, 1 Cor. 15\40, 15\48-49, Phil. 2\10, 3\11, 2 Tim. 4\18, Heb. 3\1, 6\4, 8\5, 9\23, 11\16, 12\22. (Cp. for evil powers at 3\10, 6\12.) Strong's g2032, equiv. of Heb. שמים (*shamayim*), Strong's h8064, Gen. 2\4, Deut. 7\6, 7\14, 10\15, 11\21, 26\19, 28\1, 1 Sam. 2\8, Psalm 113\7, Job 36\7, Isaiah 65\17, 66\22-23. Cp. οὐρανός (*ouranos*), Strong's g3772, Mat.

So in Paul's opening to the Ephesians he was telling them that God had exalted them in every spiritual exaltation which has been named "among the most exalted." This is the key: it is perfectly in line with passages such as Romans 8\29 ("whom He knows in advance, He marks out in advance also *to be* conformed to the image of His Son, for himself to be First-honoured among many brothers") and Hebrews 11\40 ("God having foreseen something better involving us, so that they should not be complete without us"), those passages (and others) speaking of believers being marked out for exaltation with Jesus and among the prophets and apostles. God has already exalted them *now*, in advance. This is also in line with the foundation of the calling: that great proclamation by the prophet Moses for the sons of Israel to be "above all peoples" (Exodus 19\5-6) and "above all peoples on the face of the Earth" (Deuteronomy 7\6, 7\14, 28\1), and echoed by Peter that they are "a nation set apart" (1 Peter 2\9-10, Exodus 19\5-6). If it were to mean blessed "in heavenly *places*", the verb would have to say "he will exalt", future – the Ephesian readers were not in "heavenly *places*", nor will they ever be. But it is not future tense – it is "having exalted", a participle, showing completion. Those same Ephesians turn up again, in the opening to Revelation (1\11, 2\1), very much on the Earth.

"Exalted *are* the submissive," Jesus said, "for they will inherit the land" (Matthew 5\5). It's the land, not Heaven, they are going to inherit, as promised to the patriarchs. And the great King David testifies:

> The heavens, *yes* the heavens, *belong* to Yahweh,
> but the Earth He has given to the sons of Adam. ~ Psalm 115\16

After all those years, no longer was I floating out to Hell from Greatham. Nor was I ascending into Heaven out of Jericho near Oxford. My feet are grounded for ever on the mysterious Earth, which same Earth Jesus will reign over (through the Angel of God and His prophets and apostles) from the heavens during the coming eon, and where Jesus will set down his nail-scarred feet on the Mount of Olives, and where he will remain. Jesus will be in the Holy City with God and with "the twelve tribes of the sons of Israel" and "the twelve apostles of the Lamb" (Revelation 21\12-14, Matthew 19\28). On the New Earth, in the New Jerusalem (Hebrews 12\22). How can man's place be in the heavens if Jesus is coming down to the Earth and reigning in the New Earth? Only one man has been to Heaven: the Lord Jesus Christ, who was taken up and led by angels. Nobody else is going.

So studying the God-authorized Books for me now, you will understand, is no longer an empty exercise about where Heaven might be and how to get up there, or where Hell might be and how to avoid it. The Earth is our home. And here I am, in my home, writing this, and my wife is in the kitchen feeding our baby girl, and our three year-old son is staring at my computer screen. My mother died three months ago, and I'll soon be back for a while in the house I grew up in. It feels as if I'm starting all over again, this time with a lump in my throat.

February 2004.
Slightly revised May 2021, June 2023.

★

ed48

3\2, and οὐράνιος (*ouranios*), Strong's g3770, Mat. 6\14. See Preface, p. xxxii. Cp. 'pillar', 1 Sam. 2\8, Gal. 2\9, Rev. 3\12

Chapter 3

A Bit of Biograph

I was brought up attending Roman Catholic Masses in a town church, and I went to a Roman Catholic grammar school. I believed in God and I thought atheists were sad and awkward people, cornering themselves in an impossible position, and I contended with them.

When in later teenage years the temptations and lusts of the world came knocking on my door, I invited them in and shut my eyes to God. But I knew ...

At the end of the 1970s I lived a few doors away from a tin-roofed shack-looking building used for Christian meetings and, through my Sunday morning hazes, I would see interesting looking characters emerging from this building, perhaps poets, musicians, painters, actors.

By December of 1979 I had moved a few miles away, but I met one of those interesting characters, an Irish folk musician. I spoke to him over several months about spiritual matters, then I asked him if I could go to one of their shack meetings. I thought it an absolute scandal I should be permitted among presumably righteous-living people, but the musician seemed curiously delighted.

On Sunday the 9th of December 1979 the eccentric and gifted Irish musician took me to a Sunday morning meeting in the shack thing. I do not remember anything about the service now, other than hearing a man reading something from John's Gospel – I wish I knew what it was – and then my being driven home in somebody's car and I was talking immensely excitedly about it all. I didn't know it immediately but did in time that I had been generated from above, as if reborn. My mind was different, my outlook, my purpose, my strong awareness of specific guilt and craving for forgiveness, my fixing on Jesus. I had begun to understand the death of Jesus. I was seeing it as the centre-point of all human history.

In those days I was managing the family bookshop, and I was staying up all hours writing poetry and painting and drawing and reading. Our dad used to talk about becoming a full-time writer. My brother and I, aged seven and nine, wrote stories and sent them to a big-name publisher. A month later we would receive a postal order for a couple of shillings. It was not, though, until 1974, having digested Keats and Eliott, that I became obsessed with reading and writing poetry.

After hearing John's Gospel in that strange building, I got myself one of those Bibles they were reading from, and I poured over it; my reading had new wings. I remember one of the leaders being surprised that, without contesting, I believed everything I was reading, particularly creation. Well why shouldn't I? It's true.

I well remember also another one of their leaders explaining to me, as we walked over the Devil's Punch Bowl at Hindhead, all about Hell and how people like my parents deserve it for not believing. He told me no Greek or Hebrew words, nor any passages to back up his ideas, only spoke about it philosophically. I did not know then about the church creeds and the Church Fathers and the Latin Vulgate, or anything about mistranslations.

I was obsessed with my Bible and took it everywhere. I made lists, indexes of themes, underlined passages, wrote question marks against anything I could not understand, and typed up a large portion of Isaiah. Somebody would tell me something or give me something to read and those would set me off on a new quest. I spoke endlessly to people about it, and I told everybody about the salvation of Jesus.

The following year, 1980, I was working on a boat in southern France, and I sat reading the

Bible on its beautiful summer beaches with all the obvious distractions. None of my boat workmates made any disparaging remarks about my Bible obsession and my spiritual leanings. One night in Antibes I bumped into a journalist I knew from my home town and we stayed in a bar talking until very late; by the time I got back to the boat, the *Conquest*, it was locked and everyone was asleep so I slept underneath an upturned row-boat on the dockside, my jumper for a pillow. Another night my workmates and I went into a bar and I was approached by a beautiful woman. When she asked me to buy her a drink I realized she was *une femme de la nuit*, so I told her the gospel of Jesus in French, the best French I'd ever spoken.

Back in England the next winter in the bookshop I told one of the church people how I would one day like to make my own translation.

In 1981 I read Francis Schaeffer's book, *How Should We Then Live? The Rise and Decline of Western Thought and Culture* (1976). I saw from Schaeffer that, from the time of the Reformation to the 20th century, in works of literature, art, music, film, theology, philosophy and science, purposeful attacks had been made against faith in the Bible and against the one true God. These grisly works influenced nations and multitudes. I wanted to know why they even get published and exhibited. I wanted to know why Christians did not produce greater works to overshadow the atheistic works. I wanted to know what a Christian could write to beat back and defeat all these godless works, and recover the mood against the word of God.

Some time around 1990 I had a dream. I saw a large trout struggling on a shallow gravel bed in a brook in Steep, Kettlesbrook, where my brother and I fished when children. I picked up the fish, and it became smaller in my hands (like the two sticks becoming one stake in the hand of Ezekiel). I put it into deeper water and it swam off into safety. With that, I left the church I'd been attending, saying I was going to concentrate on studying the Bible. This, I was told by the leaders, was "of the Devil" and they were shouting at me in gobbledygook glossolalia. I covered my face with my hands and laughed silently. It was time to go.

Around 1992 I had another inspiriting dream. I was standing on a round table in the large front room of the house I was living in. The room was crowded with many people and I was saying to them, in a voice elevated by immense excitement, "I've found the Scriptures, I've found the Scriptures!" I thought about Ezra: "And Ezra the scribe stood on a high platform of wood that they had made for the purpose, and beside him stood Mattithiah, and Shema, and Anaiah, and Urijah, and Hilkiah, and Maaseiah on his right hand; and on his left hand, Pedaiah, and Mishael, and Malchiah, and Hashum, and Hashbadana, Zechariah, and Meshullam. [5] And Ezra unrolled the scroll before the eyes of all the people, for he was above all the people, and when he opened it all the people stood up, [6] and Ezra magnified Yahweh, the magnificent Elohim. And all the people answered, 'Amen, amen!', and they lifted their hands, and bowed their heads, and worshipped Yahweh, faces to the ground" (Nehemiah 8\4-6).

Fast forward to Scotland 1997. It was there I learned the falsehood of man's having a soul that flies through the stars to mystical places after death. By this time I had a copy of Dr EW Bullinger's *Companion Bible*, and I was absorbing all its copious corrections and enhancements to the King James Bible, as well as Bullinger's 198 appendices. I already had a growing file titled *Amendments to the English Bible*. For example, my file contained these (some have since been revised): at Proverbs 2\18 "dead" should be "Rephaim". At Jeremiah 3\15 "pastors" should be "shepherds". At Acts 12\4 "Easter" should be "Passover". At 1 Corinthians 16\22 the words "Anathema Maranatha" should be separated with a full-stop. At 1 Timothy 6\10 "the love of money is the root of all evil" should be "the love of money is a root of all the evils". At Hebrews 11\3 "the worlds were framed" should read "the ages to have been framed". And so on: there were thousands more in Bullinger's *Companion Bible* and in his *How to Enjoy the Bible*.

I was walking in Scotland around some island – I think it was called Holy Island; I didn't take much notice because I was too involved in conversation. I was talking to Errol Palmer about William Tyndale. Errol was a gardener who liked to tell you the Latin name of every plant we might come across. He knew more about Tyndale than I did. We were impressed with Tyndale's nerve and vision. As we walked around the island, these things were burning inside me, like the two men on the Emmaus road who met Jesus, saying, "Was our heart not burning in us while he was talking with us on the road, and while he was opening the scrolls to us?" (Luke 24\32).

When I was home in England, I was lying on a bench by a Hampshire lake on a hot afternoon, pondering these things in my heart, and it was at that moment that it came into my head and heart that I should make a translation. So I walked home and started. The PC that I had then had only one font available, Courier, and there was no feature for italicising or underlining or emboldening.

I thought then that my translation would be a revision of the King James Bible: write in Bullinger's corrections and enhancements; get rid of "Hell" and "soul" and any other ancient pagan contraband stuff; get rid of the archaisms; get rid of the King James gibberish such as Exodus 38\4 ("he made for the altar a brasen gate of network under the compass thereof beneath unto the midst of it"); make some stylistic improvements of my own; construct good paragraphing and lineation and general good presentation; construct good subject headings for guidance; and then I'd have an accurate and readable Bible. So I thought.

That was until I got hold of Jay Green's Hebrew and Greek interlinears. In Llandudno in Wales in 1998 I met Dr Graham Thomason, a Hebrew and Greek scholar, who gave me a list of recommended books I would need for translating. Also in Wales I discovered from Rowland Wickes the works of Otis Q Sellers. And it all grew from there, the collection of lexicons and grammars, other books, the understanding, the vision. And slowly everything was becoming quite different, with discovery after discovery. This was to be an entirely different work. Now it's not a revision of anything: it's an entirely new translation. It's not even based on the same Greek texts as those of the popular versions, my translation being based on the Robinson-Pierpont Textform 2005, introduced to me by Dr Thomason.

Eventually, that first Bible I had carried everywhere fell to pieces and became unreadable. I had tried other versions but, beside my obsession, there was always dissatisfaction for me in whatever version I looked at.

Alongside the translating work, I was writing studies on words and themes, something I had already been doing before I began the translation. One of those studies became a book-length work, *What Happens When You Die*.

Much of my early translation and other work were composed on voice-activated software, which I was using following an arm injury. Voice-activated software makes errors, particularly with the early versions (they are astonishingly accurate now). In a lengthy letter to a publisher I wrote asking them to "please send my hundred pounds" but, when I printed it and proofread it, it said "please send my underpants".

Those early days at the gospel shack, travels in France, Scotland, Wales, the Lake District, seem a long time ago. How, in the 26 years and many tens of thousands of hours work since 1997, has it all happened to produce this translation? It's a modern day miracle. Truly, I do not even know myself quite how it all happened, how I managed the time.

God's providence all these years has been remarkable, beyond belief, beyond human coincidence: the fortunes in finding the right books at the right time; meeting the right people (whether helpful, or whether contradictors who prompted defences); Chris Day of Filament Publishing who has been a tireless godsend. Anybody would think it's a conspiracy.

✱

Chapter 4

William Tyndale

✷

William Tyndale (?-1536), from Gloucestershire, was the first to translate the New Testament into English, for which he was hunted down, betrayed by a friend, arrested and imprisoned, then strangled and burned near Brussels on October the 6th, 1536. Within a few years there were Bibles throughout England.

Somewhere in Cologne,
his eyes squinting
in the wicks of candles,
one of Europe's finest scholars
hunches on a desk,
and runs a hand across the surface
of the manuscript: Βίβλος
γενέσεως Ἰησοῦ χριστοῦ ...

    Excited stevedores
passed the new translations
as contraband through East End docks
and shipping traffic from the Low Countries
and Germany, and they pressed secret marks
on Bills of Lading stuffed in bags
of corn and boxes. *The book
of the generations of Jesus Christ* ...
    The ill-knighted Thomas More,
Chancellor of the king, considered it Utopian
to make his red-hot loathing
of William Tyndale the obsession
of his life. More would wear a hair-shirt
which drew his blood,
and he flagellated his own body
with knotted whips. From the Eden
of his Chelsea large estate,
he flogged his adversaries
in his garden on 'the tree of Truth',
and tortured them in chains
and stocks and fetters.
    Thomas More called Tyndale's *Newe Testament*
'the testament of Antichrist'.
More regretted that there had been no burnings
in 'ye fyre' for eight years in England:
you could smell the faggots of the righteous
burning on the pages of his writings.

With a bloodhound
on his starry trail,
William tramped the map
of northern Europe.
In a snaking alleyway in Antwerp,
two soldiers cornered him,
a Gethsemane betrayal
by Henry Phillips' pointing finger,
a poltroon with high connections
who had been hired for the kidnap
by a mysterious benefactor
whom he concealed till his death,
presumed to be the Chancellor to the king,
Sir Thomas More.
    The dungeon door
slammed like a tomb.
From the scurrying darkness
of William's rat-stenched cell,
he could hear the squabbling moorhens
in the wide waters of the moat
which slapped against the walls
of grim Vilvorde's seven-towered castle.
He heard, too, the Prelates' Catholic bells,
clanging hard as anvils against the poor,
against the illiterate plowboy,
clanging against the dead who rise.
    For their summer pageant
they led William through the market square,
they disrobed him, made him kneel,
and they scraped his hands
with glass, and subjected him
to mummeries of degradation.

A sorry procession through the jail's corridor
of Inquisitors with papal keys,
offering strange fires from Rome,
failed to persuade William
of the Canons of the Church
and that obedience to the Church is needed
for salvation. The jail-keeper and his daughter
were converted by William's witness
to the light of Christ: υἱοῦ Δαβίδ,
υἱοῦ ᾿Αβραάμ ... *the son
of David, the son of Abraham ...*

On the five-hundredth day of William's freezing solitude,
the prisoner's catarrhal throat
was stapled to a wooden pillar.
'Lord,' he mustered himself
to cry out in a dying voice,

'open the king of England's eyes!'
The hooded man, who was
the strangler of Vilvorde,
snapped the cold iron of the strangling chain
on the throat's lump.

A half gulp, checked gargles,
a starbursting of blood:
the priests and scarlet-robed cardinals,
with drooping jowls like turkeys,
and the sour doctors of theology,
wrapped in silks and ermine,
grinned through broken teeth.
        The Proceurer General, Pierre Dufief,
smirked like a broken-mouthed mocker
shouting for Barrabas,
as in a Bosch cartoon of, say, Jesus
carrying his stake.
And Pierre Dufief brought the flaming torch
to the stack of faggots and piles of straw
and brushwood heaped
around William's hemp-roped feet.

And the raging flames of the Church
crept around the feet of peace
which had fled from the hills
of Gloucestershire.

They left for the wind
a lump of carrion,
a charred form
hanging limply
from an iron noose;
trees
were beginning to turn,
and leaves fall,
in slate-grey air.

Βίβλος γενέσεως Ἰησοῦ χριστοῦ (= *biblos geneseos Jesu Christou*);
υἱοῦ Δαβίδ, υἱοῦ Ἀβραάμ (= *huiou Dabid, huiou Abraham*).
Both are citations from the opening of Matthew's Gospel.

✶

Chapter 5

The Harmonium
~ A Modern Pilgrim's Progress or Piers Plowman

★

Those were the most palindromic
of years. He didn't know this –
he just went on driving the longboat
of his heart in a backwards race
along a false sea of his own blood
whose steady drips on sharp rocks
he could barely notice.
        What he could see
from his high window, when the bell
tinkled like a village heartbeat,
was the gentle village people
in their processionals of chatter
as they walked to the stone chapel
on the hill, the problem of God
heavy on their minds.
                How could he,
on his weekends, find half a day
to withdraw himself
from the overflowing goblets
of the feasts of Belshazzar?
Was he too dull,
too pathetic in his spirit,
that he should be not desirous
of the thousand fruits
and wines on the tables
of the thousand lords, too oppressed
by some ingrowing virginity to release
loud laughter bursting from his heart
in the revels of the night?
              After the long hours
of his nights, he came back
to life in the mid-afternoons,
and he staggered outside,
smoking from his malefactions,
raising a hand to shield his eyes
from the blaze of daylight.
          One cool Sunday in December,
he took a long walk for recovery
from the night, and as he ambled on his way

a feint rain began to slant across him.
He increased his pace and rain fell
harder. He passed through an avenue
of deluge-hammered trees, and at its end
stopped at a corner of the village pond
and contorted himself underneath
a low branch-covered shelter. The drilling
of rain splashed in the pond
like six-inch nails, and when it seemed
not possible that the rain could fall
down harder, the harder down it came
in a pounding rush, until every bolt
of it shot with a weltering weight,
and it leaned like a force of wind
against the rushes and drained down in tap-fulls
off the remaining leaves of autumn.
It was as if a gang of giant demons
in the sky were bailing barrels of water
out of cloud-length boats.
The curses of the still half-drunken man
were stronger in the ear than the tempest.
He was three miles from home
and, hunched with an encrimsoned face,
he crouched below the dripping overhang.
      When the rain became less violent
he set off up the hill in the direction
of his home, and on the way he stepped
without a thought inside the chapel porch
for a moment's shelter, in hope the rain-clouds
might run out of aspiration.
Through thick glass doors he watched
the rain and the yard-wide rivulet
racing down the hill. And curious
at the soft flow of the chapel's old harmonium
droning through something from their hymn books,
he hung his coat and wiped his dripping head
and went inside their chapel
on the hill. He seated himself near the door,
and gazed and yawned through
a mildewed sermon, and half-liked
some music of their wafer-thin religion.
      His head flickered with it all
like leaves of a poplar tree.
He loved the sound of the harmonium
and was wishing for a better view
of its yellowed keys,
its manufacturer's silver metal badge,
and how the hands of the woman playing it
moved to make its chords,
and how she was pedalling on it

like a granny's sewing-machine.
        A preacher, whose look
the man did not warm to, snapped back
the clasps of a gold-edged book,
then in a peculiar and contrived voice
read a passage from the Gospels
about coins in a fishes' mouth,
and another from the prophets
concerning an image of a beast
with seven heads and ten false crowns
and who speaks blasphemous words,
and following that the unnatural-voiced
preacher read another passage
about a man coming through the skies
and with garments dyed in red
and who treads a winepress.
        That was it. That was all
that was needed by the man who was,
yet was no more. A thundering star was born
in the astrodome of his heart. It was a star
the size of an innkeeper's cowshed.
This reveller heaved himself
from the dark hearse
of his crazy living. He ran home
in his sodden shoes, wiped the rain
and sweat from his head
which drained off him like blood,
and from his bookshelves
he took down the Book
with his grandfather's name signed in it,
and he turned to the passages
he'd just listened to
and read aloud the strange words
written in a bizarre and archaic English
and he tried to comprehend them.
        He paced the hills that night
until stars slipped out like a fox with a paw raised
crouching at the edge of a field.
An owl's hoot echoed,.
He walked until the creaking
of the wind was enough to turn
the blood to ice, and on and on
he paced until a midnight host of stars
whirled about like Catherine wheels.
        The next morning, when dawn
ruffled back its curtain and stepped up
to mount her golden throne,
he walked the lower fields
while early sunlight from the broken window
of the sky sloped on the hills,

and for the first time he thought he understood
the meaning of the plain wooden cross,
the tree or stake they call
a cross, and the river of blood
that courses all humanity:
that is, that we have redemption
by means of Jesus' blood,
the forgiveness of sins,
in keeping with the outflowing wealth
of God's free and merciful goodwill,
which, he'd read somewhere,
He has lavished on us
in all wisdom and understanding.
          He purchased other versions
of that Book he'd heard, and books
about the Book in its first languages,
and he set out at the Creation prologue
in the opening book of Moses,
the divine making of the galaxies
and everything in the universe created by a word,
and the Creation of the first man
out of dust. And this new son of Adam,
son of God, pronounced aloud
the opening words which pierced his deep heart
like a flying Viking crossbow bolt on fire –
b'resheeth bara Elohim eth shamayim
ve et ha eretz –
'In the beginning God created the heavens
and the Earth.'
          This also was enough.
Over and over he repeated
the words that he wondered
why he hadn't heard before:
'In the beginning Elohim created
the heavens and the Earth ...':
b'resheeth bara Elohim, b'resheeth
bara Elohim, and he repeated
words of his imploring:
'Elohim, Elohim, Yahweh Elohim ...'
      In his first year
on time's wheel of the heavens
he returned to the stone chapel
and showed these words
to the chapel people on the hill,
and they said only that they recognized them,
or that they hadn't heard
such words before.
      By the time the local pond
was frozen over, and snow ribboned
its tree-lined edges, and the ice

crackled, and the small fish
were twitching their cold lives away,
and snow had settled on the rooftop
of the chapel and made it appear like a visitor
from some magic land, his former life
was crushed underfoot
and his speech was no longer a muttering
in the dust of death. For the noble man,
his Book was pressing this on him,
counsels noble things
and by noble things he stands.
      Now, with his former life
so crushed underfoot as a rolling cartwheel
pushes down the grass,
his former friends were unable
to rouse him back into it, though they swore
and blasted on his door to go drinking
in their cockroach joints
with the late loud rabble.
He told those who formerly had regarded him
as a prototype of their rebellious kind
that there was nothing shaking for him now
with all that night-time living and carousing,
that he was reading the Book of books
and studying and making notes,
and he had his healthy Anglo-Saxon teeth
in it, and that there are names
registered in a Book of Life.
One of these rebels exploded
and mocked him, 'Can it, Jesus freak!'
and slammed the door in his face
like a smack from a steam-shovel,
then shouted at his window,
'Look, he's gone all cosmic, man!'
and Kerouac's joke 'Books ain't no good',
and they went guffawing
down the village street, drag-footed,
the wind tearing at their coats
like border rats and broken desperados
of the night, and he watched them
disappear in the smoke and scorching wind
of their own metaphysical landscape,
and he pulled the shutter up.
      He made himself a living sacrifice
for the God and Father of Jesus Christ,
and in many years he became what the Book
revealed to him as *ho theou anthropos*,
'the man of God', unlocking truth
from the stinking dungeons
that the Book had been held captive in.

                    And in the dividing truth of the Book
he found the one true God
the prophets and apostles served,
and he discovered for himself
how the prophet Isaiah says
that Yahweh is 'the First and Last'
and 'there is no other',
and the man digging up the golden truth
figured that a runner in a race of one
comes both first and last
and there is no other runner apart from him,
and that the one true God he'd found
was not the same as the three gods
of ancient Polytheism's worship and depiction
and Platonic and Augustinian religion,
whatever the adversarial and complying
and tergiversating Thanatologists
and the Goombahs and Gothamites
and the Salamanders of Oblivion might have to say
in their foamings from the throat,
and whose phantoms stalk
the cobweb ruins of their creaking hearts.
                    And he discovered that
לעולם – *le olam* – in the Hebrew writings of the prophets
is the same as εἰς τὸν αἰῶνα – *eis ton aiona* –
in the Greek writings of the apostles:
that is to say, *le olam* represents
the same as *eis ton aiona*,
and both translate as
'throughout the eon',
that is, the duration of the coming Messianic eon,
that eon the heart of mankind
has been groaning for
since Eden's flaming swords of cherubim.
So: 'God so much loved the world
that He gave His only Son,
in order that everyone believing in him
might not suffer destruction,
but might have eonian life',
that is, they will have life in Jesus
throughout the entire duration
of his sovereign government.
And, Jesus said to Lazarus' sister Martha:
'everyone living and believing in me
will most certainly not die
throughout the eon. Do you believe this?'
           Martha believed it. He believed it.
And he discovered too that שאול – *sheol* –
in the Hebrew writings is the same

as ᾅδης – *hades* – in the Greek writings:
that is to say, *sheol* represents
the same as *hades*, the place
the patriarchs and prophets
and Israel's Messiah anticipated
for their states of death, and signifies
the grave, or place of the dead,
and so, too, the place of resurrection,
and they never mean 'hell'
and there is no word for 'hell'
in all the God-authorized Hebrew and Greek writings
of the prophets and apostles.
He decorated his Book
with such marginalia
as:
      לעולם = εἰς τὸν αἰῶνα = לעולם
and:
      שאול = ᾅδης = שאול.
All this – and the certain knowledge
of inheritance in the Eon of Jesus Christ,
the time of his kingdom, his sovereign government,
that contains the greatest joys
man's heart can ever know.
      He acquired an old harmonium
and heaved it up the stairs to his bedroom
so he could sing between his readings
and translations. His legs pumped
the pedals of the harmonium
like a joyful river on a mill:
'Rejoice, rejoice! Emmanuel
shall come to you,
just as the prophets tell.'
      He made ten thousand notes
to give himself clear references
in the linguistic complexities
of the Greek and Hebrew words and phrases.
He adhered to grammatical rules
and was astounded to find
others had not done this.
He designed indexes and cross-references
in the lexicons of Wigram, Young, Gesenius
and Bagster, weighed up the renderings
of Berry, Green and Bullinger and Bagster,
and digested the most nutritious vitamins of spirit
from Burgon, Bullinger, and Sellers.
He found errors in those too,
and made ten thousand of his own
but spat the gristle out. In every theme
he was pursuing he lined up

every clue of every passage
of the Book by his Deep Word Archaeology Method
with the organic food grown
from Translating Laws and Translating Targets,
until the passages rang out with the correctness
of their internal harmony,
sometimes surging, sometimes inching towards perfection
of its one truth and its many truths,
yet still he felt he was dragging
a thousand miles behind.
      He had his long and dark hours:
griefs as sharp as the agony
of a bone that's snapped
in seven places, griefs for the sorrow
of wasted years, circumstantial setbacks,
unsought for solitude and unanswered yearnings
for a woman, the quiet persecution
of rejection, the false reproaches,
the cooling-off that falls out
from imbalanced measures of unworthiness
and comes to all who leave
the path of worldly misery,
and he learned at times
from one or two he met
what he thought it is to be like Jesus,
yet all the time he understood too well
what it is to be unlike Jesus,
and as he stumbled towards the light
he felt the more the dark discouragement
of transgression, self-reprobation
hung over him like a thunder-cloud.
      A wretched distraction
came for a season, like a lie in Eden.
It was parcelled in the guises
of religious enthusiasm when he heard somebody
rhapsodizing about getting back,
this interloper was proposing,
to what he called 'the great doctrines
of the Reformation'.
This knocked him off
for a season – 'a time
to cast away stones,
and a time to gather stones together' –
until he kicked himself awake
and enquired of himself
what could be wrong, then,
with getting back to
the doctrines of the prophets and apostles?
And he found it out that all the stuffs
of that faulty rhapsodizer

was in other books but not the one true Book,
and their dogmas were no more than
some of the same mind-deluders
and guardians of 'the systematizing of error'
sternly warned against
in the letters of the apostle Paul.
The blindfolds fell away
and he left that hissing path.
   Every evening, every borrowed hour,
as his own silent purpose whispered at his side
like a breath hanging in the air,
he immersed himself in the magnificence
of the task of the Book, to acquire
its knowledge and to comprehend
its exclusive wisdom.
   The rebirthing exhilaration
of the discoveries of its truth and war
were sometimes almost more than
he could bear, and when he prayed and waited
and opened wider his perception,
attentive to reconsideration,
a billion billion megawatts of light
flooded in his pulsating mind.
   What he discovered was all a thing apart
from anything he had heard or come across:
the ἐπιφάνεια (*eiphaneia*), the favourable intervention
and expectation of the manifestation
of Jesus Christ, who gave himself,
redeeming men from lawlessness,
for God to purify for Himself a zealous people;
then the manifestation of the Sons and Daughters of the Books;
the wonders and struggles of
a Messianic Eon to come;
the Ezekiel's spring of water
from the House of God to heal
the waters of the world;
the final conquest of the false seed;
the pearl city with a river
and a Tree of Life.
   The Book explained to him
the mysteries of the universe,
and it answered back at the world's vain philosophy
and ridiculed the vanity
of its most exalted theories
and false heroes. He saw the jigsaw
of mankind's recorded history,
how it fits tightly in the sequences of the Eons
and divine administrations, and fixes
its axis on three days and three nights
of death and triumph,

and the two-edged sharpness of its truth
slashes across the dark curtain
of all human drama
that moves in centrifugal energy
away from that perfect triumph,
while the Book moves alone,
centripetally towards it.
        It was as when the solar wind
collides with the Earth's magnetic field
of oxygen and nitrogen atoms,
and the sky displays an aurora theatre show
of rolling colours in a miracle
of particle physics, even while
the solar wind they claim is battering the Earth
at 400 kilometres a second – all that
was only a minutest fraction of the miracle
of the Book's exquisite truth and grammar.
        The prophets saw
and heard. Now you read the Book.
This Eon is the Eon of the mind.
And no one in the world has a mind
more clear than the inheritors of the Eon
so they see right through
the world's deluding cultural
and political and religious and scientific
and pharmaceutical and cosmological
and astronomical smokescreens, Biblical science
contradicting science of the heathens.
        Season turned
on season in his labours,
and the man forgot his former life and its associations,
and for him, as the poet Homer said,
no riches can compare with being alive,
for life's spirit can't be hunted back
once it has passed the lips,
and his living became a love
of the year's flowers, the migrating birds
and raptors, and the birds
who bounced around in his garden
with their little eyes like berry seeds,
while he pursued his way through the Book
to the very last words of its Apocalypse,
which, in transliteration, reads,
Hee charis tou Kuriou emon Jesu Christou
meta panton ton hagion amen,
which is, 'The merciful goodwill
of our Lord Jesus Christ
be with all the set apart people. Amen'.
        And as with the beginning
so with the end –

he had to say it over and over,
Hee charis tou Kuriou emon Jesu Christou
meta panton ton hagion amen,
Hee charis tou Kuriou emon
Jesu Christou ...
          On Sunday mornings
from his window
when he hears the tinkling
of the chapel bell,
he sees the handsome village people
walk in their processions up the hill,
and he mutters to himself
from his favourite apocalyptic words,
Hee charis tou Kuriou emon Jesu Christou
meta panton ton hagion amen.
          After two hours of his study
he rises up to watch them
in their small and happy companies,
while they walk back down the hill
for roast beef Sunday lunches.

✶

ed16

Chapter 6

Keys of the Kingdom Holy Bible
is the most accurate and reliable translation
of the Hebrew and Greek Books
of the prophets and apostles

1. The underlying Greek Manuscripts
Keys of the Kingdom Holy Bible translation is based on the Robinson-Pierpont Byzantine Textform 2005, compiled by Maurice A Robinson and William G Pierpont, from the superior body of Majority Manuscripts, rather than the corrupt and deplete Alexandrian Minority texts. The Robinson-Pierpont Textform 2005 has early support in all directions. It is a major improvement on the Textus Receptus text, on which the King James Bible (1611) NT is based. The Robinson-Pierpont Textform represents a major advance in textual study. It has the most impressive early support and agreement from early versions and other writers over a large geographical area and over a long period of time.

2. Order of the Books
Keys of the Kingdom Holy Bible translation of the Old and New Testament has the Books in the correct order. See Chapter 22, "The Proper Order of the Books".

3. Best equivalent translation method
The translation method insists on the English being able to be translated back into the same original language, and finding the nearest and best equivalent, rather than the paraphrase system popular in modern versions.

4. Without financial aid or reward and independent
The work is done without any financial payment – and without any request for financial payment – from anybody anywhere. The work is done outside any system or organization, and from the beginning has been without any prejudice or bias other than finding out the truth from the prophets and apostles, so that the motivation is impelled aside from all tradition and institution and prejudice.

5. ORGANIC Translating Laws
and targets and the Deep Word Archaeology Study Method
Keys of the Kingdom Holy Bible has been made with the impregnable foundations of original principles for Biblical translation: the 5 Translating Laws, being the Science of **Grammar, Internal Harmony, Logic, Research, and Text** (GIHLRT in my shorthand). I like to embellish these as "Deep Grammar, Internal Harmony, Transcendent Logic, Diamond-Mining Research, and Text". The Deep Grammar means a retrieval, where possible, of the grammatical forms of words, and of the stylistic and literary grammatical structures of the original writings. None of this is evident in other translations. The Translating Laws have been done with these 3 Translating Targets in mind: **Accuracy, Clarity, Literariness** (ACL in my shorthand). The day-to-day work uses the reliable method of translation and interpretation which I call the Deep Word Archaeology Method, explained in Chapter 7. This is an internal and contextual examination of words and phrases, pioneered by Dr EW Bullinger and advanced by Otis Q Sellers.

6. Design
Narrative prose sections are in appropriate paragraphs, unlike the King James Bible which makes every verse a new paragraph, and poetical sections are lineated as poetry. All supplied words, given for English sense, are set in italics. (Feedback has been outstanding and ecstatic, even emotional. Many of these appear on the website.)

7. Contemporary language and style
Keys of the Kingdom Holy Bible is not shackled up in the prison house of unappealing archaic language. It is written in a sober style, with an ear for cadence, in a mainly formal register with occasional informal words and phrases and phrasal verbs for literary effect. This work has been done, so to speak, outside the city gates. It is not a product of "theology" colleges and seminaries, with their rigidity and self-conscious and unattractive in-house language. Large numbers in narrative sections are in figures, but in words in poetry or dialogue.

8. Hebrew names and titles of God
Whereas other versions merely have "God" and "Lord" as titles of God in the Old Testament Hebrew books, *Keys of the Kingdom Holy Bible* transliterates as many of the names and titles of God as are considered sensible. These are listed in Eonian Document 1. The Hebrew names and titles I have listed number 160, and not exhaustive. The meanings behind the names and titles are often given in footnotes and an appendix. For example, at Exodus 15\26 Yahweh Ropheka is given in the footnote as "the Lord Who heals you".

9. Pronouns
Pronouns referring to the many names and titles of God are capitalized. The *titles* of Jesus and of the Holy Spirit angel are capitalized, but *pronouns* relating to them are not.

10. Research
Extensive works have been consulted in determining meanings of words. The interlinear works of Green, Bagster, Berry, the lexical works of Gesenius, Wigram and Thayer, and the commentaries and comments of Bullinger and Sellers, to all of whom I am indebted, have been frequently consulted, and so have the many titles in the bibliography and others besides, so that many renderings are backed by authorities.

11. Companion Notes
Behind the translation, I have made over 13,000 *Companion Notes* explaining the translations and their interpretations. These were where I tried out words and phrases, drawing from other occurrences, making cross-references, and from my lexical helps and from other writers and commentators, and from other versions, as I strived to words perfect representations of God's truth. The intention had been to publish them in time, but that will be unlikely now, but I often draw from them to create the footnotes.

12. Eonian Document studies and other books to be published
I have written 360 Eonian Document studies and 10 book- or booklet-length studies which describe in meticulous detail the true meanings of words and phrases and themes of the God-authorized Books. These originate from my own need to test my conclusions. Some of these will in time, God willing, be published on the website and possibly in book form. These Companion Notes and written studies have provided the scaffolding for the translation and for the teaching.

13. Subject headings and new insights
Keys of the Kingdom Holy Bible has guided subject headings, according to the themes of Jesus and

the prophets and apostles, and not according to the traditions of ancient creeds. Because the translation is done according to grammatical rules and internal consistency and internal harmony of themes, Translating Laws and Translating Targets, there are manifold new insights into passages such as, say, prophecies concerning the twelve tribes of Israel in New Jerusalem in Ephesians.

14. No smuggled words of mythology and ecclesiology
In *Keys of the Kingdom Holy Bible* translation there are no smuggled words or notions from profane mythology, that is, no falsehoods of "Hell" and "saints" and men going off to mystical regions of outer space. *Keys of the Kingdom Holy Bible* translation has none of the ecclesiastical baggage of words which have been smuggled into other versions. When Jesus was on the Earth, and later when the apostles were writing their letters, the present universal religious system was not in existence, and such a thing was not in place until a few centuries after Jesus and the apostles when religious armies went out conquering the world, and the Protestant sects did not begin to flourish in England until Henry VIII founded the Church of England and made himself head. Ecclesiastical language of that religious system is not found in *Keys of the Kingdom Holy Bible*.

15. Vibrant words
Rather than stale and hackneyed words and religious clichés, *Keys of the Kingdom Holy Bible* looks for more vibrant and attractive words. *Keys of the Kingdom Holy Bible* translation aims to create a refreshing vocabulary for the oracles of God. Every word has burst out of my nervous system, as if, like some startled poet, every word and phrase has taken me by surprise. This Comes from intensity, labour in classical literature and poetry, research in linguistic studies, from correction, and wanting the translation to be an echo of the prophets and to be pleasing to God and Christ.

16. "Eon" and "eonian" and the true gospel of Jesus proclaimed
Keys of the Kingdom Holy Bible is the first translation to correctly and consistently render the Hebrew עולם (= *olam*) as "eon" or "eonian" (occurs 438 times), and the Greek αἰών (= *aion*) as "eon" (occurs 126 times in the Robinson Pierpont text), and αἰώνιος (= (*aionios*) as "eonian" (occurs 71 times), and the Hebrew לעולם (= *le olam*; occurs 162 times), and the Greek εἰς τὸν αἰῶνα (= *eis ton aiona*; occurs 27 times), as "throughout the eon". It renders these appropriately, according to context, but not slavishly). *Keys of the Kingdom Holy Bible* is the first translation to bring out the truth of Jesus" gospel of "eonian life" and life "throughout the eon", so that now at last the English-speaking world can read and study the correct phrasing of the real truth of Jesus' salvation and the progressive gospel of the apostle Paul. I should say, this is not the first translation to use the words "eon" and "eonian". *The Concordant Literal New Testament* was not shy of these words, but it did not always use them correctly. I have seen no translation get John 11\26 right.

17. Words rendered with integrity,
according to grammatical rules and internal harmony
Keys of the Kingdom Holy Bible is the first translation to make the bold and accurate renderings – according to the themes of Jesus and the prophets and apostles – of important words such as: ᾅδης (= *hades*), "death", "grave"; ἐπουράνιος (= *epouranios*), "most exalted", "most eminent"; γέεννα (= *Gehenna*), "the Valley of Hinnom"; שאול (= *sheol*), "death", "grave". John 1 is translated not according to the word of tradition but according to internal harmony and grammatical principles. Passages such as John 3\13, 3\15-16, 8\58 and many others are corrected from their usual mishandling. *Keys of the Kingdom Holy Bible* is translated according to grammatical rules, and not according to chanted creeds blighted with ancient error. Passive verbs

are translated as passives, actives as actives, indicatives as indicatives, infinitives as infinitives (unless the underlying language is different grammar to English; I do not claim the translation to be literal as perfect literalism from one language into another is not possible); nouns as nouns; adjectives as adjectives; so that there is no falsification. This is not the case, is not true, of the popular church versions.

18. Transliteration of ἐκκλησία (= *ekklesia*)

The word ἐκκλησία (= *ekklesia*) in other versions is almost always translated anachronistically in English versions as "church". But *Keys of the Kingdom Holy Bible* makes bold and superior renderings of the word ἐκκλησία (= *ekklesia*), sometimes transliterating it as "Ekklesia", and for plurals as "Ekklesia group", and other times translating it according to its context since it has at least five different meanings (see Chapter 17, *Ekklesia*). The transliteration is necessary as no suitable English word has been found for ἐκκλησία, and it bears no relation to the world religious system which was begun around the third and fourth centuries AD. It was not prophets and apostles, but ecclesiastical "fathers" who wrote the foundations for the world system.

19. Footnotes

A recent enhancement is the addition of 4,300 footnotes. These give citation sources, textual issues, alternative readings, and cross-references, and abbreviated explanations of Hebrew and Greek words. Since the publication of the first edition, another 900 footnotes have been added.

20 Selection of studies
included as appendices with the translation

Keys of the Kingdom Holy Bible includes a selection of appendices, with some insights and truth hidden since the days of the prophets and apostles, including the historical development of translations, and the gospel promise of "eonian life".

21. Jesus and the Holy Spirit

Jesus Christ is restored to his true status as a created man. The personality of the Holy Spirit is restored to his true status of an angel, being titled as "the Holy Spirit". The gift of the holy spirit – lower-case – πνεῦμα ἅγιον (= *pneuma hagion*) is rendered as "holy spirit", or in some constructions "the spirit of separateness", so as not to confuse it with the personality of the angel who is titled the Holy Spirit. See pages xiii-xv of *Keys of the Kingdom Holy Bible*. This is discussed in Chapter 19, "Concerning holy spirit and Holy Spirit: the two meanings of πνεῦμα ἅγιον (= *pneuma hagion*)", and the same study is on the website.

22. The restoration of the promises
and preeminence of the 12 tribes of Israel

By the processes of determining correct meanings and establishing unshakeable internal harmony, 12 words are brought to light which wonderfully restore to the patriarchs and prophets the promises of land and preeminence with God, so that these can once again be found in the pages of the New Testament. (See Chapter 25.)

✸

Chapter 7

The Deep Word Archaeology Study Method:
concerning Acts 2\31 and the grave
and John 1\3 and the gospel

✶

Principles of the Deep Word Archaeology Study Method
The Deep Word Archaeology Study Method never takes for granted any popular or personal opinion. It is built on foundations. This restoration work, this recovery of the divine books, is carried out according to sciences of Targets, Laws, and Results. To describe the project of Translation Truth, the Deep Word Archaeology:–
1. **3 Translating Targets** of Accuracy; Clarity; Literariness. (These Targets neither stated nor apparent before.)
2. To achieve those targets by **5 Translating Laws** of Grammar; Internal Harmony; Logic; Research; Text. (These Laws neither stated nor apparent before.)
3. To produce **Results** not achieved before, the full recovery of Divine Structure, the right books in the right order and right groupings; of Divine Literary Beauty, their literariness, their literary and language devices; of Divine Truth, their true teachings. (These Results not stated nor apparent before.)

"A three-fold cord is not quickly broken" (Ecclesiastes 4\12).

The divine *structure* is a divine signature that the Bible writings are God-breathed like no others. The divine *beauty*, its literariness, draws attention to the divine *truth*. His revealed *truths* are incontestible. ORGANIC food of the gardens of God. Not PROCESSED lab meat.

The Deep Word Archaeology Study Method adopts a comprehensive approach to translating and studying the God-authorized Hebrew and Greek Books. Deep Word Archaeology can be adopted by any seeker of deep truth prepared to get hold of the right study tools and make the necessary labours. All this takes time and an abandoning of wasteful worldly indulgences, mainstream television, radio, cinema, newspapers, idleness, sloth.

The method is to line up all internal evidence of any word or phrase or theme. In order to do this, the method pays first attention to grammar: every occurrence, translation, the language and meaning, determining this from the first mentions, the grammatical form, what is figurative and what might be non-figurative, and other uses and their contexts. It considers the writer and audience, how God was dealing with men at the time of writing (consider Jesus mocking Greek mythology and the Pharisees in Luke 16, regarding Hades), distinguishing between what was written *for* us and what was written *to* us. It makes use of the best available lexicons and commentaries (see Bibliography and Chapter 1) and of logic and common sense.

It also takes advice and makes consideration of what others have said, whether respected or not. The method takes regard not for long-held opinions, but for gathering all these internal evidences, then makes what the great manuscript scholar John Burgon somewhere called "a calm consideration of the facts". Because of this gathering and lining up of evidence, the Deep Word Archaeology Method is able to adapt, correct itself, and make progression. This is a matter not of any traditional opinion, but of integrity, diligence, and truth.

This approach is not new. These criteria are evident in the writings of Dr EW Bullinger and Otis Q Sellers. And centuries ago Miles Coverdale (1488-1569) had this to say: "It shall greatly help you to understand Scripture if you mark not only what is written or spoken, but of whom, and to whom, with what words, at what time, where, to what intent, with what circumstances, considering what goes before, and what follows."

⚖

An example of the Deep Word Archaeology Method: Acts 2\31 & 2\27
At Acts 2\31 the King James Bible has Peter say of Jesus "his soul was not left in hell". This suggests Jesus somehow became detached from his dead body and a part of him went into a mythical region of eternal and tormenting flames. This, we are told, happened while he was in the grave for three days and three nights and, according to the King James' Luke 23\43, he was also in Paradise (so in three places). How can we gain understanding of it?

The first reaction of gaining meaning and understanding is to question the translations of the key words which, in this case, are obviously "hell" and "soul". Are these the correct rendering of the Greek words in the manuscripts from which they were translated?

The word the King James translators rendered as "hell" is ᾅδης (= *hades*). In Greek mythology Hades was an underworld. But Peter's use of ᾅδης (= *hades*) at Acts 2\31 is in the context of resurrection, for the next verse says: "This Jesus God raised up, of which we are all witnesses" (Acts 2\32). Peter was citing and commenting on Psalm 16\10 of David – and he was proclaiming the resurrection of Jesus from the grave. The King James Bible renders that part of Psalm 16\10 as "For thou wilt not leave my soul in hell." The word it translates as "hell" is שאול (= *sheol*).

In Peter's citing of Psalm 16\10 he used the word ᾅδης (= *hades*) as the equivalent of David's Hebrew word שאול (= *sheol*). So, in order to understand the Greek word ᾅδης (= *hades*), we first have to interpret the Hebrew word שאול (= *sheol*). When we go to the first mention of this Hebrew word שאול (= *sheol*) we find a passage concerning Jacob: "And all his sons and all his daughters rose up to comfort him, but he refused to be comforted, and he said, 'For I will go down to the grave [שאול (= *sheol*)], mourning for my son' " (Genesis 37\35). What could be more obvious? How stupid and unlearned it would be to translate שאול (= *sheol*) here as "hell". Even the sloppy King James Bible has "grave". As if Jacob thought he would suffer eternal torments in an (imaginary) underworld of punishing fire just because he lost his son! Any translation other than words meaning "grave" or a place of burial of the dead would be an abomination. In that case, the Hebrew word שאול (= *sheol*) means "grave". If we look at every occurrence of שאול (= *sheol*) we find that it is always linked with death and is used in the contexts of death and sometimes also of resurrection. It has no connotation of fire and the torments of "hell". Nor, indeed, does any word from the Books of God have any connotation at all of any place called "hell". And to translate *sheol* anywhere as "hell" is an abomination. So is it abomination with *hades*.

So, we make this ecstatic deduction:

1. שאול (*sheol*) = grave at Genesis 37\35;
2. שאול (*sheol*) = grave at Psalm 16\10;
3. שאול (*sheol*) = ᾅδης (*hades*), (Psalm 16\10 with Acts 2\31, 2\27);
4. therefore, as שאול is "grave", then ᾅδης also is grave.

If we look at every occurrence of ᾅδης (= *hades*) we find that, like שאול (= *sheol*), it too is always linked with death and is used in the contexts of death and resurrection. For example, in Paul's passage about the resurrection he cites the prophet Hosea:

Where, oh death, *is* your sting?
Where, oh grave, *is* your victory?   ~ 1 Corinthians 15\55

Once again, in the Hebrew of Hosea 13\14, from where Paul's citation comes, the word "grave" is שאול (= *sheol*), and in the Greek of Paul the word "grave" is ᾅδης (= *hades*), so that שאול (= *sheol*) and ᾅδης (= *hades*) are shown to be interchangeable.

The word ᾅδης (= *hades*) occurs 11 times between Matthew and Revelation: Matthew 11\23, 16\18, Luke 10\15, 16\23, Acts 2\27, 2\31, 1 Corinthians 15\55, Revelation 1\18, 6\8, 20\13, 20\14. Now, at every occurrence we have an unmoveable principle for translating it, and we will not be writing silly and sloppy renderings such as "hell".

I say that ᾅδης (= *hades*) always means "grave". The Deep Word Archaeology Study Method, though, examines every occurrence in its context. There is one exception, and that is at Luke 16\23. In that context it is different and certainly represents the belief in an underworld. In Jesus' satirical story about the rich man and Lazarus, Jesus was mocking the Pharisees' adoption of Greek mythology into their system of theology, which nullified the commandment of God (Matthew 15\7). This satiricl story deliberately mocks mythology. Jesus ended his satirical story by speaking of resurrection: "If they do not hear Moses and the prophets, not even if somebody should rise from among *the* dead will they be persuaded" (Luke 16\31). Jesus then straightaway told his disciples his opinions of those who teach such mythologies as truth: "He said to the disciples, 'It is inevitable but that snares should come, but woe to through whomever they come! It would be better for him if a millstone turned by a donkey were hanged around his neck and he should be thrown into the sea, rather than that he should be a cause of stumbling to one of these lowly *people*' " (Luke 17\1-2).

The Pharisees' teaching about death and the after-life was false and a snare and a cause of stumbling. In the context of the use of the Greek word ᾅδης (= *hades*), Jesus deliberately used it to represent an horrific difference between his teaching and that of Greek mythology mingled with religion. God's Books are not books of mythology: they stand hard in opposition to myths.

So, the passage we began with, Acts 2\31, is falsely rendered with "hell". That the Greek word ψυχή (= *psuchee*) and its Hebrew counterpart נפש (= *nephesh*) do not mean "soul", and that ψυχή (= *psuchee*) is best rendered in Acts 2\31 as "dead body", can be discovered by the same Deep Word Archaeology shown to discover that שאול (= *sheol*) and ᾅδης (= *hades*) do not mean "hell". The Hebrew word נפש (= *nephesh*) certainly means "dead body" or "corpse" at Leviticus 19\28, 22\4, Numbers 5\2, 6\6, 6\11, 9\10, 19\11. And its equivalent, the Greek word ψυχή (= *psuchee*), also has to mean "corpse" or "dead body" at Revelation 6\9. So therefore the Greek word ψυχή (= *psuchee*) at Acts 2\31 also means "corpse "or "dead body".

Acts 2\31 ought to read, in full:

[God], foreseeing this, spoke of the resurrection of the Christ, so that his dead body was not left in the grave, nor did his flesh see decay.

Perfect! All about death and resurrection.

So too should the King James Bible's wording at Acts 2\27 be adjusted. It has "thou wilt not leave my soul in hell". That should be "You will not abandon my dead body in the grave". This is confirmed by the second part of the verse: "nor will you allow Your Holy One to see decay". Peter is the speaker and his subject is the resurrection of Jesus Christ. To import Babylonian mythology into Peter's speech is an abomination. For, if while he was supposed to be dead in the grave Jesus was actually alive in the fictional place where you burn in eternal torment, then he has not suffered death as the sacrificial lamb – and no sacrifice for sin has been made. The King James Bible wrecks the gospel hope.

John 1\3

With this passage I will work the other way round: begin with my translation and its reasonings, then discuss the King James Bible translation so that the effects of the translators' thinking can be understood. John 1\3:

Everything arose through it, and apart from it there arose not even one thing that has arisen.

That wording would probably be quite unfamiliar to readers – but it should not be so. It should always be that way and nobody anywhere should ever expect anything different.

I'll go through the first clause, then summarise the second, for enough will have been shown. First we have a pronoun, πάντα (= *panta*), meaning "everything". This is governed by the verbs that follow it. The first verb is ἐγένετο (= *egeneto*), which is singular aorist active intransitive stative, having the familiar meaning "came to pass", "happened", "arose". Then we have the preposition διὰ (= *dia*), which is "through", or "by means of". This is followed by the pronoun αὐτοῦ (= *autou*), which is masculine singular, showing by means of what it was that "everything arose". We have to go back to John 1\1 where we find λόγος (= *logos*), "the word", which also is masculine. So: "everything arose through it" – the word of God.

In the second clause there are two verbs: ἐγένετο (= *egeneto*), the same as the verb in the first clause. And then the second verb is γέγονεν (= *gegonen*), which is singular perfect active intransitive stative. In the contexts these mean, similarly, "arose" and "has arisen".

So John's prologue is telling us that everything in the account that he has written has arisen through the word of God. In his closure he makes a similar testimony that what he writes is true (see John 21\24-25).

Now look at John 1\3 in the King James Bible:

"All things were made by him; and without him was not any thing made that was made."

The King James Bible opens with a plural pronoun. And it has a plural imperfect passive transitive verb "were made", but ἐγένετο (= *egeneto*) is not the verb "to make" or "create" – that word would have been ποιέω (= *poyeo*) or κτίζω (= *ktizo*) – and the verb is neither plural, nor passive, nor imperfect, nor dynamic, nor transitive. Then the King James Bible has "him", which connects with its "Word" in verse 1, but notice that they have capitalised it, quite wrongly, without justification. Note that "the Word" is not a title of Christ. At his return Jesus will be titled "the Word of God", but not "the Word". The King James Bible translators have done it to give the impression it is about Christ. Then, come to verse 3 and they've turned him into the creator, by altering the meaning of the verb and by altering it from singular active aorist intransitive into plural passive imperfect transitive. The other two verbs in the King James Bible's John 1\3, "made" and "was made" are, once again, the wrong verb for making or creating, and they've been turned into singular passive.

The word of God is His verbal communication. For example, Jesus said to God, "Your word is truth" (John 17\17). Peter speaks of "the word of the gospel" (Acts 15\7). Ephesians 1\13 says, "the word of truth, the gospel of your salvation". James 1\18 speaks of "a word of truth".

We also need to consider the opening phrase of John 1\1, "<u>In the beginning</u> was the word". What "beginning" is this? The first thing to look at is the openings of the other Gospel accounts. So in Mark we find that he opens with reference to the beginning of the proclamation of the gospel, as we would expect: "<u>The</u> beginning of the gospel of Jesus Christ, *the* Son of God". Luke does the same: "just as those who, <u>from *the* beginning</u>, having become eye witnesses and servants of the oracle, handed *those things* on to us" (Luke 1\2). Phillipians 4\15, similarly speaks of "<u>the</u>

beginning of the gospel". This is John's reference point at John 1\1. Hebrews 6\1 speaks of leaving "the discussion of the beginning of the Christ". The King James translators, though, wanted us only, it seems, to reach right back to creation in Genesis 1\1, because they supported the three gods as one god system. John 1\1 does echo Genesis 1\1, it is true, but only in that it opens with the same three words. Its subject matter is not the same. John is discussing not creation but, rather, the declared word and plan of God.

John opens his first letter in a similar way: "That which was from *the* beginning, that which we heard, that which we saw with our eyes, that which we gazed on and our hands touched concerning the oracle of life" (1 John 1\1-2). Similarly at 1 John 2\7: "Brothers, I do not write a new commandment to you, but an old commandment which you had from *the* beginning. The old commandment is the oracle that you heard from *the* beginning." He also uses "beginning" at 1 John 2\13, 2\14, 2\24, 3\11, 2 John 5, 6.

We know, then, that the King James Bible has altered grammatically the forms of words in John 1\3. Further, we know it cannot be true that Jesus was around from the beginning of time because Hebrews 3\1-2, translated properly, says Jesus was "faithful to Him having created him". Jesus was created inside the young Israeli virgin Mary (properly Maria) at the time of the announcement to her by the angel Gabriel. (Mary, who gave birth to Jesus, was not alive at the time of Creation either.) And we know that Jesus is not the creator because Genesis 1\1 says that "Elohim created the heavens and the Earth" (Genesis 1\1). Jesus is not Elohim. Elohim created Jesus. Elohim is the Father. Jesus is the Son. The Son is not the Father. The Son is not his own Father. It is interesting that Hebrews 6\1 says, "having, therefore, left the discussion of the beginning of the Christ ...".

Application

As a translator you cannot accurately translate the scrolls of God without also spending many years writing with exploration about the themes of the prophets and apostles, and then applying your translations to those studies. Until those studies are completed, the translations are no more than a wine-case of theories. It is in making those studies, and using your translations for them, and when passages are aligned with other passages, that your errors are thrown up and the lights can shine.

ed17

Chapter 8

John 11\26 with Genesis 3\4

✶

Verse with Keys of the Kingdom Holy Bible translation and comment	Latin Vulgate, c. 390; – King James Version, 1611; Revised Version, 1881	Comment
Genesis 3\4 And the serpent said to the woman, "You will certainly not die!" Comment: The one called the serpent was tempting Eve to eat a fruit which God said would bring death. There must have been something in it nutritionally malicious which menaced the metabolism, perhaps the first cancer. God drove Adam and Eve out of the garden to prevent access to the fruit of the Tree of Life. Presumably there was an antidote which would enable them to live "throughout the Eon" (Genesis 3\22-24). John 11\26 And everyone living and believing in me will most certainly not die throughout the eon. Do you believe this? Comment: Jesus raised Martha's brother Lazarus, and he spoke to Martha concerning resurrection "in the last day", and he made the promise of "eonian life". These facts of death, resurrection, and eonian life set straight the lie that the serpent spoke to Eve. In the coming Kingdom we will put on immortality. We are not immortal. Jesus' phrase εἰς τὸν αἰῶνα means "throughout the eon".	Latin Vulgate et omnis qui vivit et credit in me non morietur in aeternum credis hoc [= and all who live and believe in me will not die in eternity do you believe this] KJV And whosoever liveth and believeth in me shall never die. Believest thou this? RV And whosoever liveth and believeth in me shall never die. Believest thou this?	Jerome's John 11\26 phrase "non morietur in aeternum" in the Vulgate means "will not die in eternity". This does not represent the Greek, and is not what Jesus said, and it masks Jesus' promise of eonian life. And it maintains the serpent's lie to Eve that she would not die. At the end of John 3\16, for ζωὴν αἰώνιον Jerome wrote "vitam aeternam" – "eternal life". His "will not die in eternity" is the same error that is in today's popular versions. So the false gospel dates back as far as the day of Jerome. As well as the Vulgate's masking the gospel promise of Jesus, the Jesus of the KJV and RV at John 11\26 also refutes the certainty of death with the bald lie, "shall never die". For the truth is, there is no word "never" in the Greek of John 11\26. Jesus did not say "never die". The Jesus of the KJV and RV continues the tradition of the serpent's Eden gospel: "you will never die". The KJV and RV, through a fake Jesus, affirm the serpent's lie. The lie of the serpent that "you will certainly not die" has been perpetuated by his agents in all the world through the falsehood of the "migration of the soul", the lie that at death the "soul" passes straight to Heaven or Hell or Purgatory. The real truth of God that man's place is on the Earth (Psalm 115\16, Matthew 5\5) and that there is no memory or sound in the grave "where you go" (Ecclesiastes 9\6-10, Psalm 6\5) is contradicted by the religious system. Men of religion have invented their own preferred ideas. The false translations put words into Jesus' mouth, making him hiss the serpent's lie, and therefore create "another Jesus" and "a different gospel" by "a different spirit" (2 Corinthians 11\4). This is possibly the worst act of translating ever made. It promises a lie; misrepresents Jesus as a liar and not understanding death; it likens him to the serpent in Eden; it repeats the serpent's lie to Eve; and conceals the gospel promise.

✱

Not without irony from our viewpoint, Jerome wrote to Pope Damascus, "[W]hy not go back to the original Greek and correct the mistakes introduced by inaccurate translators, and the blundering alterations of confident but ignorant critics, and, further, all that has been inserted or changed by copyists more asleep than awake?"

It is interesting to note that Jerome claims there were already mistakes being "introduced by inaccurate translators", even so early, and referring to "blundering alterations", and "ignorant critics".

If only Jerome had done what he suggested, and gone back to the original Greek and corrected the mistakes before him, then English versions might have been spared many falsehoods that they copied and inherited from Jerome's own translation. Perhaps Jerome was speaking deviously, in order to excuse himself or justify his own "blundering alterations" made to flatter Pope Damascus.

✱

ed21

Chapter 9
Samuel and the Woman of Endor

✦

The narrative of Samuel and the woman of Endor appears in 1 Samuel 28. This is the text of 1 Samuel 28/7-20:

[7] Then Saul said to his servants, 'Find me a woman, an expert of mediumship, so that I can go to her and make enquiry of her.'

And his servants said to him, 'In fact, there is a woman, an expert of mediumship, in Endor.'

[8] And Saul disguised himself, and put on other clothing, and he and two of the men with him went, and they came to the woman at night, and he said, 'I ask you, divine for me through mediumship, and bring up for me him whom I will name to you.'

[9] And the woman said to him, 'Look, you know what Saul has done, how he has cut off the mediums and magic men out of the land. Why then do you lay a snare for my life, to cause me to die?'

[10] And Saul swore to her by Yahweh, saying, '*As* Yahweh lives, no punishment will come on you for this thing.'

[11] Then the woman said, 'Whom shall I bring up to you?'

And he said, 'Bring me up Samuel.'

[12] And when the woman saw Samuel, she called out with a loud voice, and the woman spoke to Saul, saying, 'Why have you deceived me? For you *are* Saul.'

[13] And the king said to her, 'Do not be afraid, for what have you seen?'

And the woman said to Saul, 'I saw a messenger ascending out of the ground.'

[14] And he said to her, 'Of what form *is* he?'

And she said, 'An old man comes up, and he *is* covered with a mantle.'

And Saul perceived that it *was* Samuel, and he stooped with *his* face to the ground, and bowed himself.

[15] And Samuel said to Saul, 'Why have you disquieted me, to bring me up?'

And Saul answered, 'I *am* bitterly distressed, for the Philistines are making war against me, and Elohim has departed from me, and He answers me no more, neither by prophets, nor by dreams, so I have called you so that you can make known to me what I should do.'

[16] Then Samuel said, 'Why then did you ask me, seeing that Yahweh has departed from you and become your enemy? [17] And Yahweh has done for Himself as He spoke by my hand, for Yahweh has torn the kingdom out of your hand and given it to your neighbour, to David, [18] because you did not listen to the voice of Yahweh, nor did you execute His fierce anger against Amalek. For that reason Yahweh has done this thing to you this day. [19] In addition, Yahweh will also deliver Israel with you into the hand of the Philistines, and tomorrow you and your sons *will be* with me. Yahweh will also deliver the army of Israel into the hand of the Philistines.'

[20] Then Saul fell, the fulness of his stature, motionless on the ground, and he was bitterly afraid because of the words of Samuel, and there was no strength in him, for he had eaten no food all day, nor all night.

[21] And the woman came to Saul, and she saw that he was severely troubled, and she said to him, 'Look, your handmaid has listened to your voice, and I have put my life in my hand, and I have listened to your words that you spoke to me. [22] Now therefore, please listen also to the voice of your handmaid, and let me set a piece of bread before you, and eat, so that you might have strength when you go on your way.'

~ * ~

This account is cited as "proof" by those who want to hold onto the Platonic and religious system, implying that there is some intermediate state between death and resurrection. The claim is that a woman of the dark occult was able to bring Samuel back from the dead and communicate with him, and that Samuel himself appeared to Saul.

However, an examination of the passage reveals that such an interpretation makes no consideration of the full context of the passage. It is not difficult to dismantle the fake notion that Samuel's "soul" or "spirit" returned from heavenly regions to appear to Saul. Such a notion is loaded with impossibilities and inconsistencies. Man does not have a detachable, unscrewable "soul" or "spirit". The ancient myth of man having such a thing comes not from the prophets and apostles of God. Peter said, "David did not ascend into the heavens" (Acts 2\34). Jesus said, "And nobody has ascended into Heaven" (John 3\13).

Samuel – if the alleged appearance had been Samuel, which it was not – said, "Why have you disquieted me, to bring me up?" (28\15). Those words denote a bringing *up*, not *down* from heavenly regions, where mythology likes to say the dead go. Also, those words say "me", not "my soul" or "my spirit" which would be the words of a religious story. Furthermore, if Samuel really was raised, who raised him? Can a medium have such powers? Only God can raise the dead, not some occult-working woman from Canaanite Endor.

What has perplexed many should not perplex us who follow the project of Translation Truth. The King James Bible has it that Saul asks his servants to find him "a woman that hath a familiar spirit" (28\7). But first we have בָּאַל (*bahgal*, Strong's Concordance reference number h1169), which is "mistress" at 1 Kings 17\17, Nah. 3\4. Here we can write that as "expert" (as someone might be a master of their craft, she is a mistress of hers). So: "a woman, an expert". And then we have אוֹב (= *ohv*, Strong's Concordance reference number h178). It occurs in this account at 28\3, 28\7, 28\8, 28\9. Gesenius says of it: "[Versions of] LXX. almost always render אבות [plural] by ἐγγαστρίμυθοι, ventriloquists, and correctly; because ventriloquists, amongst the ancients, commonly abused this art of inward speaking for magical purposes" (p. 182). So: "a woman, an expert in mediumship" and ventriloquism. NOT the King James Bible's "a woman that hath a familiar spirit".

Mediumship is forbidden, evil, a lie.

The woman called out and told Saul that she had seen "a messenger ascending out of the ground" (28\13). She described to him "an old man ... covered with a mantle" (28\14), and Saul "perceived" that it was Samuel (28\12). The "familiar spirit" was speaking in a way that, in the ears of Saul, imitated the voice of a prophet.

The word "messenger" is deceitfully rendered "gods" in the King James: "I saw gods ascending out of the earth" (1 Samuel 28\13). When the woman said what she saw, Saul replied, "Of what form *is* he?" This indicates that she saw a singular one, "he", not a plurality, "gods". The word rendered "gods" is אלהים (= *elohim*), which is usually "Elohim", and sometimes "gods" and "idols", but it cannot be "gods" here. (Of course, she did not see anybody. She was lying.)

The word אלהים is also used for "angel" or "messenger" (Psalm 8\5, 86\8, 97\7 and 97\9 with Hebrews 1\6). This sense of "a messenger" fits Saul's response, asking, "Of what form *is* he?" It fits with the woman's character whose operations were through the lying spirit which was in her personality-type, psychological make-up, her evil profession. The best rendering of אלהים here seems "messenger". A singular rendering is needed.

---

1. As unhelpful here as is the KJV, the Jewish Publication Society translation *Tanakh* (1985) renders אלהים here as "a divine being", which is also its paraphrased rendering for "sons of God" at Genesis 6\2 and 6\4. That is inaccurate, without justification, unhelpful, and misleading.

The word "messenger" is put for man or men in such places as Matthew 11\10 Mark 1\2, 1 Corinthians 11\10, Galatians 3\19, Hebrews 13\2, Jacob (James) 2\25, 2 Peter 2\4, Jude 1\6. Messenger. Simply a man.

Because of the woman's character, it is also logical to describe the character of the woman as evil. She lies that she sees a spirit appear as "an old man ... covered with a mantle" (28\14), a description to resemble Samuel, a deceit which would not be the practice of an angel of God. Certainly, God did not raise Samuel from the dead in order to deceive Saul. Nor is there such a thing as a post-death "soul" by which Samuel could have appeared.

Whoever Samuel heard was an impersonator. That is how lying pretenders work. Either the woman had the skills of ventriloquism, projecting her own voice in a different mode. Or she had an actor in her employment to act up the part. It was not the voice of long-dead Samuel from the grave.

Saul died for this transgression of "consulting a medium" (1 Chronicles 10\13, with Leviticus 19\31, 20\6, Deuteronomy 18\10-12), a hardly likely doom if God had sent an angel, or had raised Samuel from the dead, to speak to Saul, or if the "soul" of Samuel had been sent back by God to speak to Saul. Her practice of witchcraft is rebellion against God with penalty of death (Exodus 22\18). When the woman described the אלהים, the messenger, Saul "stooped with *his* face to the ground and bowed himself" (28\14), an action deserving of death for a king of Israel (Deuteronomy 13\5).

The entire incident is one of deception. The skills of the woman enabled her to mislead Saul that the prophet Samuel was speaking. Mediums and witchcraft work by deception lies, and invention. All make-believe.

Where the account says, "the woman saw Samuel" (28\12), and "Samuel said to Saul" (28\15, 28\16), we should allow the writer's intention that it was through the agency of the woman. The clause "Samuel said to Saul" is written from Saul's deceived perspective. In reporting journalism, the woman's agency might be signified with speech marks in this way: "And 'Samuel' said to Saul", the speech-marks around Samuel signifying, "You know what we mean: it wasn't actually Samuel himself, but the woman herself or an impersonator, speaking and deceptively claiming to be Samuel."

It was not the prophet Samuel who appeared, for he was, and still is, in the grave, and he will have no life until the resurrection (Acts 2\29). Samuel was a prophet, and Saul had already acknowledged that God was not answering him through prophets (28\6, 28\15), so God was certainly not going to speak to Saul the oracles of a prophet through witchcraft and necromancy.

If Saul actually saw anybody, it was an actor. The word "perceived" at 28\14 is ידע (= *yada*), which has the meaning of intellectual understanding, rather than visual sight. It could also be translated as "knew", "discerned" or "understood" (as it is in many places, including at 26\12, 28\1-2, 28\4 et cetera). Gesenius' *Hebrew-Chaldee Lexicon* (p. 333) says of ידע (= *yada*): "to perceive, to acquire knowledge, to know, to be acquainted". We should say, then, that Saul perceived in his mind, from what the woman said, that it was Samuel whom she was (misleadingly) trying to describe. Saul did not see anybody, for he asked the woman, "what have you seen?" and "Of what form *is* he?"

We must not be deluded as Saul was deluded. She did not see Samuel either. She was lying. Neither did she see anybody at all. There was a voice, but whose was it? Certainly not that of the prophet Samuel raised from the dead by a witch! How deluded in the mind must we be to think that a witch could raise a prophet of God from the dead. Only one immersed in the teachings of the apostate church system could allow themselves to believe that.

Is it not curious that the woman was able to speak seemingly prophetic words to Saul about his turning away from God (28\16-19) at a time God was not answering him through prophets (28\6, 28\15)? Similarly, God allowed "a lying spirit" (a lying *person*) to persuade king Ahab to his doom: "And [the spirit] said, 'I will go out, and I will be a lying spirit in the mouth of all his

[Jehoshaphat's] prophets' " (1 Kings 22\19-24, 2 Chronicles 18\18-23), "spirit" put for the person or the messenger. Ahab's destruction was God's intention.

We cannot say here how the woman of Endor was able to communicate the things she did, because we are not told. She might have overheard such things elsewhere. Perhaps what she said was common knowledge, as *The Companion Bible* astutely indicates at 28\16, with the comment "Nothing was said but what was well known before".

When the alleged spirit asked Saul why he had "disquieted" him (28\15), this was all part of the deception: Saul had sought a Canaanite witch, the incident was at night (28\8), Saul was faint with hunger (28\20), ideal conditions for deception.

It might be argued that the text says "Samuel said to Saul", so why not just accept literally what is written? The answer is that there was deception at work (and the usual mistranslating by the King James Bible). The text also says the woman, operating by occultic deception, saw – *claimed* to see – "a messenger" who was in a disguised form passing off as Samuel. One of these two statements has to be modified in order to accommodate the other. They cannot both be held literally. To insist that Samuel actually appeared demands unreasonable modifications of the whole passage, which is why such an interpretation is an error of literalism and – in historical terms – of post-Babylonian Myth and Magick.

If we prefer to believe Samuel himself did appear and speak, then we have to credit a woman with the ability to raise a prophet of God out of his death state. What deceived the wayward Saul and a medium woman should not deceive us also. Endor was a Canaanite stronghold (Joshua 17\11-13). The Canaanites were known for their evil occultic practices.

A lying woman from Endor cannot raise the dead. Samuel is dead and buried and he will be raised by God in the resurrection. It was not Samuel who appeared – or seemed to appear – to the woman of Endor. Samuel is in the grave and without any consciousness until the resurrection. As Peter spoke of David: "he both died and was buried, and his tomb is among us until this day" (Acts 2\29). And, for an additional dismantling of post-Babylonian mythology, "nobody has ascended into Heaven" (John 3\13).

"God raises the dead" (2 Corinthians 1\9).

*

ed68

Chapter 10

Those Pillars of Antiquity

✶

Where are the temples of ancient Greece and Rome? Aye, where are they? And why those fluted pillars in broken heaps, collapsed roofs, the piles of rubble of, say, the Parthenon?

Does anybody wonder?

The drama should begin at Eden. It's one of the greatest stories. Rebel messengers put it out that the one who was to them the Benevolent One in Eden was disclosing to Adam and Eve what secret knowledge the Malignant One had been withholding through his jealousy.

And so it came to be that God and the serpent were cunningly reversed. It was God the Evil One who restricted Adam and Eve, and forbade them to taste the fruit of the knowledge of good and evil, and it was the serpent, the Benevolent One, who offered the fruit of the good knowledge. The one called "Elohim" was considered ungenerous and malignant, while the serpent was the redeemer who emancipated Adam and Eve from God's yoke, and gave them the required fruit of knowledge. This is borne out in profane history. But the truth is told in the writings of God's prophets. The Book of Genesis says, "all flesh corrupted their way on the Earth" (Genesis 6\12).

When Cain clubbed Abel down for his sweet offering of sacrifice to God, the apostates on the side of Cain taught, and still teach, that he was a sacred priest, and that Abel's murder was a sacrifice, a ritual act for the benefit of the community, to cleanse and bless the land with sacrificial blood.

After that time, "the sons of God", descendants of Adam, named as the בני האלהים (*bene ha-Elohim*), saw the beautiful daughters of other men and had seed by them and the Nephilimic people were born, giants and titans. Only Noah's line was untainted by evil seed: "Noah was a righteous man, untainted in his time" (Genesis 6\9). Some say the Adamic people were taking wives outside the Adamic line. To wipe out the evil breed God drowned them in the Flood and saved Noah.

In the Babylonian Mysteries, the man Noah was presented as a god with two heads which looked away from each other, because he was said to have two lives – before the Flood, and after it. The apostates wanted to preserve the order of the old world. From this came the myth of Janus and the myth of mermaids. The divine saving of Noah was distorted into a legend that a beast called Oannes emerged out of the sea and civilized the Babylonian people. The beast was worshipped in the name of Dagon, the fish-god.

Because the serpent was considered to be a great spiritual enlightener, he was identified with the Sun. Infants were considered the most acceptable burnt sacrifice to the Sun-god, so the priests and people burned their sons and daughters in the fire as a sacrifice to Moloch (Isaiah 30\33, Jeremiah 7\31, 32\35). The priests of Nimrod ate the flesh of their sacrifices. Priests of Baal were called "Cahna-Baal". From those priests, the priests of their lord Baal, comes "cannibal".

The apostates became powerful and mighty in the land of Babel, especially under Nimrod, son of Cush. The people of the kingdom were under a single dominion and the kingdom was extended under one unifying language so they built a city and tower dedicated to worship of the heavenly bodies. But the Angel of Yahweh reported back to God and He confounded their language in order to block the progress and He caused them to be scattered over the Earth and the demonic building plan had to be abandoned.

After Nimrod died, initiates into the Mysteries entered the temple in total nakedness, on the annual date of Nimrod's birth. The building appeared resplendent with light and radiant fire, then it was plunged into blackness, with rumbling thunder, lightning and dreadful bellowings. The building seemed to shake around them. Terrible apparitions astonished the trembling spectators, accompanied by trick voices of priests behind a screen. In this secret system of the Mysteries, everything was contrived in a sophisticated theatre of phantasmagoria, to wind the minds up of the initiates and novices so that, having surrendered to the priests, they might receive anything the priests would tell them. On a distant wall a mass of light transformed into a visage, which a loud voice proclaimed as Nimrod, and it declared, "The lord of all the Earth is born."

By the time of God's messiah the priests and religious teaching in the capital of the promised land had been taken over by Canaanites and an Edomite King, Herod the Great, child-killer. That messiah, anointed one of God, called Jesus and the Christ, warned them that they will be held accountable for all the righteous blood poured out on the Earth going back to Cain. His apostles after him, from around 26 to 66 AD warned of rebels who proclaimed a parallel and pseudo gospel. The apostle Paul wrote of "another Jesus ... a different spirit ... a different gospel" (2 Corinthians 11\4), and of false prophets opposing the prophets and apostles.

*

The survey leaps forward to the Roman Emperor Constantine. The power had been switched from Babylon. With his hoax conversion to religion by a vision of a cross in 312 AD, as a strategy for military and political expansion, Rome was able to switch its attack from bloodthirsty persecution to a strategy for a world delusion, with a view to universal domination. After his hoax conversion vision, he had his wife Fausta suffocated in a boiling bath, and executed his son Crispus, his brother-in-law Licinius, and Licinius's son.

While true worshippers and the scrolls of the prophets of God remained, an outward and adulterated version of religion had been concocted by deceivers, false men, pseudos. The new formal religion was legalized in 313, and Constantine consolidated his empire. In 325, at the Council of Nicea, the creeds of the polytheistic religion were founded – and made compulsory, under threat.

In 378 came the master stroke. Bishop Damascus of the Church of Rome was made the Pontifex Maximus of the Pagan Mysteries religion, and he took quiet possession of Keys of Janus, double-faced Janus who lives in both worlds: Bishop and Pontifex Maximus.

The new Pontifex was anxious to appease followers of the former Pagan pontiffs, and consequently he was willing to concoct or revise every dogma necessary to maintain popularity on both sides. Seeking to unite the ancient Mysteries with the new religion, Damascus went mining like a mole in the dark with the religious rulers so they could introduce their doctrines into public light. In their attempt to cover up discrepancies between the two, they sought to make up similarities. Truth was of no concern. The question was how to maintain the power structure of the *kosmokrators*, the world rulers and the authorities.

Pope Damascus had a translation of the oracles of the prophets and apostles twisted into his own tongue. Words and phrases were fidgeted and doctored in order to perpetuate the amalgam with the ancient Mysteries.

By the year 431, the Pontiff felt able to make the proclamation that Keys of Janus represented the symbolic keys given to Peter the apostle. They were considered the actual keys. Initiates into the Mysteries were instructed from the Book Petroma, and the office was turned into Pope Peter of Rome, though the apostle Peter did not go to Rome. From the mere jingle of words, Paganism and the adulteration were mixed, mixed by double-faced Janus who lives in both worlds.

The new Roman Pope, successor of the Babylonian kings, was said to be incapable of error and he was invested with the same powers as the Babylonian pontiffs. The chair of the Pagan Pontifex was acclaimed the actual chair of Peter, and he took the Papal mitre of Dagon, the fish-god of the Babylonians and Philistines, and put on the costumes of their priests. Celibacy for priests became an ingrained dogma, so that no upkeep of the family could gobble up the Roman coffers, and customs of the Mysteries were continued. And any debauchery was permitted.

Rich and poor hailed the new worship. They filled the new churches and were able to bring along their Mysteries practices unchallenged: the magic formula of three godheads, wafer gods, a god inside a man, salaried priestcraft, buildings, sacraments, baptismal regeneration, eternal fires, claims of *"vitam aeternam"* (eternal life) and *"non morietur in aeternum"* ("shall not die in eternity"), immortal souls departed from the body, souls received in Heaven, feast days, demonstrations of phoney miracles, stigmata, and other hoax Mysteries inherited from ancient Babylon. And so they made their invocations to the gods and goddesses of antiquity in the incensed and perfumed ceremonies and decadently opulent and gaudy festivals of the palatial Vatican churches, resplendent in their forms.

The doctrines of Plato became the doctrines of Augustine, making a new religious form out of human philosophy in one of the worst books ever written, *De Civitate Dei Contra Paganos (On the City of God against the Pagans)*, which city was, of course, Rome. Augustine's father was a Pagan, and his mother a Christian. Augustine was a double-faced Janus.

Armies of the *kosmokrators* stampeded across the world and missionaries went out in religious togas into all the world, and gave new names, some stolen from the Scrolls of God, to the Mysteries practices they found already there. Wherever those Roman missionaries went, it was Babylon coming home to Babylon. They found the same gods with different names, and new ones were added and christianized with the names of deities and saints.

The blinding theatres of phantasmagoria, in place of voices and apparitions, were transferred into new creeds and practices, mangling the writings of the prophets and apostles. And so the temples of antiquity were allowed to crumble into ruins. Down came the old, and up went the new, ecclesiastical architectures, century by century, age by age, Roman and non-Roman. The old teachings of the gods of antiquity have been broadcast ever since through those polyglot architectural satellites, in every village of the world.

And so tourists today walk round and round those Pagan Mysteries ruins, gazing this way and that with cameras and great wonder, clicking away at clues for the greatest smokescreen in the world.

✱

ed37

Chapter 11

Crows

✶

Perhaps that crow out in the road
poking at the scarlet guts of a rat
disembowelled by some speeding car
is the son of the crow
who was the son of the crow
of the sons of the sons of the sons of the crows
among the other "Fowls of the Air"
who feasted on Henry Garnet who sang sweetly
and who, hiding in a house near Worcester,
a secret refuge with false walls and rooms and trapdoors
and concealed stairs, was holed up in the darkness with a friend,
two men crouching in a cramped false chimney,
too small for even one of them to stand,
and took with them marmalade
and they were fed hot liquids through a straw poked between the walls,
and when the agents of the King came
the two men in the chimney crawled out after eight days looking half-alive,
and the sight terrified the government agents,
and Garnet's legs were swollen terribly,
and in the end it was the smell of their own accumulated faeces
that drove them down,
and Henry Garnet, confessor priest to the gunpowder plotters,
in the late spring of 1606, at the order of King James,
was tortured, then dragged face-down and backwards by a horse
from the Tower to St Paul's churchyard
where he was tormented under the inquisition of two translators of the King James Bible,
George Abbot and John Overall,
the noose ready, the axe leaning on the block,
and he was "hanged up by the Neck between Heaven and Earth",
then castrated, disembowelled and quartered
with the executioner's sharp and ready axe
and "his Bowels and inlay'd Parts taken out and burnt"
and his head cut off,
and the crowd groaned and mumbled
at the sight of a good man murdered for no good reason,
"and the Quarters were set up in some high and eminent Place
to become a Prey for the Fowls of the Air".

✶

ed112

Chapter 12

The exaltation of the man and woman of God compared with post-Babylonian myths

The Prophets and Apostles of God	World religion system
"*The* Lord our God is one Lord" – Deuteronomy 6\4 Mark 12\29	An upperworld of three called gods
"You are dust, and you will return to dust" – Genesis 3\19	A mysticism of never dying and of disembodied migrating souls flying through outer space up to God's temporary hiding-place in Heaven
"For in death *there is* no remembrance of You. Who in the grave is going to give You thanks?" – Psalm 6\5	
"For in the grave where you go *there is* no work, nor device, nor knowledge, nor wisdom" – Ecclesiastes 9\10	
"a time is coming in which all those in the graves will hear his voice, and they will come out" – John 5\28-29	
"For God so much loved the world that He gave His only Son, in order that everyone believing in him might not suffer destruction, but might have eonian life" – John 3\16	rejection of "the coming eons" and of the promise of resurrection and eonian life
"And everyone living and believing in me will most certainly not die throughout the eon" – John 11\26	
"The heavens, *yes, the* heavens, *belong to* Yahweh, but the Earth He has given to the sons of Adam" – Psalm115\16	floating to Heaven, to live for eternity in God's temporary hiding-place in Heaven
"… they will inherit the land" – Psalm 37\9-11, Matthew 5\5	
"Exalted *be* the God and Father of our Lord Jesus Christ, Who has exalted us with every spiritual exaltation among the most exalted in Christ" – Ephesians 1\3	
"He also raised *us* up together, and seated *us* together among the most exalted *who are* in Christ Jesus, [7] in order that in the coming eons He might show the transcendent wealth of His merciful goodwill in kindness towards us in Christ Jesus" – Ephesians 2\6-7	
"… the living God … is the Saviour of all men, especially of believers" – 1 Timothy 4\10	An underworld of fire, devils, and unsaved men in unceasing torments
"the eonian fire, which has been prepared for the slanderer and his messengers" – Matthew 25\41	
"Every passage *is* given by inspiration of God, and *is* profitable	A world

for teaching, for conviction, for correction, for discipline in righteousness, in order that the man of God can be complete, thoroughly equipped for every good work" – 2 Timothy 3\16-17

of buildings, rituals, and positions and respectability

"and, having been made complete, you are in him who is the fountainhead of all prime leadership and power"
– Colossians 2\10

"And the things that you have heard from me by means of many witnesses, set these down before faithful men who also will be competent to teach others" – 2 Timothy 2\2

A theology of "systematizing of deception" (Ephesians 4\14)

"having blotted out the handwriting of the decrees which was against us, which was in opposition to us, and he has removed it out of the way, having nailed it to the stake" – Colossians 2\14

"... no longer may we be infants, tossed here and there, and carried about with every wind of teaching, in the roguery of men, intent on craftiness, intent on the systematizing of deception" – Ephesians 4\14

"For if, indeed, he who comes proclaims another Jesus whom we did not proclaim, or if you receive a different spirit which you did not receive *from us*, or a different gospel which you did not accept *from us*, you put up with *him as* commendable" – 2 Corinthians 11\4, Galatians 1\6

"As we said before, and now I say again, if anybody proclaims to you a gospel contrary to the one you received, let him be anathema" – Galatians 1\9

*

ed23

Chapter 13

Grammatical Bedevilments and Myths in the King James Bible

✶

Here and there there are a few excellently translated words and phrases in the King James Bible, which I defend. Alongside those there are hosts of clumsy passages which perpetuate myths and delusions, jingles of words, which have given incorrect information about God and salvation to centuries of generations.

This document is a table of a selection of King James Bible's copious bedevilments. There are hundreds of bedevilments in the King James Bible regarding the eons / ages, the gospel promise of eonian life, who Jesus is, who the Holy Spirit is, and more.

The King James translators were either spiritually blinded to the truth, or they were unwilling to translate accurately – and therefore willing to translate inaccurately – because the underlying Hebrew and Greek do not support the results of their work. Blinded *and* unwilling.

First and important occurrences	King James Bible (KJV)	Keys of the Kingdom Holy Bible (KTK)	Effect of KJV blunder
1. Nouns – Hebrew			
Genesis 2\7 נפש (= *nephesh*)	'soul'	'being'	Gives the impression, from the ancient Mysteries, of mortal man being undying and eternal.
Genesis 3\22 עולם (= *olam*)	'ever'	'eon'	The KJV turns a noun into an adverb, a grammatical violation. Masks the truth about the eons which God has arranged (Hebrews 1\2, 11\3).
Exodus 24\13 Numbers 4\12 Numbers 4\47 Ezra 7\24 1 Chronicles 9\28 2 Chronicles 7\6 ~ several words used	'minister', 'ministering' 'ministry'	'attendant', 'service', 'servant', 'hand'	Supports the world religious system.
1 Samuel 27\10 פשט (= *pashat*)	'Whither have ye made <u>a road</u> to day?'	'Where have you made <u>a raiding trip</u> today?'	This is the only place the KJV has the word 'road' and it's wrong. As if David would build a road during wartime, and build it in a day. Comedy.

Isaiah 14\9 רפאים (= Rephaim)	'the dead'	'the Rephaim'	The Rephaim were one of the Canaanite tribes whom Abraham found in the land (Genesis 12\6). Isaiah 17\5 has the phrase 'the Valley of Rephaim', which the KJV has correctly. Also at Isaiah 26\14, 26\19, Psalm 88\10, Proverbs 2\18, 9\18, 21\16. Clumsy error. Inconsistency.
Psalm 9\17 שאול (= sheol)	'The wicked shall be turned into hell'	'The wicked man will be turned into the grave'	Even more clumsy in KJV is 'thou wilt not leave my soul in hell' (Psalm 16\10, Acts 2\27, 2\31). The impossible myth of never-ending fire.
Psalm 37\9, 37\11, 37\22, 37\29, 37\34 ארץ (= eretz)	'the meek shall inherit the earth'	'the submissive will inherit the land'	This statement by David is a reminder of God's promise to the patriarchs and prophets of the land allotted to the 12 tribes of Israel. To speak of inheriting 'the earth' is meaningless, and has no force as a reminder of the promise to the patriarchs. Yet at Psalm 37\3, the same Psalm, the KJV correctly has the word as 'land'. Why is it inconsistent? It does the same at Matthew 5\5. Destroys the link with the patriarchs. Internal conflict.
Daniel 9\24 עלמים (= olamim), plural form of עולם (= olam)	'and to bring in everlasting righteousness'	'and to bring in the righteousness of the eons'	Turns a plural noun, 'eons', into a singular adjective, 'everlasting', a grammatical violation. It also pulls off this same eon-dodging strategy at 1 Timothy 1\17. Masks the vision of the coming eons, and masks the true gospel promise of eonian life.
1 Chronicles 21\1 שטן (= satan)	'And Satan stood up against Israel and provoked David to number Israel'	'And an adversary stood up against Israel, and provoked David to number Israel.	2 Samuel 24\1 says: 'the anger of Yahweh burned against Israel, and He caused David to be moved against them to say, "Go and number Israel and Judah" ', so that the שטן is shown to be God Himself. So, in effect, the KJV calls an act of God an act of Satan. The word שטן only ever means 'enemy' or 'adversary'. There is no roving monster called 'Satan'. Blasphemy. Mythology.

2. Nouns – Greek	KJV	KTK	Effect of KJV blunder
Matthew 4\1 διάβολος (= *diabolos*)	'Then was Jesus led up of the Spirit into the wilderness to be tempted of the <u>devil</u>'	'Then Jesus was led up by the Spirit into the wilderness to be put to the test by the <u>slanderer</u>'	This word διάβολος is neither a name nor a title for anybody, as 2 Timothy 3\3 and Titus 2\3 show, where used concerning humans. It is an adjective (masculine) acting as a substantive (noun). Occurs 38 times. The KJV has 'the devil' (lower-case) for every occurrence, except at Revelation 12\9 where it has 'the Devil' (capitalized); 'slanderers' (which is good) at 1 Timothy 3\11; and 'false accusers' (which is good) at 2 Timothy 3\3 and Titus 2\3. It is linked with σατανᾶς (= *satanas*), occurring in the same phrases at Revelation 12\9 and 20\2. There is no Hebrew or Greek word which translates into a roving monster called 'Satan' and 'the Devil'. Mythology.

Matthew 4\15 ἔθνος (= *ethnos*)	'The land of Zabulon, and the land of Nephthalim, by the way of the sea, beyond Jordan, Galilee of the <u>Gentiles</u>'	'Land of Zebulon, and land of Naphtali, road of *the* sea, across the Jordan, Galilee of the nations'	This first occurrence of ἔθνος, in citation of Isaiah 9\1-2 concerning northern tribes of Israel, shows that 'Gentiles' is a bad translation. The house of Israel to the north were broken in Covenant and considered by God 'not My people' (Hosea 1\9-10, 2\23) and Jesus had come to rescue those 'lost sheep' (Matthew 15\24 Acts 5\31) with a New Covenant. 'Gentiles' is a loaded word. It signifies non-Israelite. Paul uses ἔθνος in reference to Israel at Romans 11\13, 11\25-26, concerning those who had been 'not My people', but were now 'My people' and 'Sons of the living God'. Paul says that when 'the fullness of the nations has come in, and so all Israel will be saved, as it has been written' (Romans 11\25-26), showing that those 'nations' are part of the reconciled sons of house of Israel, completing the reconciliation. Even in the KJV itself, "Gentile" is shown to be not a permanent status of race, for it has "ye were Gentiles" and "in time past Gentiles" (1 Corinthians 12\2, Ephesians 2\11). From this mistranslation we get the false construct of 'Jew and Gentile', rather than the understanding of 'Judahite and Greek' representing the house of Judah and the house of Israel. God's rescue plan for the 12 tribes of Israel seems forgotten in the New Covenant writings of the KJV.

Matthew 5\5 γῆ (= gee)	'they shall inherit the <u>earth</u>'	'they will inherit the <u>land</u>'	This statement by Jesus is a reminder of God's promise to the patriarchs and prophets of the land allotted to the 12 tribes of Israel. As at Psalm 37\9-11, to speak of inheriting 'the earth' is meaningless, and has no force as a reminder of the promise to the patriarchs. Turn from the writings of the Old Covenant to the writings of the New Covenant, and everything about the promises to the 12 tribes seem to be forgotten. Destroys the link with the patriarchs. Internal conflict.
Matthew 5\22 γέεννα (= gehenna)	'hell'	'<u>the Valley of Hinnom</u>'	The impossible myth of never-ending fire.
Matthew 11\23 ᾅδης (= hades)	'hell'	'<u>the grave</u>'	The impossible myth of never-ending fire.
Matthew 12\18 ἡ ψυχή μου (= hee psuchee mou)	'Behold my servant whom I have chosen; my beloved, in whom <u>my soul</u> is well pleased'	'Behold My servant whom I have chosen, My Richly Loved One in whom <u>I Myself</u> have found delight'	This is one of three thundering bungles by the KJV men: that man has a detachable 'soul' (Matthew 10\28); that Jesus has a detachable 'soul' (Matthew 26\38, John 12\27); and that God has a detachable 'soul' (Matthew 12\18). Supports the world system.
Matthew 16\18 ἐκκλησία (= ekklesia)	'<u>church</u>'	'Ekklesia'	Ekklesia is the equivalent of David's קהל (= qahal), 'assembly' of 'the seed of Jacob', those 'called together'. Ekklesia is 'called out' (Psalm 22\22-25 with Hebrews 2\12). Supports the world religious system.
Matthew 16\23 σατανᾶς (= satanas)	'Get the behind me, <u>Satan</u>: thou art an offence unto me'	'Get behind me, <u>adversary</u>! You're a snare to me ...'	Jesus would not call his friend Peter by the name of a fictional monster. The word σατανᾶς here could not be more clearly shown to have the meaning of 'adversary', 'enemy' in its occurrences. Mythology.

Reference	KJV	Alternative	Comment
Matthew 20\26, Luke 1\2, Acts 1\17, Romans 12\7, 13\6, 15\8, Hebrews 1\14, 8\6, Luke 1\23, Acts 1\17, 6\1 ~ several Greek words used	'ministry' 'ministration'	'servant' 'work' 'servant' 'officiating service'	Supports the world religious system.
John 1\1 ὁ λόγος (= *ho logos*)	'the Word'	'the oracle'	By its imposed capitalization of 'Word' (not capitalized in the Greek), it gives the impression that ὁ λόγος is a title of Jesus, but the declared oracle of God and of the gospel; Mark 1\1, Luke 1\2. Post-Babylonian polytheism.
John 3\13 ὁ ὢν ἐν τῷ οὐρανῷ (= *ho hon en to ourano*)	'the Son of man which is in heaven'	'the Son of Man, who is in the Heavenly One'	Jesus was talking to a priest in Jerusalem. KJV makes him say he was in Heaven at that same moment! Comedy.
John 7\35 Ἕλλην (= *Hellēn*)	'will he go unto the dispersed among the Gentiles, and teach the Gentiles?'	'Is he about to go to the diaspora of the Greeks and then teach the Greeks?'	Astounding! The KJV men have altered the meaning from 'Greeks' to 'Gentiles', even though they are described as 'the diaspora' (the dispersed tribes of the house of Israel who had not returned after the captivity). Proper nouns (names) are the easiest work for a translator. These 'Greeks' were Israelites, as the context makes clear. See also John 12\20, Acts 17\4, 'Greeks' going to worship at the Festival. The KJV repeats the error at Romans 2\9, 2\10, 3\9, 1 Corinthians 10\32, 12\13, yet has the word right in other places. Internal inconsistency. Turns Israelites into non-Israelites.
Acts 1\20 ἐπισκοπή (= *episkopee*)	'bishopric'	'office'	Supports the world religious system.
Acts 2\27 ᾅδης (= *hades*)	'thou wilt not leave my soul in hell'	'You will not abandon my dead body in the grave'	According to the KJV, then, while Jesus was supposed to be dead for three days and three nights he was actually in the fictional place called "hell", therefore he did not die at all. Also at Acts 2\31. Takes away the death of the sacrificial lamb; destroys hope for mankind.

Acts 7\45 Ἰησοῦς (= Jesus)	'Jesus'	'Joshua'	Ἰησοῦς is the Greek form for 'Jesus', but Stephen is recounting the history of Israel from the days of Abraham. The successor to Moses was Joshua, but the KJV put 'Jesus' as his successor. Also wrong at Heb. 4\8. But they got it right elsewhere, so this is blunder. Comedy.
Acts 12\4 πάσχα (= paska)	'Easter'	'Passover'	Supports the world religious system.
Romans 1\16 Ἰουδαῖος (= Ioudaios)	'to the Jew first, and also to the Greek'	'both to the Judahite first, then to the Greek'	Always in the KJV translated as 'Jew'. But, because of the general mistaken associating of 'Jews' as representing all 12 tribes of Israel, to translate it as 'Jew' is misleading. It is much better as 'Judahite', enforcing that it stands for the tribe of Judah. The other reason for 'Jew' being so unhelpful is that, used in apposition to 'Gentile' when it should be 'Greek', it forces the impression Paul is talking about non-Israelites.
Romans 2\9, 2\10, 3\9, 1 Corinthians 10\32, 12\13	'the Jew first and also of the Gentile'	'of Judahite first, and of Greek'	In all these passages the KJV has altered the word 'Greek', to 'Gentile', as it also did at John 7\35, yet has the word right in other places.
1 Corinthians 10\11 αἰών (= aion)	'upon whom the ends of the world are come'	'On them have come the ends of the eons'	Turns a plural noun, αἰώνων (= aionon), 'eons', into a singular noun, 'world', and changes the meaning. Also at Hebrews 9\26. αἰών (= aion) does not mean 'world'. Only because it has been wrongly put as 'world' and 'worlds' (??) in KJV do some stiff-necked commentators object it means 'world'. Our English words 'eon' and 'eonian' are derived from it. Masks the vision of the coming eons.
Philippians 1\1 ἐπίσκοπος (= episkopos)	'bishop'	'overseer'	Supports the world religious system.
Philippians 1\1 διάκονος (= diakonos)	'deacons'	'attendants'	Supports the world religious system.

	KJV	KTK	Effect of KJV blunder
1 Timothy 1\17 αἰών (= aion) in plural form αἰώνων (= aionon)	'the King eternal'	'the King of the Ages / Eons'	Turns a plural noun, αἰώνων = aionon), 'Eons' (or 'Ages'), into an adjective, 'eternal'. It also pulls off this same eon-dodging strategy at Daniel 9\24. Masks the vision of the coming eons.
1 Timothy 3\1 ἐπισκοπή (= episkopee)	'bishop'	'office'	Supports the world religious system.
1 Timothy 3\10 διακονέω (= diakoneo)	'deacons'	'attendants'	Supports the world religious system.
Hebrews 1\2 αἰών (= aion)	'by whom also he made the worlds'	'through whom also He designed the eons'	Turns an abstract noun, 'eons', into a concrete noun, 'worlds'. There is only one world. Also at Hebrews 11\2. Comedy.
Hebrews 4\8 Ἰησοῦς (= Jesus)	'if Jesus had given them rest'	'If Joshua had caused them to rest'	Ἰησοῦς (= Jesus) is the form for Jesus, but the whole context here is that Joshua did not give the people rest from works in the promised land, and that rest is now given in Jesus. KJV implies Jesus DID NOT give them rest, but the point of the passage is that Jesus DID give them rest. See also Acts 7\48. Implies failure by Jesus.
Hebrews 9\26 αἰών (= aion)	'but now once in the end of the world hath he appeared'	'but now, once, towards the completion of the eons, he has been revealed'	Turns a plural abstract noun, αἰώνων (= aionon), 'eons', into a singular concrete noun, 'world', and changes the meaning. Why? Also at 1 Corinthians 10\11. Masks the vision of the coming eons.
Hebrews 11\2 αἰών (= aion)	'Through faith we understand that the worlds were framed by the word of God'	'By faith we understand the eons to have been framed by an oracle of God'	Turns an abstract noun, 'eons', into a concrete noun, 'worlds'. There is only one world. Also at Hebrews 1\2. Comedy.
3. Adjectives – Hebrew	KJV	KTK	Effect of KJV blunder
Genesis 9\16 Daniel 12\2 et cetera עולם (= olam)	'everlasting'	'eonian'	Noun acting adjectivally. Masks the truth of the eons God has arranged. And masks the gospel promise of eonian life.

Exodus 19\6 קָדוֹשׁ (= kahdosh)	'holy'	'set apart'	God's promise to the sons of Israel is that they are to Him 'a nation set apart'. To say that they were 'holy' is in conflict with God's divorcing them and making a New Covenant with them. There can only be one 'set apart' people. Separateness cannot be shared.

4. Adjectives – Greek	KJV	KTK	Effect of KJV blunder
John 3\16 αἰώνιος (= aionios)	'everlasting'	'eonian'	Masks the truth of the eons God has arranged. And masks the gospel promise of eonian life, life in the coming eons.
Romans 1\7 ἅγιος (= hagios) (Occurs over 60 times, first at Matthew 27\52)	'saints'	'set apart people'	'Saints' gives the image of Renaissance paintings of disciples with their feet off the ground and plates behind their head. Apply the correct meaning, then the link with Exodus 19\5-6, concerning the sons of Israel, is restored. These are Israelites, those set apart. Conceals Israel's preeminence in the mind and plans of God.
Ephesians 1\3 ἐπουράνιος (= epouranios) (Also at 1\20, 2\6, 1 Corinthians 15\48)	'heavenly *places*'	'the most exalted'	Gives the impression men go to Heaven, supporting the world religious system. Furthermore, breaking the link with Exodus 19\5-6, Deuteronomy 7\6 et cetera, of the 12 tribes being above all nations on the Earth (Revelation 21\12-13, Deut. 7\6).

5. Pronouns – Greek	KJV	KTK	Effect of KJV blunder
John 1\3 αὐτοῦ (= autou)	'him ... him'	'it ... it'	Tries to make it refer back to ὁ λόγος (= ho logos) as Jesus. Polytheism.

6. Verbs – Hebrew	KJV	KTK	Effect of KJV blunder
Exodus 24\13, 28\35 Daniel 7\10, Psalm 9\8, 2 Chronicles 24\14 ~ several Hebrew words used	'minister'	'serve', 'service'	Supports the world religious system.

	KJV	KTK	Effect of KJV blunder
Micah 5\2 (supplied verb)	'But thou, Bethlehem Ephratah, *though* thou be little among the thousands of Judah, yet out of thee shall he come forth unto me that is to be ruler in Israel; whose goings forth *have been* from of old, from everlasting'	'But you, Bethlehem of Ephrathah, *although* you are too little *to rank* among the districts of Judah, yet out of you will come for Me *one who is* to become Ruler in Israel, and his proceedings *will be* from of old time, from the days of the Eon'	This is a futuristic vision. A verb has to be supplied to make English sense of the Hebrew. The KJV's supplying of the past tense 'have been' makes Jesus seem an eternal mystical being. Note also the bad style in 'yet out of thee shall he come forth unto me that is to be'. Polytheism: the post-Babylonian three gods as one god system.

7. Verbs – Greek	**KJV**	**KTK**	**Effect of KJV blunder**
Matthew 2\2 προσκυνέω (= *proskuneo*)	'[we] are come <u>to worship</u> him'	'we have come <u>to pay honour</u> to him'	Makes Jesus seem God. Polytheism.
Matthew 4\11 Acts 13\2, 20\34 Romans 15\16 1 Corinthians 9\13 2 Corinthians 9\10 Ephesians 4\29 Philippians 2\25 Colossians 2\19 1 Timothy 1\4 Hebrews 1\14 ~ several Greek words used	'<u>minister</u>'	'<u>attended</u>'	Supports the world religious system.
Matthew 23\3 ποιεῖτε (= *poyeite*) indicative verb	'<u>do</u>' [imperative verb]	'<u>you do put into practice</u>' [indicative verb]	Uses an imperative verb where context demands an indicative. Encourages inappropriate obedience to leaders.
Matthew 26\45-46 Mark 14\41-42 καθεύδετε (= *katheudete*) and ἀναπαύεσθε (= *anapauesthe*) Matthew 26\45-46 Mark 14\41-42	'<u>Sleep on</u> now, and <u>take your rest</u> ... the hour is at hand ... Rise, let us be going'	'<u>Are you</u> still <u>sleeping</u> and <u>taking your rest?</u> ... the hour has drawn near ... Rise up, *and* let us be going'	Just when the thugs are coming to arrest Jesus, the KJV has Jesus tell his disciples all at once both to 'Sleep' and 'rise' – and that after he had just been ticking them off for sleeping. Comedy.

Matthew 27\64 ἐγείρω (= *egeiro*) in its passive form ἠγέρθη (= *heegerthee*) This verb occurs in passive forms at: Matthew 8\15, 9\25, 11\5, 11\11, 14\2, 25\7, 27\52, 27\63, 27\64, 28\6, 28\7, Mark 2\12, 6\14, 6\16, 16\6, 16\14 (in participle form), Luke 24\6, 24\34, John 2\22, 21\14, Acts 9\8, Romans 4\25, 6\4.	'... He is risen from the dead'	'... He has been raised from the dead'	What is a passive verb form, ἠγέρθη, KJV wrongly has as mid-voice. Perhaps this was done in order to force the impossible mystic view that Jesus somehow raised himself, in which case he could not have died and then there is no salvation. But Jesus said to John, 'I became dead' (Rev. 1\18). He was raised from death, not some mystic half-life. KJV echoes the Vulgate which has 'surrexit'. Yet the KJV has this verb correctly as passive at Matthew 11\5, Romans 4\25, 6\4. Mysticism. Polytheism.
Matthew 28\19 πορευθέντες (= *poreuthentes*), aorist optative participle	'Go ye' [imperative verb]	'In your having gone' [participle]	The pretence has been forced that this is a command to all and sundry, and that anybody can apply this passage to themselves and leave their homes and go off as a 'missionary'. This has cost well-meaning lives to the breaking of families, damaged children, and knives of savages.
John 1\3 ἐγένετο (= *egeneto*), active singular	'were made ... made ... was made'	'arose ... arose ... has arisen'	What are active aorist and perfect tense singular intransitive stative verbs the KJV doctors into passive imperfect plural transitive statives, then a passive imperfect singular transitive dynamic, in order to give the impression Jesus is the Creator, in conflict with Genesis 1\1 et cetera. Polytheism: the three gods system.
John 1\10 ἐγένετο (= *egeneto*), active singular	'the world was made by him, and the world knew him not'	'the world has come to be through him, yet the world did not know him'	What is an active aorist intransitive stative verb the KJV fiddles into a passive imperfect transitive verb, in order to give the impression Jesus is the Creator, in conflict with Genesis 1\1. Polytheism: the three gods system.

Chapter 13 — Grammatical Bedevilments and Myths

	KJV	KTK	Effect of KJV blunder
John 8\58 γενέσθαι (= *genesthai*) aorist infinitive verb	'Before Abraham was, I am'	'before Abraham is to appear, I Am'	KJV changes an infinitive verb into a finite imperfect verb. Gives an impression of Jesus as an eternal mystical being. Yet they were able to put γενέσθαι as an infinitive at Mark 1\17, Luke 21\28, John 1\12, Acts 26\28, and elsewhere (but wrongly as 'be made', finite passive, at John 5\6, and wrongly as 'be done', finite passive, at Revelation 22\6). Mysticism. Polytheism.
Roman 9\3 εὔχομαι (= *euchomai*), here as ηὐχόμεν (= *euchomai*), imperfect tense or conditional mood	'For I could wish that myself were accursed from Christ for my brethren, my kinsmen according to the flesh'	'for I used to vow for I myself to be a curse from the Christ – for the sake of my brothers, my countrymen in relation to flesh'	This is 1st person singular imperfect, but is in the same form in the conditional mood. Rendered in KJV as present conditional, 'I could vow', which gives the notion Paul could die or suffer to be the saviour for the sins of rebellious Israelites. But salvation is through Christ. Sense dictates Paul is saying he used to be glad to be cursed from Christ. See Acts 23\12-21, 26\9-11, 1 Timothy 1\13. Mysticism.
Hebrews 3\2 ποιέω (= *poyeo*); here an aorist participle, ποιήσαντι (= *poihsanti*), so literally 'having created'.	'[Christ Jesus]; Who was faithful to him that appointed him'	'[Jesus Christ], faithful to Him having created him'	This is a common verb for create or make or cause (Heb. 1\2, 1\3, 1\7 Revelation 12\15, 14\7 et cetera). KJV's 'appointed' masks that Jesus is a created man. At Hebrews 1\2, the word used for God appointing Jesus is τίθημι (= *titheemi*). Hebrews 1\2 has 'designed', ποιέω (= *poyeo*), in apposition to 'appointed'. Avoiding that Christ is a created man.
2 Peter 2\4 ταρταρόω (= *tartaroo*), verb	'cast down to hell'	'swallowed underground'	KJV smuggles in the notion of 'hell'. The impossible myth of eternal fire.

8. Adverbs – Hebrew	KJV	KTK	Effect of KJV blunder
Genesis 3\22 לעלם (= *le olam*)	'for ever'	'throughout the eon'	Masks the eons God has arranged.

Isaiah 45\17 עולמים (= olamim)	'everlasting'	'for the eons'	Turns a plural noun into an adjective. Masks the eons God has arranged.
Isaiah 45\17 עד־עולמי עד (= ad ole me ad)	'world without end'	'throughout the eon and its duration'	KJV says 'world without end', which is not true. And it conflicts with its own 2 Peter 3\10 'the earth ... and the works that are therein shall be burned up'; and its own Revelation 21\1 'I saw a new heaven and a new earth: for the first heaven and the first earth were passed away'; and its own Matthew 13\39 (et cetera), which says (incorrectly) 'at the end of the world'; and its own 1 Corinthians 8\13, which says (incorrectly) 'while the world standeth'. Further clashes at Ecclesiastes 1\4, Ephesians 3\21. Internal conflict. Masks the eons God has arranged (Hebrews 1\2, 11\3).
Psalm 23\6 לארך ימים (= le orek yamim)	'for ever'	'for the length of days'	The word 'duration' is ארך (as in 'the length' of the ark at Genesis 6\15). The word ימים is 'days'. The same phrase is at Psalm 21\4, 91\16, 93\5, Job 12\12. David means for his lifetime and for the Messianic eon of his hope, not 'for ever' as KJV. David will not be in the House of Yahweh for ever, because in the New Jerusalem there is 'no Sanctuary' (Revelation 21\22). Lack of understanding about David's life and future inheritance.
Psalm 133\3 et cetera עד־העולם (= ad ha olam)	'for evermore'	'throughout the duration of the eon'	Masks the eons God has arranged.
Ecclesiastes 1\4 לועלם (= le olam) = 'throughout the eon'	'the earth abideth for ever'	'the Earth remains throughout the eon'	KJV says 'the earth abideth for ever'. Conflicts with its own Matthew 13\39 (et cetera), 'the end of the world', 1 Corinthians 8\13, 'while the world standeth'. See also Isaiah 45\17, Ephesians 3\21. Internal conflict.
Daniel 2\4 לעלמין (= le alamin)	'for ever'	'throughout the eon'	Turns a noun into an adverb. Masks the gospel promise of eonian life.

9. Adverbs – Greek	KJV	KTK	Effect of KJV blunder
Matthew 6\13 εἰς τοὺς αἰῶνας (= eis tous aionas)	'for ever'	'throughout the eon'	Turns a noun into an adverb. Masks the gospel promise of eonian life.
Matthew 13\39 συντέλια τοῦ αἰῶνός (= sunteleia tou aionos)	'the end of the world'	'*the* completion of the eon'	KJV's version clashes with its own Isaiah 45\17 and Ephesians 3\21, which say 'world without end'. Masks the eons God has arranged. Comedy.
John 4\14 οὐ μὴ ... εἰς τὸν αἰῶνα (= ou me ... eis ton aiona)	'never'	'certainly not ... throughout the eon'	KJV turns two adverbs and a three word prepositional phrase into a single word adverb. (Also John 11\26.) Adds to Scripture, and takes away from Scripture. Masks the eons God has arranged. And masks the gospel promise of eonian life.
John 9\32 ἐκ τοῦ αἰῶνος (= ek tou aionos)	'since the world began'	'since of old'	Here the Greek is well rendered idiomatically in the context. But the KJV does badly in style and sense: there is no word 'world' and no word 'began'. Somebody opening the eyes of a man born blind could not have been 'heard of' before the world began. Comedy.
John 11\26 οὐ μὴ ... εἰς τὸν αἰῶνα (= ou me ... eis ton aiona)	---	'most certainly not ... throughout the eon'	KJV omits to translate these two adverbials in John 11\26, and instead inserts a random word 'never' which is not represented by any Greek word in the text. (Also John 4\14.) Adds to Scripture, and takes away from Scripture. Eternal and undying man. Conceals the gospel promise.
Acts 3\21 ἀπ' αἰῶνος (= ap aionos)	'since the world began'	'from of old'	Here the Greek is well rendered idiomatically in the context. But KJV does badly in style and sense: there is no word 'world' and no word 'began'; there have not been prophets since the world began. See also 1 Corinthians 2\7, 2 Timothy 1\9 and Titus 1\2. Comedy.

Romans 16\25 [Romans 14\25 in KTK, based on a different Greek text] χρόνοις αἰωνίοις (= kronois aioniois)	[Romans 16\25 in KJV] 'revelation of the mystery, which was kept secret since the world began'	[Romans 14\25 in KTK] 'an unveiling of a mystery kept in silence in eonian times' (or '... in times of the ages')	KJV does not represent a single word of the Greek. Conflict with KJV's own 1 Corinthians 2\7, Ephesians 3\5, 3\9-10, 2 Timothy 1\9, Titus 1\2 which say the mystery and the gospel were 'ordained' and 'promised' and was 'given' 'before the world began'. KJV does not have a single word right here It does not represent the Greek. There are no Greek words in the passage for 'since', 'the', 'world', and no verb 'began'. Internal conflict. Conceals the fact of the coming eons.
1 Corinthians 2\7 πρὸ τῶν αἰώνων (= pro ton aionon).	'a mystery ... which God ordained before the world'	'a mystery ... kept hidden ... which God has marked out beforehand, in advance of the eons'	Changes a plural abstract noun, αἰώνων, 'eons', into a singular concrete noun, 'world', changing the meaning. In conflict with its own Romans 16\25 and Ephesians 3\5. It does not represent the Greek. The only word KJV has right is 'before'. There are no Greek words in the passage for 'the' or 'world'. It's made up. Conceals the fact of the coming eons.
1 Corinthians 8\13 εἰς τὸν αἰῶνα (= eis ton aiona)	'while the world standeth'	'throughout the eon'	In conflict with KJV's Isaiah 45\17 and Ephesians 3\21, which say 'world without end'. KJV does not represent the Greek. There are no Greek words in the passage for 'while', 'the', or 'world'. The only word the KJV has right in this phrase is 'the'. Internal conflict. Conceals the fact of the coming eons.
Ephesians 3\21 τοῦ αἰῶνος τῶν αἰώνων (= tou aionos ton aionon)	'world without end'	'the duration of the eons'	In conflict with KJV's Matthew 13\39 and 1 Corinthians 8\13. See also Isaiah 45\17, Ecclesiastes 1\4. KJV does not have a single word right here It does not represent the Greek. There are no Greek words in the passage for 'world', 'without' or 'end'. It's all made up. Internal conflict. Conceals the fact of the coming eons.

2 Timothy 1\9 Titus 1\2 πρὸ χρόνων αἰωνίων (= pro kronon aionion)	'his own purpose and grace, which was given us in Christ Jesus before the world began'	'His own purpose and merciful goodwill given to us in Christ Jesus in advance of eonian times'	The KJV can only manage 'given us in Christ before the world began'. Neither of the KJV's words 'the', nor 'world' nor 'began' are in the Greek. And it makes no sense: how can you be given anything 'before the world began'? The KJV's Titus 1\2 also has 'promised before the world began', but who would be there to promise it to? These are in conflict with the KJV's Romans 16\25 1 Corinthians 2\7 which say the gospel 'was kept secret since the world began' (wrong in those passages also). In conflict as well with KJV's Ephesians 3\5, 'in other ages not made known'; in conflict with its Ephesians 3\9, 'from the beginning of the wold hath been hid in God'; in conflict as well with its Matthew 13\35 speaking of 'things kept secret since *the* foundation of *the* world order'. The 'eonian times' here are *future*. KJV does not represent the Greek. Masks the gospel of eonian life. Masks the eons God has arranged. Puts the future into the past. Calvinism.
10. Prepositions – Hebrew and Greek	**KJV**	**KTK**	**Effect of KJV blunder**
Genesis 3\22 לְעוֹלָם (= le olam)	'for ever'	'throughout the eon'	עוֹלָם (= olam) is a noun, 'eon', not an adverb 'ever'. The 'for' should be 'throughout'. Masks the truth about the eons God has arranged.
John 1\1 πρός (= pros)	'the Word was with God'	'the oracle was pointing to [or, in relation to] God'	The Greek word 'with' is μετά (= meta). KJV tries to make out, along with its corruption of λόγος (= logos) in this verse by capitalizing 'Word', that Jesus was with God in the beginning of time. Polytheism: the three gods system.

	KJV	KTK	Effect of KJV blunder
John 6\51, 6\58 et cetera εἰς (= *eis*) in the phrase εἰς τὸν αἰῶνα (= *eis ton aiona*)	'he shall live <u>for ever</u>'	'he will live <u>throughout</u> the eon'	Eternal and undying man. Yet the KJV has this preposition εἰς correctly once as 'throughout' at Ephesians 3\21.
2 Thessalonians 1\12 'of'	'according to the grace of our God and the Lord Jesus Christ'	'in harmony with the merciful goodwill of our God and <u>of</u> the Lord Jesus Christ'	The words 'the Lord Jesus Christ' are all genitive. KJV omits the second 'of' in order to make it seem as if Jesus is God. Also at Titus 2\13, 2 Peter 1\1. Polytheism.
Titus 2\13 'of'	'glorious appearing of the great God and our Saviour Jesus Christ'	'magnificence of the Mighty God, and <u>of</u> our Saviour Jesus Christ'	The words 'our Saviour Jesus Christ' are all genitive. KJV omits the second 'of' in order to make it seem as if Jesus is God. See 2 Thessalonians 1\12. Polytheism.
2 Peter 1\1 'of'	'righteousness of God and our Saviour Jesus Christ'	'righteousness of our God and <u>of</u> the Saviour Jesus Christ'	In the Greek TR text of the KJV, there is also 'our' before the word 'God' but KJV omits to translate it. (In RP text there is no 'our' before 'Saviour'.) The words 'Saviour Jesus Christ' are all genitive. KJV, though, omits the second 'of' in order, presumably, to make it seem as if Jesus is God. KJV got it right in verse 2, though, where it has 'of God, and of Jesus ...' – so why not in verse 1? Polytheism.

11. Definite article	**KJV**	**KTK**	**Effect of KJV blunder**
1 Timothy 6\10 'the'	'For the love of money is <u>the</u> root of all evil'	'For the love of money is <u>a</u> root of all the evils'	KJV adds 'the' to 'root', but it is not in the Greek texts. Money was not the cause of evil in Eden, nor is it the cause of all evils. And 'evils' is plural. False teaching.

12. Punctuation	KJV	KTK	Effect of KJV blunder
Luke 23\43 comma	'Verily I say unto thee, To day shalt thou be with me in paradise'	'Truly, I say to you this day, you will be with me in the paradise.'	KJV has the comma in the wrong place; it comes AFTER 'this day', not BEFORE, as shown beyond argument in the same expression at Mark 14\30, Deut. 4\26, 4\39 et cetera. Also, the 'Paradise of God' is not yet: it's the New Jerusalem in the new Earth (Revelation 2\27, 21-22), after this Earth's system has been turned over by fire (2 Peter 3\12). The lie that Paradise is already in existence. The lie of eternal and undying man.
1 Timothy 3\15-16 comma / full-stop	'But if I tarry long, that thou mayest know how thou oughtest to behave thyself in the house of God, which is the church of the living God, the pillar and ground of the truth. 16 And ...'	'although I might delay – in order that you might know how you ought to conduct yourself among *the household of God, which is the Ekklesia of the living God. A pillar and foundation of the truth* [16] and ...'	KJV puts the full-stop in the wrong place, too late in the sentence, and opens verse 16 with 'And'. This gives the effect that 'the church' is the pillar of the truth, not Jesus Christ.

13. False capitalizations	KJV	KTK	Effect of KJV blunder
Matthew 1\20 and elsewhere πνεῦμα ἅγιον (= *pneuma hagion*) 'holy sprit'	'the Holy Ghost'	'*the* holy spirit'	KJV indiscriminately capitalizes, without regard to context, unable to distinguish between the Angel of God, who is the Holy Spirit, and the power and nature of God and Christ. Commitment to polytheism.
Romans 8\9 and elsewhere πνεῦμα (= *pneuma*), 'spirit'	'But ye are not in the flesh, but in the Spirit, if so be that the Spirit of God dwell in you'	'You though, are not in flesh, but in spirit, if, indeed, *the* spirit of God inhabits you'	At Matthew 3\6, John 14\26 et cetera 'the Spirit of God' is a title for the Angel of God (see Isaiah 63\9-11). But 'the spirit of God' here stands for the renewed nature of the believer, the spirit of the mind. KJV at Romans 8\9 capitalizes 'spirit', making it seem that their third God lives in people's bellies. Polytheism. Mysticism of gods in the fat of men's bellies.

14. Words untranslated	KJV	KTK	Effect of KJV blunder
John 11\26 οὐ μὴ ... εἰς τὸν αἰῶνα (= ou me ... eis ton aiona)	- - - (no equivalent)	'most certainly not ... throughout the eon'	The KJV has 'never' in this verse, but there is no word for 'never' in John 11\26. The Greek word for 'never' is οὐδέποτε (= oudepote), and that word is not in John 11\26. This means there are 5 words in the Greek left untranslated. Taking away from the oracles of God (Revelation 22\18-19). Masking the gospel promise of eonian life and believers not being subject to death in the future eon.
2 Peter 3\18 εἰς ἡμέραν αιῶνος (= eis hemeran aionos)	'To him be glory both now and _ _ _ for ever'	'To him be magnificence, both now and throughout *the* day of *the* eon'	The Greek has the adverbial phrase εἰς ἡμέραν αιῶνος (= eis hemeran aionos), which, simply enough, is 'throughout *the* day of *the* eon'. The first and last words mean 'throughout' and 'eon', which the KJV wrongly has as 'for ever'. The middle word, ἡμέραν, which means 'day', the KJV has ignored. Taking away from the oracles of God (Revelation 22\18-19). Ignoring the coming eon.

15. Words added	KJV	KTK	Effect of KJV blunder
- - - (no equivalent)	'Saint Matthew ... Saint Mark ... Saint Luke ... Saint John ... Saint John the Divine'	- - - (no equivalent)	What is all this 'Saint Matthew'? There is no man or woman in all the writings of the prophets and apostles called 'Saint' anybody. Adding to the oracles of God (Revelation 22\18-19). Where it has 'saints' in passages such as Ephesians 1\1, which should be 'holy people', it masks the connection with Exodus 19\5-6, 1 Peter 2\9-10.

1 John 5\7-8 ἐν τῷ οὐρανῷ ὁ πατήρ ὁ λόγος καὶ τὸ ἅγιον πνεῦμα καὶ οὗτοι οἱ τρεῖς ἕν εἰσι καὶ τρεῖς εἰσιν οἱ μαρτυροῦντες ἐν τῇ γῇ	'in heaven, the Father, the Word, and the Holy Ghost: and these three are one. And there are three that bear witness in earth.'	- - - (no equivalent)	Rogue insertion without textual foundation, as is well-known.
16. Order of the Hebrew and Greek Books	KJV	KTK	Effect of KJV blunder
The Hebrew Books are in a divinely established order: 'the Law of Moses, and the Prophets, and the Psalms' (Luke 24\44). Jesus also spoke of 'the blood of the righteous Abel to the blood of Zechariah' (Matthew 23\35). Abel is in Genesis 4\2 and Zechariah is in 2 Chronicles 35\8.	Gen., Ex., Lev., Num., Deut., Josh., Judg., 1 & 2 Sam., 1 & 2 Kings, 1 and 2 Chr., Ezra, Neh., Esth., Job, Ps., Prov., Ecc., Song, Is., Jer., Lam., Ezek., Dan., Hos., Joel, Amos, Obad., Jon., Mic., Nah., Hab., Zeph., Hag., Zech., Mal.	'The Law': Gen., Ex., Lev., Num., Deut. 'The Prophets': Josh., Judg., 1 & 2 Sam., 1 & 2 Ki., Is., Jer., Ezek., Hos., Joel, Amos, Obad., Jon., Mic., Nah., Hab., Zeph., Matthew, Mark, Hag., Zech., Mal. 'The Psalms': Ps., Prov., Job, Ruth, Lam., Ecc., Dan., Ezra, Neh., 1 & 2 Chr.	The KJV order is an annoying mess. This mess is repeated in other translations, with hardly any exceptions. See Chapter 22. The divine order is structured. KJV includes the disharmonious and hostile Song of Songs and Esther. See Chapter 28. Awkward reading. Awkward finding.
1. Four Gospels and Acts. 2. Other apostles' 7 letters. 3. Paul's 14 letters. 4. Revelation	Matthew, Mark, Luke, John, Acts, Rom., 1 & 2 Cor., Gal., Eph., Phil., Col., 1 & 2 Thes., 1 & 2 Tim., Tit., Phil., Heb., James, 1 & 2 Peter, 1 & 2 & 3 John, Jude, Rev.	1. Four Gospels and Acts: Mat., Mark, Luke, John, Acts; 2. Other apostles' 7 letters: Jacob (James), 1 Peter, 2 Peter, 1 John, 2 John, 3 John, Judah (Jude); 3. Paul's 14 letters: Rom., 1 Cor, 2 Cor., Gal., Eph., Phil., Col., 1 Thes., 2 Thes., Heb., 1 Tim., 2 Tim., Tit., Phil.; 4. Rev.	The KJV order is an annoying mess. This mess is repeated in other translations, with hardly any exceptions. See Chapter 22. The divine order is structured. Awkward reading. Awkward finding. (NB. The KTK held back from this NT ordering in first edition.)

| 17. Speech marks | ~ There are no speech marks in the KJV~ | Speech marks are an essential help, as is paragraphing. | Awkward reading, as is its lack of paragraphing. |

18. Word order at 2 Chronicles 4\16	KJV	KTK	Effect of KJV blunder
	'... and all their instruments, did Huram his father make to king Solomon for the house of the LORD <u>of bright brass</u>'	'... and all their instruments <u>of bright bronze</u> his master craftsman Huram made for king Solomon for the House of Yahweh.' Or syntactically, using dashes: '... his master craftsman Hiram made – for king Solomon for the House of Yahweh – <u>of bright bronze</u>'	Who is this 'LORD of bright brass'! The failure to construct clarity overspills into comedy. The comma after 'instruments' is grammatically incorrect, creating expectation of a sub clause. Comedy.

*

Chapter 14

Why the Bible is True

♦

1. Source

⁴ But in answer, he said, 'It has been written: "Man shall not live by means of bread alone, but by every utterance proceeding through the mouth of God." '

~ Matthew 4/4, Deuteronomy 8/3

We cannot have any creation without a creator. If that creator does not put His truth down into words over several centuries, how would we know who He is and what He is like, and how He would have us conduct our lives?

The fact is, the creator has indeed put His truth down into words over several centuries, through several writers, and through several forms of writing. So we are not without a divine law book. And these writings can be tested.

The first question that needs answering concerning the writings of the prophets and apostles of God is how did those most wonderful of all writings originate. Why should they be accepted as God-given?

They expressly state they are God-given. For example, Moses says that God Himself wrote the first commandments on tablets with His own finger: "And He gave to Moses, when He had made an end of communing with him on Mount Sinai, two tablets of Testimony, tablets of stone, written with the finger of God" (Exodus 31\18).

As nobody has seen God (Genesis 48\15-16, Exodus 33\20, John 1\18), then we can presume that the two tablets said to be written by the finger of God were handed to Moses by the Angel of God. That Angel is God's chief representative. Similarly, Jesus said he was driving out demons by "the finger of God", the phrase "finger of God" meaning by the power of God and so Jesus was the representative and agent of God's power (Luke 11\20).

Then there are countless statements that say that "God spoke", "the Lord says", "the Lord says this", "the word of God came". Jeremiah introduces his book: "The words of Jeremiah ... to whom the word of the Lord came during the days of Josiah" (Jeremiah 1\1-2).

And how did those words come to the prophets and apostles? The Angel of God, who is God's Holy Spirit (Isaiah 63\9-11), spoke to them. For example, Ezekiel writes: "And the Spirit came up to me when he spoke to me. And he ... said to me ... 'the Lord says this' " (Ezekiel 2\2-4, 3\24-27). That "Spirit", "the Angel of God", is God's principal messenger. He told Ezekiel what God wanted to say. King David received his words from the same Angel of God: he prayed, "do not take Your Holy Spirit from me" (Psalm 51\11); "Where can I go from Your Spirit?" (Psalm 139\7), the "Spirit" being the Angel of God. Jesus said that David spoke (wrote) "by means of *the* Spirit" (Matthew 22\43).

The apostles Peter and Paul had the same confidence that they received their oracles from the Angel of God. Paul writes: "the Spirit speaks in persuasive words" (1 Timothy 4\1), that Spirit being the Angel of God. And "Every passage *is* given by inspiration of God" (2 Timothy 3\16). And Peter writes that to the prophets "it was revealed by means of *the* Holy Spirit sent from Heaven" (1 Peter 1\12); and "prophecy was not brought about at any time by any will of man, but, being directed by *the* Holy Spirit, the holy men of God spoke" (2 Peter 1\20-21).

There is no doubt about the source. God gave the message to His angels – the Angel of God and the angel Gabriel and the angel Michael – and the angels took it to God's prophets and apostles, and the prophets and apostles took it to the people.

Paul received instruction from Jesus: "I neither received it from man, nor was I taught *it*, but *I received it* through a revelation from Jesus Christ" (Galatians 1\12).

The prophets and apostles and scribes – Nehemiah, for example, is called a scribe: (Nehemiah 8\4) – knew that they were truly speaking from God. Haggai says: "the word of the Lord came by the prophet Haggai" (Haggai 2\1).

No other book makes any such claim that numerous authors have been visited by angels of God, authorized by the one true God, to deliver messages of righteousness.

2. The writers knew their own authority from God

Paul, in order to show that his Christ-given authority as an apostle means that he speaks from God, writes: "we speak *the* wisdom of God" (1 Corinthians 2\6); and "to the married I command – not I, but the Lord" (1 Corinthians 7\10); and "to the rest I myself speak, not the Lord" (1 Corinthians 7\12).

And Peter speaks: "remember the words having been spoken by the holy prophets, and of your commandment of the apostles of the Lord and Saviour" (2 Peter 3\2). As they are apostles, their writings form part of the God-authorized Books.

3. Unity of the writings

The writers recognized each other's writings as being God-authorized, just as their own writings also were. Ezra cited Jeremiah (Ezra 1\1); Daniel cited Jeremiah (Daniel 9\2) and Moses (Daniel 9\11); Paul cited Jesus (1 Timothy 5\18); Paul cited Genesis, Exodus, Leviticus, Deuteronomy, Samuel, Isaiah, Jeremiah, Hosea, Malachi, the Psalms, Job, Proverbs; Peter cited Paul (2 Peter 3\15-16). Jesus referred to "the Law of Moses, and the Prophets, and the Psalms" (Luke 24\44). From Matthew to Revelation the apostles and Jesus together made at least 300 citations of the prophets.

The writings of the prophets and apostles and scribes have an extraordinary degree of internal harmony in both their continuance and in their thematic agreements, a cohesion which would not be possible in the most sophisticated designs of man. At the opening of Exodus the Hebrew conjunction ו (= *ve*), "now" or "and" connects Exodus with Genesis. Then the same connections are seen in Leviticus and Numbers.

4. Internal Harmony and Cohesion

All the major themes are repeated, often citing each other, often adding further understandings.

Of themes, Moses, for example, says that "God created the heavens and the Earth" (Genesis 1\1); Jeremiah says, "He created the Earth by His power" (Jeremiah 10\12); Paul speaks of "The God having created the world and all things in it, He being Lord of Heaven and Earth" (Acts 17\24); John also speaks of God having "created Heaven and the Earth, and the sea, and springs of waters" (Revelation 14\7). Daniel speaks of a time of 70 sevens (Daniel 9\24); Jesus hints at this figure 70 sevens: "Jesus said to him, 'I say to you, not up to seven times, but up to seventy times seven'" (Matthew 18\22). It speaks frequently of the scattering of the 12 tribes of the sons of Israel (Deuteronomy 30, 2 Thessalonians 2\1). And there are a thousand and more deep and multi-layered agreements throughout the 64 Books. The miraculous and faultless internal harmony of the books of God is a major guiding principle for translators, as illustrated in the preface to *Keys of the Kingdom Holy Bible*.

5. Jesus knew the writings would be preserved

Jesus said: "For truly I say to you, until Heaven and the Earth pass away, not one iota nor one merest ornament will in any way pass from the law until all will come into being" (Matthew 5\18). And he said: "this generated word will by no means pass away until all the things such as this arise. [35] Heaven and the Earth will pass away, but my words will certainly not pass away"

(Matthew 24\34-35).

The 37 Hebrew Books from Genesis to 2 Chronicles (the correct order) are the right books, and no other deserves its place among them. The 27 Greek Books are also the right books and no other deserves place among them: other "gospels" and "letters" are not written by God's recognized prophets or apostles or scribes and therefore lack divine authority; they are not in harmony with the 64 God-authorized, God-approved and received books.

No, there no missing books, no Vatican hidings, no missing Enoch, no missing Apocrypha, no "777 missing books", no "666 missing books". We have all that we need.

6. Jesus knew the writings of the prophets and apostles would go into all the world

Jesus said: "Wherever this gospel will be proclaimed in all the world" (Matthew 26\13). He also said, "So has it been written, and so must the Christ suffer in this way and rise out from among *the* dead on the third day, and submission and forgiveness of sins be proclaimed in his name to all the nations, beginning from Jerusalem" (Luke 24\46-47). And, indeed, the Books of God spread through the Western world like no other writings.

7. Jesus cited the writings of Moses and the prophets as authoritative

Jesus cited and named Moses in early Genesis (Matthew 19\4-5, Luke 5\14). He cited the Law (Matthew 5\21, 5\27 et cetera). He cited David and the prophets (Matthew 21\13, 21\16, 21\42). He cited the Psalms and spoke of the authority of all the writings in this passage: "Jesus answered them ... the Scripture cannot be broken" (John 10\35), "the Scripture" there standing for all that had been written in the Old Covenant Books of God. He also referred to the whole of the writings in this way: "These *are* the words that I spoke to you while I was with you, that all things must be fulfilled which have been written in the law of Moses, and the Prophets, and the Psalms concerning me" (Luke 24\44). Luke also writes: "And beginning from Moses and from all the prophets, he gave them an understanding of all the things in the scrolls concerning himself" (Luke 24\27).

8. The writings were accepted by the people of God as being from God

The prophet Daniel accepted the writings of Jeremiah and Moses as being God-authorized, calling them "the scroll of truth" (Daniel 10\21, 9\2, 9\11, 9\13).

The scribe Nehemiah read the Law of Moses to the people (Nehemiah 8\1-3).

The writings were accepted by the people of God as being God-authorized: "And these [of Berea] were more noble-minded than those in Thessalonica, who received the word with all readiness of mind, closely examining the scrolls daily, whether these things held up that way" (Acts 17\11); "having received from us the reported word of God, you received *it* not *as* a word of men, but just as it truly is, the word of God, Who works effectually also in you who believe" (1 Thessalonians 2\13).

And the writings were also circulated among the people of God: "And when this letter is read among you, arrange that it is read among the Ekklesia group of Laodiceans as well, and that you yourselves likewise read the *letter* from Laodicea" (Colossians 4\16); "I adjure you by *the* Lord for this letter to be read by all the set apart brothers" (1 Thessalonians 5\27).

9. Some prophetic words of the prophets and apostles have already come true

It has come true about a birth through a virgin: "Now all of this came about in order that what was spoken by the Lord through the agency of the prophet might be fulfilled, where he says, 'Mark this: the virgin will be with a child, and she will give birth to a son, and they will call his name Emmanuel,' which, being translated, is 'God with us' " (Matthew 1\22-23). This was spoken by the prophet Isaiah: "the virgin will be pregnant, and she will give birth to a son, and she will call his name Emmanuel" (Isaiah 7\14).

It has come true about Jesus coming out of Egypt: "[Joseph] stayed there until the death of Herod, so that what was spoken by the Lord through the agency of the prophet might be fulfilled, saying, 'Out of Egypt I called My son' " (Matthew 2\15, fulfilling Hosea 11\1).

Jesus' death was a fulfilment of prophecy, for, speaking of his imminent murder, Jesus said to his incredulous disciples, "How, then, will the scrolls be fulfilled that it must come about in this way?" (Matthew 26\54) – if, that is, angels intervened and rescued him.

Jesus spoke of false Christs, false teachers, false prophets, fear, anxiety, wars and rumours of wars, nations rising against nations, famines, plagues, earthquakes, persecution, betrayal, lawlessness, tribulation, then signs and wonders to deceive, love grown cold (Matthew 24\4-24, Luke 21, Mark 13). The apostle Paul spoke of times of apostasy, hypocrisy, consciences branded with iron, forbidding to marry, abstaining from certain foods, dangerous times, love of money, boasters, blasphemers, disobedient to parents, slandermongers, traitors, lovers of pleasure(1 Timothy 4\1-3, 2 Timothy 3\1-5). The apostle Peter warned of scoffers and mockers coming in the end-times.

10. There are multiple witnesses of the one truth about the one true God

The 64 books were written by at least 30 different authors, prophets, scribes and apostles. These are all in agreement about every point. If there are different things said, it is because God spoke to men in different ways in different eons.

There are over 5,000 preserved manuscripts of the Greek New Testament books: one manuscript by one author would be enough to excite and convince historians about secular historical matters.

11. Acts of creation and miracles

No other book has such unusual and colossal acts of God, nor such a range: the creation of the entire universe; the creation of the first man, made of dust, and the first woman; a flood to cease the activities of predatory rebels; a sea parting in order to save a persecuted race; a floating axe-head; a jar of oil that never ran out; the foretold birth of Jesus, Cyrus, John the Baptist; the Sun turning back; a virgin giving birth; water changed into wine; the sick and lame and demoniacs cured; the dead raised; great prophetic prayers by godly women; the Messiah saying he would be killed and raised after three days; his tomb sealed securely but an angel rolling it away; his appearing to his friends; prophets taken into the skies by angels; miraculous gifts of foreign languages; vicious-natured religious men shutting apostles in jail and their being let out by angels; the prophecy of a period of 49 sevens; the latter days described in advance and the Messiah's return; the imprisonment of the slanderer and his destruction; a cashless society; the burning of this Earth's system and the appearing of a new worldly system and the rulership of God and Christ; a city of gold with gates of pearl and a river of the water of life and a tree with healing fruits.

Just as dramatic as all these is the miracle of the new nature that is generated in the believer by an operation of God.

All these were written in perfect harmony over about two thousand years. No other book could even dare to attempt such a scope of wisdom, teaching, truth, and divine acts, historical and prophetic, over such a period of time.

12. The answers to all mankind's problems

All man's deepest philosophical questions about himself and the universe and all his emotional problems are answered in the Books of God: if there is a God and what He is like; where man comes from; who he is; why he is here; why he is like he is; how he should behave and why; why he dies; what is life for; what happens after death; where all the creation comes from and what will happen to it – everything we need to know.

These writings describe the thoughts and emotions and ways of man, with all his psychological make-up in a way many fathoms deeper than any book does, and they alone offer salvation from God, through one Saviour, sacrificed for men by God, Jesus Christ.

13. Unlike any other book
The collected writings of the prophets and apostles are unlike any other writings, having such a variety of literary and spoken forms. There is a variety of history, prose narratives, poetry, prophecy, meditations, dramas, wise sayings, vital genealogies, commands, advice for living, parables. Nor is there any other book with the historical scope of the eons, each one introduced by prophetic acts or statements: indeed, "we understand the eons to have been framed by an word of God" (Hebrews 11\3). And: "[God] at *the* end of these days spoke to us by means of *His* Son whom He appointed heir of all things, through whom also He designed the eons" (Hebrews 1\2).

14. Archaeological findings
Archaeological findings have again and again been given meaning by what is written in the prophets and apostles. There have been astounding archaeological findings, which, from the 1840s, have uncovered ancient civilizations with names and descriptions of kings and peoples and characters and places and towns which were previously only known from the Bible, illuminating many of its narratives. These include Noah and the Flood, Babel and Calah (Genesis 10\10-11), Ur, Abraham, the Nile Delta, Nineveh, Canaanite Baal worship, giants' beds, King Solomon's vast stables, and much much more. Such findings inspired one researcher to exclaim that "The Bible is right after all".

15. The word of God can change us quicker than anything else
The words of God and Christ can change a man in an instant: "And *when* they heard, they were stabbed to the heart, and they said to Peter and the other apostles, 'What shall we do, men, brothers?' " (Acts 2\37).

For indeed, "the word of God *is* living, and powerful, and sharper than any two-edged sword, piercing even to division of natural and spirit, of both joints and marrow, and *is* a discerner of thoughts and intentions of *the* heart" (Hebrews 4\12).

"And they said, 'Believe in the Lord Jesus Christ, and you will be saved, you and your house.' And they spoke to him the word of the Lord, and to all those in his house. And having taken them along at the same hour of the night, he washed off their wounds, and he was baptised, he and all his household, straightaway" (Acts 16\31-33).

The word of the gospel of God and Jesus changed me in an instant in 1979 when I heard John's Gospel read.

In addition, from the words of God the regenerated believer has a spiritually-activated and inexpressible exuberance, a divine love, and a peace that transcends all human understanding. These are not the fountains of the wisdom of man. They are impossible without the express penetration into the mind of the pure word of God.

All these things are because the word of God is "like a fire ... and like a hammer *that* breaks the rock in pieces" (Jeremiah 23\29). "His word runs very quickly" Psalm 147\15).

16. The hard truth
The Bible does not flatter us or its heroes. A book written by the hand of men would lionise and make celebrities of its authors' favoured individuals or groups. The prophets and apostles made

no such favourtisms. The fact that some love these writings and some hate them shows that they are not the word of man: if they were only man's wisdom they would flatter man instead of convicting him of sins against just laws. No book is so loved, no book so hated.

DH Lawrence, English novelist and poet, for example, wrote a book on how he hated the Book of Revelation (one of my favourites). I heard of a pop singer who tears up Bibles on stage. On the other hand, many holy men and women of God have given their lives for defence of the Bible. And rightly so.

This book of books has to be smuggled into countries with Christ-hating governments. This love and hate alone speaks that they are from the mind of God and not the mind of man. These writings, and these alone, are from God.

17. Bible Numerics: the ultimate divine signature

Embedded in the divine writings are extraordinary patterns of numbers. This is a specialist subject, demonstrating, for example, there are extraordinary repetitions of prime numbers, and palindromic (back-to-back) repetitions. For example, the numeric value of Genesis 1\2 is 1369 (37x37). Of John 1\1 it is 3637 (39x93). And just in those two verses, there is far, far more to it than just those figures.

This ultimate divine signature is a sign. It's a sign that no human could have written the Biblical writings, nor would have been able to choose to do so. It's all from God.

ed94

Chapter 15

The Septuagint

The *Septuagint* is a Greek translation of the Old Testament Hebrew Books. Some scholars exalt it above the Hebrew of the Masoretic text, the Hebrew text from which English translations of the Old Testament are principally made. Some scholars claim it was made before the time of Jesus, in the third century BC, in 70 days by six men of each of the twelve tribes of Israel, under the order of Ptolemy II Philadelphus (285-247 BC). I do not believe that and reject it as myth *The Septuagint* is often a poor work, atthough useful. It most probably appeared around the 2nd century AD. Jerome said it was from the same hand as the (corrupt) Greek manuscript Vaticanus (B). Even Fenton Hort, a man on the post-Babylonian side, said that *The Septuagint* and Greek New Testament manuscripts A and B and ℵ (Sinaiticus) are "the same manuscript Bibles".

Some of the apostle Paul's citations of the prophets are not exact citations of the original Hebrew. That is nothing abnormal regarding citations. Citations do not have to be exact to be a genuine reference or allusion. For example, the prophet Isaiah says (in translation from his Hebrew):

> ⁷ How beautiful on the mountains
> are the feet of him who brings good news,
> who proclaims peace,
> who brings good news of good things,
> who proclaims salvation,
> who says to Zion, 'Your God reigns!' ~ Isaiah 52\7

But when Paul cites this in his letter to the Romans he cites it loosely, surely from memory, as (in translation from Paul's Greek):

> ¹⁵ How beautiful are the feet
> of those announcing the gospel of peace,
> of those announcing the gospel of excellent things! ~ Romans 10\15

It is widely held that the differences are because Paul was citing *The Septuagint* version of Isaiah 52\7. This is said because Paul's Romans 10\15 seems to be similar to *The Septuagint* version of Isaiah 52\7. Bagster's translation of *The Septuagint* version of Isaiah 52\7 reads:

> ¹⁵ I am present, as a season of beauty on the mountains,
> as the feet of those announcing good news of peace,
> as one preaching good news!
> For I will publish your salvation,
> saying, oh Zion, your God will reign!

We see the same processes at, for example, Isaiah 10\22 and Romans 9\27-28, and in over 80 reported other allusions where *The Septuagint* is close to the wording of Jesus and the apostles.

Commentators throw up their hands and say, "Look, Christ and Paul cited *The Septuagint!*" They exalt *The Septuagint* as the guiding Scriptures of Jesus and the apostles. Whereas it is wise to say that the reverse is true: *The Septuagint* cited Jesus and Paul. Then all that was needed was that *The Septuagint* should be distributed in copies, with mythologies and fables following in its serpent's dusty trail.

Paul's citation of Isaiah 52\7 is similar to *The Septuagint's* Isaiah 52\7, because whoever wrote *The Septuagint* – whether Origen or some other – when he came in his work to translating Isaiah 52\7 (from Hebrew into Greek), simply went to Paul's Greek at Romans 10\15 and wrote what he could of Paul's version into his own translation of Isaiah. And the author of *The Septuagint* did the same in other places: he stole from the Greek versions in the Gospels and the apostles' letters, and copied what he could into his own book. That process saved him the job of a bit of translating.

Suspicious, therefore, is the common notion that Jesus and Paul made citations from *The Septuagint*. Rather, *The Septuagint*, where it could, cited Jesus and the apostles. The translators should, instead, have translated the Hebrew of the prophets.

Some misguided commentators have uttered greater praises for it than they have for the real Hebrew text.

The historian Josephus, in his *Antiquities of the Jews*, makes a hysterical claim that a book of the law was completed in 70 days by 72 men in the time of the high priest Eleazar (72 men; yet the fable says 70). Josephus, though, refers to only the books of the law being completed, not *all* the Hebrew books. Certainly, then, Josephus was referring to something else, a translation of the law. Indeed, there was a Greek version of the Pentateuch around before the time of Jesus, which Philo quotes from.

Any idea that the whole of the Hebrew books, Genesis to 2 Chronicles, could be translated well in 72 days is an idle dream. If men attempted such a task, their hurried work would be poor. The King James Bible took over 50 men 8 years, and it was still shoddy. Understanding the Bible takes decades. Translating it takes decades. As I make plain at the end of Chapter 7, The Deep Word Archaeology Study Method, it is not possible to accurately translate the Scrolls of God without also spending many years writing satisfactorily about the themes of the prophets and apostles and then applying your translations to those studies. I've spent decades of study, (and still not fully satisfied), yet we are supposed to believe that 70 men could translate accurately in 70 days. It did not happen. The 50 King James Bible men had 8 years and failed. Authentic translation takes decades.

The Septuagint, though, is useful at times as a check. The years in Genesis 5 and Genesis 11, for example, must be correct in *The Septuagint*, but wrong in the Masoretic text.

There is spooky mythology surrounding the authorship of *The Septuagint*. The mythology was possibly created – if not perpetuated – by Augustine in his book *The City of God*. He says the translators of *The Septuagint* "did not differ ... in a single word ... [nor] in the order of words", and that the translators "were prophets" and inspired. Augustine was prone to other inventions. Another myth-maker about *The Septuagint* was the letter of Aristeas. It invents fake names, falsifies historical facts, and has been rejected as a forgery.

Jesus and the apostles would not have esteemed – and did not esteem – any Greek and foreign translation above their scrolls that would have been available to them in the Temple and the synagogues of Israel. Only Levites were allowed to write from the Books of the Law (Deuteronomy 17\18, 31\25-26), so that fact too makes the mythology void.

The Septuagint is poor at Isaiah 52\7. It is also poor in places where it inaccurately cites Jesus and the apostles. *Translating* Isaiah inaccurately is not the same thing as *citing* Isaiah loosely, which is permissible by anybody. We do that all the time ourselves in conversation and writing.

The only time the writer of *The Septuagint* could have jiggered with the Hebrew text to make it seem to agree with Jesus and the apostles would have been *after* the whole body of the Greek Books had been completed and then distributed in collections. If Hort was right that *The Septuagint* and the manuscripts A and B and א – which are Alexandrian – are "the same manuscript Bibles", then it seems safest to date *The Septuagint* as around the 2nd century AD.

The reality of *The Septuagint* is that it does not line up with the citations by Jesus and the apostles; its mythology is a fraud; it adds words; it takes out words; it has inadequate renderings; it has doctrinal differences; it gets figures wrong (Ezekiel 45\1 should have the figure "ten thousand", but *The Septuagint* has "twenty thousand"); it makes blunders (Amos 9\12 of *The Septuagint* has "men" where it is probably safer with "Edom", which is אדום).

It has been suggested that the book known as *The Septuagint* was made by Origen, also author of *The Hexapla*. It has also been suggested that the myth was made because *The Septuagint* contains the Greek Apocryphal books and the perpetrators wanted to protect those. Even Samuel Bagster's introduction to his (sympathetic) *Septuagint* edition (1890) says in the introduction that it is "embellished with various fables". Bagster also says that "some books show that the translators were by no means competent to the task" and that "the book of Isaiah appears to be the very worst". Yet, we are told by the traditions of orthodoxy, Paul made citations from this "very worst" translation of Isaiah.

One yet more damning thing about the *Septuagint* is that it has the Hebrew books in the wrong order, the errant order found now in Bibles. That would not have happened in the times before Jesus and the apostles. It must have come later, under another influence. Dr EW Bullinger said it was Jerome, although perhaps it came before him.

ed5A

Chapter 16

Some fool is saying Jesus didn't exist

friend writes to me about an online article that says there was no person in history whom we know as Jesus Christ. I'll call the writer of the article Yokel Elginbrodde:

Dear Chris
I have heard before what this article says. Can you comment on it?

I reply:

Dear —
Thank you for sending that. And that – *that* – passes for scholarliness! ...

If a single ancient document were found of, say, a female slave, the archaeologists would rejoice, the museum curators would rejoice, the historians would rejoice, the newspapers and television would be full of it. Books would be written about it. Documentaries would be made. Hollywood would make a film. One single little parchment. Just one. Half a page. That would be enough. Nobody would dare to say she did not exist.

Does anybody make such a fool of himself to say that Aristotle did not exist? I think not. There is manuscript evidence for him. 5 manuscripts. Does anybody make such a fool of himself to say that Caesar did not exist? There is manuscript evidence for him. 10 manuscripts.

You would think, too, would you not, that nobody would make such a fool of himself to say that Jesus Christ did not exist. There are said to be around 5,686 pieces of Greek manuscripts of the New Testament of varying provenance and pedigree, dating back to 125 AD. On top of that, there are said to be over 19,000 ancient New Testament manuscripts in the Syriac, Latin, Coptic and other languages. Now let's add those up:

5,686 + 19,000 = 24,686 texts. [1]

Is that enough? That is more manuscript evidence than for anybody in ancient history. But hold your breath ...

Apparently, 24,686 is *not* enough. A quasi "researcher" – if you can call him that, this Yokel Elginbrodde – is telling us that Jesus Christ, God's sacrifice and our Saviour, did not exist. He says there is NO evidence for him. He says that, although Josephus wrote about Jesus, that was put in by a later editor. He has, of course, no evidence that it was put in by a later editor. He just says that it was, and that is enough for his low level type of "academic" research.

But hold on, Professor Yokel. So Jesus is in Josephus, is he? Well, that's one more piece of evidence FOR Jesus, not against. Ah ...

---

1. I have since read that the figure of New Testament manuscripts is now 5,856. So, add the 19,000 and that now makes 24,856 (4 September 2018).

Make that 24,687.

24,687 documents record the life of Jesus Christ of Nazareth, the Son of God.

Instead, Elginbrodde picks a few writers who do not or might not mention Jesus. Josephus did, so discount him. Marcion, if it is true he did not mention Jesus, does not count: he was an arch heretic.

There is more written evidence about Jesus than about any other historical man or woman of his time or before. Evidence of Aristotle, 5 manuscripts. Of Caesar, 10. And did Aristotle exist? Perhaps Yokel Elginbrodde would like to write about that. But there would be no point, would there, because Aristotle does not call sinners to submission to the God of Abraham and Isaac and Jacob, and of the Lord Jesus Christ. Nothing to gain by that. And Aristotle wouldn't care less.

So why does this Elginbrodde say "no evidence"? And where is his evidence that Josephus was later edited to include Jesus?

Yokel Elginbrodde claims that there are 126 manuscripts that have no mention of Jesus. Now let me get this clear. If anybody writes something in the first or second century he has got to mention Jesus, has he, and if he does not mention Jesus that would mean Jesus did not exist? Are there any manuscripts written in the second century which do not mention Caesar? How many manuscripts written after 1945 do not mention Winston Churchill? Billions. Does that mean that, even if there were 24,967 manuscripts which *did* mention Churchill, and there were 126 which *did not*, Churchill did not exist? Does Yokel Elginbrodde actually exist? Are there any manuscripts – 126, say – which do not mention Yokel Elginbrodde? If so, he is just an invention, a mythical character.

It is hard to imagine that anybody does exist who could bring himself to make the hostile statement that Jesus did not exist.

The article says the apostle Paul was unaware of the virgin mother, Jesus' birth, parentage, life events, work, miracles, the apostles, Jesus' arrest and trial and death. First, Paul did not need to go over all the facts of Jesus' birth and life again because that is already covered in the Gospel accounts. Second, Elginbrodde cannot have read the letters of the apostle Paul. Galatians 4\4: "born out of a woman". Er, Paul does not mention Jesus' birth? Paul quotes Jesus, he speaks of his work, he speaks of the other apostles, he speaks of Jesus' miracles, and he speaks of his death and resurrection. If Elginbrodde would like to meet me I would show him the passages and he can write an article and cite them all and admit how short-sighted he has been.

The truth and teaching and commands of Jesus are a threat to the pride and stubbornness of man because they demand submission to the holy God. That is why Yokel Elginbrodde wants to convince himself that Jesus did not even exist. That way, no adjustment of character is needed.

It is astounding how some people's minds work. Yesterday, in looking for some papers for an MOT, I found letters sent to me twenty years ago by a man with whom I had had some pleasant enough conversations. The letters were full of unexpected bile and rudeness. He invited me in one letter to come and join his religion. Those letters are alarming that anybody's mind could operate in such a contrary manner. God haters. Christ haters. But what will become of them in the end?

It is in only the case of "the man Christ Jesus" (1 Timothy 2\5) that these imbalanced theories arise. The self-righteous do not want to bow down to a righteous God and acknowledge that their hearts are bleeding and crying for His mercy and forgiveness:

Jesus said: "And this is the judgement: that the light has come into the world, and men loved the darkness rather than the light, because their works were actively evil. [20] For everybody who carries out evil hates the light and does not come to the light, so that his works might not be brought home to him. [21] But he who exercises the truth comes to the light so that his works might be brought to light, for they have been operated by God."   ~ John 3\19-21

ed101A

Chapter 17

Ekklesia

The Greek word ἐκκλησία (= *ekklesia*) occurs altogether 115 times between Matthew and Revelation. In the Gospel accounts it only occurs three times: Matthew 16\18, and 18\17 (twice). At the first occurrence, Matthew 16\18, Jesus says "I will build my Ekklesia".

I have chosen to transliterate ἐκκλησία as "Ekklesia". The King James Bible has it as "church" 112 times. At Acts 19\31, 19\39, 19\41, I have it as "assembly", in a secular manner, as does the King James Bible.

Where Hebrews 2\12 speaks of the Ekklesia, it is an echo of David in Psalm 22\22-25. This shows that "the Ekklesia" in Jesus' mind was the same "assembly" in David's mind, saying, "all you seed of Jacob, all you seed of Israel" (Psalm 22\23).

David's word for "assembly", which is קהל (= *qahal*), in general means "called together". Jesus' word ἐκκλησία, similarly, means "called out". When I think of David vowing to praise God in "the great assembly" I think of all those Israelites in the Sanctuary of God, the Temple. The letter to the Hebrews also speaks of "the Ekklesia of firstborn" (Hebrews 12\23), representing, then, the gathering together of the houses of Judah and Israel, previously at enmity, but now reconciled in Christ, those twelve tribes of Jacob in one Body. This assembly and Ekklesia is made possible by the resurrection implied in Jesus' words "I will build my Ekklesia, and gates of the grave will not overpower it".

If Matthew had written his account in Hebrew rather than Greek he would have written not ἐκκλησία but קהל (= *qahal*), so having Jesus say, "I will build my Qahal" (Matthew 16\18). In fact, I have a New Testament translated into Hebrew and that is the word it uses, קהל (= *qahal*).

I capitalise "Ekklesia" in order to emphasise its importance as an authoritative body. It is an authoritative body who will reign with God and Christ in New Jerusalem when the promise is fulfilled for the twelve tribes of Israel to become "above all nations of the Earth" (Exodus 19\5, Deuteronomy 7\6, 7\14, 28\1, Revelation 21\12-13 et cetera).

What a pity, then, that when the King James Bible translators came to the first occurrence of the Greek word ἐκκλησία they wrote "church", having Jesus say, "I will build my church".

And it does the same concerning all the Ekklesia groups, calling them "churches". The effect of "church" is psychological. It's as if, turn from the writings of the Old Covenant to the pages of Matthew and the writings of the New Covenant and it's no longer about the 12 tribes of Israel and the anticipation of the New Covenant (Jeremiah 31\31), but all about setting up a world religious system.

It is unfortunate that the English translations ever translated this word ἐκκλησία as "church". The word "church" appeared in the early English versions – John Wycliffe's translation of 1380 has it – and in English the international religion would have been called "church" before Wycliffe's translation. For centuries this has given people the impression that the writings of the apostles are all to do with an international religious movement. Multitudes have the notion that Jesus set up this vast international religious system. It was set up by the formal writings of the so-called Church Fathers, correctly called that because that is what they are, the architects of a world system of ritual-based religion. When we think of the King James Bible's "church" at Matthew 16\18, it is easy to think of architecture, collection plates, international audiences, structured leadership and preachermen in post-Babylonian costumes. It's a psychological trick. The result is that the assembly of Israel David spoke of, which is the Ekklesia Jesus spoke of, is forgotten in Matthew and the following writings about the New Covenant. But Jesus will build his Ekklesia, "the Ekklesia of firstborn" – not a universal *church* system.

I thought at one time to translate ἐκκλησία it as "the outcalling". However, it was after many years of rumination and experimenting that I decided the best way to translate ἐκκλησία is to *transliterate* it, that is, to represent it in corresponding English characters, hence "Ekklesia". The Latin Vulgate translation, also transliterates the Greek word, Latinizing it with "ecclesia". Tyndale put "congregation".

In its 115 occurrences, I perceive 4 meanings of ἐκκλησία:

1) "Ekklesia of firstborn" (Hebrews 12\23): The same as Jesus' Ekklesia at Matthew 16\18. The context of Hebrews 12\23 is: "You have ... drawn near to Mount Zion" (Hebrews 12\22-23). The Ekklesia is founded on the true rock of salvation, which is Jesus, the Messiah of Israel. The general Ekklesia members of Jesus have never assembled together because the members have been separated by time and distance. The true Ekklesia of Jesus will be brought to light at the resurrection of the righteous (John 5\29, Colossians 3\4). They will finally be together in the New Jerusalem (Revelation 21\12-14).

2) "Ekklesia groups": I have distinguished the general Ekklesia of Jesus from the local groups in the apostles' letters by referring to the latter as "Ekklesia groups", the local gatherings of believers such as "the Ekklesia group at Cenchrea" (Romans 16\1), which were authorized and overseen by the apostles and met in each others' homes;

3) "legislative body": that is, the legislative assembly of Jesus' apostles at Matthew 18\17. Moses had a legislative body of 70 elders (Exodus 24\1). Moses had authority to judge disputes, and he also had "rulers of ... thousands ... hundreds ... fifties ... tens" (Exodus 18\25-26), and these appointed men made judgements among the people. God told Moses to "bear the burden of the people" (Numbers 11\10-16). Jesus, likewise, gave his disciples authority to judge disputes among brothers (Matthew 18\15);

4) "assembly": which is any secular gathering, such as the mob of angry silversmiths in Asia at Acts 19\32, and a mob secular court at 19\39, 19\41.

Chapter 18

Elohim

Elohim is one of the Hebrew titles for Him we know as 'God'. In Hebrew it is written אלהים, and is pronounced *el-oh-heem*. Since it stands for the title of God, this word אלהים (= *elohim*) is obviously an important word to understand. It first occurs in that beautiful opening of the Book of Genesis where the prophet Moses wrote "In the beginning Elohim created the heavens and the Earth." So Elohim is the Almighty Creator of everything in the beginning of the universe. According to Appendix 4 in *The Companion Bible*, אלהים occurs 2,700 times in the God-authorized Books – the Elohim-authorized Books – Genesis to 2 Chronicles (I have not checked that figure).

The word אלהים (= *elohim*) is interchangeable with the Greek form θεός (= *theos*), also standing for the title of God. At Hebrews 1\8 Paul cites Psalm 45\6:

> "Your seat of government, oh God,
> *remains* throughout the duration of the eon."

That Psalm has אלהים (= *elohim*). Hebrews 1\8 has θεός (= *theos*), a singular form. The two words, therefore, have the same meaning.

However – and you could hardly have dreamed it up – there is contention. Some polytheists like to say that אלהים (= *elohim*) is really a plural word and therefore indicates a plurality in the "Godhead" (their word).

Think of the English word "innings": it is not always plural. It can be singular ("a good second innings"), plural ("a duck in both innings"), and metaphorical ("She had a good innings", meaning a long life). (We might also consider the word "series": there could be a single series of a detective story, singular; or there could be multiple series of detective stories, plural. The word does not change.) We see the same thing with the Hebrew word שמים (= *shamayim*): that also can be singular ("Heaven", "sky"), plural ("heavens", "skies"), and metaphorical ("God", "exalted men"). It's just the same with אלהים (= *elohim*).

As with "innings", so also with אלהים (= *elohim*).
And as with אלהים (= *elohim*), so also with שמים (= *shamayim*).
And as with שמים (= *shamayim*), so also with innings.

The word אלהים (= *elohim*) can be used in the singular, plural, and metaphorically. The fact that אלהים ends in a plural suffix ים (= *im*) does not mean that it is a plural word, just as our ending "s" does not mean that "innings" is always plural. The writers of the post-Babylonian system, though, want it as a plural form because that would back up their idolatrous polytheism, worshipping "the man Christ Jesus" as one of its gods (and worshipping the Angel of God as another of its gods).

In order to distinguish the one true God from the plurality of the Canaanites' gods, the prophet Moses said, "Hear, Israel: Yahweh our Elohim *is* one Yahweh" (Deuteronomy 6\5). This was cited by Jesus the Messiah at Mark 12\32. God also said through His prophets that "*there is* no one else beside Him" – see Deuteronomy 4\35, 4\39, Isaiah 40\3, 43\10-11, 44\6-8, 45\6, 45\18, 45\22, Zechariah 14\9 et cetera.

Jesus, Paul and James stated that "God *is* one" at Mark 10\18, Romans 3\30, 1 Corinthians 8\4-6, Galatians 3\20, Ephesians 4\5-6, 1 Timothy 1\17, 2\5, James 2\19, 1 John 5\7, Jude 25, and Revelation 4\2.

אלהים (= *elohim*) has a variety of meanings, but the most common is its singular form, as at Genesis 1\1: "In the beginning Elohim created the heavens and the Earth." Gesenius's Hebrew lexicon says, אלהים (= *elohim*) is, among its meanings, "in a singular sense, *of one god ... of any divinity*" (p. 49). In Bullinger's *Book of Job* (pp. x-xi; see also his book *The Divine Names and Titles*), he gave the following definition of Elohim: "ELOHIM is God, as the *Creator*, carrying out His *will*; God, standing in the relation of Creator to His creatures."

At Exodus 7\1 אלהים (= *elohim*) is used for "judge", singular (King James Bible has, wrongly, "god", but another version explains, satisfactorily, "in the role of God").

At Exodus 21\6, 21\22, 22\8, 22\9, 22\28, and at Psalm 82\1 and 82\6, אלהים (= *elohim*) is in the plural, "judges".

It is used in a negative sense for an idol or false "god" (Exodus 20\3, 20\23, 22\20, 23\13, 23\24, 23\32-33 et cetera). It is also in the plural form for false "gods" (Exodus 18\11, 32\1, et cetera).

It is used for "angels" or "messengers" (Psalm 8\5, 97\7, 97\9) – disputed by some as "gods", wrongly since Hebrews 1\6, 2\7, and 2\9 confirm it as "angels" or "messengers".

One thing אלהים (= *elohim*) most certainly does not mean is that the Creator "Elohim" is a plurality of gods. The name "Elohim" is interchangeable with "Yahweh" and jointly with "Yahweh Elohim", and "Yahweh Elohim" is not a plurality either. That torpedoes any sense of "Elohim" being a plurality. As early as Genesis 1\5 this is confirmed: "Elohim called the light day, and the darkness He called night."

The word of God knows nothing other than that His title "Elohim" represents a singular deity.

God (Elohim) has Moses stress to the Israelites that He is one, saying, "Hear, oh Israel: Yahweh our Elohim is one Yahweh." Or, "Hear, oh Israel: the Lord our God is one Lord" (Deuteronomy 6\4). Yet at that very point where Elohim has Moses stressed that He is not like the "gods" of the Canaanites, and that He is "one", those of the polytheistic nature claim that the word for "one", אחד (= *echad*), means a plurality. This is untrue. Gesenius says, "only one of its kind". (Usages of it at Ezekiel 7\5, and Job 23\13 demonstrate that it is "only one of its kind". It is also used as a title of God at Job 31\15, signifying "the One". When Jesus cites Deuteronomy 6\4, "... T*he* Lord our God is one Lord" [Mark 12\21], the Greek word for "one" is also peculiarly singular, εις (= *eis*), meaning "only one of its kind".

At Exodus 9\28 אלהים is used with "thunderings and hail" and is translated "mighty thunderings and hail", אלהים being "mighty" in this context. It is used in this adjectival sense of "mighty" in the description of Abraham, in his being "a mighty prince". At Genesis 30\8 the matriarch refers to her "immense / mighty struggles". At Genesis 32\1 "a mighty *force of messengers*" met Jacob. At Genesis 32\2 Jacob speaks of "a mighty camp". In all these the adjective is אלהים.

Any other "gods" are idols. And "Elohim" is just one of over 160 names and titles of the one true God. Including אחד (= *echad*), "one". And none of the others presents any plurality of gods. There is only one God. Elohim is one. Not two, not three, not seven, not nine. One. This plurality teaching must stop.

Moses instructed the Israelites: "It was shown to you so that you might know that Yahweh *is* ha Elohim. *There is* no one else beside Him" (Deuteronomy 4\35).

Chapter 19

Concerning holy spirit and Holy Spirit:
the two meanings of πνεῦμα ἅγιον (= *pneuma hagion*)

1. Introduction

There are few words in the word of God which have caused as much confusion as the word "spirit". Some have even invented another god out of it. Some have made of it a living demon or a god living inside the fat of men's bellies. Their minds have been clogged with traditions of men – and these traditions wage battles and prevent them from thinking clearly. I admit, though, that discernment of every occurrence of "spirit" is not easy, and it is a long task to understand all the meanings of "spirit". In another document I have tabulated 19 classifications of quite different meanings. This study is concerned with only two of the meanings.

Our concern is with the Greek phrase πνεῦμα ἅγιον. It is transliterated in English as *pneuma hagion*. It occurs 92 times in the New Testament. It gets translated in English Bibles, whatever it means, as "Holy Spirit", usually haphazardly capitalized, regardless of its meaning. In *Keys of the Kingdom Holy Bible* it is translated as either "Holy Spirit" or "holy spirit" or "spirit of separateness", depending on the context, in order to make distinctions in its meanings. For, whether we like it or not – as with almost all words and phrases – πνεῦμα ἅγιον (= *pneuma hagion*) does not always have the same meaning.

Dr EW Bullinger's *Companion Bible*, Appendix 101, section 14, gives a list of 52 occurrences of πνεῦμα ἅγιον (= *pneuma hagion*) which do not have the article ("the"), and, Dr Bullinger says, these refer to the *gift*, rather than to the *personality* who is the Holy Spirit:

Matthew 1\18, 1\20, 3\11, Mark 1\8, Luke 1\15, 1\35, 1\41, 1\67, 2\25, 3\16, 4\1, 11\13, John 1\33, 7\39, 20\22, Acts 1\5, 2\4, 4\8, 4\31, 6\3, 6\5, 7\55, 8\15, 8\17, 8\19, 9\17, 10\38, 11\16, 11\24, 13\9, 13\52, 19\2 (twice), Romans 5\5, 9\1, 14\17, 15\13, 15\16, 1 Corinthians 2\13, 6\19, 12\3, 2 Corinthians 6\6, 1 Thessalonians 1\5, 1\6, 2 Timothy 1\14, Titus 3\5, Hebrews 2\4, 6\4, 1 Peter 1\12, 2 Peter 1\21, Jude 20.

However, as helpful as such lists might be, I do not believe that this theory that occurrences without the article refer always to the gift is correct. Of that list, I consider that the following 3 occurrences (of 4) of πνεῦμα ἅγιον (= *pneuma hagion*) without the article – so that the article "the" has to be supplied and italicised – refer not to the gifts, but to the personality titled the Holy Spirit:

> Luke 2\25-26: *the* Holy Spirit was over [Simeon], and it was divinely communicated to
>   him by the Holy Spirit;
> 1 Peter 1\12: it was revealed by means of *the* Holy Spirit sent from Heaven;
> 2 Peter 1\21: directed by *the* Holy Spirit, the appointed men of God spoke.

The theory in *The Companion Bible* of making a distinction in whether or not the article "the" appears does not, therefore, always help us. Another theory, then, is needed. The distinction which must be made, as I will demonstrate, is this:

The phrase πνεῦμα ἅγιον is used sometimes CONCRETELY to describe a *personality*
and
sometimes ABSTRACTLY to describe an *inner gift*.

I therefore make these conventions:
First, when πνεῦμα ἅγιον (= *pneuma hagion*) is used CONCRETELY to denote the PERSONALITY, I render it as "Holy Spirit". This retains the title familiar to readers. I capitalize it this way when the meaning is the angel who is "the Holy Spirit", that is, when it is used as a title of the PERSONALITY, such as Isaiah 63\10, 63\11, John 14\26. The frequent capitalizations in other versions suggest that πνεῦμα ἅγιον (= *pneuma hagion*) is *always* the title of a PERSONALITY (their third god), but we will see the shortcoming. So there is a necessity of being responsible for removing the confusion.

Second, when it is used ABSTRACTLY to denote the apostles' EMPOWERMENT or a RENEWED MIND, I render it as "holy spirit" or, sometimes, as "spirit of separateness". [1]

Third, if there is no article το (= *to*), "the", with πνεῦμα ἅγιον (= *pneuma hagion*) in the original, I add it in and italicize it to indicate that it has been added for English sense. This can occur whether the context is the PERSONALITY of the "Holy Spirit", or the ABSTRACT gift of the "holy spirit".

2. Distinguishing πνεῦμα ἅγιον by context

i. The Holy Spirit WHO. The "Holy Spirit" who was seen [2]
Luke speaks of the event of Jesus's baptism (βάπτισμα = *baptisma*) by John the Baptist:

"And the Holy Spirit [πνεῦμα ἅγιον = *pneuma hagion*)], in a bodily form, descended over him in the manner of a dove, with a voice coming out of the sky, saying, 'You are My Son, the Richly Loved One. In you I have found delight.' "   ~ Luke 3\22

At this event, Jesus "SAW the Spirit of God descending" (Matthew 3\16). So too did John say that he "SAW the Spirit descending out of *the* sky in the manner of a dove". Others SAW him too (John 1\32-34). The Holy Spirit WAS SEEN, so this speaks of a visible being: the PERSONALITY titled "the Holy Spirit" and "the Spirit of God".

After his resurrection, Jesus told his disciples, "you will receive power *when* the Holy Spirit comes to you" (Acts 1\8). That was a promise of the PERSONALITY. Then on the Day of Pentecost, "suddenly out of the sky a ringing in the ears came like a rushing of a violent wind-

---

1. I used to have it as "divine spirit". Although there is another word which gets rendered as "divine" – θεῖος (= *theios*) Acts 17\29, 2 Peter 1\3) – I considered it justified at times to also render ἅγιον (usually rendered "holy") as "divine". That which is "holy" or "set apart" can only have a divine origin. What is gained by responsibly giving clarity and knocking out centuries of confusion is tremendous beyond expression. However, I decided to standardize it as "holy spirit", since it is not always easy to distinguish the holy spirit is empowerment for signs and wonders from the new nature, and perhaps it might prove to be a somewhat unsafe distinction. I see more advantage in having the lower-case "holy spirit" visibly contrasted with the upper-case "Holy Spirit" occurrences of πνεῦμα ἅγιον relating to the Angel of God.
~ cjs, 27 March 2019

2. The Angel who is the Holy Spirit is discussed on pages xiii-xv in "Conventions", the preface to *The Eonian Life Bible*. I have written a booklet on him entitled *Who Is the Counsellor and the Holy Spirit? The Hoax of Polytheism Exposed*, to be published, God willing, in time.

blast, and it filled the whole house where they were sitting. And divided tongues, as if of fire, were seen by them, and they rested over each one of them" (Acts 2\2-3). The phenomena of the "wind-blast" and the "fire" suggest the presence of the Holy Spirit personality. We know that this was the Holy Spirit because Jesus had already told his disciples that the Holy Spirit was going to come to them (Acts 1\8). Of course, the "wind-blast" and the "fire" were not in themselves the Holy Spirit: they were effects in physics of his presence. It reminds me of the Angel of Yahweh and the fire at the burning bush (Exodus 3).

The PERSONALITY of the Holy Spirit is also referred to by the titles "*the* Angel of *the* Lord" (Matthew 1\20); "the Counsellor" (John 14\16, 14\26); "the Spirit of Truth" (John 14\17, 15\26, 16\13); "the Spirit of God" (Matthew 3\16, 12\28); "*the* Spirit of *the* Lord" (Acts 8\39); "the Spirit of Christ" (1 Peter 1\11). He has numerous other titles in the Hebrew Books.

Being "sent from Heaven" (1 Peter 1\12), the Holy Spirit gave the oracle of God to the prophets, the "men of God" (Hebrews 9\8, 1 Peter 1\12, 2 Peter 1\21). He spoke the words of God to David (Psalm 51\11, 139\7, so David had the presence and counsel of the Holy Spirit (Matthew 22\43, Mark 12\36, Acts 1\16, Psalm 95\7-11 with Hebrews 3\7-11). He spoke the oracles of God to Isaiah (Acts 28\25-26). He spoke to Ezekiel (Ezekiel 2\2, 2\12). He spoke to the disciples (Acts 8\29, 10\19, 11\28, 13\2, 13\4, 15\28, 16\6, 16\7, 20\28, 21\4, 21\11). He conveyed Philip to another place (Acts 8\39). He conveyed John to Patmos and his visions (Revelation 1\10, 4\2, 21\10). He counselled and encouraged the Ekklesia groups (Acts 9\31). He gave witness of the apostles (Hebrews 10\15). He appointed overseers in the Ekklesia groups (Acts 20\28). He testified in every town (Acts 20\33). He spoke prophecy to Paul (1 Timothy 4\1). His name is secret and it will be revealed to believers in the coming eon (Judges 13\6-18, Matthew 28\19). He will speak on behalf of believers under interrogation in time of persecution from the enemy (Matthew 10\20, Mark 13\11, Luke 12\12). All these were acts of the angel who is titled "the Holy Spirit".

The Holy Spirit was dramatically active during the Acts period. His future work in the coming eon is described by Jesus: he will be sent to the apostles from "beside the Father" (John 15\26, 14\26) to be "alongside" and "among" the apostles (John 14\17) "throughout the eon" (John 14\16, Matthew 28\19); "he will make the facts known to the world concerning sin, and concerning righteousness, and concerning judgment: concerning sin, because they do not believe in me; concerning righteousness, because I am going away to my Father and you will behold me no more; and concerning judgment, because the ruler of this world stands judged" (John 16\8-11. See also John 14\16-17, 14\26, 15\26, 16\7-14).

Jesus made a reference to the Holy Spirit as "the Counsellor" (John 14\16, 26). The word for "Counsellor" is παράκλητος (= *parakleetos*), which is literally "called alongside". It is related to the verb παρακαλέω (= *parakaleo*), to comfort, encourage, summon, call for, or call to one's side. And it is related to the noun παράκλησις (= *paraklesis*), which is a calling near, summons, imploration, exhortation, encouragement, consolation, comfort. (The word παράκλητος also appears at 1 John 2\1 in relation to Jesus as an "advocate", or "counsellor", and is not to be confused with its use in John 14, 15 and 16.)

This "Counsellor" – παράκλητος (= *parakleetos*), "called alongside" – was called alongside the apostles and the Ekklesia groups, and he will be called alongside the apostles "throughout the eon", the days of the Kingdom, as "the Spirit of Truth" (John 14\16, Matthew 28\19). Just as he was called alongside the Israelites in the wilderness. The world will not see him, but the apostles will both see and know him, for he will be "alongside" and "among" them (John 14\16-17). He "proceeds" from "beside the Father" (John 15\26).

In all his titles, the Holy Spirit angel is referred to 116 times (in my current assessment; always under revision) in the Greek Books. He is also referred to (with at least 24 titles) 184 times (again, in my current assessment; always under revision) in the Hebrew Books. That is a total of 300 direct mentions, under his various titles, of the Angel of God who is the Holy Spirit.

The name of the Holy Spirit who is the Angel of God is secret (Judges 13\18). His name will be made known to believers in the coming eon ("the name ... of the Holy Spirit"; Matthew 28\19). Whoever might dare to speak falsely against the Angel of God does not have forgiveness throughout the eon, but is liable to "eonian condemnatory sentence" or "eonian condemnatory sentence" (Mark 3\29).

There is, for sure, much else which I could say about the Holy Spirit. For example, the Holy Spirit is also known as "the Spirit of God", who was involved with God in creation (Genesis 1\2, 1\26, Psalm 104\30, Job 26\13); "My Spirit" who could no longer "contend with mankind" (Genesis 6\3); "the Angel of Yahweh" who appeared to the patriarchs and to Hagar (Genesis 16\7-11, 22\11-18); "the Angel of God" and "Angel of His Presence" who gave safe conduct to the Israelites out of Egypt (Exodus 14\19); "the Angel" who appeared to Ezekiel (8\3, 43\5); the "Holy Spirit" who, Isaiah says, was "vexed" by Israel (Isaiah 63\10); the "Holy Spirit" spoken of by David (Psalm 51\11); "the Spirit" and "the Holy Spirit" who appeared to Jesus (Matthew 3\16, Luke 3\22); "the Spirit" who was seen by John the Baptist and others (John 1\32-33); "the Counsellor" and "the Spirit of Truth" who will accompany the disciples "throughout the eon" (John 14\16); "the Counsellor, *who is* the Holy Spirit" (John 14\26); "the Holy Spirit" who was a mediator for the disciples during the Acts period (Acts 1\8); the "Holy Spirit" who Paul said spoke "to our fathers through the agency of the prophet Isaiah" (Acts 28\25); and "the Holy Spirit" who gave the prophets the oracles of God (1 Peter 1\12, 2 Peter 1\21), who will serve the disciples "throughout the eon" (John 14\16), and who will be with them in the eon when they go about the world teaching the commands of Jesus to the nations (Matthew 28\19).

ii. The "holy spirit" WHICH. The "holy spirit" which gave divine empowerment

We do not see this divine empowerment in the same way we see it in the Gospels and the Acts. This was the empowerment for the enabling of signs and wonders. This, too, is denoted by the phrase πνεῦμα ἅγιον (= *pneuma hagion*).

The empowerment of Jesus is the model:

"And Jesus, being full of *the* holy spirit [πνεῦμα ἅγιον (= *pneuma hagion*)], returned from the Jordan."
~ Luke 4\1

It was prophesied by Isaiah that the Spirit of Yahweh would anoint and empower Jesus for his work (Isaiah 42\1, 61\1) and this anointing was fulfilled at his being baptised and identified with God (Luke 3\21-22, 4\18, Matthew 12\18) so that he was "full of *the* holy spirit" (Luke 4\1). By this anointing and power he was able to perform his signs and works of power and "he went about doing good, and healing all who were being overpowered by the slanderer, for God was with him" (Acts 10\38). He was full of "the holy spirit", not "the Holy Spirit". No angel was living inside Jesus.

Before his being taken up by angels into the heavens, Jesus told his disciples that they would be "baptised with *the* holy spirit [πνεῦμα ἅγιον (= *pneuma hagion*)] after not many days from these" (Acts 1\5), and that they would receive "power from on high" (Luke 24\49). Then we see the 12 being "filled with *the* holy spirit" and speaking in Mediterranean languages (Acts 2\4). We know that this "holy spirit" was power because Jesus had also told them they would receive power (Acts 1\8, Luke 24\49), as well as telling them that the person of the Holy Spirit would come to them (Acts 1\5). We also know that the spirit they were filled with was *power*, and not the *personality* titled the Holy Spirit, because they could not have been filled with a personality. Angels do not live inside humans: only a baby in the womb can do that.

When this empowerment was given to the disciples during the Acts period, they were empowered in an extraordinary way that drew attention to their message of Jesus' resurrection and offer of eonian salvation. We see Peter and John bringing healing to a lame man, with Peter saying, "in the name of Jesus Christ the Nazarene, rise up and walk" (Acts 3\6), and "And taking him by the right hand, he raised *him* up, and instantly his feet and ankle bones were strengthened. And he leaped up, *and* stood and walked, and went into the Temple with them, walking and leaping and praising God" (Acts 3\7-8), and the people were "filled with wonder and ecstasy at what had happened to him" (Acts 3\10). Paul performed a similar act, bringing healing to a lame man (Acts 14\10). Paul had such immense power from God that "even sweat bands or gowns from *contact with* his skin were put on the sick as well, and the diseases departed from them, and the wicked spirits went out from them" (Acts 19\12).

The magician Simon was "amazed" when he saw "the signs and works of power being done" through Philip (Acts 8\13). It is also said of Stephen that he "worked mighty signs and wonders among the people" (Acts 6\13). Paul was unharmed by a poisonous snake (Acts 28\3-5).

Works of divine power were also promised among all who believed: this is shown in Jesus" instructions to the 11 when he said that they would have power over demons, speak foreign languages, be unharmed by snakes and poison, and have power to heal the sick (Mark 16\16). Paul lists the various gifts which were distributed among believers: wisdom, words of knowledge, acts of faith, healing, power, prophecy, discerning of spirits, foreign languages and interpretation of them (1 Corinthians 12\3-13). Jesus said that those who received this would issue speech like "rivers of living water" (John 7\39). The holy spirit of power fell on Cornelius and his relatives and friends and it was "poured out" on them, just as, Peter said, it had also fallen on the 12 "in *the* beginning" (Acts 10\44-47, 11\15-17, that "beginning" being seen at Acts 2\4), and the result was that they spoke "with foreign languages and magnified God" (Acts 10\46). The spirit of power fell on about 12 men of Ephesus and they spoke with foreign languages and prophesied (Acts 19\1-7).

Eventually, when Paul turned to the nations, this empowerment left the apostles. Paul, who once had immense power, spoke – after the Acts period – of Epaphroditus, his "brother and companion in labour, and fellow soldier" and an "apostle", being "sick to the point of death", but Paul says not that he healed him, but that "God had mercy on him, and not on him only, but on me also, so that I might not have sorrow added to sorrow" (Philippians 2\26-27). Timothy he instructed to drink a little wine for his stomach complaint and "frequent infirmities" (1 Timothy 5\23). Paul also says that he left Trophimus "sick in Miletum" (2 Timothy 4\8). The power of πνεῦμα ἅγιον for signs and wonders had gone.

iii. The "holy spirit" WHICH. The "holy spirit" which is spiritual renewal, "the spirit of [the] mind" (Ephesians 4\23)

This also is denoted by the phrase πνεῦμα ἅγιον (= *pneuma hagion*).

Writing after the spirit-activated Acts period, Paul assured the Ephesians of:

> "the gospel of your salvation, in whom, believing also, you were marked with a seal with the holy spirit [πνεῦμα ἅγιον (= *pneuma hagion*)] of promise, [14] which is the deposit of our inheritance until the redemption of the special possession, for the enthused praising of His magnificence." ~ Ephesians 1\13-14

This is "the spirit of your mind" (Ephesians 4\23). Anybody who truly believes "the oracle of Christ" (Colossians 3\16) receives "an operation of God" (Colossians 2\12) by which he or she is said to be "marked with a seal with the holy spirit of promise". This is described elsewhere by Paul as "marked with a seal, and given ... the deposit of the spirit in our hearts" (2 Corinthians 1\22, 5\5), and "the good deposit entrusted through *the* holy spirit inhabiting us" (2 Timothy 1\14). Paul also speaks in Romans of the "spirit which inhabits us", obviously, therefore, an abstract gift (Romans 8\9, 8\11; see also 1 Corinthians 3\16, Ephesians 3\17).

The mental and emotional activities of this form of πνεῦμα ἅγιον are described by Paul:

"be filled with *the* spirit, making voice to yourselves in psalms and praise songs and spiritual songs, singing and making melody in your heart to the Lord, giving thanks at all times for all things, in *the* name of our Lord Jesus Christ, to Him Who *is* God and Father."   ~ Ephesians 5\18-20

This type of πνεῦμα ἅγιον, an inner gift, an ABSTRACT thing, is not, then, the same as the first type, the PERSONALITY of the Holy Spirit angel. It is *not* a personality, and these days, in this age, it does *not* empower believers in the same way that Jesus and his apostles were empowered. It governs our emotions and thoughts – if we let it – and it enables us to understand spiritual things, that is, those things which are written in the God-authorized Hebrew and Greek Books (see 1 Corinthians 2\14-15).

Of this inner spirit, the spirit of the mind, Paul speaks of being rejuvenated "by the spirit of your mind" (Ephesians 4\23). And he says, with ironic understatement, "I think I have the spirit of God" (1 Corinthians 7\40) – so Paul must mean an inner spirit. He could not "think" he had an angel, a spirit being! How could you *"have"* a spirit who is a personality? He means God's nature, character, the gift of a renewed inner spirit. He wished for the Ephesians to be "strengthened with might in the inner man, through [Jesus'] spirit" (Ephesians 3\16), that is, Jesus' nature.

This type of "holy spirit" is also described by Paul as πνεῦμα Θεοῦ (= *pneuma Theou*), "*the* spirit of God", and as πνεῦμα χρισςτοῦ (= *pneuma Christou*), "*the* spirit of Christ". Paul says: "You though, are not in flesh, but in spirit, if, indeed, *the* spirit of God inhabits you. But if anybody does not have *the* spirit of Christ, he is not his. ¹⁰ But if Christ *is* in you, the body *is* dead because of sin, but the spirit *is* life because of righteousness" (Romans 8\9-10). This "spirit of God" and "spirit of Christ" are not to be confused with similar titles of the Holy Spirit who is the Angel of God. This "spirit of God" inhabits believers: angels do not go down men's throats! This "spirit", though, is in them as a renewed mind. Jesus said that he is "in the Father" (John 10\38): "the Father *is* in me, and I in Him": that means a Father and Son relationship, not personalities living inside.

3. Chaos and conflicts if we fail to differentiate

It does not take any nous (from the Greek word, νοῦς = *nous*, "mind") to perceive that there is a strong difference in these meanings of πνεῦμα ἅγιον. And it does not take any nous to perceive what a peril and confusion of mind it would be if we were to make the pretence that they are the same. Were we to do so, we would be walking around falsely imagining that the personality called the Holy Spirit was "inhabiting us", that this Spirit, this Angel of God, had clambered down our throats and was somehow making a life for himself squeezed somewhere into our brains or between our ribs. Like a baby in the womb.

And were we to dream up such mystical hocus-pocus, we would have to wonder how he could also be inhabiting anybody else at the same time! – something we do not have to wonder because he does not live inside anybody anywhere. In addition, were we to have this perilous confusion of mind, we would be walking around imagining that we ought to be performing the same "mighty signs and wonders" that the apostles performed during the Gospel and Acts period.

Instead of suffering such affliction of mind and confusion, though, what we can have is "a sound mind" (2 Timothy 1\7) and spiritual sanitation.

Some occurrences of πνεῦμα ἅγιον are not easily discerned, but these are my current opinions on some of those occurrences.

4. Sensible consideration of passages relating to "spirit"

<u>John 7\39 and Matthew 1\18-20</u>
Jesus spoke about "the spirit which [not "who"] those believing in him were about to receive, for πνεῦμα ἅγιον was not yet *given*, because Jesus had not yet been magnified" (John 7\39). So πνεῦμα ἅγιον would not be given until *after* Jesus' resurrection. Yet before Jesus was even born, the angel Gabriel had already said to Maria that a child would be born to her "through the agency of πνεῦμα ἅγιον" (Matthew 1\18-20, Luke 1\35). But how could this be if the πνεῦμα ἅγιον was not yet given? Gabriel was speaking of an event by God, a dramatic empowerment – ABSTRACT – which would create the miracle of Maria's virgin conception. Jesus was speaking of a gift – also ABSTRACT – which would flow "out of his inside" (John 7\38) and which "those believing in him" would receive as a permanent gift of renewal (John 7\39). Jesus could not possibly have been speaking of the PERSONALITY because only the ABSTRACT gift of πνεῦμα ἅγιον which he spoke of could flow "out of his inside", or out of anybody else's inside. The giving of πνεῦμα ἅγιον which he was speaking of was the general giving, as he said, to "those believing in him". He said that it – "it", not "he" or "He" – would be given to "those who ask" (Luke 11\13).

<u>"filled with πνεῦμα ἅγιον"</u>
A few special individuals – John the Baptist (Luke 1\15), Elizabeth (Luke 1\41), Zecharias (Luke 1\67), and Jesus himself (Luke 4\1) – were filled with πνεῦμα ἅγιον *before* Jesus' resurrection. John the Baptist was filled with πνεῦμα ἅγιον from birth (Luke 1\15); he was an exceptional man, the prophet Jesus ranked above all the prophets. The 12 disciples also (Acts 2\4), and others, were likewise "filled". None of these individuals were filled with the PERSONALITY of πνεῦμα ἅγιον. They were filled with the ABSTRACT gift. You cannot be filled with another being, so what they were filled with was the ABSTRACT power of God.

This means, then, that the spirit which Jesus said was going to be given was something new. This is reflected in the words of John the Baptist who said, "It is true that I baptise you in water towards submission. But the one coming after me ... will baptise you in the holy spirit" (Matthew 3\11). That baptism in spirit is the spirit we need to be saved. It is the superior baptism to the one John performed.

<u>Seen, descended, communicated, being blasphemed, speaking</u>
When Jesus was baptised, "πνεῦμα ἅγιον" descended from the sky over Jesus (John 1\32). It was "divinely communicated" to Simeon "through the agency of the πνεῦμα ἅγιον" that he would see Jesus (Luke 2\25-26). Jesus spoke about "the blasphemy concerning the πνεῦμα ἅγιον" (Matthew 12\31-32, Mark 3\28-30). He told the disciples that under arrest they would be given what to speak and that it would not be "you who speak, but the πνεῦμα ἅγιον" (Mark 13\11). Now consider all those. What is ABSTRACT cannot be seen, cannot descend from the sky, cannot communicate, cannot be blasphemed, cannot speak. So all these are references to the PERSONALITY of the Holy Spirit. What a thundering blunder of logic we would be making if we failed to differentiate these passages as referring to the PERSONALITY.

<u>John 20\22</u>
After Jesus' resurrection, the disciples received the ABSTRACT gift when he "breathed" on them and said, "Receive *the* holy spirit" – obviously ABSTRACT because you cannot breathe out another PERSONALITY.

<u>Acts 2\33, 10\45, Romans 5\5: πνεῦμα ἅγιον "poured out"</u>

In these passages, the holy spirit – both of empowerment (Acts 2\33, 10\45) and of a renewed mind (Romans 5\5) – is spoken of as being "poured out". You cannot pour out a PERSONALITY. God can, though, and did, pour out ABSTRACT gifts.

1 Corinthians 6\19
Paul said to the Corinthians, "your body is a temple of πνεῦμα ἅγιον", therefore a "temple" of something ABSTRACT. For your body, the temple of your own personality, cannot also be the temple of another PERSONALITY. How foolish it would be to pretend that another being was somehow clambering about inside our own body. As if the Angel of God could have an existence in many people's bodies. It's all a fable.

Somebody told me Jesus lives inside him. I asked him how Jesus, in the heavens, could be living inside him. I asked him how Jesus, in the heavens, could be living in millions of people at the same time. I asked him how Jesus, in the heavens, is stated by Peter as having to remain in the heavens until the restoration of all things (Acts 3\21). He said it was "a miracle"! I wonder what part of him he thinks Jesus lives in.

Ephesians 1\13, 4\30
Paul spoke to the Ephesians of being "sealed" with the "πνεῦμα ἅγιον of promise". You cannot be sealed with another some*body*. You can only be sealed with some*thing*, something ABSTRACT.

2 Timothy 1\14
Paul spoke to Timothy of the "πνεῦμα ἅγιον inhabiting us" (also at Romans 8\9, 8\11 (twice), 8\16). Again, this is obviously the ABSTRACT gift, what Paul calls the spirit "of the inner man" (Ephesians 3\16). By this πνεῦμα ἅγιον believers are renewed (Titus 3\5).

πνεῦμα ἅγιον linked with ABSTRACT nouns
πνεῦμα ἅγιον and wisdom (Acts 6\3);
πνεῦμα ἅγιον and power (Acts 10\38);
πνεῦμα ἅγιον and faith (Acts 11\24);
joy and πνεῦμα ἅγιον (Acts 13\52, 1 Thessalonians 1\6);
righteousness and peace and joy in πνεῦμα ἅγιον (Romans 14\17);
power and πνεῦμα ἅγιον (1 Thessalonians 1\5);
purity, knowledge, long-suffering, kindness, πνεῦμα ἅγιον,
      and unfeigned love (2 Corinthians 6\6).

All those are, then, ABSTRACT, referring to the gift. It would be strange fire in these passages to mix ABSTRACT nouns with a PERSONALITY. So they all refer to the ABSTRACT gift.

Acts 1\5 and 1\8
Just before his ascension into the skies, Jesus told the disciples, "you will be baptised πνεῦμα ἅγιον after not many days from these" (Acts 1\5). He also told them "you will receive power *when* πνεῦμα ἅγιον comes to you" (Acts 1\8). What is the difference? At Acts 2\1-4 we read that "there was a ringing in the ears ... like a rushing of a violent wind-blast, and it filled the whole house where they were sitting. And divided tongues, as if of fire, were seen by them". So you can tell that there was the presence of the PERSONALITY of "the Holy Spirit" (and presumably he was seen) because of the effects of his presence shown in verse 2.

The passage goes on: "they were all filled wit πνεῦμα ἅγιον, and began to speak with other languages as the spirit was giving them utterance." So the PERSONALITY appeared to the 12, and they were filled with the ABSTRACT gift, then the gift of the PERSONALITY enabled them to speak Mediterranean languages in order to proclaim Jesus' resurrection and the gospel. Therefore, both Acts 1\5 and 1\8 came to pass: the PERSONALITY πνεῦμα ἅγιον appeared, and the ABSTRACT gift πνεῦμα ἅγιον was received.

5. A few anomalies

Matthew 3\16 and Acts 2\4
When Jesus was publicly baptised (βαπτίζω = *baptizo*), the Holy Spirit angel appeared. When the 12 were baptised in the holy spirit (ABSTRACT), the Holy Spirit (PERSONALITY) also appeared (Acts 1\8, 2\2-4). The Holy Spirit (PERSONALITY) was connected with Jesus and the apostles. However, when others in Acts were baptised in the holy spirit (ABSTRACT) there is no appearance mentioned of the Holy Spirit angel (PERSONALITY). This difference was, I presume, because Jesus and the apostles are exalted in authority. The 12 will be judges and rulers in Israel in the coming eon (Matthew 19\28, Revelation 21\12-13). They will have authority to forgive sins and to withhold forgiveness for sins (John 20\21-23).

Matthew 28\19-20 and Mark 16\14-18
In Jesus' instructions in the Mark passage he says that those who believe and are "baptised" (βαπτίζω = *baptizo*) with (or into), God would manifest "signs", that is, power over demons, power over sicknesses through the laying on of hands, immunity to snakes and poisons, and speaking "new languages". These signs were seen in the Acts period among those who believed and were βαπτίζω (= *baptizo*) in the holy spirit – so, concerning the Mark 16\16 baptism instructions, the act of being "baptised" (βαπτίζω) included being baptised in the holy spirit.

In Jesus' instructions in the Matthew passage he told the 11 to "disciple all the nations, "baptising [βαπτίζω (= *baptizo*)] them into the name of the Father, and of the Son, and of the Holy Spirit, teaching them to observe all things which I have commanded you." This is different to the Mark passage. There is little resemblance. There is no mention of any manifestations. And, although there is a baptism into the πνεῦμα ἅγιον it is a "relating", "identifying" (βαπτίζω = *baptizo*) into the "name" of the PERSONALITY called the Holy Spirit, not a baptism into the ABSTRACT gift which is the spirit of divine empowerment. So while the Mark passage is a baptism into divine empowerment, the Matthew passage is a baptism or relating into the "name" of the Holy Spirit.

Why are these different? The baptism into empowerment shown in the Mark passage was fulfilled during the Acts period when there was a great outworking of signs and wonders, even among the Corinthians (1 Corinthians 12). The word βαπτίζω (= *baptizo*), baptise, identify, relate, appears in 1 Corinthians and Galatians, but it does not appear in the later letters of Paul, except the "one baptism" in Ephesians 4\5. So the instructions in the Mark passage were fully carried out and the manifestations were seen. We see nobody after Acts being baptised into divine empowerment: neither the words nor the manifestations are seen. What comes after Acts is Paul's gospel, that proclamation which he called "my gospel" (Romans 2\16, 14\24 (16\25 in other versions), 2 Timothy 2\8), given to him by the resurrected Jesus.

As for the Matthew passage, we see nobody at all in the whole of the God-authorized Greek Writings being related into "the name" of the Holy Spirit angel. What is his name? We do not know even now. It has been held secret (Judges 13\18). Jesus concluded his instructions by saying, "I am with you all the days, until the consummation of the eon". This shows us that the

Matthew instructions to the 11 are for them to carry out in the coming eon. This aligns with John 14\16: "And I will ask the Father, and He will give you another Counsellor, so that he might continue with you throughout the eon." The Matthew authorization was not an instruction for their own time, nor is it an instruction for the present time (it was spoken to the 11). Instructions for believers today are in the later letters of Paul.

John 20\22
After proving his resurrection to his disciples, Jesus said to them, "Peace to you. As the Father has authorized me, I also authorize you." And when he had said this he breathed on *them*, and said to them, "Receive *the* holy spirit (πνεῦμα ἅγιον = *pneuma hagion*)]. Whoever's sins you forgive, they are forgiven for them. Whoever's you retain, they are retained."

There is no other occurrence of Jesus' breath being referred to as πνεῦμα ἅγιον it is not the same as the twelve's later baptism in the holy spirit: that was to empower them for signs and to be witnesses (Luke 24\49, Acts 1\8). πνεῦμα ἅγιον in John, though, was a specific empowering, stated to be the authorization of the 12 as judges over men's sins.

Matthew 3\16 and Acts 19\6: ἔρχομαι (= *erchomai*)
Matthew says that when Jesus was "baptised" (βαπτίζω = *baptizo*) publicly with God he saw the Holy Spirit [πνεῦμα ἅγιον] "descending ... and alighting over him". The verb "alighting" is ἔρχομαι (= *erchomai*). When Paul laid hands on some men of Ephesus, "*the* holy spirit [πνεῦμα ἅγιον] came on them, and they were speaking with foreign languages and prophesying". The word rendered as "came on" is also ἔρχομαι (= *erchomai*).

So we see that this word ἔρχομαι is used for the PERSONALITY by Matthew, *as well as for* the ABSTRACT gift by Luke in Acts if, that is, I have discerned it correctly.

It might be argued, then, that this same word ἔρχομαι used with πνεῦμα ἅγιον could suggest that πνεῦμα ἅγιον has the same meaning in both passages. However, context must dictate interpretation. At Jesus' baptism, the Holy Spirit was seen by Jesus and by others. At the Ephesian men's receiving πνεῦμα ἅγιον, there is no suggestion of the Holy Spirit being seen, or of him making any appearance; and the holy spirit came by the laying on of Paul's hands: the mere laying on of hands would be unlikely to bring an angel down from the skies.

The appearance of the Holy Spirit was a special event for Jesus and the 12 because of their exalted authority. Why, then, should this word ἔρχομαι not be used for both the appearing of a PERSONALITY and also for the coming of an ABSTRACT gift? We do such things in our own language all the time, applying a word to different contexts. Apply a bandage; apply a word; apply for a job; apply for permission; apply to context; apply with discernment.

The holy spirit of empowerment "fell"
The Book of Acts speaks of the holy spirit "falling" on believers in Samaria (8\16) and on Cornelius and his party (10\44, 11\15). The Greek word for this "falling" is ἐπιπίπτω (= *epipipto*). Could this "falling" suggest a similarity to the Holy Spirit descending as at Jesus' baptism, and that it was the PERSONALITY, the Holy Spirit, coming to them and not the ABSTRACT holy spirit of empowerment? No – but why not?

As with ἔρχομαι in the section above, there is nothing in these cited occurrences of ἐπιπίπτω (= *epipipto*) to indicate that any PERSONALITY was seen or made any appearance – and remember, the Holy Spirit is a visible angel. Many words have many meanings, and can only be interpreted by context. You only have to look at Thayer's marvellous Greek lexicon to see many pages describing some Greek words' many meanings. Why should the writers not use the same words for different events, just as well as using synonymous words? Take our English word "come". How many meanings and contexts might it have? For example, come, come along, come away, come back, come by, come come!, come forward, come in, come nine o'clock, come now!, come off, come off it, come on, come onto, come out, come over, come round, come to, come to nothing, come-uppance, come with, when it comes to it.

The Greek word ἐπιπίπτω (= *epipipto*), meaning "fell", is also used in other contexts, both concrete, personal and abstract. A "trance came [= ἐπιπίπτω] over" Peter (Acts 10\10); "mist and darkness fell [= ἐπιπίπτω] on" Barjesus (Acts 13\11); "fear came [ἐπιπίπτω] over" some Ephesians (Acts 19\17); and "Paul went down and fell [ἐπιπίπτω] on" Eutychus (Acts 20\10).

6. A divinely intended overlap

If this πνεῦμα ἅγιον has 2 different meanings – the Holy Spirit and Angel of God; and an abstract gift of divine empowerment for miraculous powers and a renewed mind with the spirit of separation in the inner man – why, it might be asked, has God allowed the same phrase to be used for both?

I have described in another study 19 classifications of the word "spirit". That demonstrates what a vigorous and polysemous word "spirit" is, whether רוח (= *ruach*) in Hebrew or πνεῦμα (= *pneuma*) in Greek. I have to assume that there is an intended overlap in the two meanings of πνεῦμα ἅγιον in that each has its source in God.

We have seen how the Greek word πνεῦμα – our equivalent of "spirit" – is used to describe divine personalities. Jesus said of God that He is "spirit" (John 4\24). The words we translate as "spirit" and "Spirit", defining the Angel of God and God Himself, also happens to be the Greek word synonymous with empowerment. And it also happens to be the Greek word which describes the character or nature of "the spirit of separation". Distinguish and discern them we must.

The "spirit" which is the "spirit of your mind" (Ephesians 4\23) cannot be the Holy Spirit angel who was seen.

The Spirit who was seen cannot be the spirit of empowerment which believers were filled with and which came sometimes by the laying on of apostles' hands (Acts 5\12, 6\6, 8\17-19, 14\3, 19\6, 19\11-12, 28\8, 2 Timothy 1\6).

*

7. Display of distinctions

For a visual display of distinctions of "Holy Spirit" and "holy spirit" and "the spirit of separateness", here is a table of a few occurrences of equivalents from both the Hebrew and Greek Books. Note well: this is only a *selection* of occurrences of πνεῦμα ἅγιον and רוח קדש, both meaning either "holy spirit" or "Holy Spirit".

	Hebrew Books equivalent	Greek Books examples
1. Personality of the Holy Spirit angel (= *who, he*)	The Hebrew *equivalent* of πνεῦμα ἅγιον – which is קדש רוח (= *ruach qodesh*); occurs only three times: Isaiah 63\10, 63\11: "But they rebelled and they vexed His Holy Spirit" "Where is He Who position His Holy Spirit among them?" Psalm 51\11: "do not take Your Holy Spirit from me"	John 14\26 the Counsellor, *who is* the Holy Spirit, whom the Father will authorize in my name, that one will teach you all these things, and bring all these things to your remembrance Acts 13\2 As they were serving the Lord and fasting, the Holy Spirit said ...
2. Divine empowerment for signs and wonders (= *which, it*)	– – – no occurrences of קדש רוח (= *ruach qodesh*) refer to divine empowerment – – – But Exodus 35\31-33 has this: He has filled him with the spirit of God, in wisdom, in understanding, and in knowledge, and in all types of workmanship, [32] and to devise embroidered works, to work in gold, and in silver, and in bronze, [33] and in the cutting of stones, to set *them*, and in carving of wood, to make all kinds of skillful work	Acts 13\9 But Saul (also Paul), filled with *the* holy spirit, set his eyes on him Acts 19\6 And *when* Paul laid *his* hands on them, *the* holy spirit came on them, and they were speaking with foreign languages and prophesying
3. The spirit of separateness, the renewed mind: (= *which, it*)	– – – no occurrences of קדש רוח (= *ruach qodesh*) refer to a renewed mind – – – but the prophet Ezekiel spoke of "a new heart and a new spirit" ("spirit" being רוח (= *ruach*); (Ezekiel 18\31, 11\19, 36\26-27)	Romans 14\17 For the realm of God is not eating and drinking, but righteousness, and peace, and exuberance in *the* holy spirit Ephesians 1\13-14 you were marked with a seal with the holy spirit of promise, which is the deposit of our inheritance until the redemption

9. The 92 occurrences of πνεῦμα ἅγιον (*pneuma hagion*)
Here is a tentative breakdown of the 92 occurrences of the phrase πνεῦμα ἅγιον. Remember, this does not mean that the distinctions do not occur by other names, such as simply "spirit", for they do – but these lists are only all the occurrences of πνεῦμα ἅγιον. From these lists you can make tables of the passages and their contexts. I have made investigatory tables of many occurrences of "spirit" and "Holy Spirit" in *Who is the Counsellor and the Holy Spirit? The Hoax of Polytheism Exposed.*

The CONCRETE occurrences of πνεῦμα ἅγιον denoting the PERSONALITY of the Holy Spirit:
Matthew 12\32, 28\19;
Mark 3\29, 12\36, 13\11;
Luke 2\25, 2\26, 3\22, 12\10, 12\12;
John 14\26;
Acts 1\2, 1\8, 1\16, 5\3, 5\32, 7\51, 9\31, 10\38, 13\2, 13\4, 15\28, 16\6, 20\23, 20\28, 21\11, 28\25-26;
2 Corinthians 13\14;
Hebrews 3\7, 6\4, 9\8, 10\15;
1 Peter 1\12;
2 Peter 1\21.

Total, = 34

The ABSTRACT occurrences of πνεῦμα ἅγιον denoting divine empowerment, and a renewed mind, which is "the spirit of separateness":
Matthew 1\18, 1\20, 3\11;
Mark 1\8;
Luke 1\15, 1\35, 1\41, 1\67, 3\16, 4\1, 11\13;
John 1\33, 7\39, 20\22 (compare Luke 24\49);
Acts 1\5, 2\4, 2\33, 2\38, 4\8, 4\31, 6\3, 6\5, 7\55, 8\15, 8\17, 8\18, 8\19, 9\17,
    10\44, 10\45, 10\47, 11\15, 11\16, 11\24, 13\9, 13\52, 15\8, 19\2 (twice), 19\6;
Romans 5\5, 9\1, 14\17, 15\13, 15\16;
1 Corinthians 2\13, 6\19, 12\3;
2 Corinthians 6\6;
Ephesians 1\13, 4\30;
1 Thessalonians 1\5, 1\6, 4\8;
2 Timothy 1\14;
Titus 3\5;
Hebrews 2\4;
Jude 20.

Total, = 58

✶

Chapter 20

Understanding Isaiah 9\6

♦

The topic of Isaiah 9\6 arose in conversation last night. This has of course been used to prop up an agenda. This is the Keys of the Kingdom translation of Isaiah 9\6:

> For a child is born for us; a son is given to us
> and the government will be on his shoulder
> and his name will be called wonderful counsellor,
> mighty ruler, founder of the eon, prince of peace.

The Hebrew for the titles or epithetical ascriptions by the prophet Isaiah to the promised Messiah is שר־שלום אבי־עד גבור אל יועץ פלא (= *pehleh yahgatz, el gibor, abi ad, sar shalom*), "wonderful counsellor, mighty ruler, founder of the eon, prince of shalom".

This is about the Messiah, Jesus.

I contend with the traditional ways of translating the two phrases אבי־עד (= *abi ad*) and גבור אל (= *el gibor*). The first, אבי־עד (= *abi ad*), usually gets rendered as "everlasting Father". The second, אל גבור (= *el gibor*), usually gets translated as "Mighty God". But these are about the Messiah, so these renderings must be contested.

We know that the King James Bible translators were not expressly commissioned to discover the truth of the prophets and apostles of God and Christ. They upheld the Hell and three gods system, migrating souls in Heaven, and devils. But careful studiers of the word of God know that the Messiah is the created Son of God and, therefore, that we must translate the phrases אבי־עד and אל גבור according to revealed truth.

1. אבי־עד (= *ahvi ad*)

The King James Bible has the phrase אבי־עד (= *ahvi ad*) as "the everlasting Father". Such a phrase, in relation to the Messiah, is loaded with post-Babylonian Mysteries agenda. Jesus Christ is not his own Father! What the King James Bible men represented as the adjective "everlasting" is in fact frequently used by the prophets as a noun, עד (= *ad*). It is also sometimes used as a preposition, an adverb, and a conjunction, and occasionally as an adjective. Here, though, it cannot be an adjective. It must be a noun. And the noun that it must be is "eon". For just one example of many, at Isaiah 65\18 the phrase עדי־עד (= *ade ad*) is well rendered as "from eon to eon" in the clause "be glad and rejoice from eon to eon". The prophets looked forward to "the coming eons" (Ephesians 2\7), when the land would be under the jurisdiction of God and not political gangsters and banking billionaires. So at Isaiah 9\6 I render the phrase אבי־עד (= *ahvi ad*) as "founder of the eon". If could also be "Architect of the Eon".

To translate the word עד (= *ad*) as an adjective such as "everlasting" is contextually wrong and grammatically wrong. The usual Hebrew word for "father" is אב (= *ahv*). In Isaiah 9\6, though, the form of this word is אבי (= *ahvi*). Davidson's Hebrew lexicon describes this as the "construct" state of אב (= *ahv*); (see p. 3 and also p. 76 in section 45 after its Preface). It must be followed by "of" something. The English equivalent would be "father's", that is, it is a genitive. And since we know that עד (= *ad*) 134 times carries the meaning "eon", then that is what we have here: "the Founder of the Eon".

The word the King James Bible translators have as "father" is אב (= *ahv*). (See Strong's Concordance reference number h1.) Isaiah is giving descriptions and titles of the Messiah. Of course the Messiah is not God or the Father, but he is, rather, the anointed man of God, the anointed Son of God. He is the inheritor of all things and all things will flow from him in the 1,000 years. The deep meaning of the Greek αἰών (*aion*), Greek equivalent of Hebrew עולם (*olam*), connects with flowing. Rivers named "Avon" are related to αἰών. The word אב (*ahv*), usually "father" can also mean "founder", "nourisher", "teacher". Gesenius says, "the word *father* has often a much wider meaning". He includes "any ancestor", "founder", "first ancestor", "bringer up", "nourisher", "master", "teacher", "possessor". The Lord Jesus Christ is "the founder of the eon", or "architect of the eon".

The Keys of the Kingdom translation has the following footnote concerning this:

founder of the eon: אבי־עד (*ahvi ad*). Strong's h1 + h5702. Genitive construct state of אב (*ahv*); followed by 'of' + עד (*ad*), noun (over 100 times as 'eon', 'age', 'duration' (see 9\7); (not an adjective 'everlasting' as KJV). Gesenius concerning אבי: 'the word *father* has often a much wider meaning ... any ancestor ... founder ... first ancestor ... bringer up ... nourisher ... master ... teacher ... possessor'. The Messiah as 'the last Adam', 'the second man', is founder, architect, father even, hence 'Firstborn', of the coming eon (John 3\16, 11\26, 1 Cor. 15\45-47, Col. 1\16-23, Heb. 1\2, 11\3). Eg cp. אב at 1 Sam. 24\11 (David to Saul) as 'father' meaning 'lord', 'master'. Strong includes 'head', 'founder', 'originator', 'ruler', 'chief'

2. אל גבור (= *el gibor*)
The King James Bible puts these two words together at Isaiah 9\6 as "the mighty god": loaded with agenda of the Mysteries campaign, as if the Son of God were also God the Father Himself. That woeful phrase for the Messiah creates internal disharmony. It is true that the phrase also occurs at Isaiah 10\21 where it does refer to God and not to the Messiah, and there I translate it as "Mighty El" – but that will not do for the Messiah. It disturbs the internal harmony of the word of God and it destroys the context. The first word, אל (= *el*), (Strong's Concordance reference number h410), certainly does have the frequent meaning of "God". However, like "Elohim", it has other meanings too. Gesenius (p. 45) describes it as "strong", "mighty", "a mighty one", "a hero", "might", "strength". So it is not just a matter of *translation*, but also of *interpretation*. In other places the King James Bible has אל as "power" (in the phrase "in the power of my hand" at Genesis 31\29 and in "in our power" at Nehemiah 5\5); "gods"; "god"; "mighty"; "goodly"; and "idols".

The second word, גבור (= *gibor*), (Strong's Concordance reference number h1368), is the regular word for "mighty". Gesenius describes it as "strong", "mighty", "impetuous", "a chief", "military commander". The King James Bible also has it as "strong"; "valiant men"; "men"; "mighties"; "mightiest"; "strongest"; and "mighty men". Since Jesus said, "All authority in Heaven and on Earth has been given to me" (Matthew 28\18), we can assume this power and authority to him in the title אל גבור (= *el gibor*). So the two words are synonyms. This gives an intense phrase in the same manner as "King of kings" and "Lord of lords" (1 Timothy 6\15, Revelation 19\16), which could also be put as "mighty King".

At Genesis 2\17 there occurs the phrase מות תמות (= *mot tamut*), which Bullinger (*Companion Bible*, p. 6) puts as literally "dying thou shalt die", the literary figure of "polyptoton" (many inflections), "the repetition of the same part of speech in different inflections". What might appear tautologous is put for effect, the effect of emphasis. In other words, words with the same or similar meanings put in apposition to each other for the purpose of emphasis. Moses is using a repetition of the verb מות (= *mooth*).

At Leviticus 27\28 (and many other places), there is קדש קדשים (= *qodesh qodesh*), "holy + holy" (the second "holy" is in a plural form – the first as we read it, left to right –), Strong's Concordance reference number h6944. This is rendered in KTK as "especially dedicated", sometimes in other places as "Sanctuary".

At Acts 7\34 a similar idiom is seen in the Greek ἰδὼν εἶδον (= *idon eidon*), "I have clearly seen", literally "seeing I saw".

That, I believe, is the case with אל גבור (= *el gibor*) – a figure put for emphasis. We can put the two words together as something like "mighty ruler", or "mighty god" ("god" only permissible in the sense of "to whom the word of God came", John 10\35, hence a prophet). This now creates internal harmony with Jesus' saying "All authority in Heaven and on Earth has been given to me" (Matthew 28\18), given to him by God. Jesus is not God. God is God. God cannot be tempted. Jesus was tempted. God cannot die. God is immortal. Jesus died. If Jesus is God, then Jesus raised himself. And if he raised himself, then he did not die. And if he did not die, there is no sacrifice for sin – and the world is doomed.

Chapter 21

The Development of the God-authorized Books
translated into English
from the Hebrew Masoretic Text
and
the Greek Byzantine Majority Texts

✦

The Anglo-Saxons began the first English translations, made only in parts. John Wycliffe (1320-1384) and William Tyndale (?-1536) made complete translations, and were murdered for their work. Since Wycliffe's first complete English translation, 636 years ago, there have been over 150 English versions. *The Concordant Version*, by AE Knoch (1926), commendably has "eonian life" and "ecclesia"; it understood Romans 9\3; it had a fair go at John 1\1; it almost got John 11\26 right; but it is based on deplete manuscripts; has traditional errors; its John 17\5 is ungrammatical; it is archaic; it mixes tenses; and has curiosities ("log of life"; "flying creatures") and numerous other problems. One million copies of the *Revised Standard Version* (based on a non-Byzantine text) are said to have been sold on the first day of its publication on the 30th of September 1952. Since that version, over 90 English versions have been made, many of them no more than paraphrases based on deplete manuscripts.

The Law and Prophets and Psalms, Genesis to 2 Chronicles,
written in Hebrew and Aramaic
by the God-authorized prophets and scribes,
starting with Moses (probably about 1400 BC),
probably completed by about 500 BC;
preserved in Hebrew Masoretic Scrolls

∎

The Gospel Accounts and the Letters and Revelation
written in Greek
by the God-authorized apostles,
probably completed by about 68 AD;
preserved in Greek Majority (Byzantine) texts

∎ [← Latin Vulgate, principally Jerome,
c. 390 AD]
∎
∎

Early English Anglo-Saxon versions:
Caedmon's Paraphrase (7th century);
Aldhelm, Abbot of Malmesbury, translation of Psalms (8th century);
Egbert (?-766), translation of Gospels (8th century);
Bede, an Abbot, translation of Gospel of John (735);
King Alfred the Great's Psalms (9th century);
Aldred, The Lindisfarne Gospels (10th century);
Aelfric, sections of the Hebrew Books (10th century)
The Wessex Gospels, also known as West Saxon Gospels (c990)

∎

Wycliffe Bible (John Wycliffe, 1380, revised & completed 1384, 1388-90);
translated from the Latin Vulgate,

the first full *hand-written* English manuscripts;
Wycliffe was declared a "heretic" and his writings banned;
died of a stroke 1384; in 1428 Pope Martin V commanded Wycliffe's body
to be exhumed and burned and his ashes to be scattered in the River Swift;
"You say it is heresy to speak of the Holy Scriptures in English.
You call me a heretic because I have translated the Bible into the common tongue
of the people. Do you know whom you blaspheme?"

■

■

William Tyndale's New Testament (1526, 1534);
first translation into English
directly from the Greek manuscripts;
first New Testament *printed* in English;
murdered by strangling and burning in 1536:
"If God spare my life, I will see to it that the boy who drives the plowshare
knows more of the scripture than you, Sir";
described as "the architect of the English language"

■

Coverdale Bible (1535);
sourced from Tyndale, Latin and Luther's German versions;
first *complete printed* English Bible

■

John Rogers, pseudonym Thomas Matthew (1537, 1549);
first version translated wholly from the Hebrew and Greek,
composite of own work and Tyndale's and Coverdale's;
second complete Bible printed in English;
Rogers burned in 1555

■

Taverner Bible (Richard Taverner, 1539);
mostly revision of Matthews Bible;
first Bible allowed for public use

■

Great Bible (Miles Coverdale, 1539, revised 1541);
worked mostly from Tyndale, Apocrypha,
Latin Vulgate, and German versions

■

Geneva Bible (1560);
Calvinist; first Bible with verse numbers

■

■

Bishops' Bible (1568);
mostly work of English bishops

■

Rheims New Testament (1582);
Roman Catholic version; from the Latin Vulgate

■

■

Douai Old Testament (1609);
OT Roman Catholic version; from the Latin Vulgate

■

Douai-Rheims Bible (1610);
first complete Roman Catholic version; from the Latin Vulgate

■

King James Bible (1611);
also known as the Authorised Version;

influenced by Latin Vulgate;
Calvinist; ordered by King James 1 in 1604, the work of about 54 men;
revised 1629, 1638, 1762, 1769

■

Robert Aitken (1734-1802);
first English Bible printed in America

■

Noah Webster (1833);
mainly revision of KJV; sometimes called The Common Version

■

Young's Literal Translation (Robert Young, 1862)

■

The Englishman's Greek New Testament Interlinear (Samuel Bagster, 1877)

■

■ [← new form of attack launched by
Westcott and Hort, from deplete Greek
manuscripts, The Revised Version, 1881]

■

Interlinear Greek-English New Testament (GR Berry, 1897)

■

The Holy Scriptures (JN Darby, 1890)

■

The Book of Job (EW Bullinger, c1910?)

■

The Companion Bible (EW Bullinger, 1921)
a King James Version, a pioneering work with countless corrections,
enhancements, and 198 appendices

■

The Interlinear Bible: Greek-English (Jay P Green, Sr., 1980);
and Hebrew-Greek-English (Jay P Green, Sr., 1986)

■

Revised Authorized Version, New King James Version (1979, 1982)

■

The Resultant Version: a translation of Ephesians
with notes (Otis Q Sellers, c1980)

■

The 21st Century New King James Version (1994)

■

Analytical-Literal Translation (Gary Zeolla, 1999-2001) **A**

■

English Majority Text Version (Paul Esposito, 2010?) **B**

■

Far Above All (online, Graham Thomason, 2020) **C**

■

The Eonian Life Bible, New Testament, 2017 edition, 2019 revised edition with footnotes,
and 2021 edition (Christopher Sparkes) **D**

■

Keys of the Kingdom Holy Bible (Christopher Sparkes, 2022) **E**

~ ✹✹ ~

ed3

A, B, C, D, E: All these in NT are based on the Greek Robinson-Pierpont Textform

Chapter 22

The Divine Order of the Books
(revised from First Edition of KTK)

✦

We know from words of Jesus the divine order of the Hebrew Old Covenant writings: **"the Law of Moses, and the Prophets, and the Psalms"** (Luke 24\44). This specific statement describes the divinely-established arrangement of the Hebrew books in three structural divisions. Jesus also spoke of **"Abel to ... Zechariah"** (Matthew 23\35); that is, from the time of Abel in Genesis 4\2 to the time of Zechariah in 2 Chronicles 35\8, the last Hebrew book. This structure Christ described is confirmed in any Hebrew Bible. The correct order makes finding books in the Old Covenant writings easy because it is in three logical sections, whereas the current disarrangement in English translations is wrong, illogical, and unhelpful, creating an annoying mess of the divine structure.

There is no such internal statement describing the divinely-established order of the Greek books of the New Covenant writings. However, for those who have ears to hear, there is an order which displays the signature of divine design. The beautiful divine order is reflected in the majority of New Testament manuscripts. The so-called "Church Fathers" followed it.

The Robinson-Pierpont Greek text, on which *The Keys of the Kingdom Holy Bible* is based, reflects this order. Robinson and Pierpont comment on this ordering: "Individual manuscripts present the New Testament books in various arrangements; nevertheless, a particular Greek "canonical order" seems to have been popular during early transmissional history. This order is partially evidenced within various early papyri and manuscripts, and occurs in the fourth-century Festal Letter of Athanasius (AD 367) and the list of canonical books attributed to the Laodicean Council (AD 360/363) ... The individual books within each category follow the familiar order ... [William HP] Hatch shows that this order is found among early and geographically diverse Greek manuscripts, fathers, and versions, and was retained among some manuscripts over many centuries" (Robinson and Pierpont, pp. xvi-xvii, and footnote).

Unfortunately, some apostates along the way, Latin Vulgate era, altered the divine arrangements, disobedient to the heavenly vision, so we have been seduced into not even questioning the orders – let alone the inclusions – in English Bibles.

The *internally divine-set order* of the Old Covenant Hebrew books is this grouping of three: **1. "The Law of Moses"**: Genesis, Exodus, Leviticus, Numbers, Deuteronomy; **2. "The Prophets"**: Joshua, Judges, 1 & 2 Samuel, 1 & 2 Kings, Isaiah, Jeremiah, Ezekiel, Hosea, Joel, Amos, Obadiah, Jonah, Micah, Nahum, Habakkuk, Zephaniah, Haggai, Zechariah, Malachi; **3. "The [Books of the] Psalms"**: Psalms, Proverbs, Job, Ruth, Lamentations, Ecclesiastes, Daniel, Ezra, Nehemiah, 1 & 2 Chronicles. (Concerning the Song of Solomon and Esther, see Chapter 28.)

Happily, the New Covenant Greek books also have an *internally divine-set order* of a grouping of three. The 5 books of the Gospels and Acts, a new Pentateuch, – like "five smooth stones out of the brook" to strike the stupid brow of Goliath (1 Samuel 17\40); but for the wise 5 is also the number of "grace" (see Bullinger, *Number in Scripture*) – stand between the two groupings of three either side of it. In the divine arrangement, the individual books follow the familiar *groupings*. However, the *order* within the groupings in their text is not the same: **1. Four Gospels and Acts**: Matthew, Mark, Luke, John, Acts of the Apostles; **2. Other apostles' 7 letters**: Jacob (James), 1 Peter, 2 Peter, 1 John, 2 John, 3 John, Judah (Jude); **3. Paul's 14 letters**: Romans, 1 Corinthians, 2 Corinthians, Galatians, Ephesians, Philippians, Colossians, 1 Thessalonians, 2

Thessalonians, Hebrews, 1 Timothy, 2 Timothy, Titus, Philemon; **4. Revelation**.

The structural overview in the following chart exhibits divine patterns. The other apostles were "apostles before [Paul]" (Galatians 1\17), appointed to "the circumcision", that is, the house of Judah (Galatians 2\7-9), harmonising with the word going out to "the Judahite first" (Galatians 2\7, Romans 1\16, 2\9-10). It came from apostles who themselves were "Judahites by nature" (Galatians 2\15). The letters of Paul following the other apostles' letters harmonises with Paul's saying he, with others, were to go "to the nations" (Galatians 2\8-9). After the word having gone to "the Judahite first", Paul then turned to the nations (Acts 28\28, Romans 1\16). This is described by Paul as "then to the Greek", the "uncircumcision", the uncircumcised dispersion of the house of Israel (Romans 1\16, 2\9-10, Ephesians 2\11, John 7\35, 12\20).

As William Petri puts it in his Preface: "Yahweh Elohim did not intend it to be the other way round, with Paul being placed ahead of James, Peter and John" (p. xv).

Paul's having been called as an apostle after the others (Galatians 1\17), it is fitting that his letters follow theirs. The letter to Hebrews stands between 2 Thessalonians and 1 Timothy, separating Paul's local Ekklesia letters from those to individuals. There is also, in the divine arrangement, divine patterning concerning numbers. The Hebrew books total 37 (a divine patterning number, a primary; see Appendix 7); and the Greek total 27 books (3x3x3), 3 a number of *divine perfection* and *completeness*. The total of books numbers 64 (8x8). The total of books, also the divisions, either side of the Gospels and Acts numbers 22 (representing the 22 characters of the Hebrew alphabet). The divisions either side of Luke – declaring "peace on Earth" (Luke 2\14) – number 24 (representing the 24 characters of the Greek alphabet). All the divisions number 49 (7x 7). Coincidence? All this is a delight, though of little surprise, to those who understand the Creator, He Who has been pleased to leave His dazzling signature in everything everywhere.

NB. On the website there is a chart exhibiting a DIVINE SIGNATURE in the CORRECT ORDERING of the 64 books of the divinely inspired writings.

✱

ed4

CHAPTER 23. THE EONS DISPLAYED ~ EONS PAST, THE PRESENT EON, & THE EONS COMING (*not proportionate time-scales*)
1. The "eons past" (Isaiah 63\16, Psalm 77\8, 93\2, Romans 14\24); and "the present eon" (Galatians 1\4)

Creation / Restoration of Earth	Flood		Exodus Red Sea		Jesus Christ "Son of God". Writings of Apostles.	Destruction of Jerusalem AD70	Apostasy, religious systems
Pre-Adamic	Adam & Eve rebellion & sin	Noah	Patriarchs, "the fathers", Abraham, Isaac, Jacob, Joseph promise of land (Gen. 13\15, 26\3, 28\4, 28\13, Deut. 30\5)	Moses & the prophets: law & Covenant with Sons of Israel (Ex. 19\5-6)	John the Baptist	Jesus Christ & atonement for sin promise of land restated (Mat. 5\5) law restated (Mat. 5 to 7) apostles chosen (Mat. 10); signs New Covenant (Mat. 26) death & resurrection; Acts period Paul ends Judahite privilege to hear gospel first Heb. 8\9) & goes to dispersion	present eon of darkness (Gal. 1\4, Eph. 6\12) & the day of man (1 Cor. 4\3); Church Fathers & "apostatizing" (1 Tim. 4\1) & international religious system; invisible true Ekklesia of Christ;
				God's divorce from Israel (Jer. 3\8, Hos. 1\9-10,			
1. PRE-ADAMIC EON		**2. ANTEDILUVIAN EON**	**3. PATRIARCHAL EON**	**4. MOSAIC EON**			**5. EKKLESIA EON (joint Body of Christ)**

2. The "eons coming" (Ephesians 2\7)

favourable intervention   Jesus' return & magisterial presence (παρουσία, *parousia*)
of God & Jesus (ἐπιφάνεια, *epiphaneia*)   "1,000 years consummated"   & "Paradise of God" (Rev. 2\27, Luke 23\43, Rev. 20) →   →   →   →

"Day of Yahweh"   "Day of Christ" (Phil. 1\6, Rev. 20), "coming eon" & "the Kingdom"; "first resurrection" (Mark 10\30, John 11\26, Mat. 3\2, Rev. 20)
& God (Is. 13\6,   New Covenant with Judah & Israel fulfilled in marriage supper (Luke 13\29, Heb. 9\15, 10\16, Rev. 19\7-9); adversary shackled (Rev. 20)
Rev. 1\10)   present system burned (1 Cor. 7\31, 2 Peter 3\10); the παρουσία (*parousia*); White Throne; New Jerusalem (Rev. 21, Gal. 4\26, Eph. 2, Heb. 12\22)
attack on Jerusalem   "twelve tribes of the Sons of Israel" ruling with God and Jesus over all nations (Ex. 19\5-6, Mat. 19\28, Eph. 1\3, 2\6, Rev. 21\12-14)
"days of vengeance"   new heavens & Earth for new rulership & administration (Luke 19\17-19, 2 Peter 3\12);
(Luke 21\22)   saved "nations" close by (Rev. 21\24-26); no death or sorrow (Rev. 21\4)
appearance of Elijah (Mal. 4\5-6)
tribulation (Rev. 13)

6. DAY OF YAHWEH EON   7. DAY OF CHRIST EON
8. NEW HEAVENS AND NEW EARTH EON (divine rulership; consummation; death abolished; God "all in all")

1. Pre-Adamite → Adam *2. Antediluvian* → Noah *3. Patriarchal*: Abraham, Isaac, Jacob & → arising of Edomite adversary → *4. Mosaic*: Moses, first Covenant with Sons of Israel, law & prophets; John; Jesus; apostles; new "better Covenant" → *5. Age of Ekklesia* of Christ & all authority in him; Paul, apostle to dispersed (Romans 1\16, 2\9, 2\10, John 7\35 et cetera); "present eon of evil and darkness" & church fathers (Gal. 1\4, Eph. 6\13, 1 Tim. 4\1) → *6. Day of Yahweh*: Elijah (Mal. 4\5); tribulation → *7. Day of Christ*: divine "favourable intervention" (ἐπιφάνεια, *epiphaneia*) & first resurrection; marriage supper (Luke 13\29); adversary shackled; establishment of 1,000 years (symbolic immortality & divine rulership); short release hostile "Gog and Magog"; Jesus' 2nd coming (παρουσία, *parousia*); magisterial presence on Earth (παρουσία, *parousia*); day of judgement; "Great White Throne" & "Book of Life" (Acts 17\31, Rev. 20\11-15); lake of fire refinement (Rev. 20, 1 Cor. 3\15)

→ *8. New heavens & new Earth*: consummation; Paradise of God; "12 tribes of the Sons of Israel" & 12 apostles reigning with God & Christ; no death; God "all in all", Jesus in Greek, Ἰησοῦς (*Iesous*), has numeric values of 10+8+200+70+400+200, = 888 (Ap. 7).

In "the day of Christ", also called "the last day" (John 11\24-26), those in Christ are raised into immortality, having incorruptible resurrection minds and bodies, like that of Christ. The 12 tribes of the Sons of Israel will reign with God and Christ in the Holy City, the New Jerusalem, "the Paradise of God" (Rev.2\27, Luke 23\43), ruling over the nations, promised since Moses on Sinai (Ex. 19\5-6, Mat. 19\28, Eph. 1\3, 2 Tim. 2\12, Rev. 21\12-14).

ed19

Chapter 24

The True Meanings of αἰών (aion) and αἰώνιος (aionios)

'Where *is the* disputer of this eon?'
~1 Corinthians 1\20

There's an old English word "aeon". Contemporary spelling prefers "eon". An "eon" is a long period of time, in Geology a major division of time, subdivided into eras. In such secular measurements its boundaries are vague. In the divine measurement, though, the boundaries of an eon are distinct, having a known beginning and a known end, marked by events and by the proclamations of prophets and apostles of God.

The Greek word αἰών (aion) means "eon"
Our English word "eon" is derived from the Greek word αἰών (aion), Strong's Concordance reference number g165. This is one of the most important words for everybody in the world to understand, for the coming Kingdom of God and Christ is often referred to as "the eon" (such as Isaiah 9\6). It occurs 126 times (in the RP text; 128 in the TR text, with two extra occurrences at Rev. 5\14), the first at Mat. 6\13. This Greek word αἰών is a simple word to translate. It means "eon", "age", defining, just as it does in English, a time dimension. In 100 of its 126 occurrences I have translated it as "eon", "age", or, plural, "eons", "ages".

Often only the rendering "eon" is really good enough. In some cases "age" is the right alternative, but that will not always be quite right, as that can suggest a shorter time, as in "the age of Dostoyevsky", and is ambiguous ("a good age", "New Age"??); "era" is too short; "epoch" is too short and does not have the right connotation. Our word "eon" is the derivation, meaning, and translation of αἰών.

For example, Jesus spoke of "the eon that is coming" (Mark 10\30, Luke 18\30). So did Paul (Heb. 6\5, Eph. 1\21). Paul spoke of "the present eon of evil" (Gal. 1\4) and "this eon of darkness" (Eph. 6\12), which is our present time. Paul spoke also of "the coming eons" (Eph. 2\7), which are the 1,000 years and then "the day of God" (Rev. 20\2-7, 2 Peter 3\12) in the new Earth. Paul would not have spoken of "the present eon" (Gal. 1\4, 2 Tim. 4\10) if there were not other eons to come.

Thayer comments: "probable is the conjecture ... that αἰών is so connected with ἄημι *to breathe, blow*, as to denote properly *that which causes life, vital force*; ... *age* (Lat. *Aevum*, which is αἰών with the Aeolic digamma), *a human lifetime* (in Hom., Hdt., Pind., Tragic poets), *life itself*" (pp. 18-19). Otis Q Sellers gives a fine analysis of αἰών in his Seed & Bread articles nos. 126, 127 and 128 "*What Does Aiōn Mean?*" He relates it to "Avon" and flowing: "The idea of "outflowing" is the thread that runs so true through every occurrence of the word *olam* and continues on through the word *aion*. In many passages this knowledge will bring great beauty and new meanings. Note this in Psalm 9:7 where we are literally told: 'Jehovah shall sit as a King outflowing [*olam*]'" (Seed & Bread 127). And Sellers says: "I do not believe that there is any word in the English language that will express the truth contained in the word *aion* so that it can be used to translate it. When we come upon a situation such as this, the proper course to follow is to transliterate (carry them over) these words, anglicizing them as a rule into more easily handled forms. This has already been done, and the words *eon* and *eonian* will be found in the dictionary. Then when we find the true idea that *aion* represents, by the use made of it in the Word of God, we can use the simple term *eon* to express it" (Seed & Bread 126).

What this *abstract noun* αἰών (*aion*) does not translate as "ever" or "for ever": it is not an *adverb*, and αἰών does not mean a concept of eternity. Nor does it translate as "for ever and ever", or "evermore". Nor does the *abstract noun* αἰών mean the *concrete noun* "world". Yet those are how the KJV sloppily translates it.

The KJV & popular versions concerning αἰών

The translators of the *King James Version* (KJV), 1611 – concealing Jesus' gospel promise of "eonian life" – translated αἰών in 8 different ways: "ages" (twice); "course" (once); "end" (once); "eternal" (twice); "ever" (51 times); "evermore" (3 times); "never" (7 times); "world" or "worlds" (39 times). And 22 times they mischievously ignored it. Not once did they translate it correctly as "eon".

The KJV 39 times has αἰών as "world" or "worlds", which is a concrete *space* dimension, but αἰών is an abstract *time* dimension. Not one single time does αἰών mean "world". The Greek for "world" is κόσμος (*kosmos*), Strong's Concordance reference number g2889, not αἰών. The word αἰών is an *abstract noun* – and nothing could be more abstract than a long measurement of time. κόσμος is a *concrete noun* – and nothing could be more concrete, could it, than the mass of the world?

The KJV and many others also sloppily translate αἰών as "ever" or "evermore" or "never" ("ever" with a negative); (61 times in the KJV). But again, αἰών is an *abstract noun*, not an *adverb* of time. It also twice has the noun αἰών as an *adjective*, "eternal", and once as the *noun* "end" – badly wrong in both.

Just three of the KJV's renderings αἰών are acceptable: twice as "ages" (Eph. 2\7, Col. 1\26), and once idiomatically as "course" (Eph. 2\2).

By the KJV's slovenly blunders, both God's arrangement of the eons and His precious gospel promise of "eonian life", life in the coming Messianic eon or age, have been masked. These absurd renderings – perpetuated in version after version – have held the world back, prolonging suffering. It is my conviction that the event of the eon will not come without a bold and prophetic announcement. Eon-marking events of God have been signalled in advance by prophets. The prophet Amos wrote that "Adonai Yahweh does nothing unless He reveals His secret counsel to His servants the prophets. The lion has roared – who will not fear? Adonai Yahweh has spoken – who can but prophesy?" (Amos 3\7).

At Mat. 13\38-39 we see Jesus say of his parable of the tares that "the field represents the world [κόσμος]" and "*the* harvest represents *the* completion of the eon [αἰών]". We could not wish for a sharper distinction between these two Greek words. The KJV, though, puts both words as "world", spoiling Jesus' explanation: both the field *and* the harvest cannot represent the world.

At John 11\26-27 there are both words αἰών, "eon", "age", and κόσμος, "world": Jesus spoke of life throughout the *timespan* of the eon (αἰών), and Martha spoke of his having come into the *concrete* world (κόσμος), showing the difference of the words, but the KJV men failed or refused to see that.

At Acts 3\21, the Greek text has the phrase ἀπ' αἰῶνος (*ap aionos*), which is "from of old", using αἰών (*aion*) idiomatically, and referring to God speaking through His holy prophets "from of old". The KJV, though, has that Greek phrase as "since the world began", but no words with any of those meanings are in the Greek; and it wrongly renders αἰών as "world"; and, further, the KJV's words are wrong in their contexts here as well because there have not been "holy prophets" since the world began. The first prophet was Enoch, who was the "seventh from Adam" (Jude 14, Gen. 5\18-23).

At Acts 15\18, the Greek text again has the phrase ἀπ' αἰῶνός (*ap aionos*), which, again, is idiomatic and is "from of old". But the KJV wrongly has it as "the beginning of the world", yet no words with any of those meanings match any of the Greek words.

At 1 Cor. 2\7, Paul speaks of the wisdom which God has marked out beforehand, "in advance of the eons / ages". The KJV, though, only managed that as "before the world", so that αἰών is wrongly put as "world", a plural is put as a singular, so that the eons are concealed, or strangely put into a distant past.

At 1 Cor. 3\18-19 there are the two clauses: "If anybody among you thinks *himself* to be wise in this eon [αἰών]" and "the wisdom of this world [κόσμος] is foolishness with God".

So we have "this eon" followed by "this world". Nevertheless, the KJV translators did not drop their refusal to translate αἰών as "eon" or "age", and they stuck to their rendering of "world". Both phrases they put as "this world". If Paul had meant "world" in both places he would have written κόσμος in both places.

At 1 Cor. 10\11, Paul says of idolaters, "on them have come the ends of the ages", signifying a certain imminent judgment (Mat. 24, Mark 13, Luke 21). But the KJV men were only able to manage that as "upon whom the ends of the world are come". So they translated αἰώνων, "eons", "ages", plural, as "world", singular, and their insistence on αἰών as "world" found them out, since they could not sensibly write "the end of the worlds". There are not "worlds", plural. So they pulled off a dodge and wrote it as singular.

At Eph. 3\9, the Greek has the phrase ἀπὸ τῶν αἰώνων (*apo ton aionon*), which is "from the eons". The KJV has that as "from the beginning of the world", but that does not in the slightest measure reflect the Greek or the lesson, since the word αἰώνων is "eons", *plural*, not "world", *singular*.

Eph. 3\11 has "*the* purpose of the eons", αἰών being in the genitive plural, αἰώνων, but the KJV conjures "eons" plural into an *adjective*, "eternal", wiping out Paul's point.

Eph. 3\21 is particularly interesting. The Greek has the phrase τοῦ αἰῶνος τῶν αἰώνων (*tou aionos ton aionon*), meaning literally "the eon of the eons [ages]", but better rendered, in my view, as "the duration of the eons". The KJV translators, though, put that as "world without end", but there is no Greek word there for "world", no Greek word for "without", and no Greek word for "end". The KJV – repeated at Isaiah 45\17 – is made worse in that it has contradictory phrases such as "the end of the world" at Mat. 13\39 and elsewhere (14 times altogether). So, the KJV has two contradictory phrases: "world without end" and "at the end of the world". And both are wrong.

Col. 1\26 has the phrase "the mystery having been hidden from the eons / ages". Imagine trying to make the plural of αἰών in that phrase mean "world" or "ever": "the mystery which has been hidden from the evers" (grammatical nonsense), or "from the worlds" (What "worlds" would those be? There is only one world). At least the KJV has "ages" there.

At 1 Tim. 1\17 Paul describes God with the majestic title "King of the Eons / Ages", the noun αἰών being plural (that is, αἰώνων *aionon*). The KJV has that as "King eternal", twisting a plural *noun* into an *adjective*. Without an understanding of the coming eons, our vision of the future and our inheritance in Christ is nullified, smeared out.

Heb. 1\2 and 11\3 state clearly that God "designed the eons" (αἰῶνας, plural), meaning that He has framed all the past and present and coming eons, divisions of time marked by His different ways of speaking to and dealing with mankind. However, in these two verses the KJV translators put "he made the worlds" and "the worlds were framed", but there is only one world. Also, when speaking of the creation of the heavens and the Earth, or the Earth in relation to the heavens, the Greek usually uses γῆ (*gee*, "Earth"; see Mat. 5\18, 11\25, Acts 4\24, 14\15, 17\24, 1 Cor. 8\5, Eph. 1\10, 3\15, Col. 1\16, 1\20, Heb. 1\10, 2 Peter 3\7, 3\13, Rev. 6\13, 14\7, 20\11, 21\1). Just twice it uses κόσμος in relation to creation (Acts 17\24, Rom. 1\20). Furthermore, γῆ and κόσμος, in such contexts, appear in the singular: one Earth, one world. There are, though, several eons, several ages. Hebrews 1\2 and 11\3 concern *arranging* – not *creating* – the arranging and framing of the eons, not the creating of the world. αἰών most certainly does not mean "worlds".

In addition, if more fixed certainty were wanted that αἰών does not mean "world", then Eph. 2\2 and Heb. 9\26 most happily provide that certainty. For in both those verses both words occur, αἰών, "eon", and κόσμος, "world". Ephesians 2\2 has both words in the same phrase, "the eon of this world", so the KJV men were forced to make a distinction – even *they* would not write "the world of this world" – and so they wrote "the course of this world".

Heb. 9\26 has the two phrases *"the*

foundation of *the* world [κόσμος]", "world" singular, and "*the* completion of the eons [αἰών]", "eons" plural. Hence it's absurd to want both κόσμος and αἰών as "world" singular; yet that is exactly what the KJV does have, having "the foundation of the world" and "the end of the world" – wrong in number, and as if, absurdly, Jesus' death was at the end of the world.

At Heb. 11\3 and 11\7 we yet again see the clear distinctions: "the eons [αἰών] ... have been framed by ... God" and "Noah ... condemned the world [κόσμος]". Noah did not condemn what God designed and framed! But the KJV says "the worlds were framed". Which *worlds*? Contrast Genesis 1\1.

Heb. 13\8 says "Jesus Christ yesterday and today *is* the same, and throughout the eons [ages]". For that last phrase, though, all the KJV could manage was "for ever". To represent a *plural noun* with an *adverb* "ever" is curious mischief indeed. How can a plural *abstract noun* become an *adverb*? What happened to the eons God designed?

All these are subjects of simple and straightforward grammar, logic, and truth. There are many more such blunders in the KJV with the word αἰών. There is one good way which the KJV men refused to translate αἰών – and that is "eon", "age", the way it ought to be translated. It is not difficult Greek!

The Hebrew word עולם (*olam*), and the Chaldee word עלם (*alam*) both mean "eon" and are the equivalents of the Greek word αἰών

The word αἰών is the Greek equivalent of the Hebrew word עולם (*olam*), Strong's Concordance reference number h5769, and of the Chaldee word עלם (*alam*), Strong's h5957, which both mean "eon". The noun עולם occurs 438 times in the Hebrew Books, first at Gen. 3\22; not even once does the KJV manage to translate it as "eon". The Chaldee noun עלם occurs 19 times (in Daniel and Ezra), first at Daniel 2\4; not even once does the KJV manage to translate that as "eon".

In Exodus and Leviticus the KJV makes reference to statutes as being "everlasting" and "for ever" (עולם). But they are not "for ever", since they will have completion and be forgotten in the New Jerusalem on the New Earth.

At Isaiah 45\17, the Hebrew word עולם is in the plural, עולמים (*olamim*), and means "for the eons". The KJV, however, translates it as "everlasting", an *adjective* clumsily put for Isaiah's *adverbial phrase*.

Also in Isaiah 45\17 there is the phrase עד עד־עולמי (*ad oleme ad*), "throughout the eon and its duration". The KJV has it as "world without end", which is wrong linguistically, wrong contextually, and wrong thematically – not a word of the Hebrew there means either "world" or "without" or "end". This is the same blunder the KJV has in Eph. 3\21 where it also has "world without end", creating a clumsy contradiction of its own phrase "end of the world" in other places.

At Isaiah 64\4, the Hebrew has the phrase למעולם (*leme olam*), which is well rendered as "from of old", using עולם ("eon") idiomatically. But the KJV translates the phrase as "since the beginning of the world", but that reflects not a word of the Hebrew, and is wrong contextually.

Ecc. 3\11 has God has "set the eon in their heart" – signifying that we all long for a golden age. But the KJV, by its refusal to put עולם as "eon", has that clause as a curiosity, "he hath set the world in their heart", which is without meaning.

The Greek word αἰώνιος (*aionios*) means "eonian"

Our beautiful English word "eonian" is the adjective form of "eon". (There is also an old adjective, "eval". Think of "medieval", from Latin *medius* middle + *aevum* age.) The Greek αἰών, too, has an adjective form, αἰώνιος (*aionios*), Strong's g166, and it means "eonian", "age-enduring", that is, relating to and enduring for an eon, for a defined age. It occurs 71 times. I dispute that it means "eternal", for it is used with fire and no fire can be eternal (Mat. 18\8, 25\41). Not even once does the KJV have αἰώνιος correctly as "eonian", or even "age-enduring".

Mark 10\30 and Luke 18\30 have the phrase "in the eon [αἰών] which is coming, eonian [αἰώνιος] life". But the KJV has these as "in the world to come life everlasting". So the *noun* αἰών ("eon") they twisted to "world", and the *adjective* αἰώνιος ("eonian") they put (somewhat but not altogether reasonably) as "everlasting". This twisting thieves from the believer the knowledge of the true inheritance in Jesus, life in the coming Messianic age or eon. No wonder the phrase of the real gospel promise of "eonian life" is alien to the ears of so many.

If the KJV men wanted αἰών as "world", then they should have been consistent and had its adjective form αἰώνιος as "worldly", and translated the gospel phrase as "worldly life", and so at Mark 10\30 and Luke 18\30 they should have written "in the world which is coming, worldly life".

The phrase χρόνοις αἰωνίοις (*kronois aioniois*), Strong's g5550+g166, meaning "eonian times" or "times of the eons [ages]", magnificently illustrates and demands that αἰώνιος has to mean "eonian" or "age-enduring" or sometimes "enduring", but not "eternal". The phrase χρόνοις αἰωνίοις occurs at Rom. 14\24 (RP text; 16\25 in the KJV's TR text), 2 Tim. 1\9 and Titus 1\2, where the adjective αἰώνιος is linked to the plural noun "times", χρόνοις. It would be senseless to translate χρόνοις αἰωνίοις as "eternal times", since eternity can have no pluralities, and "eternal times" would be a curiosity without sense, yet one modern version does exactly that. There are no times before eternity, and there are no times after eternity: it has no pluralities. Even the KJV men recognized the senselessness of writing "eternal times". But instead of "eonian times" they invented something else and wrote the ragged phrase "before the world began". Not one of those KJV's words represents a single word of the Greek (I thought the idea was to translate the Greek), all of them wrong linguistically, thematically, and contextually; nor are they what the writer Paul was saying; nor are they true to the facts. And if this promise of life were, as the KJV has it in Titus 1\2, "promised before the world began", to whom, then, was it spoken as promised if the world was not even made? Again, in contradiction of itself, at Rom. 16\25 the KJV says that the gospel was "kept secret since the world began", but then in 2 Tim. and Titus the KJV says that the gospel was promised "before the world began". In contrast, having χρόνοις αἰωνίοις correctly as "eonian times" or "times of the eons / ages" makes perfect sense in its occurrences; fits its contexts; is what Paul meant; is true to the facts. I suggest "in advance of the times of the eons" mean the gospel was preached to the patriarchs (throughout Genesis) and to Moses (Ex. 19\5-6), for Titus describes it as the life "God promised in advance of eonian times" (Titus 1\2).

I translate αἰώνιος as "eonian" or "age-enduring" or "enduring" in all but four of its 71 occurrences where in those occurrences its usage seems idiomatic. At 2 Cor. 4\17, 4\18, 5\1 I translate αἰώνιος as "age-enduring" because it's set in apposition to "temporal". At Philemon 15 I translate it as "permanently" because, unusually, Paul uses it adverbially.

The KJV has the adjective αἰώνιος as "eternal" 42 times, "everlasting" 25 times, "for ever" 1 time – and as a noun, "world", 3 times which is injurious in concealing the fact of the coming eons on Earth, and consequently masking the truth of the gospel promise, "in the eon which is coming, eonian life".

The Greek phrase ζωὴ αἰώνιος (*zoe aionios*) means "eonian life"

The phrase ζωὴ αἰώνιος, Strong's g2222+g166, occurs 44 times in the New Testament, the first at Mat. 19\16. Its meaning is "eonian life" or "age-enduring life". Jesus gives explanation of that as knowing both himself and God: "And this is eonian life: that they might know You, the only true God, and him whom You have authorized, Jesus Christ" (John 17\3; also 1 John 5\20). Jesus also spoke of it as the future life: "in the eon that is coming, eonian life" (Mark 10\30, Luke 18\30). The famous gospel promise at John 3\15-16 of "everyone believing in [Jesus] ... might have eonian life" is life in "the eon that is coming", the "eon" being the Kingdom of

God and Christ. That is the gospel Jesus and Paul and the other apostles proclaimed.

The KJV for this phrase ζωὴ αἰώνιος (*zoe aionios*) alternates randomly between "eternal life" and "everlasting life", unable to make up its mind. Salvation is of course everlasting. While it is most certainly true that believers in God and Jesus will – after resurrection – have life without end, life throughout the coming ages ("a golden age" in secular parlance), and in "the day of God" in the renewed Earth (2 Peter 3\12), that was not the point being made. The point being made in the gospel promise is that those in Jesus have the promise of life in the long-expected new eon foretold by the prophets, when the Messiah will reign over Israel and the Earth. This is the expectation of "eonian life", living throughout the entire course of the coming ages, whereas those who have lived against God and Jesus will not have life in those ages. This is the true gospel. What will happen after "the day of God" we are not told; perhaps it will be that way for ever.

There is the same gospel promise of "life throughout the duration of the eon" spoken by David (Psalm 133\3). And it is the same gospel promise of "eonian life" spoken by Daniel (Daniel 12\2), "eonian life" represented by לחיי עולם (*le chaye olam*), Strong's h2416+h5769, the Hebrew's equivalent of the Greek ζωὴ αἰώνιος.

It is the greatest reward and privilege of all to receive life throughout the coming Messianic eon, but those against Jesus reject that privilege and they will not have that life. The words ζωὴ αἰώνιος (*zoe aionios*), meaning "eonian life", ought to be constantly on the lips of every exuberant believer in the true God and Jesus Christ.

The Greek phrase εἰς τὸν αἰῶνα (eis ton aiona) means "throughout the eon"

The Greek phrase εἰς τὸν αἰῶνα (*eis ton aiona*), meaning "throughout the eon", has its Hebrew equivalent in לעולם (*le olam*), which first appears at Gen. 3\22 and appears 162 times in all. The Greek phrase εἰς τὸν αἰῶνα (*eis ton aiona*), "throughout the eon", appears 27 times.

This promise of life "throughout the eon" is shown exactly or implied in the words of Jesus at John 4\14, 6\51, 6\58, 8\35 (twice), 8\51, 8\52 (reported speech), 10\28, 11\26, 12\34, 14\16, 1 John 2\17. At John 11\26, Jesus said to Martha, "everyone living and believing in me will most certainly not die throughout the eon. Do you believe this?" Yes, it is the fact. The KJV, however, has Jesus promising Martha that whoever believes in him "shall never die. Believest thou this?" As a matter of fact, no, that cannot be believed at all. It is not true. Even Jesus himself died for three days and three nights. And everybody since has died and gone into the grave, and they await resurrection, whether believer or not. The words of the KJV are not true. They make Jesus' promise a lie.

In John 11\26 (and 10\28) the two phrases meaning "most certainly not" and "throughout the eon" represent five Greek words, οὐ μὴ ... εἰς τὸν αἰῶνα (*ou me ... eis ton aiona*). But the KJV only translated those five Greek words as one word, "never". One word for five words leaves four words untranslated. Words out of their meaning; a wrong word; words left untranslated; internal disharmony. That is not the right approach to go about translating the great oracles of the Son of God. There is a Greek word for "never", οὐδέποτε (*oudepote*) – Strong's g3763; see Mat. 7\23, 1 Cor. 13\8 et cetera – but it does not appear in John 11\26. When Jesus meant "never" he said "never": for example, "Have you never [οὐδέποτε] read ...?" (Mat. 21\16, 21\42).

In John 11\26 Jesus did not say "never" and he did not mean "never" because it would have made his statement untrue. The Greek way to say "never" is not by the two phrases οὐ μὴ and εἰς τὸν αἰῶνα (which often appear independently, meaning "most certainly not" and "throughout the eon"). The KJV's "never" is a blunder, a poisoning at the root of the promise of Jesus, shipwrecking at every point the resurrection and his gospel promise. The KJV's having Jesus say that men "will never die" is the same lie the serpent told Eve in Eden (Gen. 3\4): "You will not surely die". So the KJV puts the lie of the serpent into the mouth of Jesus.

Where in John 11\26 the KJV wants the *abstract noun* αἰών as the *adverb* "ever", it constructs nonsense. Furthermore, in the phrase εἰς τὸν αἰῶνα the KJV is omitting to translate the definite article τὸν. It is also omitting to translate the preposition εἰς (which it manages once to have correctly as "throughout" at Eph. 3\21). And, if it wants αἰῶνα as "ever", then it should have "throughout the ever", grammatical nonsense. Nonsense too if it wants αἰών as world: "will ... not die throughout the world" is semantic gibber.

This is the truth, though: Jesus said, "I give them eonian life, and they will most certainly not suffer destruction throughout the eon" (John 10\28, 3\16).

And as Jesus had to correct the traditions of the scribes who mangled the law, so do we have to correct the scribes today who have mangled the law and say to them: You have heard it said that whoever believes in Jesus "will never die". But truly I tell you today, whoever believes in Jesus will be resurrected, Sons and Daughters of God, and then they will most certainly not die throughout the coming Messianic eon.

The phrase εἰς τὸν αἰῶνα could be well translated idiomatically as "permanently" at 1 Cor. 8\13, so reading "I would certainly not eat flesh permanently [εἰς τὸν αἰῶνα]", but it is preferable to let the hyperbole of "throughout the eon" remain. The phrase might also be idiomatic (but maybe not?) as at John 13\8, concerning the washing of Peter's feet, but, once again, it is preferable to let the hyperbole remain.

αἰών can sometimes be translated as "duration"

In the opening of his letter to the Galatians, Paul has the phrase "throughout the durations of the eons" (Gal. 1\5). The Greek of that is εἰς τοὺς αἰῶνας τῶν αἰώνων (*eis tous aionas ton aionon*). This could be rendered literally as "throughout the eons of the eons", but is more meaningful as "throughout the durations of the eons".

The same phrase – with minor variations – also appears at Eph. 3\21 ("the duration of the eons"), Phil. 4\20, 1 Tim. 1\17, 2 Tim. 4\18, Heb. 1\8 ("the duration of the eon"), 13\21, 1 Peter 4\11, 5\11, Rev. 1\6, 1\18, 4\9, 4\10, 5\13, 5\14 (in TR text, not RP text), 7\12, 10\6, 11\15, 14\11, 15\7, 19\3, 20\10, 22\5.

In the Heb. 1\8 occurrence of the phrase Paul is citing Psalm 45\6-7, so his Greek reflects the Hebrew, which is לעולם ועד (*le olam va ed*), a phrase first occurring at Ex. 15\18. Two different Hebrew words are used in that, עולם (*olam*) and עד (*ad*), so "duration" and "eon" seem the sensible renderings, strengthening the case for "duration of the eons" in Paul's writings – hence they are reflected in my renderings of the Greek phrase (and its two variants) εἰς τοὺς αἰῶνας τῶν αἰώνων (*eis tous aionas ton aionon*).

The true gospel promise

The promise of the coming eon is also expressed as "the Kingdom of God" (Luke 4\43), and "the Kingdom of the Exalted / Heavens" (Mat. 3\2). See both "Kingdom" and "eon" at Isaiah 9\6. Resurrection and life throughout the coming eon are the true hope of the "sons of the resurrection" (Luke 20\36), the Sons and Daughters of God.

As Jesus said, "Labour ... for the food enduring into eonian life, which the Son of Man will give you" (John 6\27).

A new eon is on its way – hear the hoofbeats! – as the prophets and apostles declare, and we are hurtling towards it. This will be the sovereign rulership of God, the Kingdom of God and Christ. Then Jesus returns to the Earth, and after that, as John tells us six times, there will come the 1,000 years (Rev. 20\2-7), and then "the day of God" (2 Peter 3\12) which is the New Earth and New Jerusalem (Rev. 21 and 22). Rejoice!

Concordance of how I've translated the 126 occurrences of αἰών

as "**eon**", "**age**" (60 times) or "**eons**", "**ages**" (40 times) (total: = 100 times): Mat. 6\13, 12\32, 13\22, 13\39, 13\40, 13\49, 21\19, 24\3, 28\20, Mark 3\29, 4\19, 10\30, 11\14, Luke 1\33, Luke 1\55, 16\8, 18\30,

20\34, 20\35, John 4\14, 6\51, 6\58, 8\35 (twice), 8\51, 8\52, 10\28, 11\26, 12\34, 13\8, 14\16, Rom. 1\25, 9\5, 11\36, 12\2, 14\26, 1 Cor. 1\20, 2\6 (twice), 2\7, 2\8, 3\18, 8\13, 10\11, 2 Cor. 4\4, 9\9, 11\31, Gal. 1\4, 1\5, Eph. 1\21, 2\2, 2\7, 3\9, 3\11, 3\21, 6\12, Phil. 4\20, Col. 1\26, 1 Tim. 1\17 (twice), 6\17, 2 Tim. 4\10, 4\18, Titus 2\12, Heb. 1\2, 1\8, 5\6, 6\5, 6\20, 7\17, 7\21, 7\24, 7\28, 9\26, 11\3, 13\8, 13\21, 1 Peter 1\23, 1\25, 4\11, 5\11, 2 Peter 2\17, 3\18, 1 John 2\17, 2 John 1\2, Jude 1\13, 1\25, Rev. 1\6, 1\18, 4\9, 4\10, 5\13, (twice in TR text at 5\14, but not in RP text so not included), 7\12, 10\6, 11\15, 14\11, 15\7, 19\3, 20\10, 22\5;

as **"of old"** (4 times): Luke 1\70, John 9\32, Acts 3\21, 15\18;

as **"duration"** (2 times): Eph. 3\21, Heb. 1\8;

as **"durations"** (20 times): Gal. 1\5, Phil. 4\20, 1 Tim. 1\17, 2 Tim. 4\18, Heb. 13\21, 1 Peter 4\11, 5\11, Rev. 1\6, 1\18, 4\9, 4\10, 5\13 (not in RP text at 5\14), 7\12, 10\6, 11\15, 14\11, 15\7, 19\3, 20\10, 22\5.

The 45 occurrences of "eonian life"
Dan. 12\2, Mat. 19\16, 19\29, 25\46, Mark 10\17, 10\30, Luke 10\25, Luke 18\18, 18\30, John 3\15, John 3\16, John 3\36, 4\14, 4\36, 5\24, 5\39, 6\27, 6\40, 6\47, 6\54, 6\68, 10\28, 12\25, 12\50, 17\2, 17\3, Acts 13\46, 13\48, Rom. 2\7, 5\21, 6\22, 6\23, Gal. 6\8, 1 Tim. 1\16, 6\12, 6\19, Titus 1\2, 3\7, 1 John 1\2, 2\25, 3\15, 5\11, 5\13, 5\20, Jude 21.

✶

ed23

Chapter 25

Twelve words mistranslated,
concealing the twelve tribes of Israel
~ destroying the narrative of God's promises
to His ancient people

♦

The great and manifold translation errors in the English Bibles derail every major doctrine of the prophets and apostles. Every major theme is disturbed: who God is; who Jesus is; creation; God's words to Eve; God's words to Cain; the flood; who the Holy Spirit is; what the holy spirit is; man's structural identity; man's eternal destinies; election; Christ's death and resurrection; his New Covenant; the identity in the New Testament of the house of Israel and God's faithfulness to them; the gospel promise of life on Earth in the coming eons; finance; God's promise to the patriarchs of the land; what Paul's work really was.

The great and manifold translation errors also derail the promises by God to the tribes of Israel and, therefore, make a denial of His faithfulness under the New Covenant with the house of Judah and the house of Israel.

This corruption of the word of God has been continued by no end of so-called scholars and commentators. I'll describe here the mistranslation of 12 words – 4 Hebrew words and 8 Greek words – which nullify the narrative of God's faithfulness to the twelve tribes of the sons of Israel.

1. קדוש (= *qadowsh*), Strong's Concordance number h6918; inferiorly translated as "holy" at, for example, Exodus 19\6
The Hebrew word קדוש (= *qadowsh*) is usually translated as "holy". However, "holy" is better translated and better understood as "set apart". Its first occurrence is in God speaking through Moses and saying to "the sons of Israel" at Exodus 19\5-6:

"Now, therefore, if you will surely obey My voice and keep My Covenant, then you will be a treasure acquired for My own possession above all nations, for all the Earth *is* Mine. ⁶ And you will be to Me a kingdom of priests, and <u>a nation set apart</u>. You shall speak these words to the sons of Israel."

The sons of Israel were to become a nation, "a kingdom", whom God would set apart from all other nations and people – "a nation set apart". They are set apart as the special treasure of God, set apart from all other nations and peoples.

The King James Bible, though, has the phrase "holy nation". But to describe Israel as a "holy nation" suggests a quality of righteousness. Was the prophets' perpetual testimony concerning Israel not otherwise? But to describe Israel as "a nation set apart", as it should be, suggests that God is making a distinction concerning this nation which He has not made with other nations. To say "a holy nation" does not exclude Israel from all other nations, but to say "a nation set apart" does exclude all other nations. And it should exclude all other nations because, as the previous verse says, Israel was to be God's "own possession above all nations" (Exodus 19\5). These words were addressed to "the sons of Israel".

Further, when קדוש (= *qadowsh*) is translated correctly, we see "you shall be קדוש, for I am קדוש" (Leviticus 11\44), which is "you shall be set apart, for I am set apart". Any individual or body of people called to God must be set apart to Him, and set apart also from other individuals and bodies of people. Throughout the word of God we see men and women called to be set apart to God.

To translate קדוש as "holy" concerning Israel destroys the fact of Israel being set apart to God in a way which no other nation is set apart. To translate קדוש correctly as "set apart" makes a distinction between Israel and other nations. God deals with the sons of Israel in a way that He deals with no other people or nation.

2. ἅγιος (= *hagios*), Strong's Concordance number g40; inferiorly translated as "holy" at, for example, 1 Peter 2\10
Nor is "holy" the best meaning of the Greek adjective ἅγιος (= *hagios*) or its associated verb ἁγιάζω (= *hagiazo*). These also are not best represented in the English translations as "holy". "Separateness", "dedication", being "set apart" and "appointed" represent better understandings of their meanings.

ἅγιος (= *hagios*) is the Greek equivalent of the Hebrew word קדוש (= *qadowsh*).

At 1 Corinthians 3\3-4 Paul calls his readers "flesh-natured". Yet in his opening at 1\2 and at 3\17 he addresses them as ἅγιος – so "holy", a word associated with righteous mindedness, hardly seems an appropriate meaning for ἅγιος. What he was addressing them as was "set apart people". Paul usually addressed his letters to "the set apart people" (Romans 1\7, 1 Corinthians 1\2, 2 Corinthians 1\1, Ephesians 1\1, Philippians 1\1, Colossians 1\2), creating a link going back to the words of Moses at Exodus 19\5-6.

At 1 Corinthians 7\34 we see ἅγιος as "set apart": "The unmarried woman cares for the things of the Lord, so that she might be set apart both in body and in spirit".

Similarly, the verb ἁγιάζω (= *hagiazo*) is much better as "to set apart". So at Matthew 6\9 and Luke 11\2: "may Your name be set apart". That is, set apart from all the names of false gods and idols. At 1 Peter 3\15 we see ἁγιάζω as "set apart" – "set apart the Lord God in your hearts".

At 1 Thessalonians 3\13, for the associated noun ἁγιωσύνη (= *hagiosunee*) it is not "holiness" but "separateness", Paul saying, "establish your hearts as blameless in separateness before God and our Father". That speaks to my heart! Believers are called to be separate from the world's religious systems and philosophies. And at Hebrews 12\14: "Pursue peace with everybody, and being set apart [or, separateness], without which nobody will see the Lord."

Now, when we come to 1 Peter 2\9, a magnificent internal harmony is established if we translate ἅγιος correctly. Peter's words are an obvious echo of the words of Moses at Exodus 19\5-6, Peter saying:

"You, though, are a chosen race, a royal priesthood, <u>a nation set apart</u>, a people destined to be a special possession in order that you might proclaim the virtues of Him Who has called you out of darkness into His wonderful light."

and from Exodus 19\5-6:
"... you will be a treasure acquired for My own possession above all nations, for all the Earth *is* Mine. [6] And you will be to Me a kingdom of priests, and a nation set apart."

Peter was writing to the dispersion of Israel (see 1 Peter 1\1). By Peter's words we know that the sons of Israel, the house of Jacob, have not been abandoned to become irrelevant in God's plan, as some allege, and we see that God is still seeing through His promises made to the sons of Israel. So we are not surprised when we see "the names of the twelve tribes of the sons of Israel" in the New Jerusalem (Revelation 21\12). Not only do we see God's faithfulness, but also a beautiful internal harmony between the words of Moses, the words of Peter, the addresses in Paul's letters, and John's vision of the New Jerusalem.

Translating these words and their associates as "holy" in every occurrence is one thing. But some translators do a worse thing. I'm looking at a contemporary version. It opens Ephesians with "to the saints who are in Ephesus". And so do many versions write the word "saints" instead of "set apart people". A "saint" is a fictional monk-dressed figure in a painting, with feet off the ground and a plate behind his head. When the translation is corrected with "set apart people", then the connection with Exodus 19\6 and 1 Peter 2\9 – and everything in between – is restored. So is God's faithfulness to His people Israel restored. "Saints" wrecks it.

3. ἐκκλησία (= *ekklesia*), Strong's Concordance number g1577;
mistranslated as "church" at, for example, Matthew 16\18
See Chapter 17. The word ἐκκλησία (= *ekklesia*) concerns those of whom Jesus said "I will build my Ekklesia" (Matthew 16\18). Hebrews speaks of the same "Ekklesia of firstborn" (Hebrews 12\23), those Hebrews, the twelve tribes, the seed of Isaac, reconciled in Christ. They are "the Ekklesia who are his body" (Ephesians 1\22-23).

This "Ekklesia of firstborn" is the "great assembly" (Psalm 22\25) spoken of by the prophet David:

²² I will declare Your name to my brothers;
I will praise You in the assembly.
²³ You who stand in awe of Yahweh, praise Him;
all you seed of Jacob, glorify Him,
and revere Him, all you seed of Israel ...
²⁵ My praise *will be* of You in the great Ekklesia [assembly].   ~ Psalm 22\22-25

We know that this is the Ekklesia, because it is cited in Hebrews:

¹² I will declare Your name to my brothers;
in the presence of the Ekklesia I will sing praise to You.   ~ Hebrews 2\12

This Ekklesia, then, is the "assembly" spoken of by David. David's word for "assembly" is קהל (= *qahal*), which, in general, means "called together". Ekklesia also means "called out". When I think of David vowing to praise God in "the great assembly" I think of all those Israelites in the Sanctuary of God, praising God with a mighty sound and wonderful instruments.

If Matthew had written his account in Hebrew rather than Greek he would have written not ἐκκλησία but קהל (= *qahal*), so having Jesus say, "I will build my Qahal" (Matthew 16\18). I have a New Testament translated into Hebrew and that is the word it uses, קהל (= *qahal*).

Paul's Ekklesia is that same assembly as David's "Ekklesia of firstborn" (Hebrews 12\23). Paul, in his travels, called together Ekklesia groups, Qahals, we might say, to Anglicize the word.

I (perhaps somewhat eccentrically) capitalise ἐκκλησία as "Ekklesia" in order to emphasise its importance. It is an authoritative body who will reign with God and Christ in New Jerusalem when the promise is fulfilled for the twelve tribes of Israel to become "above all nations of the Earth".

However, in translations such as the King James Bible, the Ekklesia of Jesus is described as something different. It has him saying of his Ekklesia, "I will build my church". And it does the same concerning all the Ekklesia groups, calling them "churches". The effect of this is that the mind switches from Israel and no longer thinks of David and the Israelites in the Sanctuary, but of European church buildings with mixed audiences. So the word "church" to any English speaker gives an image of a building, one of the buildings and gatherings of Christendom in their various forms. But none of those buildings and gatherings is a representation of the Ekklesia and remnant of Jesus Christ, being mixed with strange teachings, strange practices, mediators, idolatrous icons, post-Babylonian costumes, several or even many people among all this neither believing nor understanding.

The word "church" appeared in the early English versions – Wycliffe's translation of 1380 has it – and the citadels of Christianity had been in existence for hundreds of years before Wycliffe, so images of buildings and mixed gatherings are a long and deep heritage. (Wycliffe, though, must be excused, indeed heartily congratulated and rewarded for his opposition to the authorities, and for his heart for his people.)

The words "church" and "churches" do not suggest the Ekklesia Jesus prophesied, nor the קהל (= *qahal*) David prophesied, nor the Ekklesia Paul envisioned (Hebrews 2\12), who are the same "Ekklesia of firstborn", the seed of Isaac, the house of Jacob. They represent something quite different in the minds of men. To use them in the writings of the New Covenant is a damn in the river of life. It snips the golden thread of the wonderful narrative of the twelve tribes of Israel. It derails the whole story, and fabricates a new narrative.

The word "church" gives justification to the international religious system. But Jesus will build his *Ekklesia*, "the Ekklesia of firstborn", not "*the European and International church of anybody*".

The Ekklesia is the house of Jacob, the twelve tribes – and Jesus "will reign over the house of Jacob throughout the eons" (Luke 1\33). Jesus said to his disciples that when he has taken his seat of government they will sit down with him "on twelve thrones, ruling over the twelve tribes of Israel" (Matthew 19\28). Furthermore, in his vision John saw in new Jerusalem the names "of the twelve tribes of the sons of Israel" and "the twelve apostles of the Lamb" (Revelation 21\12-13).

4. שמים (= *shamayim*), Strong's Concordance number h8064; mistranslated as "heavens" at, for example, Deuteronomy 11\21

Deuteronomy 11\20-21 says this:

"And you shall write them on the doorposts of your house, and on your gates, [21] so that your days might be multiplied, and the days of your children, in the land that Yahweh swore to your fathers to give them, as the days of the <u>exalted *people*</u> on Earth."

The word represented in translation as "exalted *people*" is שמים (= *shamayim*). This is the usual word for "skies" or "heavens". Here it only has meaning if we understand it as "exalted *people*".

This is the continuation in the narrative of God's promise to Abraham that He would make him into "a mighty nation" (Genesis 12\2), and to Moses that the sons of Israel to be "a nation set apart" Exodus 19\5).

However ... where Deuteronomy 11\21 speaks of the sons of Israel in the phrase "the days of the exalted *people* on Earth", the King James Bible has the curious phrase "the days of the heavens upon the earth". This is meaningless, even comical, and it derails the narrative of the promotion of the sons of Israel being "high above all nations on the Earth". The days of the heavens upon the Earth ...? It's nonsense. How many readers make sense of that?

This word שמים only has meaning at Deuteronomy 11\21 if it's understood as "the exalted people" who are the sons of Israel.

Deuteronomy 7\6 says to the sons of Israel: "you *are* a people set apart to Yahweh your Elohim. *It is* you Yahweh your Elohim has chosen to be a special people for Himself, <u>above all peoples on the face of the Earth</u>."

Deuteronomy 7\14 says to the sons of Israel: "<u>You will be exalted above all people</u>."

Deuteronomy 10\15 says to the sons of Israel: "Yahweh delighted only in your fathers, to love them, and He chose their seed after them, you <u>above all peoples</u>, as *it is* this day."

Deuteronomy 11\21 says to Israel: "your days might be multiplied, and the days of your children, in the land that Yahweh swore to your fathers to give them, as the days of <u>the most exalted men on the Earth."

Deuteronomy 28\1 says to Israel: "Yahweh your Elohim will set you high above all nations of the Earth." (Yes, this was conditional, but God has made a new and better Covenant.)

At Deuteronomy 11\21 the phrase "the days of the exalted *people* on Earth" is looking ahead to that great day when Christ will take his throne, and with him will be the twelve tribes of the son of Israel ruling over the Earth as an authoritative body with God and Christ (Luke 1\33, Matthew 19\28, Revelation 21\12-14). [1]

5. and 6. ἐπουράνιος (= *epouranios*), Strong's Concordance number g2032;
mistranslated as "heavenly *places*" at, for example, Ephesians 1\3
and its associate word οὐρανός (= *ouranos*), Strong's Concordance number g3770;
mistranslated at, for example, Matthew 3\2

The Greek word ἐπουράνιος (= *epouranios*) is a derivative of οὐρανός (= *ouranos*), the frequent word for "sky", "the heaven".

At Matthew 18\35 Jesus uses ἐπουράνιος for his Father in the phrase "the Heavenly One" or "the Most Exalted One". At 1 Corinthians 15\48 and 15\49 Paul uses it for Jesus in the phrase "the Most Exalted One". And at 1 Corinthians 15\48, Ephesians 1\3, 2\6, 2\20 and Hebrews 8\5 Paul uses it also for "the most exalted men". And at Philippians 2\10 Paul uses it for "heavenly beings" which might denote angels or exalted men or both.

In Paul's letter to the Ephesians, some English translations have for ἐπουράνιος (= *epouranios*) the phrase "heavenly *places*", having Paul saying such strange things as God has blessed us "in heavenly *places* in Christ" (1\3). Some of these sources italicize the word "places", so admitting that they have added it. Others do not even do that. It gives the impression that Paul's audience will one day be in those "heavenly *places*", which is untrue: "they will inherit the land" (Matthew 5\5, Psalm 37).

"Heavenly *places*" does not make any sense. First, Jesus is coming to the Earth. Second, nobody is going into the heavens. Third, what is a "heavenly place in Christ"? It's nonsense.

The word they are translating in such a strange way is ἐπουράνιος (= *epouranios*). Apart from Otis Sellers' *Resultant Version*, which, similarly, has "the most elevated", only it seems, *Keys of the Kingdom Holy Bible* has wanted to translate this word properly.

The Greek word ἐπουράνιος does not mean "heavenly *places*". Nobody is going into the heavens. Many pray for the return of Jesus to the Earth from the heavens, yet at the same time they are taught that they are going into the heavens!

What Paul was saying at Ephesians 1\3 should read like this:

"Exalted *be* the God and Father of our Lord Jesus Christ, the one having exalted us with every spiritual exaltation *which is* among the most exalted in Christ."

The word for "most exalted" is ἐπουράνιος (= *epouranios*). At Ephesians 2\6 Paul says:

---

1. שמים (= *shamayim*) has a variety of meanings, as at Daniel 4\26, for example, where "Heaven rules" is put for "God rules", "Heaven" there being שמים. At Isaiah 1\2 the prophet exclaims, "Hear, you heavens [שמים] and you Earth!"; "heavens" and "Earth" are put, by the literary figure of metonymy, for those beings who inhabit them. At Deuteronomy 4\26 Yahweh says to Moses, "I call the heavens and Earth to witness against you". We have the same metonymic use of Heaven in English when we say "Heaven knows!", by which we mean "Only God knows". For further such metonymical uses in the word of God, see, for example, Genesis 2\4, Deuteronomy 11\21, 30\19, 31\28, 32\1, Isaiah 1\2, 13\13, 44\23, 65\17, Jeremiah 6\19, 14\22, 22\29, Micah 1\2, 6\2, Haggai 2\6, 2\21, Psalm 33\8, 50\4, 50\6, 89\29, Job 15\15, Daniel 4\26, Luke 15\18, John 3\12, Hebrews 12\25-26, 2 Peter 3\10, Revelation 12\12, 18\20, 21\1.

"He also raised *us* up together, and seated *us* together, among the most exalted in Christ Jesus, in order that in the coming eons He might show the transcendent wealth of His merciful goodwill in kindness towards us in Christ Jesus."

Again, the "most exalted" is ἐπουράνιος (= *epouranios*). And at Ephesians 2\20:

"[He raised Christ] from the dead and seated *him* at His right hand, among the most exalted, over and above all prime rulership, and forces of power, and might, and sovereignty, and every name having been named, not only in this eon, but in the one coming as well, and He subordinated all things under his feet, and appoints him as fountainhead over all these for the Ekklesia."

And what is all this but a restating of the promise to Israel to be positioned "above all nations on the Earth"? And that promise stand? Does the "purpose of God in relation to election remain"? Yes, so it is written at Romans 9\11: "in order that the purpose of God in relation to election might remain"

Paul speaks again of this preeminence, saying, "who are Israelites, whose are the adoption, and the preeminence, and the Covenants" (Romans 9\4). And Paul speaks to Timothy, "if we endure [with Christ], we will reign together with him" (2 Timothy 2\12).

And this echo Peter's phrases: "the chosen race, a royal priesthood, a nation set apart, a people destined to be a special possession" (1 Peter 2\9, echoing Exodus 19\5-6).

John speaks also of "a kingdom, priests to God", and saying, "you made them kings and priests to our God, and they will reign over the Earth" (Revelation 1\6, 5\9-10).

Indeed, the reconciliation with God of the remnant of Israel, of the Ekklesia of Christ (Matthew 16\18), "the Ekklesia of firstborn" (Hebrews 12\23), is certain through his sacrifice.

Paul speaks further of preeminence at 1 Corinthians 15\48, saying: "and as is the Most Exalted One, so also are the most exalted *men*". (That is, we now bear his image.) The "Most Exalted One", Jesus, is ἐπουράνιος (= *epouranios*) – and the "most exalted *men*" – is also ἐπουράνιος, in its nominative plural masculine form. However, the altered versions have such strange things as "and as *is* the heavenly, such are they also that *are* heavenly"! Whatever does that mean, to be "heavenly"? I do not know. Such alteration, first, removes the implication of the preeminence of the seed of Isaac and, second, sticks men in outer space, a long way from where Christ will be when he returns to Earth. And, by that, the promise to the seed of Isaac is annulled.

Paul's Ephesian readers will one day take their places among "the most exalted in Christ", who are "the Ekklesia of firstborn", and David's "Qahal", who are the "seed of Jacob", the "seed of Israel" (Psalm 22\23).

The Greek word ἐπουράνιος (= *epouranios*) is a derivative of οὐρανός (= *ouranos*), the Greek equivalent of שמים (= *shamayim*). Jesus used this word οὐρανός (= *ouranos*) as a substantive (adjective acting as noun) for the Father in the phrase "the Heavenly One", which is an adjunct to "the Father", making the full phrase "your Father, the Heavenly One", or "your Father, the Most Exalted One" (Matthew 6\14, 6\26, 6\32). At Luke 15\18 οὐρανός (= *ouranos*) is put for God in the clause "I have sinned against the Exalted One". At Revelation 12\12 we read "Rejoice on account of this, *you* heavens and you who tabernacle among them. Woe to those who inhabit the Earth and the sea!" So here we have it spelled out for us that "heavens" is put for those who inhabit them. At Colossians 1\23 οὐρανός is rendered in *Keys of the Kingdom Holy Bible* as "Supreme Monarch" and as "supreme monarch" at Acts 2\5.

At John 3\13 the altered versions have Jesus speak of himself as "the Son of man which is in heaven". And, according to these versions, there he was standing in Jerusalem saying he was "in heaven"! Their translation is foolish. That should be "the Son of man, who is in the Heavenly One", or "in the Exalted One". Then all the mysticism is buried in the sea, where it should be.

So, οὐρανός is "Heavenly One" or "Exalted One".

32 times there occurs the phrase "the Kingdom of the Exalted". This, once again, reminds us of the continuing narrative of the exaltation of the sons of Israel. However, this phrase is usually translated as "the kingdom of heaven" (Matthew 3\2 et cetera), putting into the mind some future mystical kingdom in that unknown place in the sky where God is now in hiding until the end of the 1,000 years. The word the King James Bible and others translate as "heaven" is, once again, οὐρανός (= *ouranos*). However, we who know the word of God understand that the future life is on Earth. Nobody is going into the heavens. Christ is coming to Earth. Then God Himself will come to Earth to be in the New Jerusalem. Instead of "the kingdom of the heavens", *Keys of the Kingdom Holy Bible* has "the Kingdom of the Exalted", for this is exactly what the coming kingdom is about: the rulership of the twelve tribes of Israel with God and the Lord Jesus.

ἐπουράνιος (= *epouranios*) also occurs at Ephesians 3\10 and 6\12 concerning the enemies of God, once for all the demonstrating what a hopeless translation "heavenly *places*" ever was!

"in order that now the manifold wisdom of God might be made known, through the Ekklesia, to the prime rulers and the forces of power among the most eminent."   ~ Ephesians 3\10

and:

"because the combat for us is not against blood and flesh, but against the prime rulers, against the forces of power, against the world rulers of this age of darkness, against the spirits of evil among the most eminent."   ~ Ephesians 6\12

These occurrences of ἐπουράνιος (= *epouranios*) are about "the most eminent" among earthly kings and rulers. The phrase "among the most eminent" is the exactly same phrase I have translated as "among the most exalted" at Ephesians 1\3, 2\6. (I used "eminent" the second time to distinguish from "exalted" the first time.) Imagine if *epouranios* really meant "heavenly places" – the earthly kings and rulers in heavenly places.

7. Ἰουδαῖος (= *Ioudaios*), Strong's Concordance number g2453; mistranslated as "Jew" at, for example, Matthew 3\2

Ἰουδαῖος (= *Ioudaios*) [1] occurs 195 times. It first occurs at Matthew 2\2, describing Jesus as "King of the Judahites".

It is the word most frequently translated as "Jew" and "Jews". "Jew" is slang for a member of the tribe of Judah, a Judahite. *Thayer's Greek-English Lexicon* gives this as the adjective "Jewish".

Jesus, "King of the Judahites", was born in Judah, the land of the house of Judah. Matthew 2\6 speaks of "Bethlehem of Judah", citing Micah. Jesus is "the lion of the tribe of Judah" (Revelation 5\5). Jesus said, "salvation is out of the Judahites" (John 4\22).

Judaea, of the Judahites, had become a separate nation from Israel in the north and they had even been at war with each other, and had been in enmity (Ephesians 2\14-16). That is why the New Covenant declared by the prophet Jeremiah would be "with the house of Israel and with the house of Judah" (Jeremiah 31\31, Hebrews 8\8). This is why the prophet Hosea spoke concerning the two houses: "Then the sons of Judah and the sons of Israel will be gathered together, and they will appoint over themselves one head" (Hosea 1\11, John 10\16, 2 Thessalonians 2\1).

Those said to be waiting for redemption in Israel, Simeon (Luke 2\25), Zacharias (Luke 1\5), Joseph of Arimathea (Luke 23\50), were Judahites. The apostles were Judahites. Anna (an exception as an Asherite, from a few returnees from the captivity) "spoke about Him to all those waiting for redemption in Jerusalem" (Luke 2\36-38). The word Judahite included the two tribes who had returned from exile, Judah and Benjamin. We know this because Paul said he was of

---

1. Find on page 842 of Wigram's Greek-English Concordance. Wigram wrongly has Mark 1\5 in his list under 2453. He also has it – correctly – under 2448-49, where it should be. He put it under both numbers.

the stock of Benjamin, and he also said, "I am in fact a Judahite man" (Acts 22\3). He said, "We, Judahites by nature", indicating birth (Galatians 2\15). He describes himself, being an Israelite, as, "out of the people of Israel; of the tribe of Benjamin; a Hebrew out of the Hebrews" (Philippians 3\5).

Judaea, the land of the Judahites, was at that time occupied also by Canaanites and Edomites. The Herod dynasty were Edomites. They took advantage of the captivity of Judah and moved into Judaea. Esau, who is also Edom (Genesis 25\30, 36\1), married Canaanite women, against the instructions of his father. Jesus contended with hostile serpents and wolves, so he said that the scribes and Pharisees had stolen the seat of Moses (Matthew 23\1), and that those who persecuted the prophets were guilty of "all righteous blood poured out on the Earth, from the blood of the righteous Abel to the blood of Zechariah" (Matthew 23\34-36), reckoned, therefore, as Canaanites, those going back to the murder of Abel. Jesus warned his "sheep" (the house of Jacob) of "wolves" who would deliver the sheep "into the hands of the Sanhedrins, and they will scourge you in the synagogues" (Matthew 10\16-17). They brought in their own religion, "the tradition of the elders" (Matthew 15\2). Paul spoke of his "previous manner of life in the religion of the Judahites, how with surpassing zeal I was persecuting the Ekklesia of God ... and I was advancing in the religion of the Judahites" (Galatians 1\13-14). He spoke of "pseudo brothers" (Galatians 2\4), and warns of being judaized (Galatians 2\14). Jesus also warns against "those who declare themselves to be Judahites, and are not, but are a synagogue of the enemy" and "they lie" and are accusers and persecutors (Revelation 2\9-10, 3\9). These are obviously a different body from "the sheep". Jesus spoke of those who "do not believe because you are not my sheep" (John 10\26). If "not my sheep", then it is not that they were not his sheep because they did not believe, but that they were not even his sheep in the first place and that is why they did not believe, not being of the house of Jacob, בית יעקב (= *bayith Yakob*).

Yet all these were known as Judaeans, or Judahites, or "Jews".

So hardened did Paul find those of Judah that he turned from them to another body of people, the dispersion of the house of Israel.

"Jew" is used these days to signify anybody of Israel. People speak of "the Jewish nation". But it is not so in the word of God. People say things like "when the Jews were in Egypt", but it is not so in the word of God. It says "sons of Israel" or "children of Israel". The New Covenant distinguishes between the house of Israel and the house of Judah (Jeremiah 31\1, Hosea 1\11, Hebrews 8\8).

The Greek word 'Ιουδαῖος (= *Ioudaios*) is used by Paul 25 times:

Romans 1\16: both to the Judahite first, then to the Greek;
Romans 2\9: both of the Judahite first, and of the Greek;
Romans 2\10: both for the Judahite first, and for the Greek;
Romans 2\17: you who are called a Judahite, and you rely on the law;
Romans 2\28: he is not a Judahite who is one in outward appearance;
Romans 2\29: he is a Judahite who is one inwardly;
Romans 3\1: What, then, is the advantage of the Judahite;
Romans 3\9: we have previously convicted both Judahites and Greeks;
Romans 3\29: Or is He the God only of Judahites and not of the nations as well;
Romans 9\24: ourselves also whom He called, not only from among the Judahites;
Romans 10\12: there is no difference between Judahite and Greek;
1 Corinthians 1\22: Judahites ask for a sign and Greeks search for wisdom;
1 Corinthians 1\23: to Judahites a stumbling block, and to Greeks foolishness;
1 Corinthians 1\24: but to those designated, both Judahites and Greeks;
1 Corinthians 9\20: to the Judahites I became as a Judahite, so that I might gain the Judahites;
1 Corinthians 10\32: without offence, neither to the Judahites nor Greeks;
1 Corinthians 12\13: we are all baptized into one body, whether Judahites or Greeks;

2 Corinthians 11\24: I received forty stripes minus one from Judahites;
Galatians 2\13: "the rest of the Judahites also played the hypocrite;
Galatians 2\14: If you, being a Judahite, live in the custom of the nations, and not as Judahites;
Galatians 2\15: We, Judahites by nature;
Galatians 3\28: there is neither Judahite nor Greek;
Colossians 3\11: there is neither Greek nor Judahite;
1 Thessalonians 2\14: you also suffered similar things from your own countrymen, just as they also do from the Judahites.

In English versions Ἰουδαῖος is generally translated as "Jew". It is closer and correct as "Judahite", in order to soundly signify the house of Judah. Ἰουδαῖος (= *Ioudaios*) represents both Judah and Benjamin (and Levites). It is not a synecdoche for all 12 tribes of Israel. There are other tribes, and to signify those are the other tribes Paul uses two other word, the word ἔθνος (= *ethnos*), and Ἕλλην (= *Hellēn*), as we will come to see.

Unfortunately, because of two errors, the word "Jew" in the altered versions is seen as signifying all twelve tribes of Israel. First, because of how it is used now; second, because of the fake phrase "Jew and Gentile" in the letters of Paul in the altered versions. There is no phrase "Jew and Gentile" in the word of God. It does not occur. The deception, the false translation "Jew and Gentile", robs all twelve tribes of the promises of God. It denies His faithfulness expressed constantly through the prophets and apostles and through Jesus. It wrongly counts all twelve tribes as being "Jews", that is, Ἰουδαῖος (= *Ioudaios*). Jesus and his disciples were in Judah, and Jesus said "salvation is out of the Judahites" (John 4\22). This links with Paul's saying, "to the Judahite first" (Romans 1\16, 2\9, 2\10). Then there were the northern tribes of the house of Israel.

There was a settlement of Judahites (Judah and Benjamin) in Rome. Paul wrote to them as "called to be set apart people" (Romans 1\7). The phrase "Covenant breakers" (Romans 1\31) prohibits his letter from being addressed to non-Israelites. (In Romans, Paul makes addresses first to the Judahites, then to the nations who are the dispersion of Israel.) Paul says "you are called a Judahite" (Romans 2\17). He speaks of them having the scrolls, the law, circumcision (Romans 2\17-19). He asks, rhetorically, "What, then, is the advantage of the Judahite? Or what is the profit of circumcision?" He is talking to "the house of Judah". And he answers "Much from every standpoint, primarily because they were entrusted with the words of God" (Romans 3\1-2). Those in the land of Judah heard first.

The other tribes, who were scattered, were considered as foreigners, nations, the dispersion, sojourners, exiles, strangers, uncircumcision. The Judahites, therefore, had, Paul said, "the advantage ... from every standpoint". The dispersion, though, were "without Christ, having been made alien from the citizenship of Israel, strangers from the Covenants of promise" (Ephesians 2\12). Because of the enmity between Judah and Israel, who had become two separate nations, there was what Paul describes as "the middle wall of partition" (Ephesians 2\14). The scattered northern tribes of Israel were also known as "the uncircumcision" and "the dispersion" (John 7\35, 1 Peter 1\1), who had been "in time past the nations in flesh", and they were "known as uncircumcision by those known as the circumcision in flesh made by hands" (Ephesians 2\11). Judah considered themselves superior. But now those "strangers" in Ephesus had become, through Christ, "no longer strangers and sojourners, but fellow citizens of the set apart people, and the household members of God, built on the foundation of the apostles and prophets, Jesus Christ himself being the foundation cornerstone" (Ephesians 2\19-20) – wholly Israelitish language. They were from the OTHER TRIBES *NOT* NAMED AS "JUDAHITES".

In conclusion, it is not so much that the translation of Ἰουδαῖος as "Jew" is directly wrong, it being slang for a member of the tribe of Judah, a Judahite, but it's the standard comprehension of "Jew" as representing all twelve tribes which is wrong. "Jew" is not a synecdoche for all twelve tribes. Towards that understanding it is much better translated as "Judahite". That is also close to a transliteration, as it represents the "d" and is three syllables, which the slang word "Jew" fails to do.

8. and 9. ἔθνος (= *ethnos*), Strong's Concordance number g1484; mistranslated as "Gentile" at, for example, Romans 9\24:
and גוי (= *goy*), Strong's Concordance number h1471; mistranslated as "Gentile"
The King James Bible correctly and fairly translates גוי (= *goy*) as "nation" 374 times and as "people" 11 times. However, 30 times it translates it as "Gentiles", and 143 times as "heathen". Those were naughty impositions. The word "nations" is free of bias and is not a value judgement, as is "people". But the words "Gentiles" and "heathen" are loaded with bias and value judgement. How did the translators know that in certain passages in, say, Isaiah, by גוי (= *goy*) the prophet did not mean the scattered tribes of the house of Israel?

When the apostle Paul cited the prophet Isaiah, saying, "There will emerge the root of Jesse and the one raised up to rule the nations; nations will put their trust in him" (Romans 15\12), the entire business of his letter has concerned Israel and Judah. Paul cited that from Isaiah 11\10. The King James Bible translators in that passage wrote "to it shall the Gentiles seek" (strangled grammar). That, then, by the King James reading, insists that Isaiah signified non-Israelites. Isaiah meant Israelites. It is only appropriate to remove the bias and translate the word as "nations", then you cannot be wrong.

Similarly, Jesus cited Isaiah 42\1-4, concluding, "nations will set their hope in his name" (Matthew 12\21). In both passages the King James Bible has "Gentiles". But Jesus said he had been sent for "the lost sheep of the house of Israel" (Matthew 15\ 24). It might be argued (by somebody who cannot bear to hear the King James Bible criticised) that the dispersed Israelites, having become "not My people" (Hosea 1\10), no longer under Covenant, were known as "nations" so it makes no difference. But it *does* make a difference: they had been "not My people", but the God of Abraham, Isaac and Jacob would make a new and better Covenant with them. They were Israelites, not "Gentiles". They were no longer "not My people", but were "Sons of the living God" (Romans 9\25-26, 1 Peter 2\10). "Gentiles" is just wrong.

From the Greek word ἔθνος (= *ethnos*) come our words "ethnic", "ethnicity", and "ethnically", members of a certain race type. This should be reflected in the translation and understanding of some occurrences of ἔθνος (= *ethnos*) in the New Testament writings – sometimes it refers to races of non-Israelites, and sometimes to refer to the dispersion of the house of Israel.

The first occurrence of ἔθνος (= *ethnos*) is at Matthew 4\15: "Land of Zebulon, and land of Naphtali, road of the sea, across the Jordan, Galilee of the <u>nations</u> ..." (citation from Isaiah 9\1-2). The word "nations" in that is ἔθνος. Zebulon and Naphtali are of the twelve tribes of Israel (Revelation 7\6-8), yet they are described as ἔθνος, "nations". This first occurrence shows us that the exiled northern tribes, that is, the house of Israel, is sometimes referred to as "nations". But the King James Bible has "Gentiles", implying non-Israelites, but that is not correct because Zebulon and Naphtali are Israelite tribes. "Gentiles" is an *interpretation*, not a *translation*. As an interpretation it is harmful to the internal harmony of the prophets and apostles. "Gentiles" is a very bad translation and just wrong.

At Romans 9\24 Paul speaks of "ourselves also whom He called, not only from among Judahites, but also from among the nations". Here "nations" is set in apposition to the tribe of the Judahites. So we easily deduce that "the nations" are the other Israelite tribes, the dispersion of the house of Israel. For Paul is talking about those "whom He called", and the called people are the set apart people, the sons of Israel. Paul then cites the prophet Hosea to explain that those "nations" at 9\24 are those who had become "not My people" but are now "called sons of the living God" (Romans 9\25-26). And Paul continues, "Isaiah cries out over Israel"

(Romans 9\27). So "the nations" at 9\24 is all about Israel. Peter, addressing the dispersion (1 Peter 1\1), also speaks of them as having been "not a people, but now they are people of God" (1 Peter 2\10, citing Hosea 1\9-10, 2\23). These were Israelites.

At Romans 11\25-27, Paul says: "... blindness in part has happened to Israel until the fullness of the nations has come in, and so all Israel will be saved, as it has been written: 'The Deliverer will come out of Zion, and he will turn away ungodliness from Jacob. And this will be the Covenant from Me to them' ..." If the fullness of "the nations" (ἔθνος) means that as a consequence "all Israel will be saved", and ungodliness "will be turned from Jacob", and this is God's "Covenant", then these "nations" are Israelites. Indeed, Paul was addressing "the nations": "For I say to you, to the nations – since I am indeed an apostle of the nations ... if somehow I might perhaps provoke to jealousy my flesh, and I might save some from among them" (Romans 11\13-14). The house of Judah would be jealous of the house of Israel receiving the message of redemption. Paul refers to this at 1 Thessalonians 2\16, the Judahites "preventing us from speaking to the nations so that they might be saved". In saying "my flesh" at Romans 11\14, Paul is referring to Benjamin and Judah (Paul was from Benjamin: Romans 11\1), known collectively as Judahites, those he specifically addresses at 2\17 – 3\9 and following. The entirety of Romans chapter 11 discusses the breaking apart and the reconciliation of Judah and Israel, of old time hostile to one another, and still in Paul's time hostility remained, and with bitter pride and jealousy from the Judahites.

Therefore "all Israel" (Romans 11\26) means all twelve tribes, and "the nations", the ἔθνος at Romans 11\25, means the dispersion of the house of Israel. These are the dispersion of whom Paul says "God is able to graft them in again" (Romans 11\23). That can also be translated "graft them back in". Commentators usually ignore that adverb "again" at the end of that sentence. It shows that Paul is speaking of Israelites who once had been under Covenant.

And among all this Paul says, "the good pleasure of my own heart and my prayer to God for Israel is for salvation" (Romans 10\1). He is speaking about the house of Israel.

In fact, every occurrence of ἔθνος (= *ethnos*) in Romans is a reference to the house of Israel. So is every occurrence of it in all the letters of Paul and Peter and John a reference to the dispersion.

We have established that Paul was addressing the set apart people in Ephesians, and establishing them as preeminent, high above all nations of the Earth, in his saying that they were seated "among the most exalted in Christ Jesus" (Ephesians 1\3, 1\20, 2\6). Then Paul says to them, "remember that you, in time past the nations in flesh, were those known as uncircumcision" (Ephesians 2\11). Here "the nations" are those ἔθνος (= *ethnos*) of the scattered tribes of Israel, as in Paul's letter to the Romans. They had been, because of the divine divorce pronounced by Jeremiah and Hosea, "alienated from the citizenship of Israel, and strangers from the Covenants of promise" (Ephesians 2\12). They were those who had once been "far-off" but are now "made near" (Ephesians 2\13). Through Christ the hostility between Judah and Israel was dealt with, for Christ had "broken down the middle wall of partition, having annulled by his flesh the enmity ... so that he might in himself transform the two into one new man, making peace, and so that he might reconcile both to God in one body ... peace ... to those far-off and to those near" (Ephesians 2\14-17;), that is, to Israel and Judah. Now "both" – Israel and Judah – "have access to the Father", so that the Ephesians were "no longer strangers and sojourners, but fellow citizens of the set apart people, and the household members of God, built on the foundation of the apostles and prophets, Jesus Christ himself being the foundation cornerstone, in whom every building being harmoniously framed together is growing into a dedicated sanctuary in the Lord, in whom you also are being built together into a residence of God" (Ephesians 2\18-21). Such building imagery is referring to "the city of the living God, the heavenly Jerusalem" (Hebrews 12\22), for, he says, "He has prepared a city for them" (Hebrews

11\16). All Israelitish language. All about the tribes of the sons of Israel. The "nations" in Ephesians 2\11 represent the scattered house of Israel.

The address in Ephesians "to those far-off and to those near" was spoken by Peter to Israelites (Acts 2\39). It was spoken by Isaiah to Israelites (Isaiah 59\17). It was spoken by Daniel to Israelites (Daniel 9\7). It concerns the houses of Judah and Israel.

The scattered tribes of the house of Israel, then, were known as "uncircumcision". Peter calls them "strangers and exiles" (1 Peter 2\11). They were also known as "the nations", ἔθνος (= *ethnos*) (Ephesians 2\11).

Acts 10\36 concerns the word of God to "the sons of Israel", and Luke says "the gift of the divine spirit was poured out on the nations as well" (Acts 10\45), so these "nations" also are "sons of Israel". See also Acts 11\1, 11\18.

In Antioch the apostles "went into the synagogue on the day of the Sabbaths" and, after the reading of the law and the prophets, Paul addressed them, "Men, Israelites, and those revering God, listen. The God of this people chose our fathers" (Acts 13\14-17), and then "Men, brothers, sons of the race of Abraham" (Acts 13\26). Then, "when the Judahites had departed out of the synagogue, the nations were pleading that the declarations might be spoken to them on the intervening Sabbath" (Acts 13\42). The nations, then, were brothers, Israelites, sons of the race and seed of Abraham. On the following Sabbath the Judahites "on seeing the crowds, were filled with envy" and Paul and Barnabas said "we turn to the nations. For the Lord has commanded this to us: 'I have appointed you as a light to the nations' " (Acts 13\44-47). Paul's work, then, as a light to the nations, was to the scattered tribes of the house of Israel. It can be presumed this will extend to the whole world in the coming eon (Matthew 28\19-20).

At Acts 18\4 Luke says that Paul "reasoned in the synagogue Sabbath by Sabbath, and he was persuading both Judahites and Greeks", those "Greeks", then, being Israelites, in synagogues on Sabbaths, the nations. Again at Acts 18\6, Paul said, "From now on, I will go to the nations." This was after the Judahites opposed him. At Acts 28\28, having just cited Isaiah 6\9-10, Paul said, "Let it be known to you, then, that the salvation-bringing message of God has been authorised to the nations, and they will hear." These nations we now know as the dispersion, the scattered tribes of the house of Israel. Not "the Gentiles", which indicates non-Israelite; which is how commentators mistakenly take it. Indeed, as Paul says, "Or is He God only of Judahites, and not of the nations as well? Yes, of the nations as well ... Do we, then, make the law of no effect through faith? May it not be! Rather, we establish the law" (Romans 3\29-31). Establishing the law to nations! Therefore, dispersed Israelites who had become "not My people" at one time, but the believing remnant will now be reconciled through Christ and are "My people". Peter speaks of this, saying, "you ... who at one time *were* not a people, but now people of God" (1 Peter 2\9-10, citing Hosea 1\9-10, 2\23).

At Romans 11\11, Paul says, "through their offence, salvation has come to the nations in order to provoke them to jealousy. Now if their offence is the wealth of the world, and their decline is the wealth of the nations, how much more is their fullness" – the nations here being the dispersion. That provoking "to jealousy" describes the house of Israel's reconciliation provoking the jealousy of Judah, the house of Judah having rejected Christ and assassinated the prince of glory.

Paul calls himself "an agent of Christ Jesus for the nations", discharging like a priest the gospel of God, in order that the offering up of the nations might be accepted, it being set apart in the spirit of separateness" (Romans 15\16). All this "Christ has operated through myself for obedience of the nations, by word and deed, and the power of signs and wonders" (Romans 15\17-19). All about the Israelites.

At 1 Corinthians 12\2 Paul says, "You know how when you were the nations." This Ekklesia in Corinth, then, *had been* "the nations", but were not so now. Therefore being "nations" was not a permanent status in the way that ethnicity is. The King James Bible's "Gentiles", having the meaning of non-Israelite, is inappropriate. The Corinthians were not non-Israelites. The Corinthian Ekklesia had been meeting in a synagogue, as Luke says that Paul "reasoned in the synagogue Sabbath by Sabbath" (Acts 18\4). Similarly, Paul said to the Ephesians "you, in time past the nations in flesh" (Ephesians 2\11). ἔθνος (= *ethnos*), then, was a spiritual condition determined by the prophet Hosea indicating a rejected people of God, but now, through Christ, reconciled.

In the King James Bible and the other altered versions they translate ἔθνος as, variously, "heathen", "nations", "people" (Acts 8\9, Romans 10\19) and "Gentiles". The word "heathen" is just the opinion of translators, not a translation of the Greek word, and is disregarded. Even if true, it is an interpretation. And "Gentiles" is just wrong.

The word "Gentiles" comes from the Latin word *gentilis* which is from *gens* meaning "a clan, a number of families connected by common descent, and the use of the same gentile name" (*Cassell's Latin Dictionary*, 1990 edition). In general English usage and, indeed, by most Bible readers, "Gentiles" is considered to mean non-Israelite (or, as they would probably say ignorantly and inaccurately, "non-Jewish"). But we have seen from Matthew 4\15, Romans 11\13, 11\25 and Ephesians 2\11 that the ἔθνος – "nations" – are in these occurrences anything but non-Israelite; they represent the dispersion, the scattered tribes of the house of Israel.

At Romans 1\13 Paul says "in order that I might have some fruit among you also, in the same way as among the remaining nations". Those "nations" represent the dispersion of the tribes of Israel.

Therefore, every occurrence of ἔθνος must be discerned internally – not by tradition, nor by the word "Gentiles". The word "Gentiles", because it is understood as non-Israelite, is error and creates destruction. It makes the promises and faithfulness of God to His people Israel of no effect – but to that destructive notion Paul says, "It is not as though the oracle of God has taken no effect" (Romans 9\6, Galatians 3\17). The word "Gentiles" creates the delusion of a false gospel implying that Paul went off to non-Israelites and that, therefore, God had forgotten the dispersion of the house of Israel.

10. Ἕλλην (= *Hellēn*), Strong's Concordance number g1672; mistranslated as "Gentile" at, for example, John 7\35

Ἕλλην (= *Hellēn*) occurs 27 times. It means "Greek". From it is derived the English adjective Hellenistic, meaning Grecian, of Greek nature. Being a proper noun, with an English heritage to boot, there is hardly a word in the entirety of the word of God which could be easier to translate. In all a translator's work few words could give him less trouble than translating this word. However, that is not the story in the altered versions.

Here follows all the occurrences of Ἕλλην (= *Hellēn*), with comments. The first occurrence is the most instructive and provides a key for understanding every occurrence.

John 7\35: "the Judahites said among themselves, 'Where is he going to go that we will not find him? Is he about to go to the dispersion of the Greeks and then teach the Greeks?' "
Comment: "the dispersion of the Greeks". In its first occurrence we see who these Greeks were: the dispersion of the house of Israel. The King James Bible has "the dispersed among the Gentiles, and teach the Gentiles", adding "among", and twice changing "Greeks" to "Gentiles". It is illegal to alter the Scriptures of God. The enemies of Jesus were murmuring and wondering if he was going to go and make proclamation to the dispersion. The "dispersion of the Greeks" were certainly Israelites. This phrase "the dispersion of the Greeks" is the key to understanding Paul's work to the Greeks. But if proper nouns such as Ἕλλην (= *Hellēn*) are the easiest was to translate, the King James Bible translators were unable to translate it here, incompetent,, or, perhaps, they were unwilling and not able to let themselves write "Greeks". Either way, they

changed it to "Gentiles", destroying the foundation of understanding "the dispersion of the Greeks".

John 12\20: "And there were some Greeks among those going up to worship at the festival."
Comment: This festival was the Passover (John 12\1). Who were these Greeks who were coming to worship, then, but "the dispersion of the Greeks"? Israelites.

Acts 14\1: "And in Iconium it came to fall on them to enter together into the synagogue of the Judahites, and to speak in such a way for a large number of Judahites and Greeks to believe."
Comment: Who were these Greeks who were assembling in a synagogue with members of the tribe of Judah but "the dispersion of the Greeks", fellow Israelites? All this is disrupted by the false assumption that "Jews" – instead of "Judahites" – is a synecdoche for all Israelites, rather than being of the tribe of Judah.

Acts 16\1-3 "[Paul] arrived in Derbe and Lystra, and there was a certain disciple there, Timothy by name, son of a certain Judahite woman, a believer, and of a Greek father, ² who was of good reputation among the brothers ... ³ Paul wanted him to go with him, and he took *him and* had him circumcised on account of the Judahites who were in those places, for they all knew that his father was a Greek."
Comment: The teachers of the word of tradition would distinguish between the Judahite mother and the Greek father as being "Jewish" (in their minds wrongly as any Israelite) and "Gentile", but this is error. The distinction between Judahite and Greek, in the passages already cited, is a distinction between Judahite and "the dispersion of the Greeks". Timothy's mother was from the tribe of Judah and his father was from the dispersion of the house of Israel.

How do we know that Timothy's Greek father was an Israelite?

First, his father was "of good reputation among the brothers", so he was a "brother" Israelite.

Second, he was circumcised, so he was a brother Israelite.

Third, the references to "Greeks" in Acts concern synagogues and the law and the Sabbath and the scrolls and circumcision. They were Israelites.

Fourth, Deuteronomy 7\3-6 forbids the sons of Israel to marry outside their race. Any child produced by an illegal mixed-race marriage (miscegenation) was called ממזר, a *mamzer* (Deuteronomy 23\2). A *mamzer*, "one of non-legal birth" – the King James Bible has "bastard" (oh dear) – was not allowed to enter the assembly of Yahweh, nor were his descendants, for 10 generations. I do not think Timothy was a *mamzer*! If Timothy was a *mamzer*, why was he allowed among the assembly and of good reputation? And why was he allowed to be circumcised? Why even *was* he circumcised? The prophet Ezekiel rebuked Israel for allowing foreigners into the Sanctuary: "House of Israel, enough of all your abominations, ⁷ in that you have brought in sons of foreigners, uncircumcised in heart, and uncircumcised in flesh, to be in My Sanctuary, to profane it, My House ... Adonai Yahweh says this: 'No foreigner, uncircumcised in heart, nor uncircumcised in flesh, shall have entrance into My Sanctuary, nor any son of a foreigner among the sons of Israel' " (Ezekiel 6-9).

Acts 17\4: "some from among them were convinced, and threw in their lot with Paul and Silas, as well as a large number of people of the worshipping Greeks."
Comment: This is preceded by "they came to Thessalonica where there was a synagogue of the Judahites. And in keeping with what was customary with Paul, he went in among them, and for three Sabbaths he reasoned with them from the scrolls" (Acts 17\1-2). So, in the synagogue of Thessalonica there were "scrolls" and "worshipping Greeks". Once again, obviously Israelites of "the dispersion of the Greeks". The Thessalonican Ekklesia were Israelites.

Acts 18\4: "[Paul] reasoned in the synagogue Sabbath by Sabbath, and he was persuading Judahites and Greeks."
Comment: This was in Corinth. So the Corinthians to whom Paul wrote his letters were Israelites, assembling together in a synagogue, members of the house of Judah and the house of Israel. Paul's letter to the Corinthians is addressed to "the Ekklesia group of God which is in Corinth, set apart in Christ Jesus, designated as set apart people" (1 Corinthians 1\2, Exodus 19\5-6). Israelites.

Acts 18\17: "Then all the Greeks seized Sosthenes, the president of the synagogue ..."
Comment: Again, the point is there were Greeks in the synagogue, so they were Israelites.

Acts 19\10: "And this happened over two years, so that all the inhabitants of Asia heard the oracle of the Lord Jesus, both Judahites and Greeks."
Comment: So those in Paul's journeys, the recipients of his letters, were members of the tribe of Judah and members of the dispersion of the Greeks, who were from the dispersion house of Israel.

Acts 19\17: "And this became known to all, both Judahites and Greeks living in Ephesus, and fear came over them all, and the name of the Lord Jesus was magnified."
Comment: See also Acts 18\19: "And [Paul] came into Ephesus and left them there, but he himself went into the synagogue and conversed with the Judahites." Those believers in Ephesus to whom Paul sent his letter assembled in a synagogue and were members of the house of Judah and of the dispersion of the Greeks. This is why his letter is addressed to "the set apart people who are in Ephesus" (Ephesians 1\1), an Israelite audience. Disruption of the promises of God to the tribes of Israel seeps in when the altered versions refer to "Jews and Gentiles" and "saints". The house of Judah and the house of Israel were meeting together in a synagogue in Ephesus, designated by Paul as "set apart people". No wonder, then, that Paul is able to say that Christ had "broken down the middle wall of partition" (Ephesians 2\14).

Acts 20\21: "[in Ephesus Paul was] testifying both to Judahites and Greeks submission towards God, and faith towards our Lord Jesus."
Comment: Paul's testifying here was to "the leaders of the Ekklesia" of Ephesus (Acts 20\17). We understand now the Judahites and Greeks among the Ephesian Ekklesia were Israelites.

Acts 21\28: "[the Judahites were] calling out, 'Men, Israelites, help! This is a man who teaches everyone everywhere against the people and the law and this place and, in addition, he brought Greeks into the Temple, and he has defiled this dedicated place.' "
Comment: This is the jealousy of Judah against the house of Israel. Paul brought Greeks into the Temple, they were saying. Well then, those Greeks were Israelites, "the dispersion of the Greeks".

Romans 1\14: "I am debtor both to Greeks and to foreigners, both to the wise and to the unwise."
Comment: Those Greeks in Acts, all Israelites. The "foreigners" were probably the Maltese who were good to Paul (Acts 28\1-10).

Romans 1\16: "I am not ashamed of the gospel of the Christ, for it is the power of God for salvation for everybody who believes, both to the Judahite first, then to the Greek."
Comment: Paul said this in Jerusalem. It was, then, not Jesus himself who would go to "the dispersion of the Greeks" (John 7\35), but his agent Paul.

Romans 2\9-10: "tribulation and anguish on every mind of a man who works evil, both of the Judahite first, and of the Greek, but magnificence, honour, and peace for everybody who works good, both for the Judahite first, and for the Greek."
Comment: This speaks of the curse and judgement on any unbelieving from among the 12 tribes of Israel, and the honour and exaltation on the believing from among the 12 tribes.

Romans 3\9: "What then? Do we have preeminence? Undoubtedly not, for we have previously convicted both Judahites and Greeks to be under sin."
Comment: Paul is asking, rhetorically, if the Judahites have preeminence because they still had circumcision and "were entrusted with the oracles of God" (Romans 3\1-2). Paul says "we" because Judah is reckoned with his tribe of Benjamin. All the tribes of the sons of Israel are under sin, and being called to reconciliation with God, and with one another, through Christ. At Romans 9\4 it is shown that "Israelites" have "the preeminence".

Romans 10\12: "There is no difference between Judahite and Greek. For the same Lord of all is rich to all who call on Him."
Comment: They are all sons of Israel. There should never have been division between them.

1 Corinthians 1\22: "Judahites ask for a sign and Greeks search for wisdom."
Comment: Such was their nature. Greeks had a tradition of searching for wisdom, whereas the Judahites recalled the mighty acts of God, the signs and wonders.

1 Corinthians 1\23: "we proclaim Christ hanged on a stake: to Judahites a stumbling block, and to Greeks foolishness."
Comment: To sceptical and unbelieving Greeks it is "foolishness" because of their tradition of searching for wisdom, but the simplicity of the gospel message did not appeal to their vanity.

1 Corinthians 1\24: "to those designated, both Judahites and Greeks, we proclaim Christ, the power of God, and wisdom of God."
Comment: Those designated are those called by God as "the nation set apart" (Exodus 19\5, 1 Peter 2\9-10). The "sons of Israel" (Exodus 19\6).

1 Corinthians 10\32: "Become without offence, neither to the Judahites nor Greeks, nor to the Ekklesia groups of God."
Comment: This concerns the witness to those outside – so other members of the tribe of Judah and "the dispersion of the Greeks" (John 7\35), the dispersed of the house of Israel.

1 Corinthians 12\13: "For in one spirit also are we all baptized into one body, whether Judahites or Greeks, whether slaves or freemen. And we were all made to drink from one spirit."
Comment: The reconciliation of Judah and Israel, now baptized into one body of sons of Israel.

Galatians 2\3: "However, not even Titus who was with me, being a Greek, was compelled to be circumcised."
Comment: Timothy's father was of the dispersion of the Greeks (Acts 16\1 with John 7\35, 12\20 et cetera), sons of Israel. For Paul to emphasize "not even" Titus, Titus must be an Israelite.

Galatians 3\28: "There is neither Judahite nor Greek. There is neither servant nor freeman. There is neither male nor female. For you are all one in Christ Jesus."
Comment: This continues: "And if you are Christ's, then you are a seed of Abraham, and heirs

in keeping with a promise" (3\29). Both the Judahites and the Greeks were "the seed of Abraham", therefore sons of Israel. "Gentiles" cannot be the seed of Abraham! Only those in Christ are counted as seed. For Paul says "not all those of Israel are of Israel. Nor, because they are seed of Abraham, are all sons, but 'In Isaac a seed for you will be called.' That is, these Sons of God are not sons of the flesh, but sons of the promise, counted as seed" (Romans 9\6-8). Those not in Christ are not reckoned, that is why Paul says "if you are Christ's, then you are a seed of Abraham, and heirs in keeping with a promise" (Galatians 3\29).

Colossians 3\11: "there is neither Greek nor Judahite, circumcision nor uncircumcision, foreigner, Scythian, servant, freeman. Christ."
Comment: All made one, baptized into one body. Greeks and Judahites we have concluded as Israelites. The circumcision and uncircumcision we have concluded as Israelites (Ephesians 2\11). Those reckoned foreigners are "the nations" whom we have concluded as Israelites (Ephesians 2\11 et cetera). Servant and freeman are also Israelites; there is no reason to think otherwise. What about the Scythians? They also were from among the dispersion of Israel. There is enough history on this. While in captivity in Babylon the Israelites became known by various names, one of which was the Scythians.

We see from these occurrences that the word "Greek" is often used in apposition to "Judahites". Of the 27 occurrences of Ἕλλην (= *Hellēn*), only 5 of them are not set in apposition to "Judahites" (John 12\20, Acts 17\4, 18\17, Romans 1\14, Galatians 2\3). This apposition of Judahite and Greek is because the entirety of the New Testament is about the reconciliation of the tribes of the sons of Israel to God, and their reconciliation to each other, baptised into Christ in one body. They are now under a new and better Covenant.

There is hardly a word that could be more simple for translators than the Greek word Ἕλλην – the Greek word – meaning Greek, a proper noun. Proper nouns are the easiest to translate because there is *no alternative*. There might just be a question of spelling and decisions about whether to *translate* or *transliterate* (I have transliterated the Hebrew names and titles of God, rather than translate them.)

However – you could hardly believe it – this is not how translators have seen it. At John 7\35 the King James Bible translators did something quite extraordinary. They wrote this: "will he go and to the dispersion among the Gentiles, and teach the Gentiles?" They added "among", and they changed the meaning of this very simple word Ἕλλην into "Gentiles". But that means non-Israelite, yet these were "the dispersion of the Greeks", very much Israelites. That King James rendering of "Gentiles", then, disrupts the entire thread about "the dispersion of the Greeks" which we have seen in John's gospel, Acts, and the letters of Paul.

If only they had been consistent in their skulduggery. At John 12\20 they wrote: "And there were certain Greeks among them that came up to worship at the Festival". Why did they correctly write "Greeks" here, but "Gentiles" at John 7\35? My first principle of translating is Grammar. The second is Internal Harmony. The third and fourth are Research and Logic. The King James men had no such principles. What they seem to have done is write what they thought it meant, or what they *wished* it actually said, what they thought the writer must have thought because that is what the translators believed.

The King James men got it right throughout Acts. They got it right in Galatians. And they got it right in Colossians. At 1 Corinthians 1\22, 1\23 and 1\24 they got it right. But at 1 Corinthians 10\32 they wrote "neither to the Jews, nor to the Gentiles". It should be "neither to the Judahites, nor to the Greeks". Why did they put "Gentiles"?

In writing "Jews" and "Gentiles" they are constructing a mythology of Israelite and non-Israelite. The New Covenant was with "the house of Israel and the house of Judah", not with "Jews and Gentiles".

And there is worse. At Romans 1\16 and 10\12 the King James men got it right. But at Romans 2\9, which says "for the Judahite first, and for the Greek" they wrote "of the Jew first, and also of the Gentile". Yet at 1\16 they had written "to the Jew first, and also to the Greek". At 2\10 they did it again: "to the Jew first, and also to the Gentile". And at 3\9 they did it again, writing "both Jews and Gentiles". It should be "both Judahites and Greeks". Why could they not translate this simple word with any consistency?

There were problems: they translated the entire Bible in the space of only eight years; they were rushed by their employer, King James; they were paid for their work; there were 50 of them in committees; they were not men of the spirit; they were churchmen, bishops, robed academics; they upheld the post-Babylonian mythologies; they were among the persecutors of Separatists who had to flee the country; and, above all, they were working for King James, not God. They did not understand what they had in their hands with the scrolls of God.

11. ארץ (= *eretz*), Strong's Concordance number h776; mistranslated as "earth" at Psalm 37\11

The Hebrew word ארץ (= *eretz*) occurs many times in the Old Covenant writings. It first appears in the opening of Genesis: "In the beginning God created the heavens and the ארץ" – Earth. In many places, though, it has to be understood in context, since it can mean variously, " Earth", "land", "country", "ground", and even the people on the Earth (such as Genesis 2\4, Isaiah 1\2, Jeremiah 6\19). Discernment and the establishing of internal harmony are needed to determine what the writer means by ארץ (for example at Jeremiah 4\27-28).

At Psalm 37\3 David exhorts his readers to "Live in the land [ארץ], and feed on His faithfulness." To say "live in the Earth" would be silly. They have no choice about that. At Psalm 37\11 David says, "the submissive will inherit the land, and they will delight themselves in the abundance of shalom." At 37\22, he says "those exalted by him will inherit the land, and those cursed by him will be cut off." These are forceful reiterations of the promises to the patriarchs and the prophets to possess – inherit – the land defined in its boundaries and promised by God to the sons of Israel.

Yet what do the translations say? The King James gets it right at Psalm 37\3. But at 37\11 it has "But the meek shall inherit the <u>earth</u>." And at 37\22 it has "For such as be blessed of him shall inherit the <u>earth</u> ..." Why have they changed from "<u>land</u>", which is correct, to "<u>earth</u>"? And what does it mean to "inherit the earth"? God has given Jesus Christ authority over the Earth. Nobody else can say that they are going to inherit the Earth. The King James destroys the reminder to the Israelites of their possession of the promised land.

12. γῆ (= *gee*), Strong's Concordance number g1093; mistranslated as "earth" at Matthew 5\5

The Greek word γῆ (=*gee*) is the equivalent of the Hebrew word ארץ (= *eretz*). At Matthew 5\5 Jesus cites Psalm 37\11: "Exalted *are* the submissive, for they will inherit the γῆ" – land – reminding his audience of the promise to the patriarchs and prophets of the promised land, defined in its boundaries.

However, once again the King James has "they shall inherit the earth." It should be *land*. Any concept of inheriting the planet makes little sense. The planet is the inherited property of Jesus Christ and is under his governance, and so will it remain until he hands everything back to the Father, when everything has been put right.

Jesus' reference to the promises of the land would remind his audience of those promises to the patriarchs centuries before, and reiterated by the prophets. So the King James Bible destroys the continuity of the promises to the sons of Israel of the land. This "inherit the earth" is so well-known and read so often, and is often cited without question, yet many Christians think that they're going to live in the heavens anyway (despite knowing that Jesus is coming to Earth!), so "inherit the earth" is doubly, trebly, meaningless.

In the mistranslations of these 12 words, it all seems as if, after the Old Testament, Matthew's gospel begins something new: as if it is not about the twelve tribes of Israel any more; as if the hostility between the house of Judah and the house of Israel has all been mysteriously forgotten; as if when Paul and the other apostles went travelling it was with a universal message, and the preeminence of Israel was no longer of any importance or effect; as if God has forgotten the promises to the twelve tribes of Israel; as if God's purpose in relation to election is forgotten; as if the long-time and idolatrous enemy nations of Israel were suddenly included in the New Covenant. Whereas Paul says, "the purpose of God in relation to election might remain" (Romans 9\11). But you would think from the King James Bible that the New Testament is all about churches trying to get to Heaven to see their "trinity".

Yet, despite all the translation blunders, there are some diligent searchers of the oracles of God who have understood the truth about the promises to Israel in Matthew to Revelation. Other nations are not Israel; and they will not be, as the twelve tribes of Israel will be, "above all other nations on the Earth" (Exodus 19\5-6, Deuteronomy 7\6, 7\14, 28\1, 2 Timothy 1\12, Revelation 21\12-26 et cetera); we speak of Israel of the Bible, not modern Israel. Other nations are not called to be an authoritative body in the New Jerusalem, of which John saw a vision of "the names inscribed which are names of the twelve tribes of the sons of Israel" and the names "of the twelve apostles of the Lamb" (Revelation 21\12-13).

Now, who those twelve tribes of the sons of Israel are is another matter for another time.

ed215A

Chapter 26

What are demons?

1. The concept of "demon" has changed since antiquity

I was brought up in a church with the conscious imagination of a roaming universal ubiquitous monster called Satan who is said to be a fallen angel and who inhabits a vast (and fictitious) chasm called "Hell".

This teaching never ceased throughout all my later church life and Biblical studies. So was it with the general concept of demons and evil spirits.

I was surprised when in 1979 I began to read in the Bible that demons were said to be expelled from people by a word from Jesus. I struggled to understand whatever they could be, where they had come from and how they could get inside people in the first place. When does it happen and how? Are people born with it? Where did these things get created? Where does the word of God tell of their creation? Nobody could answer. They just called them fallen angels.

Nowhere could it be more problematic than the case of the man with the "Legion" of demons which are said to have afterwards gone into pigs (Mark 5\1-17). How could so many "demons" have all been inside one man?

Then there is Maria Magdalen, "out of whom", Mark says, Jesus "had expelled seven demons" (Mark 16\9). Imagine ... seven different devil personalities all crowding inside a woman at the same time. What a jostle for space, wriggling around inside. If devil personalities, why could she not feel the wriggling around of them all, even see the movements in her body? How can we understand this?

If an evil spirit, some fallen angel or a monster or something, were to inhabit a human body how would it breathe? How could it have existence? Where exactly in the body? What would it eat and drink? What would it do all day? Would it get bored? What would it do for company? Why would it prefer to live inside a person?

That popular concept of other living personalities having an existence inside a human body is similar to the mystical teaching that three deities live inside its followers. The Father (Who is God) is not physically omnipresent (is He inside a trout's fins? the handle of a jug?). Jesus (who is human himself, and is not omnipresent) must remain in the heavens "until *the* times of restoration" (Acts 3\21). The Holy Spirit angel (who is not omnipresent either) is also currently in the heavens and will return to the Earth to give instruction to the apostles during the coming eon (John 14\16, 14\26, 15\26, 16\7-10). What existence could God or Jesus or the Holy Spirit angel have if they were squeezed up inside the guts and blood of some dirty human? It's all curious mysticism, all that about gods in the fat of men's bellies.

The Greek word δαίμων (*daimon*) gives us our English word "demon". Thayer's Greek Lexicon says of δαίμων (*daimon*): "In Grk. auth. *a god, a goddess, an inferior deity*" (p. 124). That description certainly fits my understanding of "the gods" described in the writings of Homer. We see this worldview of the Greeks when Paul was in Athens and, as Luke records, "some philosophers of the Epicureans and of the Stoics engaged him in conversation, and some said, "What might this babbler want to say?", and others, "He seems to be a proclaimer of foreign demons" (Acts 17\18). The last phrase could also be rendered "a proclaimer of foreign gods", or "a proclaimer of foreign idols".

That ancient idolatrous worldview is reflected in Corinth. Paul told the believers there: "what the nations sacrifice they sacrifice to idols, and not to God, and I do not want you to be partakers with idols. You cannot drink a cup of *the* Lord as well as a cup of idols. You cannot partake of a table of *the* Lord as well as of a table of idols" (1 Corinthians 10\20-21). The word I've put as "idols" in those verses – obviously meaning false gods – is δαιμόνιον (*daimonion*), standing for the Greek gods of antiquity.

In Paul's day the pagan Greeks in Corinth were still making sacrifices to the gods of antiquity.

Homer glamorized in poetical fiction the Greek's sacrifices to idols, speaking often of thighbones in juices and roasting goat flesh and bowls of rich wine prepared and offered to the gods ("hecatombs" are large public sacrifices of many animals):

> The troops ... to Apollo by the barren surf
> ... carried out full-tally hecatombs,
> and the savour curled in crooked smoke towards heaven.   ~ *The Iliad*, Book 1

> ... young men filled their winebowls to the brim,
> ladling drops for the god [Apollo] in every cup.   ~ *The Iliad*, Book 1

> But now that god
> had gone far off among the sunburned races
> ... to be regaled by smoke of thighbones burning,
> haunches of rams and bulls, a hundredfold.
> He lingered, delighted at the banquet side.   ~ *The Odyssey*, Book 1

> And when I had finished my prayers and invocations
> to the countless dead, I took two sheep and cut their throats
> and let the dark blood drain into the pit.
> Immediately the ghosts came swarming around me
> up out of Érebus.   ~ *The Odyssey*, Book 11

The Greek world was influenced by these fictional glamorizations. At the time when Paul warned his Corinthian brothers and sisters of the "cup of idols" and the "table of idols", the culture of the city of Corinth was riddled with idol worship.

The prophet and apostle John on the island of Patmos wrote of a time coming when a form of idolatry will be set up, possibly worldwide: "And the rest of the men who were not killed by these plagues did not even unburden themselves from the works of their hands so that they should not worship the idols, or the golden and silver idols, or the brass and the stone and the wooden idols, which are able neither to see, nor to hear, nor to walk" (Revelation 9\20). The word rendered in that as "demons" is δαιμόνιον (*daimonion*), signifying "idols", as in the phrase which follows it, "golden and silver idols".

The word "demon" has come to change its meaning from the days of Greek antiquity. Or, rather, it has been changed, on purpose, by those of mystical and irrational minds. I think it is fair to say that the majority of Christians would describe demons as evil spirits, probably fallen angels, who inhabit, live inside, the bodies of certain wicked or mentally unwell people. A simple show of this is in the King James Bible at Matthew 17\18 which says of Jesus healing a boy with epilepsy, "Jesus rebuked the devil; and he departed". The crafty King James translators have put "devil" for "demon", playing on the pagan mythology of "the Devil" and evil devils, and they have called the boy's disorder "he", not "it". The demon is expressed as "he", some devil personality who had been hiding in the boy until Jesus drove him out.

With that imposed King James view I wholly disagree. I had long struggled to make sense of it.

2. Five meanings of "demon" in the New Testament

I consider that in the New Testament writings the word "demon" represents 5 things: 1. idols; 2. psychotic disorders; 3. demonized people, demoniacs; 4. fictional devil persons ruled by a fictional "Beelzebub"; 5. false teachers. I'll expand those:

> 1. idols, false gods, things of idolatry, as in demon worship; they do not see, hear, speak, walk (Psalm 115\4-7, 135\15-17, Daniel 5\23, Revelation 9\20; they are "the works of the hand of a man (Psalm 115\4), "nor is there breath in their mouths" (Psalm 135\17);

> 2. a neurological, or psychotic disorder, or moral derangement, or unfortunate illness disturbing and controlling the character and nature of the person. A person under the power of a demon is a person with a mind controlled by a destructive energy, having vain imaginings. It needs the healing and correcting power of Jesus. In the 21st century modern medicine can sometimes control these conditions, giving the poor sufferer relief, but it cannot cure them;

> 3. by the figure of metonymy, representing the demonized person, "a demoniac";

> 4. only occasionally by the Pharisees (and in Jesus mocking them) as devil persons ruled by a fictional "Beelzebub";

> 5. Paul warns of times of those giving themselves over to "adhering to deceiving spirits and teachings of demons" (1 Timothy 4\1). Just as the word "spirits" here refers so obviously to people, so, by parallelism, does "demons" refer to people. It could not refer to anything else. Nobody else stands up in pulpits teaching. They are men and women diseased of mind, teaching things of religion that are "earthly, natural, demonic", knowing only of religion that is from "the spirit which is naturally resident in us" (Jacob (James) 3\15, 4\5). Blind leaders.

Its general, most frequent meaning, in the writings of the apostles of Jesus is the second of those. To be said to be possessed by a demon meant to have a psychotic disorder, psychosis, derangement, dark and distorted thinking causing suffering, destructive energy, mental disorder, dethroning of reason.

Our word "demon" is simply a transliteration of the Greek δαίμων (*daimon*, Strong's Concordance reference number g1142), occurring at Matthew 8\31, Mark 5\12, Luke 8\29, Revelation 16\14, 18\2. The other Greek noun for "demon" is δαιμόνιον (*daimonion*, Strong's Concordance reference number g1140), occurring about 60 times, first at Matthew 7\22.

That which is "demonic" in the eyes of God is all that opposes Him. The demon is an idol of the mind, something governing it negatively, destructively. It is in opposition to the ordered and healthy and righteous mind we can have through Jesus. It is a false deity. Idol. A demon. The apostle Jacob (James) describes this perfectly for us, speaking of that which is "earthly, natural, demonic", and "the spirit which is naturally resident in us [and] begins to words in the" (Jacob 3\15, 4\5).

Despite what has become of the word "demon", I think it better for now to render it in the usual transliterated form, "demon". What is needed for now is probably not so much a new translation for the word but a proper understanding, as Jesus understood it. And when a new, correct, understanding is established, there should come a time when we can securely make a new translation for it.

The understanding that I propose for a future time for the word "demon" is "psychotic disorder" (and sometimes "idol", as I have already rendered it in places). In time I would be happy to use that phrase, "psychotic disorder" – or something like it – in my translation for δαίμων and its related words.

How perfectly, then, the designation of "demons" as psychotic disorders describes Maria Magdalen as having been delivered from "seven demons". Perhaps "seven demons" was a general idiomatic expression. Or, as conventional teaching might have it, did seven devil personalities go running out of her throat? How had they been in her metabolism, considering that there are no vacuums in the human body? And where did they exit from? Nostrils? Mouth? Ears? The pores of her skin? Her knees? Face? No, nobody had been living inside her; there were only her skull and guts and metabolism and blood and bones – and her own habitual evil thoughts until Jesus healed her. Most likely she was delivered from seven unrighteous and disordered patterns of thinking that controlled her life, imaginings of her mind which were unrighteous, wrong, unstable.

Only God can create. So why would He create little evil creatures, like those in certain medieval frightening paintings? I suggest the popular image of them comes from art made against the second law of the Covenant: "You shall not make for yourself any carved image, nor any likeness of anything in the heavens above, nor in the Earth beneath, nor in the water under the Earth. [5] You shall not bow yourself down to them, nor serve them, for I, Yahweh your Elohim, *am* a jealous El, charging the iniquity of the fathers on the sons to the third and fourth *generation* of those who hate Me, [6] and showing kindness to thousands of those who love Me and keep My commandments" (Exodus 20\4-6, Deuteronomy 5\8-10). If anybody should think these things are "fallen angels", first, there is no such concept in the word of God. Second, look at descriptions of angels. Do those live inside people?

We have in English the idiom "battling his demons", meaning the struggles inside his head, his own destructive flaws of character. This is taken generally as a figure of speech, a metaphor. If we understand "demon" as a psychotic disorder, or a negative and destructive mental energy, then the idiom "battling his / her demons" is no longer a figure of speech but a literal description of such a man's internal struggles. It is how we should understand his struggles: he is battling against his psychotic disorders, his negative and destructive mental energies. His dethronings of reason. His lack of mental order leading to sane and balanced judgments and living.

3. Examples of idols, psychotic disorders, demonized people

All this makes perfect sense when we look at a list of the people Jesus healed: "they brought to him all who were sick, people with various diseases and oppressed by torments, and those who were under the power of demons, and lunatics, and paralytics, and he cured them" (Matthew 4\24). There are two groups in that: those with physical disabilities and those with mental disabilities. Some were physically sick; some mentally sick, "oppressed", "under the power of demons", "lunatics", people whose reason had been dethroned.

All this makes sense when we read of men saying about Jesus, "He has a demon and is raving mad" (John 10\20). DEMON = RAVING MAD. To those men a demon was a matter of an imbalanced mind. Some said of Jesus, "These are not the declarations of one under the power of a demon. Is a demon able to open eyes of *the* blind?" (John 10\21). In their asking "Is a demon able ...?" the word "demon" is personified to represent the whole person, meaning a person of a deranged mind, a demonized person, a demoniac.

Matthew 9\21-33 records that "it so happened that they brought to him a dumb man under the power of a demon. And when the demon had been expelled, the dumb man spoke, and the crowds were amazed, saying, 'Never has it been seen like this in Israel.' " Astonishing! This incompetence of his mind prevented the man from speaking. Jesus, however, freed the man's mental capacities so that he was able to find the power of speech he had lacked all his life. The "power of the demon" was a mental disability. The transmission from brain to speaking faculty was made clear. And "when the demon [the mental derangement] had been expelled", the man spoke. This "demon" was not some living devil personality, but a disorder of the mind, somehow disconnecting his mental faculties so that they were not able to transmit to his tongue the proper instructions to issue speech. Jesus healed that. The derangement was expelled, removed in him. So he spoke; his tongue was loosed.

Mark 1\34 says that Jesus "healed many who were badly sick with various diseases, and he expelled many demons, and he would not allow the demons to speak because they had knowledge of him." The "demons" here are put metonymically for the disordered people whom Jesus cured. It's a figure of speech meaning "the demonized people", demoniacs. If those "demons" were actually devil personalities, then why are they not spoken of as being seen after Jesus' had expelled? Mark recounts of unclean spirits, "whenever the unclean spirits saw him, they fell down before him and called out" (Mark 3\11); Mark is referring to the "many" with "afflictions" whom Jesus healed. The "unclean spirits" means the unclean-natured people who came to him for healing.

At Luke 8\29 we read this of a man: "the unclean spirit ... many times ... had held him in its grip, and he was being kept under guard, shackled with manacles and in foot chains, but he would break the shackles *and* be driven by the demon into uninhabited places." The man had lost power over his mind and its destructive derangement would take over normal senses and shunt him around into "uninhabited places", presumably away from other people. But by the doctrines of conventional teaching, there was some other living entity having existence inside the man and it was telling him what to do. How can another living entity have its existence inside a human? What a foolish imagination that is. And how could this other living entity instruct its host without words heard?

Some Jews said to Jesus, "Were we not right in saying that you are a Samaritan, and you have a demon?" (John 8\48). Jesus answered, "I myself do not have a demon, but I honour my Father" (John 8\49). To be a Samaritan, one from Samaria, would mean allegiance to a different god, a foreign god, hence "a demon", an idol. Jesus, though, said that he honoured his Father, the one true God. He did not serve a foreign god, was not an idolater, did not have a demon, an idol, a false god.

When an apostle of Jesus uses the word "demon" it is necessary to consider the particular writer's context. In opposing polytheistic lies about God Jacob (James) says: "You acknowledge that God is one. You do well. Even the demons acknowledge *that*, yet shudder!" (Jacob (James) 2\19). Even the deranged mind believes that God is one! What ignominy for those who say God is three. The "demons" stands for "the demonized persons", demoniacs. And false teachers. Whom did Jacob have in mind?

At Luke 10\17 we read that seventy disciples boasted to Jesus that "the demons are subject to us through your name". The "demons" represent demonized people.

Matthew 8\31 and Mark 5\12 record "the demons" as pleading with Jesus, "If you expel us, allow us to go off into the herd of pigs". The demons are personalized, as if it's the psychotic disorder speaking, rather than the demonized man himself. The psychotic disorder – or disorders, plural – are given to the pigs which are unclean animals and should not have been farmed in Israel under Mosaic law.

What John describes as "the spirits of demons, performing signs" (Revelation 16\14) are also "unclean spirits" which he saw coming "out of the mouth "of the Dragon and of the Wild Beast and of the False Prophet (Revelation 16\13). I take these as demonized men (and women) who "out of the mouth" speak things which are against the truth of God.

When John saw the collapse of Babylon he described it as "a residence of demons, and a prison of every unclean spirit" (Revelation 18\2). Babylon has, therefore, collapsed over all its false prophets and false teachers who have opposed God and Jesus, and it has become a residence of demonized people, people with unclean characters. Those who were otherwise better natured had already escaped, having been ordered: "Get out of her, My people" (Revelation 18\4).

4. Beelzebub

The blind leaders of Israel who made themselves enemies to Jesus accused him of driving out demons by "Beelzebub, ruler of the demons" (Matthew 10\25, 12\24, 9\34, Mark 3\22, Luke 11\15-19). This could just about be interpreted as their figure of hyperbole, because they also said that they thought that Jesus was "out of his mind" (Mark 3\21).

However ... however ... it seems that the deluded rulers had drunk down the falsehoods of mythology – just as they had done regarding departed souls, "Hades" and "the garment-fold of Abraham" (Luke 16\27-23). Jesus corrected them, saying he expelled demons from people by "the Spirit of God" and "the finger of God" (Matthew 12\28, Luke 11\20).

The leaders' accusation that the work of the Spirit of God was the work of Beelzebub was rebuked by Jesus as a defamation which could not receive forgiveness, "not in the present eon, nor in the *eon* coming" (Matthew 12\32).

5. Driving away our demons

And who among us does not have some sort of demons (of varying severity) against which – not against *whom* – we struggle?

We all have our own failings to struggle against, personal failings, together with the constant struggle against the false teachings and philosophies of the world and its natural religion. Paul speaks of such things coming about "in latter times", of which the Spirit of God had warned him:

"Now the Spirit speaks in persuasive oracles that in latter times some will apostatize from the faith, adhering to deceiving spirits and teachings of demons, [2] in hypocrisy of liars, having been branded in their conscience with a branding iron, [3] forbidding to marry, to abstain from foods that God created for taking with thanksgiving by believers and those fully knowing the truth." ~ 1 Timothy 4\1-3

Those "deceiving spirits and ... demons" are put for false teachers, demonized people.

The word of God through Jacob (James) defines the great contradistinction between what is of God and what is against Him, and what is against Him is "demonic", a product of a disordered, unhealthy, deranged mind, having bitterness, harbouring lies, committing foul acts, lacking peace and gentleness and kindness and wisdom, not having the love of God in their hearts. Jacob (James) says:

"[13] Who *is* wise and intelligent among you? Let him, out of good conduct, show his works in meekness of wisdom. [14] But if you have bitter jealousy and contention in your hearts, do not boast injuriously and lie against the truth. [15] Such wisdom is not coming down from above, but *is* earthly, natural, demonic. [16]

For where jealousy and contention *are*, there commotion and every foul act *arise*.
[17] But the wisdom from above is first pure, then peaceable, gentle, yielding, full of mercy and good fruits, without partiality, and unfeigned. [18] And *the* fruit of righteousness is sown in peace by those making peace."
~ Jacob (James) 3\13-18

Paul says, "God did not give us a spirit of cowardice, but of power, and of love, and of a sound mind" (2 Timothy 1\7). That "sound mind" is only found in a mind which has fully submitted itself to the truth of God and the righteousness of Jesus. In that "power" and "love" and "sound mind" are found everything that overcomes whatever is "earthly, natural, demonic" (Jacob (James) 3\15).

6. Further thoughts

Demons are unrighteous habits of thought and behaviour. I think of them inside the circle of our cranium, tiny things on little chairs and wearing thrones, sometimes swirling round our thoughts. I personify them, visualise them, only as a way to understand them.

No living thing can live inside a man or woman or child; that concept is nonsense. Even the fictional mythology of Homer's poetry does not have the demons living inside home's heroes and heroines.

There is nothing in the word of God about the creation of "demons" as living entities, nor about the existence of them as living entities. They are forces of mental energy creating psychotic disorders and lusts which are hostile to the commandments of God.

There is no concept of fallen angels in the word of God. When we see "Sons of God" in the New Testament writings we do not doubt that it is a reference to the righteous elect. And in the prophet Hosea we recognize that "Sons of the living God" is a reference to the righteous elect. So too in Genesis chapter 6 is the phrase "Sons of God" a reference to the righteous elect. So is it also in the opening chapters of the prophet Job. (The only exception is Job 38\7 where "sons of God" is a poetical reference to stars.) Genesis 6 is nothing to do with the mythology of "fallen Angels". So demons cannot be said to be fallen angels. Anyway, how could an angel or a legion of angels – live inside a human, let alone *fit* inside a human? It's all a fairy story.

Arguments in favour of them actually existing are always from stories. The human imagination is deeply susceptible to horror and fancy and delusion. Damn the films and artworks breaking the second law of the Covenant.

We must rely on the word of God only. So does the word of God describes the creation of "demons"? No. Where could they have come from, then? How could any living entity exist inside a human? It couldn't. It is beyond all logic.

We need them out! Pretending they are real personalities who have to be ordered out is ineffective. The only way to overcome our unrighteous habits of thought and behaviour is by prayer and willing submission to the words of God and Jesus, and often by spiritual help (by counselling the word of Jesus) from others. Talking to our habits of unrighteousness, shouting at them, and ordering them to come out will not work. You can't shout at sins and expect them to go away. The narratives of the miracles in the gospels happened because people were responding to the word of Jesus. That is not the same as us foolishly shouting at them.

7. A challenge

Without going to other passages, let the church preachermen prove that any of these following passages concerna "fallen angels" . I say they are all human agencies, human enemies against whom we have a struggle: –

[Jesus said] "When I was with you daily in the Temple, you did not stretch out hands against me. But this is your hour, and of the power of darkness." ~ Luke 22\53

For I am persuaded that neither death, nor life, nor angels, nor rulers, nor forces of power, nor things present, nor things to come, [39] nor height, nor depth, nor any other created thing will be able to separate us from the love of God in Christ Jesus our Lord. ~ Romans 8\38-39

... over and above all prime rulership, and forces of power, and might, and sovereignty, and every name having been named, not only in this age, but in the one coming as well. ~ Ephesians 1\21

... the combat for us is not against blood and flesh, but against the prime rulers, against the forces of power, against the world rulers of this age of darkness, against the spirits of evil among the most eminent.
~ Ephesians 6\12
[Let the reader understand that the word "spirit" is often the biblical noun for "people". In all these "spirit" is put for people: – Number 16\22, 27\16, 2 Kings 19\7, Isaiah 37\7, 2 Chronicles 18\20 ("a spirit came forward and said"), Matthew 12\43-45, Mark 3\11 ("And whenever the unclean spirits saw him, they fell down before him and called out, saying, 'You are the Son of God!' "), Luke 9\55 ("You do not know what manner of spirit you are"), 11\24-25, 1 Corinthians 5\5, 2 Thessalonians 2\2, Hebrews 12\9, 12\23, 1 Peter 3\19, 1 John 4\1. Compare Job 12\10: "In whose hand is the life of every living thing, and the breath of all flesh of man?"]

[10] at the name of Jesus every knee might bow,
of heavenly beings, and of beings on Earth
and of beings under the Earth,
[11] and every tongue make admission
that Jesus Christ *is* Lord – for glory of God *the* Father. ~ Phillipians 2\9-10

[Jesus Christ] who is at *the* right hand of God, having gone into Heaven, angels and authorities and powers having been put in subjection to him. ~ 1 Peter 3\22

And the kings of the Earth, and the high-ranking, and the military commanders, and the rich, and the mighty men, and every servant and freeman hid themselves inside the caves and inside the rocks of the mountains. ~ Revelation 6\15

... for your merchants were the magnates
of the Earth, for by your sorcery
all the nations were deceived,
[24] and in her was found blood
of prophets and set apart people
and of all those murdered on the Earth. ~ Revelation 18\23-24

[18] ... so that you can eat flesh of kings
and flesh of commanders of a thousand
and flesh of the mighty men
and flesh of horses
and of those who sit on them
and flesh of all, both freemen
and servants, and both lowly and eminent. ~ Revelation 19\18

mythology.

The "sons of Elohim" in Genesis 6 and Job are humans; no reason to make them into anything else.

As for "demons", well, what could they be? Little Heironymous Bosch things living inside us???? I do not believe we would have this concept in our heads if it were not for daft artworks of the imagination, artworks that contradict and disobey the second commandment of God: "You shall not make for yourself any carved image, nor any likeness of anything in the heavens above, nor in the Earth beneath, nor in the water under the Earth" (Exodus 20\4). Claims for their existence are always based on stories ... "I was at a seance and ..." ... "When my mum was in Kenya ..." et cetera et cetera. There are, though, powerful energies of evil, just as there are powerful energies of good (like the "daughter of Abraham" who touched Jesus' garment). The evil energies can possess our minds: strongholds of bad thought patterns – so we need the word of God to battle against these.

9. The energy of rebellion, the violence of healing

Psychotic and immoral disorders in a man's or woman's mindset control their lives, electro-neuron charges crackling over junctions signalling words, actions, directions.

How slowly these disorders are overcome in us! How will we struggle to persist in them and justify ourselves! With what reluctance and pain a man might give up alcoholic, drug, or smoking habits! Or anything else. The struggle can go on for years.

Consider the man Legion: "For [Jesus] had commanded the unclean spirit to come out of the man, for many times it had held him in its grip, and he was being kept under guard, shackled with manacles and in foot chains, but he would break the shackles *and* be driven by the demon into uninhabited places" (Luke 8\29). The man could not even live in his house.

Or consider this boy: "Lord, have pity on my son, for he's an epileptic and suffers severely, for he frequently falls into the fire and frequently into water, [16] and I brought him to your disciples and they were unable to cure him" (Matthew 17\15-16).

But it was different when people were confronted with Jesus, desperate for his help. He healed them with a word. The impact was instant. Their psychotic and moral disorders, their defects, impediments, their evil lusts were healed instantly.

It is no wonder, then, that the word of Jesus healing those violent controlling mechanisms of rebellion sometimes manifested violent reactions.

Christopher Sparkes, 2016, 2022

Chapter 27

Who or what is satan and the devil?

♦

There can be no "Devil" or "Satan" with horns who goes around the world leading people into vice they would not commit had they not been led astray by this "Devil". The Devil of John Milton's *Paradise Lost* and CS Lewis's *Screwtape Letters* is a fiction. This has been clear to me for a number of years. However, the truth that there is no universal monster who is the arch-enemy of God had not until recent years crossed my mind.

In the months of this glorious summer of 2016 I have come to the realization that there is no such character as a universal monster called "Satan" and "the Devil". This realization has come thanks to friends who have long known the Satan of the popular imagination is fiction. I grew up with the idea there is a Devil, and it amazes me I have never thought of anything or read anything or heard of anything to challenge that notion.

I regret that the 2016 editions of my published translation *The Eonian Books* and its companion volume *The Earth-Shaking Truth* both suggest possible notions of this fictional Devil. I have had to spend weeks amending my writings to rid them of this error. I want to make public apology to my readers of that edition. Thanks to God Who gives revelation to all who seek the fullness of His truth. This wonderful realization has corrected me out of errors.

I propose here three reasons why there can be no infernal monster called "the Devil".

Physically impossible
First, it is physically impossible that some alleged fallen angel could lead any human being into doing anything, unless, that is, the suggestion were made audibly and it were willingly followed. Any idea that temptations and leadings are made by some sort of heard whispering in ears is an impossible one. Equally impossible is the popular belief that this mythical figure could go around the world tempting people in, say, Hong Kong and San Francisco and Birmingham all at the same time. It's a physical and spatial impossibility. And it's not true. It doesn't happen.

How could they live this long?
If, as Paul tells us, "the wages of sin is death", how have these alleged devils and demons managed to survive for thousands of years, and not be subject to death for their sins and rebellion?

Immoral
This great myth of some universal tempter offloads people's moral responsibility for their sins against God. It says somebody else is to blame. A "Devil" made them do it. It's like the poetical fictions of Homer in which people blame their actions on "the gods".

No Biblical word which means that there's
a universal monster called "Satan" and "the Devil"
There is no Hebrew or Greek word which translates with any suggestion that there is a universal monster called "the Devil" or "Satan".

שטן (= *satan*)
The Hebrew word which gets only transliterated – rather than translated – as "Satan" is שטן (=

satan). Strong's Hebrew Concordance reference number h7854. It appears at Numbers 22\22, 22\32, 1 Samuel 29\4, 2 Samuel 19\22, 1 Kings 5\4, 11\14, 11\23, 11\25, Zechariah 3\1, 3\2, Psalm 109\6, Job 1\6, 1\7, 1\8, 1\9, 1\12, 2\1, 2\1, 2\3, 2\4, 2\6, 2\7, 1 Chronicles 21\1. In every occurrence it means "enemy", "adversary".

Nothing more shows that שטן (= *satan*) means only "enemy" or "adversary" than Numbers 22\22 and 22\32 where the Angel of Yahweh says that he himself "went out as an enemy to you"; and 1 Chronicles 21\1 and the comment on it at 2 Samuel 24\1 where the שטן (= *satan*), the adversary to Israel, is shown to be God Himself.

שטן (= *satan*) is not the name of anybody, nor is it the title of anybody. According to Gesenius, שטן always appears with the article except at 1 Chronicles 21\1. (I have not checked that.)

There is also a verb form of שטן (= *satan*), meaning "to accuse", "to oppose", "to be an adversary", occurring at Zechariah 3\1, Psalm 38\20, 71\13, 109\4, 109\20, 109\29. This verb form שטן (= *satan*) is linked to the noun and gives us information about the meaning of the noun.

The King James Bible translates the word (correctly) as "adversary" at Numbers 22\22, 22\32, 1 Samuel 29\4, 2 Samuel 19\22, 1 Kings 5\4, 11\14, 11\23, 11\25, 1 Chronicles 21\1. But the King James Bible only transliterates it as "Satan" at Zechariah 3\1-2, Psalm 109\6, Job 1\6-12, 2\1-7, 1 Chronicles 21\1. Then it *translates* the verb form at Psalm 38\20, 71\13, 109\4, 109\20, 109\29, but only *transliterates* it at Zechariah 3\1.

σατᾶν (= *satan*) and σατανᾶς (= *satanas*)

There are two Greek words which get translated as "Satan". One is σατᾶν (= *satan*). Strong's Concordance reference number g4566. It occurs only at 2 Corinthians 12\7, and means "adversary", "enemy". This word is not a name, nor is it a title. The other, more common, Greek word is σατανᾶς (= *satanas*). Strong's Concordance reference number g4567. This word also is not a name, nor is it a title. At Acts 5\3, as "hostility", for example, it's an abstract noun. At Matthew 16\23 and Mark 8\33 Jesus says it to Peter, meaning "enemy", "adversary". At Luke 13\16 I render it as "affliction". Thayer's comments include: "*adversary* (one who opposes another in purpose or act)". It's only transliterated as "Satan" in most popular versions.

Nothing more shows that the Greek form σατανᾶς (= *satanas*) does not represent a universal monster than Jesus' words to Peter, saying, "Get behind me, σατανᾶς [adversary]" (Matthew 16\23, Mark 8\33). Jesus was speaking to Peter, not invoking "Satan". Jesus would not have called his friend Peter by the name of some monstrous and hideous demon.

This word σατανᾶς and its Hebrew form שטן can be hostile people, authorities, our own sinful nature, affliction, and "antagonism" or "hostility" towards God.

διάβολος (= *diabolos*)

The Greek word which usually gets translated as "Devil" is διάβολος (= *diabolos*). Strong's Concordance reference number g1228. It needs to be understood that this word does not represent any name or title of anybody: it is strictly an adjective (masculine) acting as a substantive (noun). That it is an adjective is shown particularly at 1 Peter 5\8 where it occurs in standard adjectival form as "falsely accusing", describing the noun "adversary", making the phrase "falsely accusing adversary".

διάβολος occurs 38 times. It's usually "devil" in the King James Bible, but – inconsistently – "Devil" at Revelation 12\9, "slanderers" at 1 Timothy 3\11, and "false accusers" at Titus 2\3.

Thayer's Lexicon says: "prone to slander ... false accuser, slanderer".

Strong's Concordance says of it:

"to slander, accuse, defame ... properly, a slanderer; a *false accuser*, unjustly criticizing to *hurt* (*malign*) and condemn to *sever a relationship*. *diábolos*) is the root of the English word, "Devil" (see also *Webster's Dictionary*). *diábolos* in *secular* Greek means "backbiter", i.e. an accuser, calumniator (slanderer). *diábolos* is literally someone who *casts through*, i.e. making charges that bring down (destroy). Satan is *used* by God in this plan – as a predictable wind-up toy, playing out his evil nature."

Parkhurst is cited in Robert Roberts' *Christendom Astray* (p. 131) as saying:

"First, then, with regard to the word "devil," Cruden remarks: "This word comes from the Greek *diabolos*, which signifies a *calumniator or accuser*." Parkhurst says, "The original word *diabolos* comes from *diabebola*, the perfect tense, middle voice of *diaballo*, which is compounded of *dia*, through; and *ballo*, to cast; therefore meaning *to dart* or *strike through*; whence, in a figurative sense, it signifies *to strike or stab with an accusation or evil report.*' "

Hence, Roberts concludes: "Parkhurst defines *diabolos* as a substantive, to mean "an accuser, a slanderer," which he illustrates by referring to I Tim. iii, 11; II Tim. iii, 3; Titus ii, 3 in all of which, as the reader will perceive by perusing the passages, it is applied to human beings."

Roberts says in *Christendom Astray*:

"Sin is the great slanderer of God in virtually denying His supremacy, wisdom, and goodness, and the great ground of accusation against man even unto death. How appropriate, then, to style it THE ACCUSER, THE SLANDERER, THE LIAR. This is done in the word devil; but through the word not being translated, but merely Anglicised, the English reader, reared with English theological prejudices, is prevented from seeing it" (p. 135).

Fowler and Fowler in *Exploring Bible Language* likewise attribute "satan" and "the devil" to the indwelling spirit of rebellion which lies in the heart of all men. It is, they say,

"the 'natural man' (1 Cor. 2:14) ... 'the flesh' ... when the words devil or satan are personified they referred to man's opposition to the authority and will of God ... Jesus does not speak of the devil or satan as responsible for sins of weakness. He uses the names to personify the most fundamental sin, human pride – which rejects the authority of God's word" (pp. 145-147).

Concerning "Satan" and "the Devil", see Roberts' analysis in chapter 7 of *Christendom Astray*. Roberts exposes the myth of the Devil and Satan.

Having said all that, though, there are occurrences of διάβολος (= *diabolos*) and שטן (= *satan*) and σατᾶν (= *satan*) and σατανᾶς (= *satanas*) where I think writers and commentators such as Roberts might have commented on an individual or a group being identified. I will make this clear in the table that follows.

Table of occurrences of the one Hebrew word שטן (= *satan*) and the three Greek words σατᾶν and σατανᾶς and διάβολος

1. Occurrences of the Hebrew word שטן, Strong's Concordance number h7854

שטן is not a name or title of anybody. It is a common noun for "enemy" or "adversary". There is also a verb form of שטן (= *satan*), meaning "to accuse", "to oppose", "to be an adversary"; see Zech. 3\1, Psalm 38\20, 71\13, 109\4, 109\20, 109\29.

The King James has this variously as "Satan", "adversary", and "to withstand". It translates the noun (correctly) as "adversary" at Numbers 22\22, 22\32, 1 Samuel 29\4, 2 Samuel 19\22,

1 Kings 5\4, 11\14, 11\23, 11\25, but only transliterates it as "Satan" at Zechariah 3\1-2, Psalm 109\6, Job 1\6-12, 2\1-7, 1 Chronicles 21\1. The verb form it translates at Psalm 38\20, 71\13, 109\4, 109\20, 109\29, but only transliterates at Zechariah 3\1.

Nothing more shows that שטן means only "enemy" or "adversary" than Numbers 22\32 where the Angel of Yahweh says that he himself "went out to be an enemy to you"; and 1 Chronicles 21\1 and the comment on it at 2 Samuel 24\1 where the שטן is shown to be God Himself.

שטן	context	comment
שטן (= *satan*) Numbers 22\22	And the anger of Elohim burned because he was really going, and the Angel of Yahweh stood in the road as an adversary against him.	The Angel of Yahweh is the enemy or adversary. KJV has it correct with "adversary".
שטן (= *satan*) Numbers 22\32	the Angel of Yahweh said to him, "Why have you struck your donkey these three times? See now, I went out to be <u>an enemy</u> to you, because *your* way is perverse before me."	The Angel of Yahweh says that he himself "went out to be an enemy". The KJV has this as a verb form, "to withstand".
שטן (= *satan*) 1 Samuel 29\4	and the princes of the Philistines said to him, "Make this man return, so that he can go back to his place which you have appointed him, and do not let him go down with us into battle, in case in the battle he is <u>an enemy</u> to us."	A human enemy.
שטן (= *satan*) 2 Samuel 19\22	And David said, "What business do I have with you, you sons of Zeruiah, that this day you should be <u>enemies</u> to me?"	A human enemy.
שטן (= *satan*) I Kings 5\4	"But now Yahweh my Elohim has given me rest on every side, *so that there is* neither <u>enemy</u> nor evil occurrence."	A human enemy.
שטן (= *satan*) 1 Kings 11\14	Yahweh stirred up <u>an adversary</u> against Solomon, Hadad the Edomite. He *was* from the King's seed in Edom.	A human enemy.

שטן (= satan) 1 Kings 11\23	And Elohim stirred up *another* enemy against him, Rezon, the son of Eliadah.	A human enemy.
שטן (= satan) 1 Kings 11\25	he was an enemy against Israel all the days of Solomon (as well as the mischief which Hadad caused)	A human enemy.
שטן (= satan) Zechariah 3\1	he showed me the high priest Joshua standing before *the* Angel of Yahweh, and an adversary standing at his right hand to accuse him.	Fowler and Fowler (pp. 138-139) link this narrative with Jude 9 and 23. Fowler and Fowler comment: "[T]he vision of Zech. 3 which, as we have shown (p. 137), is a dramatic presentation of events relating to the Samaritan opposition to the rebuilding of the temple. In this little drama there is the angel of the LORD, with Joshua the high priest on his left and Satan on his right. Satan represented the Samaritan opposition to the Jerusalem Temple. Joshua, clothed in filthy garments, represented the Israelites who had adopted heathen religious practices. The drama rehearses the events described in Ezra 6: the Samaritans were severely rebuked and threatened with capital punishment and the Israelites 'separated themselves from the filth of the heathen." (p. 183). Robert Roberts comments: "The individual adversary seen by Zechariah, side by side with Joshua, represented this class-opposition to the work in which Joshua was engaged. Those who insist on the popular Satan having to do with the matter, have to prove the existence of such a being first, before the passage from Zechariah can help them; for "Satan" only means adversary, and in itself lends no more countenance to their theory than the word "liar" or "enemy" " (*Christendom Astray*, p. 126). Roberts suggests the adversary is symbolic of "a class of antagonists" and cites Ezra 3\12-3, 4\1-5 (ibid, p. 126).
שטן (= satan) Zechariah 3\2	And Yahweh said to the adversary, "Yahweh rebuke you, *you* enemy!"	A human enemy
שטן (= satan) Psalm 109\6	"Set a lawless man over him, and then an enemy will stand at his right hand."	The parallelism equates the enemy as a lawless man. A human enemy.

שטן (= *satan*) Job 1\6-12	there came a day when the sons of Elohim came to present themselves before Yahweh, and an <u>adversary</u> also came among them. Yahweh said to <u>the adversary</u>, "Where have you come from?" Then <u>the adversary</u> answered Yahweh and said, "From going around in the land, and from walking up and down in it." ... Yahweh said to <u>the adversary</u> ... <u>the adversary</u> answered Yahweh ... Yahweh said to <u>the adversary</u>	A human enemy. This very human enemy of Job is described in Job chapter 16, verses 9-14. The "Sons of Elohim" presenting themselves are an assembly of the righteous elect, just as they are in the New Testament phrases "the Sons of God". Mythology carries the notions that "Satan" and his enemies have regular meetings with God.
שטן (= *satan*) Job 2\1-7	and <u>the adversary</u> also came among them to present himself before Yahweh ... Yahweh said to <u>the adversary</u> ...Yahweh said to <u>the adversary</u> ... <u>the adversary</u> answered Yahweh ... Yahweh said to <u>the adversary</u> ... <u>the adversary</u> went out from the presence of Yahweh	A human enemy. As Job 1\6, described in Job 16\9-14.
שטן (= *satan*) 1 Chronicles 21\1	an adversary stood up against Israel, and provoked David to number Israel.	2 Samuel 24\1 says, "the anger of Yahweh burned against Israel, and He caused David to be moved against them to say, 'Go *and* number Israel and Judah' ", so that the שטן is shown to be God Himself. The KJV says "Satan stood up against Israel, and provoked David to number Israel". SO THE KJV CALLS AN ACT OF GOD AN ACT OF SATAN.
<u>summary of meanings</u>: a hostile force, an adversary, enemy, opponent		<u>summary of renderings</u>: adversary, enemy. Always human.

✱

2. Occurrence of the Greek word σατᾶν, Strong's Concordance number g4566

σατᾶν	context	comment
σατᾶν 2 Corinthians 12\7	a thorn in the flesh was given to me, a messenger of *the* enemy, in order that he might strike me	A messenger of the enemy of Christ and Paul. Other versions have "Satan", and for "messenger" they have "angel". The idea of some "fallen angel" flown in on an errand from Satan to beat Paul up from time to time has more the ring of Homeric fiction.

*

3. Occurrences of the Greek word σατανᾶς, Strong's Concordance number g4567

The King James Bible has "Satan" for every occurrence of this word σατανᾶς. It is not a name nor a title of anybody, but a common noun meaning at to root simply "enemy" or "adversary", just like its Hebrew word of origin שטן (= *satan*). Just as the Hebrew form means "enemy", and is neither a name nor title of anybody, so also does the Greek form mean "enemy".

σατανᾶς	context	comment
σατανᾶς Matthew 4\8-10	⁸ The slanderer also took him along to an exceedingly high mountain, and he showed him all the kingdoms of the world order and their glory. ⁹ And he said to him, 'All these things I will give you if you fall down *and* give honour to me.' ¹⁰ Then Jesus said to him, 'Get behind me, <u>adversary</u>! For it has been written: "You shall revere *the* Lord your God, and you shall serve Him only.	The meaning here of "satan" is determined by its occurrences at Matthew 16\23 and Mark 8\33. Jesus was rebuking an unnamed tempter, as cunning as the one called the serpent in Eden. In the same way, Jesus rebuked Peter. Some suggest the adversary here is the internal sinful nature. Jesus, it is written, was tempted in every point that we are (Hebrews 4\15). The narrative continues with dialogue: "And he said to him, 'All these things I will give you if you fall down *and* worship me.' " In light of that claim, it is worth considering the following passages concerning Jesus' power and authority: "Everything has been handed over to me by my Father" (Matthew 11\27). "Sit at My right hand until I make your enemies a footstool for your feet" (Matthew 22\44). "All authority in Heaven and on Earth has been given to me" (Matthew 28\18). "The Father loves the Son, and has given all things into his hand" (John 3\35). "For just as the Father has life in Himself, so has He also given *it* to the Son to have life in himself, ²⁷ and He has also given him authority to execute judgement, because he is the Son of Man" (John 5\26-27). "Jesus, knowing that the Father had given all things into *his* hands, and that he had emanated from God and was going away to God" (John 13\3). "All things, whatever the Father possesses, are mine" (John 16\15). The kingdoms of the world were already in Jesus' authority, so could not be in anybody's else's power to give away.
σατανᾶς Matthew 12\26 (twice)	if <u>the enemy</u> drives out <u>the enemy</u>	The parable of the house. Parable language.

σατανᾶς Matthew 16\23	Get behind me, <u>adversary</u>!	Jesus would not call his friend Peter by the name of a demonic and fictional monster. The word "satan" here is shown to have the meaning of "adversary", "enemy". Compare Luke 4\8.
σατανᾶς Mark 1\13	being tested by <u>the adversary</u>	The meaning here of "satan" is determined by its occurrences at Matthew 16\23 and Mark 8\33. In the same way Jesus rebuked Peter. See Mat. 4\10.
σατανᾶς Mark 3\23 (twice)	How can <u>an enemy</u> drive out <u>an enemy</u>?	Parable language. Mark says in this very verse: "And he called them to him, and spoke to them in parables."
σατανᾶς Mark 3\26	if <u>the enemy</u> rises up against himself	Continuation of the parable.
σατανᾶς Mark 4\15	<u>the adversary</u> comes straightaway and takes away	Our own rebellion, personified. Could also imply false teachers, deceivers. No monster of fiction mentioned or implied.
σατανᾶς Luke 4\8	Get behind me, <u>adversary</u>! It has been written ...	Personification.
σατανᾶς Luke 8\33	Get behind me, <u>adversary</u>! For you are directing your mind ...	Peter. Matthew 16\23.
σατανᾶς Luke 10\18	I watched <u>the enemy</u> falling like lightning from *his* high position.	A human enemy, unnamed, falling from his high position. Similar imagery to fall of king of Babylon (Isaiah 14\12-20).
σατανᾶς Luke 11\18	if <u>the enemy</u> is divided against even himself	Parable language. Mark 3\23.
σατανᾶς Luke 13\16	the daughter of Abraham whom this <u>affliction</u> has bound	Abstract. KJV has 'Satan', but what unfairness if some infernal monster had been permitted to cripple this woman.
σατανᾶς Luke 22\3	<u>hostility</u> arose in Judas	Also at John 13\27. I did consider whether this could be "the enemy went to Judas", but the timing at John 13\27, during the supper, seems to deny that reading.
σατανᾶς Luke 22\31	<u>the enemy</u> has made a claim on you	A human enemy of Jesus and the disciples. Threat by them of persecution and murder.
σατανᾶς John 13\27	And after the piece *of bread*, <u>hostility</u> then arose in him	As Luke 22\3. Greek has the article, but Greek often takes articles with abstract nouns.
σατανᾶς Acts 5\3	Why did this <u>hostility</u> fill your heart?	Abstract, as διάβολος (= *diabolos*) at John 13\2.

σατανᾶς Acts 26\18	to open their eyes to turn from darkness to light, and from the power of <u>antagonism</u> [or, <u>the adversary</u>] towards God, for them to receive forgiveness of sins	Abstract. There's an article in the Greek, but Greek can take articles with abstract nouns and proper nouns.
σατανᾶς Romans 16\20	the God of peace will crush <u>the adversary</u> under your feet	Probably referring to false teachers and the persecuting hostility troubling the Roman believers. Typical conquering imagery by David in the Psalms; also Luke 1\52, 1\71.
σατανᾶς 1 Corinthians 5\5	to hand such a man over to <u>the enemy</u> for destruction of the flesh	There could be added an expanding phrase, "*of the carnal mind*", in order to point the full meaning that might be intended in the passage. The "destruction of the flesh" could mean death. More likely is the enemy within, carnal lust of the mind, sinful flesh.
σατανᾶς 1 Corinthians 7\5	then you can come together again as one, so that <u>the adversary</u> does not test you	With the article. The natural lust of their own minds, sinful flesh. Abstract.
σατανᾶς 2 Corinthians 2\11	so that we should not be excessively weighed down by <u>the adversary</u>	Probably abstract, the natural rebellion and falling to temptation. Sinful flesh.
σατανᾶς 2 Corinthians 11\14	<u>the adversary</u> himself transforms himself into a messenger of light	The fierce adversary of Christ, the antichrists, the Edomites who masqueraded as super "apostles" (11\13). Any false teachers.
σατανᾶς 1 Thessalonians 2\18	we wanted to come to you, truly, I, Paul, time and again, but <u>the enemy</u> hindered us	Stated as a human enemy.
σατανᾶς 2 Thessalonians 2\9	whose presence is after the working of <u>the enemy</u> with every power, and signs and false wonders	The antichrist human enemy.
σατανᾶς 1 Timothy 1\20	Hymenaeus and Alexander whom I released to <u>the adversary</u>, so that they might be disciplined not to blaspheme	It could be abstract, the adversary within. Or it could be related to the Jewish enemy. The Greek has an article.
σατανᾶς 1 Timothy 5\15	some already have turned aside, after <u>the adversary</u>	Probably Jewish enemy. But could be the enemy within, sinful flesh.
σατανᾶς Revelation 2\9	evil speaking from those who declare themselves to be Jews and are not, but *are* a synagogue of <u>the enemy</u>	A human enemy. Usual rendering in is "a synagogue of Satan", but that masks the truth that these false Jews are the enemy.

σατανᾶς Revelation 2\13 (twice)	I know your works and where you live, the location of the throne of <u>the enemy</u>, and you hold fast to my name, and you did not deny my faith in those days in which my faithful witness Antipas was around *and* was murdered nearby you, where <u>the enemy</u> lives	A human enemy. Usual rendering is "where Satan lives", but that masks the truth that these false Jews are the enemy.
σατανᾶς Revelation 2\24	I say to you others in Thyatira – as many who do not have this teaching, who have not known the deep things of <u>the enemy</u>	A human enemy. Usual rendering is "things of Satan", but that masks the truth that hostile men and women are the enemy.
σατανᾶς Revelation 3\9	I will cause those from the synagogue of <u>the enemy</u>, those declaring themselves to be Jews and are not	A human enemy. Usual rendering is "a synagogue of Satan", but that masks the true enemy.
σατανᾶς Revelation 12\9	the terrible dragon was hurled down, the ancient serpent, the one called *the* false accuser and <u>the enemy</u>, the one deceiving the whole inhabited world	A human enemy. All the enemy within, the carnal mind.
σατανᾶς Revelation 20\2	he took hold of the dragon, the ancient serpent, who is *the* false accuser and <u>the enemy</u>, and he shackled him for a thousand years	A human enemy.
σατανᾶς Revelation 20\7	when the thousand years have been completed, <u>the enemy</u> will be loosed out of his prison	A human enemy.
summary of possible meanings: a human enemy; a personal enemy; an abstraction for man's rebellion and antagonism towards the will and authority of the one true God; personification for man's rebellious heart and mind		**summary of renderings**: adversary, adversity, affliction, antagonism, enemy, hostility

✶

4. Occurrences of διάβολος, Strong's Concordance number g1228

This word διάβολος is neither a name nor a title for anybody, as 2 Timothy 3\3 and Titus 2\3 show, where it's used concerning humans. It is an adjective (masculine) acting as a substantive (noun). Occurs 38 times. The KJV has "the devil" (lower-case) for every occurrence, except at Revelation 12\9 where it has "the Devil" (capitalized); "slanderers" at 1 Timothy 3\11; and "false accusers" at 2 Timothy 3\3 and Titus 2\3. I like the KJV's "false accusers".

Linked with σατανᾶς (= *satanas*), occurring in the same phrases at Revelation 12\9, 20\2.

διάβολος	context	comment
διάβολος Matthew 4\1	Jesus was led up by the Spirit into the wilderness to be put to the test by the slanderer	The human enemy described as an adversary at Matthew 4\10, Mark 1\13, Luke 4\8. Some say the internal struggle of the carnal mind, sinful flesh.
διάβολος Matthew 4\5	the slanderer took him along to the Holy City, and he set him on the pinnacle of the Temple buildings	As above.
διάβολος Matthew 4\8	The slanderer also took him along to an exceedingly high mountain, and he showed him all the kingdoms of the world order	The human enemy described as an adversary at Matthew 4\10, Mark 1\13, Luke 4\8. The kingdoms of the world were already in Jesus' authority, so could not be in anybody's else's power to give away. See Matthew 4\10.
διάβολος Matthew 4\11	At that the slanderer left him	The human enemy described at Matthew 4\10, Mark 1\13, Luke 4\8.
διάβολος Matthew 13\39	the enemy who sowed them represents the slanderer, and *the* harvest represents *the* completion of the eon	A human enemy, presumably the Canaanite / Edomites.
διάβολος Matthew 25\41	Depart from me, you under a curse, into the eonian fire which has been prepared for the slanderer and his messengers	All speakers against the truth of God, "the slanderer and his messengers" being a figure of hendiadys, two things put for one. But these are the "goats", therefore most likely referring to the Edomites, those described at Obadiah and Revelation 2\9 and 3\9, slanderers and accusers of the brotherhood day and night.
διάβολος Luke 4\2-3	being tested by the slanderer *for* forty days ... the slanderer said to him, "If you are the Son of God, speak to this stone so that it might become bread ..."	A human enemy. Matthew 4\8-10.
διάβολος Luke 4\5	the slanderer led him up into a high mountain	A human enemy. Matthew 4\8-10.

διάβολος Luke 4\6	the slanderer said to him, "I will give you all this authority, and all their splendour, for it has been handed over to me and to whomever I wish to give it."	A human enemy. Matthew 4\8-10.
διάβολος Luke 4\13	having ended every testing, the slanderer departed from him until a *convenient* time	A human enemy. Matthew 4\8-10.
διάβολος Luke 8\12	the slanderer comes and snatches the oracle away from their heart	A human enemy. Matthew 13\39.
διάβολος John 6\70	Jesus answered them, "Did I not choose you, the twelve? Yet one of you is a slanderer."	A human enemy, Judas. No article in the Greek. Shows "the Devil" to be human.
διάβολος John 8\44	You are out of *your* father the false accuser, and you have a will to carry out the lusts of your father.	The serpent character at Genesis 3\1, or Cain.
διάβολος John 13\2	*when* supper had finished, the slanderer had already put *it* into the heart of Judas Iscariot, *son* of Simon, that he should betray him.	Probably bribing Jewish priesthood. See Luke 22\1-6.
διάβολος Acts 10\38	Jesus from Nazareth ... healing all who were being overpowered by the slanderer	Overpowered by their own rebellious nature, or by false teachers.
διάβολος Acts 13\10	Oh *you* full of every guile and all fraud! Son of a slanderer! Enemy of all righteousness! Will you not cease to pervert the straight ways of *the* Lord?	Either descendant of, or metaphorically, "son of" being a figure of speech (called "kenning") expressing character, as in "sons of thunder" and "sons of disobedience" and "sons of uselessness". No article in the Greek.
διάβολος Ephesians 4\27	Do not let the Sun go down on your anger, nor give an opportunity to evil speaking.	Probably abstract. There is an article in the Greek, but there often is with abstract nouns. Not "the Devil"!
διάβολος Ephesians 6\11	Put on the complete armour of God, for you to be able to hold your ground against the stratagems of the slanderer.	Human enemy.

διάβολος 1 Timothy 3\6-7	not newly planted, in case, smoking up with pride, he might fall into the condemnation of <u>the slanderer</u>… He must have, though, a good testimony also from those outside, in case he might fall into reproach and a snare of <u>the slanderer</u>	The literal human enemy, who condemns the believers and is their accuser day and night. Not impossibly, though, also the internal enemy of the carnal mind.
διάβολος 1 Timothy 3\11	Wives, likewise, *must be* grave, not <u>slandermongers</u>, sober, faithful in all things	Human. No article in the Greek.
δOr the enemy withinιάβολος 2 Timothy 2\26	they might sober up again, out of the snare of <u>the slanderer</u>, having been captured by him to do his will	The human enemy, personified. Or false teachers.
διάβολος 2 Timothy 3\3	without natural affection, implacable, <u>slandermongers</u>, unrestrained, savage, despisers of good	Human. No article in the Greek. This exhibits the true meaning.
διάβολος Titus 2\3	aged women, similarly, *to be* in deportment what becomes holy women, not <u>slandermongers</u>, not enslaved to much wine, teachers of what is right	Human. No article in the Greek. This exhibits the true meaning.
διάβολος Hebrews 2\14	Since, then, as the sons are sharers of flesh and blood, he himself also in a similar way partook of the same things, so that through death he might destroy that having the power of death, that is, <u>the slanderer</u>.	Probably abstract personification. Not impossibly, though, also the slanderer of Genesis 3.
διάβολος Jacob (James) 4\7	Submit yourselves, therefore, to God, and resist <u>the slanderer</u>, and he will flee from you.	Human enemy, the wolf who will flee from the flock (John 10). And enemy within, sinful flesh.
διάβολος 1 Peter 5\8	Your <u>falsely accusing</u> adversary roams around like a roaring lion, searching for whomever it can swallow up.	Abstract, used in its proper adjectival form, agreeing with "adversary". The word "adversary" here is ἀντίδικος (= *antidikos*), Strong's g476; also at Matthew 5\25 (twice), Luke 12\58, 18\3.

διάβολος 1 John 3\8 (three times)	He who practises sin is out of the slanderer, for from the beginning the slanderer commits sin. For this the Son of God was brought to light: that he might destroy the works of the slanderer.	Probably abstract personification. Not impossibly the slanderer of Genesis 3.
διάβολος 1 John 3\10	In this the Sons of God are brought to light, and so are the sons of the slanderer.	Probably abstract personification. Not impossibly, though, the slanderer of Genesis 3.
διάβολος Jude 9	the Archangel Michael, when contending with the slanderer argued about the legislative body of Moses, did not dare bring a judgement of slandering accusation against him, but said, "The Lord rebuke you!"	Human. Aligns with Zechariah 3. Notice the "slandering accusation" in the same sentence.
διάβολος Revelation 2\10	the false accuser will certainly throw some of you into jail so that you might be tested	A human enemy.
διάβολος Revelation 12\9	the terrible dragon was hurled out, the ancient snake, the one called the false accuser and the adversary, the one deceiving the whole inhabited world.	A human enemy. Some say the enemy within, sinful nature.
διάβολος Revelation 12\12	Woe to the Earth and the sea! For the false accuser has come down to you, having terrible boiling anger, knowing that he has a short time.	Human enemy, raging against us now, the Dragon.
διάβολος Revelation 20\2	he took hold of the dragon, the ancient snake, who is a false accuser and the adversary, and he shackled him up for a thousand years	A human enemy. Some say the enemy within, personified.
διάβολος Revelation 20\10	the false accuser deluding them was hurled into the lake of fire and brimstone where the Wild Beast and the Pseudo Prophet also had been hurled, and they will be tormented day and night, throughout the durations of the eons.	A human enemy. Or the enemy within, personified.

summary of meanings: an adjective meaning accuser, accusing, evil speaker, evil speaking, false accuser, falsely accusing, slanderer		summary of renderings: evil speaking, false accuser, falsely accusing, slanderer, **slandermonger**

5. "Lucifer", a fake translation

There is one further words to discuss from the King James and other church system versions, "Lucifer", at Isaiah 14\12. The Hebrew word they translate as "Lucifer" is הילל (= *hêlēl*), Strong's Hebrew Concordance reference number h1966. To put the passage into context, the prophet is using astral – star – imagery to describe the fall and destruction of the arrogant king of Babylon (14\4). Isaiah uses the poetical imagery of metaphor, calling the proud king a "shining star" who now has "fallen from the heavens" (his once exalted position. Compare Luke 10\18). The astral imagery is extended in the phrase "son of the morning" (14\12).

Describing people as "stars" is a frequent literary device of the prophets and apostles, and of Jesus also. Isaiah had used it earlier (Isaiah 13\10). Deborah used it (Judges 5\20). Daniel used it (Daniel 8\10). Jesus used it (Matthew 24\29). John used it (Revelation 1\16, 12\4). This astral imagery in Isaiah is a reversal of Job's astral metaphor, where Job personifies stars rejoicing (not being destroyed, like the king of Babylon) in the clauses "the morning stars sang" and "the sons of Elohim shouted for joy", personifying stars as rejoicing at Elohim's creation, as if even creation itself had been in joyful wonder (Job 38\7).

Isaiah, on the other hand, depicts the king of Babylon as a star to create a metaphor of cruel and powerful rulership of the worst kind imaginable. Isaiah continues his pronouncement of destruction on the king of Babylon with the words "You are cut down to the ground". The words "shining star" in Isaiah 14\12 are from the Hebrew הילל (= *hêlēl*), which occurs only here, therefore having no precedent, and can only be translated contextually. Green has it correctly as "shining star". It could also be rendered "bright star".

The King James men, however, unfortunately failed to perceive the typical astral imagery of a star fallen from the heavens, despite having the word "stars" at 14\13, the very next verse. Instead, they imposed their ancient paganistic dogma and translated הילל (= *hêlēl*) as "Lucifer". In doing so, they broke the structure of the passage, and shipwrecked the internal harmony of a typical biblical metaphor. Furthermore in Isaiah 14, they introduced into the text a different character, for the passage concerns the king of Babylon who is defined as a "man" and "carcass" at Isaiah 14\16 and 14\19. And on this disharmonious blunder is founded the fictional mythology of "Lucifer". If they meant it as the name of the morning star, Venus, it was a careless choice. For with "Satan" and "the Devil" everywhere else, almost every reader would make the connection. There are those who describe themselves as "Luciferians", worshipers of the Devil.

6. "The ruler of this world"

One last phrase to consider is Jesus' phrase which he used three times, "ruler of this world" (John 12\31, John 14\30, 16\11). Here are the passages:

"Now is the judgement of this world. Now the ruler of this world will be thrown out." ~ John 12\31.

"No longer will I speak many things with you, for the ruler of this world is coming and he has nothing in me." ~ John 14\30

[concerning the time of the coming eon] "the ruler of this world has been condemned." ~ John 16\11

How can we identify this "ruler of this world "? Perhaps the most advantageous of the three passages for identifying the ruler is the second, John 14\30. Jesus said the ruler of this world "is coming". Well, who came for him at his arrest? Was it a Babylonian mythical monster known as Lucifer and Satan and the Devil, lashing his forked tail, and prodding with his sharpened pitchfork (where is that in the Bible?)? Here is John's description of exactly who came:

"So Judas, taking along the cohort and officers from the senior priests and Pharisees, came there with torches and lamps and weapons." ~ John 18\3

This points, then, to the false teachers and false prophets from among Jews who were Edomites, who had stolen their places in the Temple system (Matthew 23\1-2). Jesus said that the ruler "has nothing in me". I take this to mean that the ruler will find no offence, no crime, no sin. He was the innocent lamb. The word "ruler" does not have to be a single individual, but could be representative of a body of people. There is no single man or woman who is the ruler of this world. And "world" does not have to mean the entire planet. It could be regional. The Biblical world.

The Book of Revelation shows "the synagogue of the enemy", and evil adversary, and shows also "the terrible dragon" and "the enemy" and "the false accuser" (Revelation 12). In those days there will be the principal force among the ten horns and seven heads, the Wild Beast with blasphemous names on its heads (Revelation 13\1). Jerusalem is a target of control for world powers. The *Talmud* declares the Jews as the superior race, and that is the propaganda. They speak about white genocide. Loxism is the word, their belief in superiority over everybody. Rome wants Jerusalem. But God and Christ want it also.

The representatives of the evil system who came to arrest Jesus, Edomites with Canaanite blood, were, prophetically speaking, "the ruler of this world". By "world" Jesus could have been referring simply to that local order, that local social order, the pronoun "this" signifying *"this social order"*.

What about, though, when Jesus says, "Now the ruler of this world will be thrown out"? Well, this could be a prophetic statement, saying that the events to follow – his death and resurrection – will bring about their destruction. John speaks in Revelation of their being "hurled out" (Revelation 12\9, Luke 1\51). This would fit with Jesus' third statement, "the ruler of this world has been condemned" (John 16\11), Jesus speaking at that time about conditions in the future Eon; so, again, prophetically.

These passages need consideration. Certainly there is no justification in them for the Babylonian fiction monster. Some might want to consider these three passages in John concerning "the ruler of this world" as being a personification of our internal sinful nature. That too will be "condemned" and "thrown out", but did that personification come for him at his arrest, as described at John 18\3? Obviously not.

Revelation in the word of God is progressive and further light comes as we study and pray.

Conclusion

The two Greek words σατανᾶς (= *satanas*) and διάβολος (= *diabolos*) are shown to have a variety, albeit small, of meanings, including probably sometimes to signify our internal hostile nature. They appear together at Revelation 12\9 and 20\2 in the phrase "false accuser and the adversary".

We say to God in our hearts that we do not understand Him; He cannot be entir[e] as demanded; He will not provide for us; He will not forgive us; nor will He send us in our needs. The heart and mind have an impressive armoury of stratagems. All th[ese] regret and learn to overcome.

Hebrews 2\14 says this of Jesus: "Since, then, as the sons are sharers of flesh and himself also in a similar way partook of the same things, so that through death he mig[ht] that having the power of death, that is, the false accuser." This "false accuser", [of] rebellion, will be destroyed when we have our resurrection minds and bodies. For now and praise God continually and by applying ourselves to obedience and reading w[e] guard yourselves against the stratagems of the false accuser.

With all this in mind, instead of blaming a roving infernal monster from the mythology, let us reconsider.

Chapter 28

Solomon and Esther
Two issues concerning the Old Covenant Texts

The King James Bible and others have after Nehemiah a story of <u>Esther</u>, then after Ecclesiastes <u>The Song of Songs</u>. This <u>Song of Songs</u> and <u>Esther</u> have human failings in common. These works cannot be claimed as being θεόπνευστος (= *theopneustos*), "God-breathed", "God-inspired" (2 Timothy 3\16). Neither has a claim to divine inspiration. They are without divine signature and without divine quality. Neither work has the name or title of God. They are not cited anywhere in Scripture, nor do they cite Scripture; in neither is there prophet or law, divine message or command for righteousness, encouragement to walk with God, or conduct of righteousness. Both open with the smell of lust and wine. In both there are unrebuked indulgences in the worst transgressions which come from ignoring the commands of God. It was in the first and second centuries after the apostles that the Old Testament canon, and New also, began to be discussed and collated. Over two works that there was particular debate: <u>Esther</u> and <u>The Song of Songs</u>. But they found their way in. The Counter Reformation Council of Trent, 1545-1563 declared <u>Esther</u> as canonical, because it is in the Latin Vulgate, and the Council's canon included also the Apocryphal books, which we also reject as canonical, but accept as useful and of interest. The LXX version of Esther is different to the MT version, so the text is unstable.

In terms of a poem and construction, <u>The Song of Songs</u> resembles notes towards an unfinished poem. As polyphonic (many voices) poetry it is undisciplined. It switches subjects and pronouns, so that accurately ascribing identities of the apparent speakers is a matter of debate. Its ending is out of mind ("flee away ..."), peculiar and unsatisfactory, lacking the signature of divine works. It's a celebration of prostitution, adultery and drinking. It strikes blasphemously at the heart of purity to call the arts of its king's wine-laced sexual lusts analogous to God and Christ and "the church" and Mary, and theologians' other hollow attempts to justify it. (How contrary it is to Mary!) It is nothing to do with "Christ and His church". There is no prophet speaking, no God, no Christ figure, no Christ-like figure of his Ekklesia. It is contrary to the righteous conduct of the patriarchs, and to the righteous works of prophets and apostles.

It's a godless story of a lust-addicted and married Israelite king seducing a non-Israelite (1\5, 5\10) woman of his harem with flatteries, wine, and the ostentation of a thundering car (3\7), contrasting with how the godly Isaac and Jacob met and courted Rebekah and Rachel, and contrasting with the conduct of Mary and Joseph. In the midst of passion he deserts her, leaving her heart-broken and "sick with love"; she goes looking and is beaten up by his city watchmen (3\1, 5\2-8). It expresses enquiry about the pubertal development of a child (8\8). Why? It is not parable or allegory: in those respects it has invited strangled notions devoid of truth.

Weak attempts to justify it as typology only expose how blasphemous it is to align its wine-fuelled lust and highly explicit bedroom imagery (4\1-5\1) with God and Christ. In practice it does not incite any righteous conduct towards God; its effect is to incite passion and desire which might have their place elsewhere. In his vanity, the king opens his poem flattering himself by having a woman panting for his kisses and "love", he a king of lechery (6\8) into whose bedroom she has gone (1\1-3). Why should a king write a vain poem about a woman panting with lust for him? The woman whom the king has composed as panting for him has lazily neglected her work in the family vineyard, making her brothers angry (1\6). She's one of the king's harem. He brags of many women praising him (1\4). She's a bragger also (2\1, 8\10).

Solomon's authorship, if it is Solomon's, neither sanctifies nor justifies this lusty and unhealthy poem. Even if Solomon's work, it should be excluded: not every single thing that even the apostle Paul wrote is in Scripture (1 Corinthians 5\9, Colossians 4\16). Apart from those lost letters referred to, Paul would have written many things, being a scholar, but there would be much that he would withhold from publication. And so it would be with all Christians. Solomon (if the author), as a king of lechery, is no example anyway: "Solomon ... had 700 wives, princesses, and 300 concubines, and his wives turned his heart away. [4] For it came to pass, when Solomon was old, that his wives turned his heart away after other gods, and his heart was not at peace with Yahweh his Elohim like the heart of his father David. [5] For Solomon went after Ashtoreth, the goddess of the Zidonians, and after Milcom, the abomination of the Ammonites" (1 Kings 11\2-5; and see Song 6\8).

Some commentators say the woman has two lovers, the king figure and a shepherd, although 1\7-14, aligned with 1\1-4, do not easily justify that. She's boiling with lust and love for the king.

Would Jesus speak any of this adulterous harem lust and drinking poem in teaching his disciples? Would he cite 1\1-3, 2\5-7, 4\1-16, 5\1-16, 6\8, 7\10, 8\8, 8\10, 8\14? Would Isaiah, would the apostles, write this as spiritual teaching? If the poem is supposed to be a picture of "Christ and the church", would you have Jesus behaving like the poem's king, and "the church" behaving like the king's harem prostitutes? He would be no spotless saviour. Or if a Christian man today behaved like the king and said, "Oh, it's not immoral. I'm a living picture of Christ and the church." ... he would be rightly called hypocrite. Why many Christians are prepared to ditch God's commands for purity and sobriety in order to justify this unrighteous poem, and then to go so far as even to align its very unrighteousness with Christ, is a mystery, unless, perhaps, lamely to justify their favourite translation.

So too is it hypocrisy and offence to try to justify the inclusion in the word of God this unrighteous poem. It would not fit in the New Covenant writings; nor then does it fit in the Old Covenant writings. WHO BENEFITS from its inclusion? Not the body of Christ. Not the record of the inspired writings of the prophets and apostles. How wayward, then, such circulatory and helpless comments such as "[T]he Song of Solomon has always been part of the canon because what follows from this conviction is the proof for the fact that the Song of Solomon describes in poetry the love between Christ and His church" (from a Reformed theology commentator). In other words, if you believe it's in because of tradition, that proves what it means. A most extraordinary sentence, founded on sand! Even its reverse is not true (that because it is *not* about "Christ and His church" it should *not* be in). What *does* debar it from being in the word of God is that it is no more than a disorganized and unsatisfactory poem about passion, lust, and drinking, and is of no spiritual significance or benefit but, rather, is entirely disharmonious with righteous teaching ("drink abundantly": 5\1, et cetera).

If, as claimed by some, to attempt lamely to justify its inclusion, it concerns "Christ and the church", so-called, why did the apostle Paul not use it as an illustration? Solomon followed "other gods" of his many female conquests; the woman is "sick with love" for him. This "song" is a work not of the spirit, but of the flesh. That is what it's all about; and nothing else. To spiritualize it overthrows the whole of Scripture, for nothing then becomes reliable for meaning what it really means; flesh can be turned to spirit: spirit can be turned to flesh; you can say what you like and nullify everything. What is this upholding of the licentious Song of Songs but an attempt to uphold errant English translations? I suggest it is nothing more than that. Unless, of course, they do not like God's commands for obedience and purity. To overlook the poem's impurity is to apply double standards. An early Talmudic rabbi proclaimed the poem "the holy of holies". In that case, it is probably a Talmudic work. He also said, "Had not the Torah been given, Canticles would have sufficed to guide the world." Guided in what? Gustave Moreau's delicious painting *Cantique des Cantiques*, 1893, tells all you need to know of what The Song of Songs is about. Shakespeare's *Cymbeline*, with its mercy and faith, would have more place among the prophets than this adulterous and unhealthy poem. Or Geoffrey Chaucer's *Legend of Good Women*. Good women, not adulterous members of harems.

Esther: whoring with the nations As others have observed, the first thing to publish about the Babylonian tale named Esther is that it is not among the Dead Sea Scrolls. Its authorship is uncertain (despite 9\20); it might be fable (1 Timothy 1\4, 4\7, 2 Timothy 4\4, 2 Peter 1\16). It concerns the Judahites. To understand who that is, we must put into our minds the tribe of Judah, that is, the house of southern Israel who broke away from their brothers in northern Israel and were taken captive by Babylon. Their patriarch Judah is described by his father at Genesis 49\9-12. The southern tribe of Judah were taken captive by Babylon for their defilement and rebellion (2 Kings 25, Isaiah 13\16-18, Ezekiel 16, Amos 5\25-27, Psalm 137, 2 Chronicles 35\11-23). The apostle Peter centuries later visited the very small remnant of their Christ-following descendants who remained there (1 Peter 1\1, 5\13); most returned to Israel or wandered westwards.

The narrative of Esther opens with Ahasuerus, a Babylonian king of lawlessness, making displays of pomp for 180 days, then feasting with much wine. His pomp and arrogance are reminiscent of Belshazzar (Daniel 5) and the Edomite king Herod (Matthew 14\6-8, Mark 6\17-23), as, like Herod, Ahaseurus makes grandiloquent offers to Esther of "half my kingdom". When the adulterous king disposes of his wife – queen Vashti (what happens to her is not said; maybe killed off, Henry VIIIth style) – Esther, a Judahite, of all the women he tries in his new harem prepared for him, wins his favour and she is made his new queen and she defiles herself and marries the adulterous and probably murderous king, the unwisest choice of husband in all of Babylon, guilty of the slaughter and capture of her own people, as if Mary were to marry Herod after his massacre. Esther, if a Judahite, for her it was forbidden for any reason to marry outside her people (Genesis 24\3, Deuteronomy 7\3-4, Joshua 23\12, 1 Kings 8\53 et cetera; "you shall make no Covenant with them ... You shall make no marriages with them"). Ezra and Nehemiah dissolved such marriages (Ezra 9\1-12, Nehemiah 13\23-30). Expediency is rebellion also. Seduced by royal flatteries, she is disobedient to the God of her patriarchs Abraham and Isaac and Jacob.

Godly women like Deborah, Hannah, Anna, Elizabeth, Tryphena and Tryphosa, and the mother of Jesus would not have joined the procession of young women going through "purification" (2\3, 2\9, 2\12) for going into harems of Babylonian king Ahaseurus or child-murderer Edomite king Herod, in order to become their queen. Nor would those righteous women, at the offer of half a kingdom, have asked for – and made – revenge killings of many thousands, and for bodies to be strung up, as Esther does. Mordecai tears his clothes and puts on sackcloth and ashes (4\1-3), but makes no appeal to God, nor can we assume he did, for if he did it would say so; compare Jonah 3\8, Nehemiah 9\2-3, and especially Daniel 9\3: "I set my face towards Adonai Elohim, to search by prayer and requests with fasting and sackcloth and ashes". There is only "mourning" among the Judahites, fasting and weeping, sackcloth and ashes – no word of prayer.

Like the daughter of Herodias, Esther responds to Ahasuerus's Herod-like offers of "half my kingdom" by wanting killings and bodies strung up and altogether has 75,811 people killed (albeit one of them, Haman, is deserving of justice). There is no seeking the Lord God before they do this: another sin.

Where would the Judahites, in captivity in Babylon, get forces to slaughter many thousands? How would those alleged "enemies" be identified, those "hostile to them" (8\11)? There are many hostile to us, but we do not kill one of them, let alone tens of thousands of them and their sons and their "little ones and women" (8\11). The "ten sons of Haman" whom they kill (9\10) were not said to be involved in their father's plot against Mordecai and the Judahites.

It is said, "many people of the land became Judahites" (8\17). It does not say that they confess their sins and turn to the Lord God and adopt the religion of the Israelite patriarchs and Covenants. It only says they "became Judahites". There is no testimony of the commands of the Lord God so that the people might "become Judahites". If this is a true story, we are supposed to believe that, because thousands are going to be slaughtered, many changed their race. The verb for "became Judahites" is יהד (*yahad*), which is not found in the word of God, only in Esther. It is not possible to change genealogy, to become a physical member of another race. (Many make the same mistake concerning Galatians 3\7.) The Judahites – in the word of God – were the tribe of Judah, descended from Abraham, Isaac and Jacob. They could convert only to the *religion*, not the *tribe* or the *race*. People are converted only by hearing the words of God. These "many people of the land" alleged to have "become Judahites" only did so because of the king's decree that the Judahites might "avenge themselves on their enemies" (8\13) and "for fear of the Judahites" (8\17, 9\2). That is not a testimony towards following the Lord God. In the authentic Scriptures of God, the phrase "fear of the Judahites" occurs *negatively*, not *positively*, because of persecution (John 7\13, 19\38, 20\19), and is not said to make any turn to God.

Who are the 75,800? Before Haman arises against the Judahites there has been no previous mention of hostility from anybody else. How are the slaughtered mass of 75,800 supposed to be identified among other people as "enemies", especially if, allegedly, "many people of the land became Judahites"? Imagine the condemnation from critics who already dislike the apostle Paul if he had done these things. When there were plots against Paul, a man of righteousness, he did not slouch into political intrigue to have them killed, nor to have their uninvolved and innocent sons killed and strung up, then 75,800 people killed as well, including "little ones and women". Imagine the justified outrage if, in British justice, a criminal caught conspiring were hanged, and his uninvolved sons also were hanged and strung up publicly, then 75,800 of his people, all uninvolved, were slaughtered. We are better than that. Yet there follows "feasting and gladness" after the evil slaughter of 75,800.

The story calls these days "Purim, after the name of pur", so that "these days of Purim should not fail from among the Judahites" (9\26-28). The word פור (*pur*) is not a word of the Bible. The word occurs only in Esther (at 3\7, 9\24, 9\26, 9\28, 9\29, 9\31, 9\32). It is not in the books of the word of God. The Israelite practice of casting lots was for positive purposes, not to slaughter people (Leviticus 16\8, Joshua 18\6-10, 1 Samuel 14\42, Jonah 1\7, Nehemiah 10\34, 11\1, 1 Chronicles 24\31, 25\8, 26\13-14, Acts 1\26). By enemies it could be used for evil (Joel 3\3, Obadiah 1\11, Nahum 3\10, Psalm 22\18, Matthew 27\35, Mark 15\24, Luke 23\34, John 19\24). There is no record in the prophets and apostles of any such day of "Purim" being kept by them or anyone. It is not recorded in the Gospels or any New Covenant writings as being kept by Christ and the apostles. Nor, rightly, was it kept by the early Christians in the New Covenant writings. It is ignored, rightly, among Christians now, having no place with us. Esther, who cannot be ascribed as a righteous woman, and who makes no appeal to God, confirms "these matters of Purim" (9\29-32), but the *Biblical* feasts concern not mass slaughter but God's reconciliation with the house of Jacob, and they are listed in Leviticus 23. Esther has no authority from God to pronounce any feast for Israelites.

This, in the word of tradition, is supposed to be a story of God's protection for His people, but it was for unrighteousness and refusing the prophets that they were taken captive in the first place, and God did not protect them from the Babylonians. There had been no protection for the house of Israel either, when they were taken captive by Assyria. Nor were those of Judea protected from the Roman destruction of Jerusalem in AD 70. Divine protection is not unconditional. Divine protection from enemies comes from obedience (Leviticus 26\3-8, Deuteronomy 32\30, Joshua 23\10, Judges 7\7-12, 2 Chronicles 7\14, Hebrews 11\33). Esther is a story not of divine protection for anybody, but of conspiring, just as Haman does, with an evil king, rather than seeking God. Divine protection, being conditional, would not be ready for an unrighteous God-forsaking people.

The Judahites in this story obstinately disregard God. That disregard and rebellious whoring with the nations (Ezekiel 16), which is continued by Esther, was the reason for the house of Judah's captivity into Babylon in the first place.

The story of Esther probably came from the ancient Babylonian *Talmud*. Neither Mordecai nor Esther make any lament for their captivity, nor appeal to God in their threats of destruction. This is in contrast to the righteous zeal of the prophet Daniel and the apostle Paul.

Those who like and accept this story focus only on the vengeance on Haman, but forget, ignore or excuse the stew of evil, their defence a matter of misguided allegiance to the captive Judahites rather than to internal harmony of the Scriptures and the demands of righteous conduct.

There is no name or title "Elohim" in Esther. Some have seen the title "Yahweh" in Esther, buried meaninglessly in dubious codes (1\20, 5\4, 5\13, 7\5, 7\7), but these are nothing. Anybody can find apparent patterns, acrostics and codes embedded by chance in language. For example, "a prophet lived near Jerusalem" contains the name "devil" if you want to look for it. Or what can you find in this: "the people sat and ate"; or in "send a gnat as a curse"; or in "feed it to the dog"? The alleged Hebrew acrostics embedding "Yahweh" (= יהוה) in Esther, as described by *The Companion Bible*, expose them only as meaningless, random and occurring in different words: "all the wives will give" (1\20) in a backwards-reading acrostic; "let the king and Haman come this day" (5\4) in a forwards-reading acrostic; "all this profits me nothing" (5\13) in initial letters of the final letters of four words; "who is he, and where is he" (7\5) in initial letters of a forwards-reading acrostic; "that evil was determined against him" (7\7) in a forwards-reading acrostic from the initial letters. There is no pattern, no consistency and no meaning in any of that, unless strangled out of it, which you can do with any text. Doubtless other wholly unintentional codes and acrostics can be found buried in many phrases in many books. Those in Esther cannot be proved to have been deliberately done, or with any illuminating purpose, such as can be said concerning, for example, acrostics in Psalm 119. Even if the author of Esther did intend them, what do they mean? Why would you want to strangle patterns and types and symbols out of a story of unrighteous people, in order to justify its inclusion among righteous writings of the prophets and apostles?

As with The Song of Songs, what is the value of the inclusion of Esther, an uninspired and uninspiring deathly story? WHO BENEFITS? *Cui bono* (for whose good)? Not the body of Christ. Nor the record of the inspired writings of the prophets and apostles. It contradicts righteous behaviour and celebrates evil.

This work, like The Song of Songs, cannot be claimed as being θεόπνευστος (= *theopneustos*), "inspired by God", "by divine inspiration" (2 Timothy 3\16). It has no lesson from God. It is not edifying in the love of God. Its tone and spirit are alien to Biblical writings and do not read like the righteous works of the prophets and apostles. It is not cited anywhere in Scripture and it does not cite Scripture – the ultimate test. Such cross-referencing is one of the authentications of divine inspiration. The story concludes with smugness over a mass slaughter of uninvolved Persians, including "little ones and women" (8\11). It displays feasting, drunkenness, a harem, "sexual undertones ... that are deeply disturbing" (*Jerusalem Post*). Numerous Christians and scholars have rejected it as fiction and doubted or disputed it on grounds of inspiration, authenticity and usefulness, whether fiction or not. The behaviour of Esther is in contrast to Daniel, the righteous man of God. Compare Esther with Daniel who, unlike Esther, *refused* the king's table and prospered (Daniel 1\8-20). Why did Esther not do the same? How, if Esther is real, would she have responded to the rebuke of prophets?

Some commentators, including Josephus, have suggested king Ahasuerus of the story is the same as Artaxerxes who caused the rebuilding of Jerusalem to be stopped (Ezra 4\21) (although both names appear at Ezra 4\6-7); the LXX, a different and more dramatic version of the story, has him so. And if the same, that Artaxerxes, causing hostility to Jerusalem, would be the Herod-like king with whom the harem woman Esther was happy to be made his queen. If true, why is this not mentioned in either Ezra or Esther, and why did Esther's charms not influence him in *this* matter?

Should anyone regret the loss of a (questionable) story of the protection of Israelites, they can turn to the true and authentic story of the day God delivered a prayerful Israel from the Midianites with just 300 of Gideon's men (Judges 7); or the day God defended a prayerful Jerusalem from the Assyrians by His angel striking 185,000 of them (2 Kings 19\35). These were through the righteous prayers of Gideon and Isaiah, not defiant people, not celebrations of drunken feasting, not whoring with the nations, not people making an illegal marriage, not the vengeful slaughter of innocents including babies because of one inimical man. "Finally, brothers, whatever things are true, whatever things honourable, whatever things righteous, whatever things pure, whatever things lovely, whatever things of good report, if any virtue, if any praise, meditate on these things" (Philippians 4\8).

Just because <u>The Song of Songs</u> and <u>Esther</u> might have been smuggled into an OT text, just because they are in the King James Bible and its derivatives does not mean they should be there. If they can get the books of the Old Testament in the wrong order, add and take away, alter grammar, invent meanings, paraphrase, if they are men of the wrong spirit to be handling the word of God, if they can race through the translation work in a few years, then in what else, we have to ask, can they be misled? In what else can we fail to trust them? The modern versions of the international religious system even use corrupt Alexandrian Greek texts, when the preserved Byzantine texts are freely available to their translators and editors. How, then, can these popular versions also be trusted concerning the so-called canon of the word of God?

It is those having the true spirit of Christ who must decide from *internal* evidence what are God's books, and we must not shirk from that or be timid about it. From *internal* evidence it becomes quite a simple matter. It is not to early rabbis and robed bishops, nor to the Council of Trent, nor to decorated theologians from academies that we should entrust one of the most important tasks on Earth, the selection of the canon of our Scriptures. Nobody of the early centuries after the apostles had any more authority in determining what are God's book than have knowledgeable and concerned believers in Christ today. It must come finally from those having the true spirit of Christ, for those not having his spirit "are not his" (Romans 8\9) and are disqualified (although their academic contributions and histories might be valuable). They are *our* books. *We* are the custodians. Work concerning the canon, the manuscripts, and translation – as this preface demonstrates – is not a finished work, although I anticipate the canon is settled without The Song of Songs and Esther. They cannot be said to be the word of God. Nothing of righteousness and faith is lost without the impediments of these two uninspired and uninspiring books; rather, on the contrary, translations of the word of God are cleansed and purified without them, another alleluyah for translation truth.

The house of Judah was taken into captivity for disobedience and idolatry. Now, in this story, look at them. Regarding Esther being in the king's harem (2\14-17), it is written, "There shall be no prostitute among the daughters of Israel" (Deuteronomy 23\17). Her marriage to an adulterous foreign king is sin. Then chapter 9, verse 10, has it that the "ten sons of Haman" were put to death for their father's crime. This is yet more unrighteous and illegal conduct. For it is written in the holy law: "The fathers shall not be put to death for the sons, nor shall the sons be put to death for the fathers. Each man shall be put to death for his own sin" (Deuteronomy 24\16, 2 Kings 14\6, Jeremiah 31\30, Ezekiel 18\4, 18\20). Adherents to the Esther story seem unworried about that, as they seem unworried about the other illegal and unrighteous acts of the story (nor about the vices in the Song of Solomon). Esther and her companions (if the story is not fictional) were already in captivity in Babylon for transgressing God's commandments, and they pile up yet more and more transgressions, yet this is not condemned but celebrated.

The acts of righteous captives of Judah in Babylon are such as those of the prophet Daniel and his friends: refusing the king, refusing his delicacies, refusing his gods, interpreting his dreams; and making prayers and expressing faith in the God of Israel:

Daniel 1\11-13: "Daniel said ... [12] 'Test your servants ... for ten days, and let them give us vegetables to eat and water to drink. [13] Then let our faces be examined before you, our appearance and the appearance of the young men who eat the serving of the king's delicacies and, as you see fit, deal with your servants.'"

2\17-18: "Daniel went to his house, and made the thing known to Hananiah, Mishael, and Azariah, his friends, [18] so that they might pray for mercy from Elah Shamayin."

3\18: "[B]e it known to you, oh king, that we will not serve your gods, nor worship the golden image that you have set up."

6\10-11: "[Daniel] bent down on his knees three times a day and prayed, and he gave thanks before his Elah, as he had always done. [11] Then these grandees assembled, and they found Daniel praying and seeking mercy before his Elah."

6\23: "Daniel was taken out of the den, and no injury was found on him, because he had trusted his Elah."

9\3-6: "And I set my face towards Adonai Elohim, to search by prayer and requests with fasting and sackcloth and ashes. [4] And I prayed to Yahweh my Elohim and made my confession, and I said, 'Adonai the mighty and awesome El, keeping the Covenant and loving kindness for those who love Him and for those who keep His commandments, [5] we have sinned, and committed iniquity, and acted lawlessly, and we have rebelled by departing from Your commandments and from Your judgments. [6] Nor have we listened to Your servants the prophets who in Your name spoke to our kings, our rulers, and our fathers, and to all the people of the land.'"

9\20-21: "And while I was speaking, and praying, and declaring my sin and the sin of my people Israel, and presenting my request before Yahweh my Elohim, for the appointed mountain of my Elohim, [21] yes, while I was speaking in prayer ..."

10\2-3: "In those days I, Daniel, was mourning for three sevens of days. [3] I ate no desirable food; neither flesh nor wine came into my mouth; nor did I anoint myself at all until three sevens of days were fulfilled."

So are the typical behaviours of the righteous. No such passages are found in Esther. She *married* the king! Nor are they found in the seductions of the Song of Solomon. The divine attitude concerning the rebellious house of Israel was expressed to the prophet Ezekiel:

"Is it a light thing to the house of Judah that they commit the abominations that they commit here? For they have filled the land with violence, and they have come back to provoke Me to anger and, indeed, they put the Asherim to their nose. [18] Therefore I will also deal in fury. My eye will not spare, nor will I have pity and, although they cry in My ears with a loud voice, still I will not listen to them" (Ezekiel 8\17-18).

The idea of the story of Esther being divine protection is myth. Let it sink in that no protection was given when they were taken captive for their abominations and idolatry:

"And all the chiefs of the priests and the people were continually acting treacherously in all the abominations of the nations, and they defiled the House of Yahweh that He had set apart in Jerusalem. [15] And Yahweh Elohim of their fathers sent word to them by His messengers, rising early and sending word, because He had compassion on His people and His place of habitation, [16] but they kept mocking the messengers of Elohim, and they despised His words, and scoffed at His prophets, until the anger of Yahweh rose against His people until *there was* no remedy. [17] So He brought against them the king of the Chaldeans, who killed their young men with the sword in the House of their Sanctuary, and had no compassion on young man or virgin, old man or very old. He gave everyone into his hand" (2 Chronicles 36\14-17).

At least once a week I have to defend the word of God from being incomplete, when silly claims are made the Vatican hides books that should be in the Bible. God has preserved *His* books. I reject such claims of hidden books and say there are too many books: there should be 64, not 66; and the 64 reflect a divine signature. I also reject such claims by saying that those making them do not like the books that are already in the Bible, yet they want more.

✶

Chapter 29

Was the King James Bible of 1611 an unnecessary publication? The Catholic Douai-Rheims Bible of 1610 was very slightly better

✦

1. KING JAMES

The King James Bible was commissioned by the king in 1603. It was completed rapidly, and published in 1611. James's will in commissioning it was to unite and extend his empire. Never was it stated that the purpose of the translation should be a dynamic labour to recover the truths of the prophets and apostles that had been lost through the international church system. Rushed through in just 8 years, it went under only 4 edits.

James demanded of it that it is "to be read in the whole Church, and no other" (Nicholson, p. 59). Therefore, if you are not a member of what he calls "the whole Church" the King James Bible is not for you. It has on the title page, in capital letters, "APPOINTED TO BE READ IN CHURCHES". In other words, not at home by the ploughboy. And not in Puritan and other Separatist assemblies hated by the persecuting king.

King James was an initiated Freemason. There exists a mural of him kneeling at the altar of initiation at the Lodge of Scoon and Perth No. 3 Lodge in Scotland. The event happened on 15 April 1601. Doubtless he employed fellow Freemasons for his translating work. Just as Herod employed fellow Edomites in the Temple.

But more than that. King James was a filthy beast. He blasphemed Christ in words that anger me to recall. He was a homosexual of "louche sexuality" (Nicholson, p. 120). He was intrigued by the occult, and wrote about it. He could be foul-mouthed. Was given to bouts of drunkenness. Was extravagant and vain. He had 24 dishes daily brought to him for lunch (Nicholson, p. 120).

He was a persecutor of non-conformist Christians, saying he would "harry them out of the land or worse".

He was against the beautiful life-saving acts by the midwives of Egypt who were protecting the Israelite children (Exodus Chapter 1). He would presumably have sided with Pharaoh (Nicholson, p. 58). Nicholson writes: "James would have been on Herod's side" (p. 58).

It was well known king James had a lover named George.

An historian Rictor Norton writes: "While riding through the bustling streets of London from 1603 to 1621, one was liable to hear the shout 'Long live Queen James!' King James I of England and VI of Scotland was so open about his homosexual love affairs that an epigram was circulated which roused much mirth and nodding of the heads: *Rex fuit Elizabeth: nunc est regina Jacobus*—'Elizabeth was King: now James is Queen.' "

James had "a weakness for beautiful boys" (Nicholson, p. 61). Not only was the king a predatory homo. Norton writes:

"Every day [note, "Every day"] some aspiring Lord—notably Sir William Manson—would hire a troup of handsome young ragamuffin boys, scrub their faces clean with curdled milk, curl their hair, powder them and perfume them, dress them in silk and lace, and lead them in dainty procession around the throne in order to seduce the King's favour. Marvellously delighted by this display of prime mignon [sic: little flowers] at first, James quite quickly not only grew weary with surfeit, but realized that he was being made a fool of, and he gave Buckingham orders to clear the court in 1618. This marked the end of the riotous period and the beginning of a period when he would mellow, and, eventually, slide into a state of depression." (Rictor Norton, "Queen James and His Courtiers", *Gay History and Literature*, 8 January 2000, updated 9 January 2012 <http://rictornorton.co.uk/jamesi.htm>.)

I will not repeat some of the things written by king James and about him. They are vulgar. Only let it be said, he was popularly known as "Queen James".

The preface of the King James Bible is a sickly adoration of king James, whom it promotes as almost another saviour. It exhorts that King James might become "the wonder of the world in this latter age for happiness and true felicity". It addresses him with such flattery as: "Your very name is precious ... their eye doth behold You with comfort, and they bless You in your hearts, as that sanctified Person, who, under God, is the immediate Author of their true happiness. And this their contentment doth not diminish or decay, but every day increaseth and taketh your strength." To the paid translators he was "Your most Sacred Majesty".

Doubtless its Masonic and royal authority propelled the kjv-only movement.

2. THE TRANSLATORS AND THEIR ALLEGIANCE

In 1603, King James hired around 50 men to make a Bible translation. Some of these, including the chairman, were inquisitors for the king against independent non-conformist Christians, seeing them interrogated and murdered. Catholics could be hounded and dragged through the streets and cut to pieces. Puritans and Separatists, independent-minded and self-regulating Christians, men and women of the spirit, were fleeing from these vile persecutors.

James's translators were not men desperate to discover the truth of the prophets and apostles of God and Christ.

Years ago on a website article, "Which Bible Translation", I came across this:

"Most people today are totally ignorant about its translators. They were a very mixed selection of Anglican clergymen. They included brilliant scholars, as well as murderers, drunkards and adulterers. My good friends in America, especially those who believe the KJV is the one true Bible, should note that some of their ancestors, the pilgrim fathers, left this country (England) to escape persecution from some of these very men."

The proprietor of that website told me the source of his information was *Power and Glory*, Adam Nicolson (2003).

From Nicolson's book, *Power and Glory*, I found a number of the king's translators were ambitious churchmen, flesh-natured men of the flesh-natured religion. They included inquisitors, torturers, a debauched drunken pornographer. They were cruel, brutal, Calvinists, thieves, nepotists, purchasers of titles, ambitious, self-seeking careerists, sickly crawlers to royalty, lovers of wealth, intolerant, entirely worldly, ornamental, religious and ritualistic, haters and hunters of those with different viewpoints, especially haters of Catholics and Separatists.

They were on the whole an unlikeable and unrighteous brood. George Abbott, one of the translators, had 140 Oxford undergraduates arrested for not taking their hats off to him.

Some of the translators were inquisitors and persecutors of men who denied the authority of the churches' bishops. Such men, known as Separatists, were imprisoned, hung on chains, tortured, interrogated by the bishops, including the chairman of the King James Bible translators, Launcelot Andrewes, and condemned to cruel deaths, watched on by the bishops.

Catholics had to hide themselves in safe houses, crouching in chimneys and wherever they could to conceal themselves from the king's search parties.

A successful interrogation of any non-conformist was considered to be a good career move. It pleased the king. Non-conformity was considered immoral.

Richard Bancroft ruthlessly pursued Puritans which, a contemporary historian noted, "hardened the hands of his soul" (Nicholson, p. 46). Bancroft mocked and insulted the Puritans and persecuted them (Nicholson, pp. 46, 74). Such was Bancroft's anger and hatred against them he even hired spies, using bribes and threats to gain access to secret meetings. Those who refused to sign up to ritualistic conformity of the Church of England he had expelled from their ministry. These good men, these persecuted Christians, would in time become leaders of the Pilgrim Fathers (Nicholson, p. 86). Those who didn't flee to Holland were arrested and jailed in filthy rat-infested dungeons, without straw and bedding.

An 18-year-old boy, Roger Waters, was kept hanging on chains for over a year. He was interrogated by another inquisitor from the translating team, Thomas Sparkes, who tried to convince the boy Roger Waters of his supposed offence (Nicholson, pages 86-87). He was locked in a stinking pit that was nicknamed "Limbo".

When Bancroft began hiring translators for the king, Launcelot Andrewes, now Dean of Westminster Abbey, was made chairman. Launcelot Andrewes was "bewitched by ceremony" (Nicholson, p. 27), and his fingers glittered with episcopal rings (Nicholson, p. 190). He also was a persecuting inquisitor for the king. A man named Henoch Clapham criticized Andrewes, accusing him of being self-serving. So Henoch Clapham was imprisoned, refusing to agree to the retraction composed by the furious Andrewes. Clapham was kept in prison for 18 months for that.

One righteous Christian whom the inquisitors William Hutchinson and Launcelot Andrewes interrogated was Henry Barrow, a leading Separatist arrested in 1587. The righteous man Henry Barrow answered from the Scriptures, with Andrewes all the time trying to trip him up. Like the Pharisees against Jesus. Nicholson reports it: "Barrow said his imprisonment had been horrible. He had been there for three years, and the loneliness of it, the sheer sensory deprivation, the nastiness of the conditions, had sunk him deeper into depression." And: "Andrewes then uttered one of the most despicable remarks he ever made ... Andrewes's reply, witty, supercilious, a pastiche of the sympathetic confessor, told Barrow: 'You are most happy. The solitary and contemplative life I hold the most blessed life. It is the life I would choose.' "

Barrow replied, "You speak philosophically, but not Christianly."

Nicholson continues: "The poor man was lonely, longing for his friends and for a sight of the sky, from which the intolerance of the state had excluded him. Andrewes's breathtaking insouciance continued until the last." And: "the rising self-congratulatory confidence of the young Master of Pembroke College, prebendary of St. Paul's, vicar of St. Giles Cripplegate, a candidate for the bishopric of Salisbury, sweeping out of the prison parlour door, with his departing quip, his patronizing flourish: could you ask for a more chilling indictment of established religion than that?" (pp. 91-92).

The righteous Barrow was executed in 1593, saying, "These holy hands of mine are much more glorious than any of theirs."

Other persecutors among the translating team – persecutors employed by the king – were Hadrian à Saravia and Thomas Sparkes (Nicholson, p. 88). Hadrian à Saravia was involved in interrogating a Separatist by the name of Daniel Studley.

A favourite passage of the Separatist Christians was: "Come out from among them, and be separate, says the Lord, and do not touch the unclean thing, and I will receive you, and be a father to you, and you shall be my sons and daughters, says the Lord Almighty" (Nicholson, p. 90). Anathema to Andrewes, Bancroft and king James.

Another in the translating team was Richard Thompson, "a drunk pornographer" (Nicholson, p. 192), a known degenerate. He was described by William Prynne as "a debosh'd English Dutchman, who seldom went one night to bed sober" (Nicholson, pp. 99-100).

In 1608 the company of Separatists set out on the *Mayflower* for New Plymouth, tired of the struggle of living in England and of the king and his Bible-translating persecutors. They could tolerate those men no longer.

Three years later, in 1611, the King James Bible was published.

How much of the character of Christ did the translators display, then? What spiritual discernment? How could they understand anything spiritual? In the days of the Tower of Babel, these men would have been interpreters. It was said of Andrewes he would have been "chief interpreter at the Tower of Babel". Men of Babylon. Men with Babylonian teachings. Men to escape from. Before God comes down and destroys their tower.

If the spirit was not in them, how could it ever come out of them?

They were four-square on with the pillars of Babylon.

It is written that spiritual things are understood spiritually, that is, by those having the spirit of God and Christ (1 Corinthians 2\14): "the natural man does not receive the things of the spirit of God, for they are foolishness to him; nor can he know them, because they are discerned spiritually". Those not having the spirit of Christ, Paul says, are "not his" (Romans 8\9). Not Christ's.

After Constantine's hoax conversion vision, a political conversion to "Christianity", he had his wife Fausta suffocated in a boiling bath, and executed his son Crispus, his brother-in-law Licinius, and Licinius's son. King James's translating team saw true Christians murdered – at their own hand – by the state.

"You speak philosophically, but not Christianly," the righteous man Henry Barrow said to Andrewes. What wonderful answer to a devil of the flesh.

To the man of the flesh, "Spare not the rod" means to thrash a child with weapons of punishment. To the man of the spirit, "Spare not the rod" means do not fail to guide with a gentle rod of the tender Shepherd who cares for his sheep.

3. RESULTS OF THEIR WORK

Never was it stated that the purpose of the translation should be dynamic labour to recover the truths of the prophets and apostles that had been lost through the international church system.

The translators were divided into committees, to work on different sections of the Bible, which explains why many themes of the King James Bible are discordant, destroying the miraculous internal harmony of the prophets and apostles. There is disharmony in the translation, and it is even inconsistent with itself, such as, for example, "world without end" and "end of the world" (both of which are wrongly translated). It is easily apparent that the translators lacked translation principles.

They included the Apocrypha, which is not part of the inspired writings of God. There are textual issues the translators failed to resolve. Its Old Testament books are in the wrong order.

It has occultic and pagan teachings of the Mysteries religion: ghosts, Lucifer, Satan, the Devil, going into hell fire, people going to Heaven, immortality of the soul, Easter, giants, unicorn, satyrs, cockatrice; all mythological figures and concepts.

The original publication had pictures with symbols of a secret handshake, a diagram of a hierarchy structure, and the Sun of Sun Worship. Its James 3\1 has "masters" instead of "teachers".

Some of its language is incomprehensible jibberish, such as Exodus 38\4, 2 Corinthians 6\11-13). Nicholson says, "[its] language it seemed was not the language of the people" (p. 228).

Its punctuation is appalling and scruffy. I have seen better punctuation in primary schoolchildren's work.

It's Calvinistic, which was achieved by adding words not in the Greek text, "before the world began".

It does have some good words from a literary point of view, but these are not concerning the major doctrinal points.

It promotes Paul as another saviour of the Israelites (Romans 9\3).

It blasphemes God with "God forbid", reflecting not a word of the underlying Greek.

It is heavily influenced by the Latin Vulgate, especially concerning the person of Christ, of which matter I have tabulated in as many as 80 pages. The translators were given by their employers the Bishops' Bible, as David Daniell explains (which I also cite in Chapter 1, page 2):

When James 1 gave his Bible revisers the huge Bishops' Bible as their foundation, which meant that the Latin Vulgate-based Rheims version would be attractive to them, he ensured that a wash of Latinity would be spread over Tyndale's English ... The objection was not narrowly political. Powerful ecclesiastical voices throughout Europe maintained that the Latin Bible was the true word of God and that the moves of humanist scholars to press for the originality of Hebrew and Greek was a blasphemous and seditious conspiracy born of hatred. ~ Daniell, p. xxiv

It is deliberately Latin and awkward, to keep the word of God from the ploughboy. For a simple example, "Then spake Jesus" should be "Then Jesus spoke". It's not ORGANIC, but PROCESSED. It does not follow the grammatical structures of the underlying sentences of the Hebrew and Greek.

Time and again, it is PROCESSED, rather than ORGANIC. It alters grammatical forms of words, grammatical structures of phrases and sentences, meanings of words, and it adds and it takes away and it changes.

It would not translate back into the original underlying languages.

The translators altered nouns and adjectives, verbs and adverbs, pronouns and prepositions. These alterations, doctoring of the text, produced results that agree with the teachings of men of the flesh, the natural religion of the international church system – Roman and Protestant and others – and they are in conflict with the teachings of the prophets and apostles. The translation adds and takes away, an offence punishable by God, as stated in Proverbs 30\6, 2 Peter 3\16, and Revelation 22\18-19.

By doing these things the translators shipwreck every major teaching of the prophets and apostles, especially concerning the person of Christ. As I have stressed again and again, in the King James Bible translators' failure to adopt translation principles they shipwrecked the prophets' and apostles' themes of who God is; who Christ is; who the Holy Spirit is; what the holy spirit is; creation; election; salvation; our structural identity; our destiny; the gospel message; Paradise; God's words to Eve; God's words to Cain; whom Jacob met at Genesis 32\1; money; Moses; Jesus' death; Jesus' resurrection; the success of Jesus' New Covenant; what "satan" and "devil" mean; who the real enemy is; the identity in the New Testament of the house of Israel and God's faithfulness to them; the gospel promise of life on Earth in the coming eons; what the New Testament is really about; what Paul's work really was; and even the immortality of God. It blasphemes God, implying by the translators' ignorance that one occurrence of "Satan" is God. It blasphemes God with "God forbid", reflecting not a word of the underlying Greek.

The preface is a sickly adoration of King James, whom it promotes as almost another saviour.

The translators spent only eight years, saying in the preface they were "hastened" by the King; in which time it is not possible to gain understanding of the major themes of the prophets and apostles, even less so when influenced so strongly by the Latin Vulgate and carried out by men of the flesh, paid for their work by an unrighteous King interested in the occult and who had a male lover *and* a wife.

In 1997 I wrote that the Scriptures of God had fallen into the wrong hands. Nicholson wrote: "This [concerning 2 Cor. 6\11-13] is clearly a translation done by people who didn't really understand what they were translating, and in the circumstances rhythmic language and interesting vocabulary can do very little to save the situation" (p. 225).

I do not like to read or hear the King James Bible. I do not like the spirit behind it. I do not like the spirit of the man who commissioned it. I do not like the spirit of the translators. I have been looking into these things for quarter of a century. Its Jesus is "another Jesus" and its spirit is "another spirit" and its gospel is "another gospel" (2 Corinthians 11\4).

4. THE DOUAI-RHEIMS BIBLE
In 1610 the Catholics published the first complete English translation of the Bible.

It was translated from the Latin Vulgate. It contains the Apocrypha. It has the Old Testament books in the wrong order. It is Calvinistic. It shipwrecks the same themes that the Protestant King James Bible shipwrecks. It has the same "Lucifer" and "Satan" and "Devil" and "hell fire" as does the King James Bible.

However, contrary to Protestant expectations, it teaches salvation by "grace" and "faith" and not by works.

It is often stylistically better than the King James Bible.

It is properly punctuated, done with care and respect.

It has some serious passages correctly translated, where the King James Bible has blundered, especially concerning the person of Christ.

Exodus 38\4, which the King James Bible renders incomprehensible, is clear in the Douai-Rheims. (Its 2 Corinthians 6\11-13, though, is no better.) Its Hebrews 3\2 has of Jesus "faithful to him that made him", where the King James fidgets the text with "appointed", to avoid saying that God created or made Jesus. Its Genesis 3\16 has "under thy husband's power", where the King James blunders with "desire". Its Matthew 5\4 has "land", where the King James blunders with "earth". It does not change "Greek" to "Gentile" at Romans 2\9, 2\10, 3\9 (although, unfortunately, it changes it at John 7\35, 1 Corinthians 10\32, 12\13). It has "length of days" correctly at Psalm 23\6, where the King James invents "for ever". It has "Then Jesus spoke", where the King James has the comical and Latinate "Then spake Jesus"(!). Its Romans 9\3 has the verb phrase correct as "I wished myself", where the King James blunders with "I could wish that myself", reinventing and concocting Paul as a saviour of the Israelites. Its Isaiah 9\6 has the promised Messiah as "the Father of the world to come", where the King James blunders with "The everlasting Father".

It is slightly better than the King James Bible.

Protestants have no cause for pride over Catholics for their King James Bible.

With the Douai-Rheims being published in 1610, and its being better in some places than the King James Bible of 1611, and its being respectfully punctuated, was there a need for publication of the King James Bible? I have not found there to be anything of gain from it over the Douai-Rheims. Perhaps the King's men just ignored the Douai-Rheims, although Nicholson suggests they "lifted many plangent phrases" (p. 218).

With the Douai-Rheims being published before the King James Bible, the King's translators would have had time to adjust their Latin-influenced blunders, but they did not.

After the Douai-Rheims Bible was published in 1610, what need was there for the King James Bible to be published the following year, apart from, perhaps, the vanity of the King? The Douai-Rheims Bible has most of the same mistakes they wanted, although not all; they would have needed to falsify a few things and rough up the punctuation.

5. KJV-ONLY
Because the body of Christ is so wayward, there has arisen an aggressive cult of "kjv-only", some even going so far as to say it was inspired by God!! Righteous work does not proceed from evil men. God does not inspire evil men to make corruptions of the writings of His prophets and apostles.

Nothing "impure" may enter the gates of the New Jerusalem. I do not expect to be seeing the King James Bible there. It does have some good word choices here and there, which I would defend. Its prose style is often truer to the text – and less PROCESSED – than modernistic versions (which are also based on false Greek texts). But every major theme of the prophets and apostles is shipwrecked, because the translators were men of the flesh, not men of the spirit, and the intention of their work never was stated as recovering the truths of the prophets and apostles. (Has that ever been the stated intention of any of the church system Bibles?)

6. THE TRANSLATORS' ALLEGIANCE

The preface to the King James Bible exhorts that King James might become "the wonder of the world in this latter age for happiness and true felicity". It addresses him with such flattery as: "Your very name is precious ... their eye doth behold You with comfort, and they bless You in your hearts, as that sanctified Person, who, under God, is the immediate Author of their true happiness. And this their contentment doth not diminish or decay, but every day increaseth and taketh your strength." To the paid translators he was "Your most Sacred Majesty". In fact, to the people he was known as "Queen James".

The King James Bible preface says that the work is "one more exact translation of the Holy Scriptures into the *English Tongue*", implying, perhaps without realising, that it is only "one more" among others.

✱

ed2766

Chapter 30

God Is Not Flesh: Concerning 1 Timothy 3\16
(also in *TELB*, pp. ix-xii, 2021; and in KTK, pp. xii-xv)

✦

At 1 Timothy 3\16 it is necessary to depart from both the TR text and from the RP text on which my translation is based. These texts have the word θεός (= *theos*), "God", so that the King James Bible, for example, reads: "God was manifest in the flesh" (the word "the" in that clause is a saucy and unattractive addition, there being no article in the Greek). There are also, though, ancient Greek manuscripts which read ὅς ("who", or "which", or "he who", or "he"). *Keys of the Kingdom Holy Bible* follows that latter textual reading, and has "He was brought to light in flesh".

The manuscript scholar John Burgon, in his *Revision Revised*, 1883, complains of the texts which have ὅς that the neuter noun μυστήριον (= *musteerion*), "mystery", is followed by a masculine pronoun ὅς (= *hos*) (*Revision Revised*, p. 426). First though, the masculine pronoun does not have to agree with what Burgon saw as its antecedent, μυστήριον. The masculine pronoun acts as the subject of the verb δικαιόω (= *dikaioo*), meaning "was declared righteous", which follows the pronoun and points to Jesus. As antecedent, it can be either an understood reference to Jesus or a remote reference to him. There is such a remote antecedent in 1 John 3\5: "you know that he was brought to light in order that he might take away our sins" – that "he" we know is Jesus; it's just understood.

Second, Paul in Colossians 1\27 has the same construction which Burgon objected to at 1 Timothy 3\16, μυστήριον (neuter) followed by ὅς (masculine). Paul writes: "this mystery [μυστήριον] among the nations, which [ὅς] is Christ among you". That is, a neuter noun followed by a masculine pronoun, just as in 1 Timothy 3\16. Notice that "to make known ... the mystery among the nations ... expectation of magnificence" at Colossians 1\27 is a quiet echo of 1 Timothy 3\16. Notice too that the mystery relates to "Christ", not God. At Colossians 4\3 also, Paul speaks of "the mystery of Christ". So too is the *post-resurrection* Christ the subject of "the mystery" at 1 Timothy 3\16.

My 1895 edition of Westcott's and Hort's *Revised Version* (NT originally 1881) has in the margin at 1 Timothy 3\16: "The word *God* [θεός], in place of *He who* [ὅς], rests on no sufficient ancient evidence". That was a lie, and they must have known it. (Westcott and Hort's rendering of 1 Timothy 3\16 is an ungrammatical horror.) Burgon was able to cite 289 manuscripts having θεός. However, Burgon also described 6 manuscripts having ὅς. It is true that there are far more texts having θεός than there are texts having ὅς, but this is a war of truth, not a simple matter of painting by numbers.

Burgon suggested that ΘC, which is a contracted, uncial form of θεός (contracted as "a sacred name", *nomina sacra*, as some shy men might write G-d for God), got altered to OC, the contracted form of ὅς (eg, Burgon, pp. 442-3). This would be done, Burgon suggests, by the removal of the line in the theta, Θ, either blurred in time or erased deliberately, creating the appearance of an omicron, O: that would then come to be a reading in favour of ὅς. However, if any changing was done, much more likely is it that a line was later *added* to the O, omicron, of OC, to make it into a theta, Θ, done either accidentally, or pulled off deliberately by post-Nicene scribes who saw their chance. The addition of a line would be much easier to pull off than the removal of a line.

There has long been contention over whether or not there is a line in the omicron in Manuscript A. People see what they want to see. Dr. Henry Alford, another great Victorian scholar, and who wrote the lovely song *Come, Ye Thankful People, Come*, speaks of the advantage of microscopic evidence settling the dispute. Writing some two decades before Burgon, Alford had this to say of Manuscript A (his italics): "ος ... *'is now [a] matter of certainty*. The black line at present visible in the o, is a modern retouching of an older but not original fainter one, due apparently to the darkening of the stroke of an ε seen through from the other side. I have examined the page, and find that a portion of the virgula of the ε, seen through, and now corroded through, extends nearly through the Θ, not however quite in, but somewhat above, its centre, as Sir Frederick Madden has observed to me. It was to complete this that Junius made a dot ... Besides which, the mark of abbreviation above the line is modern, not corresponding with those in the MSS. Sir Frederick Madden now informs me that a very powerful microscope has been applied by Professor Maskelyne, at his request, to the passage in the MS, and the result has been that *no trace of either virgula in the* o, *or mark of contraction over it, can be discovered*. It is to be hoped, therefore, that A will never again be cited on the side of [the Received Text]" (Alford, *The Greek Testament*, Vol. III, p. 332).

Alford wrote of the satisfaction of establishing the ὅς reading at 1 Timothy 3\16: "There is hardly a passage in the N.T., in which I feel more deep personal thankfulness for the restoration of the true and wonderful connexion of the original text" (ibid, p. 333).

Textual and grammatical debates aside, the matter is easily decided on internal criteria. On purely internal evidence, the King James Bible's "God ... in ... flesh" cannot be correct. It's all out of joint: there is nothing from Genesis to Revelation to support any notion that God ever appeared in flesh. God, that is, the Father, has not ever appeared in flesh. Jesus said "God *is* spirit" (John 4\24). God is not flesh; God is spirit. In addition, Balaam said "God is not a man ... nor a son of man" (Numbers 23\19). Balaam tells us what God *is not*: a man or a son of man. Jesus tells us what God *is*: spirit. This is the exact opposite of Jesus who was *not* spirit and *is* a man, and he called himself "the Son of Man". In that case, the θεός reading at 1 Timothy 3\16 is impossible and a falsification; it disrupts internal harmony. God is not flesh. It also disrupts sense: there cannot be two who are God.

John says: "every spirit who professes Jesus Christ to have come in flesh is from God" (1 John 4\2-3, 2 John 7). It was not the Father who "came in flesh". It would make no sense for John to say that the Son came in flesh, but then for Paul to have said that God came in flesh. God is "the God and Father of our Lord Jesus Christ" (Ephesians 1\3). The Son cannot be the Father of the Son. The Son was born in flesh, and even after his resurrection he denied being a spirit, saying, "a spirit does not have flesh and bones as you see me having" (Luke 24\39), although having a spiritual body not subject to death (1 Corinthians 15\44-46). God is spirit and always was spirit, and never was flesh, and never will be flesh. No sluicegate of polytheistic spin-doctoring could ever overpower this ecstatic truth.

John Burgon, otherwise a great scholar, has much to say about his textual preference for θεός at 1 Timothy 3\16 and about the phrase "the mystery of godliness" (*Revision Revised*, pp. 497-98). He has little to say, though, about what follows in 1 Timothy 3\16, that it is all so obviously about the resurrected Son, and that it is quite irrelevant to the Father: "he was declared righteous in spirit; he was seen by angels; he was proclaimed among nations; he was believed in *the* world; he was taken up in magnificence." Who, then, was "in flesh" but the Son, "the Son of the Father" (2 John 3)? Does God need to be "declared righteous"? Who could declare Him so? Who was "seen by angels" but the Son? The angels had been seeing God ever since the day He created them. Who was "proclaimed among nations" but the Son? Who was "taken up" to be magnified in Heaven by God but the Son? Just as we "will live with him by *the* power of God", so is it also written that "Christ ... lives by *the* power of God" (2 Corinthians 13\4), and "the fountainhead of Christ *is* God" (1 Corinthians 11\3).

It might be said in accusation that I've made my doctrine ("God is spirit") then I've picked my text (ὅς). However, it would be reasonable to reply, you've picked your text (θεός), then you've made your doctrine. First, though, my doctrine is internal, and is entirely consistent internally, and it fits the context, whereas the other reading fits only an imported, external doctrine. And second, all argument is demolished without any further need of discussion by those simple words spoken by Jesus, "God *is* spirit". It is honouring to God and Christ to represent them in truth. Recall how God spoke to Job's friend Eliphaz: "Yahweh said to Eliphaz the Temanite, 'My anger glows hot against you and against your two friends, for you have not spoken of Me *what is* right'" (Job 42\7).

Now this internal solution to 1 Timothy 3\16 has been brought to light, it is time to be gladly shaking the dust of our feet on the troublesome θεός reading.

And there is yet more. Burgon wanted θεός because, dissatisfied that "God is one" (Romans 3\30 et cetera), he took it that the King James Bible reading of "God was manifest in the flesh" is some mystical statement about a divine incarnation and birth. However, 1 Timothy 3\16 certainly has nothing at all to do with any sort of incarnation and birth. The statement that Jesus "was brought to light in flesh" signifies his *post-resurrection appearances* to his disciples. The six astounding statements which describe the "mystery of godliness" – all indicated by passive verbs – are a summary of the magnificent events concerning Jesus after his resurrection, nothing at all to do with anybody's birth:

He was brought to light in flesh;	~ Mark 16\12, 16\14, John 21\14, 1 John 1\2
he was declared righteous in spirit;	~ John 20\17, 1 Corinthians 15\42-46, Hebrews 9\14
he was seen by angels;	~ Matthew 28\2, John 20\12, Acts 1\10
he was proclaimed among nations;	~ Romans 14\25, Colossians 1\27-28
he was believed in *the* world;	~ Acts 2\41, Romans 1\8
he was taken up in magnificence.	~ Mark 16\19, Luke 24\51, Acts 1\9-11

The Greek for "he was brought to light" is ἐφανερώθη (= *ephanerothee*). This word ἐφανερώθη has nothing to do with any incarnation of anybody. The word in that exact form occurs in relation to Jesus" post-resurrection appearances:[1] "After these things, he was brought to light [ἐφανερώθη] in a different form" (Mark 16\12); "Later, in their sitting together eating, he was brought to light [ἐφανερώθη] to the eleven" (Mark 16\14); "This *is* the third time now that Jesus was brought to light [ἐφανερώθη] to the disciples" (John 21\14); and, "for the life also was brought to light [ἐφανερώθη] – and *that which* we have seen and given witness to, and proclaim to you, the eonian life which was in relation to the Father, and was brought to light [ἐφανερώθη] to us" (1 John 1\2). (In the gospels the King James Bible wrongly has those as active verbs, such as "he appeared", so that the positive link to 1 Timothy 3\16 is less likely to be noticed.) The same verb is used in the active form at John 21\1: "After these things, Jesus again brought himself to light [ἐφανέρωσεν] to the disciples on the Sea of Tiberias". Luke says Jesus gave directions to the apostles "to whom with much indubitable evidence he presented himself alive after his suffering, being seen by them throughout forty days, and speaking of the things concerning the Kingdom of God" (Luke 1\2-3). These are passages we should have in mind in relation to Jesus "being brought to light" in 1 Timothy 3\16.

These post-resurrection appearances of Jesus are exactly what Paul is referring to at 1 Timothy 3\16 in his saying Jesus "was brought to light [ἐφανερώθη] in flesh". The phrase "in flesh" is

---

1. The full list of occurrences of this passive verb form ἐφανερώθη is: Mark 16\12, 16\14, John 21\14, Colossians 1\26, 1 Timothy 3\16, 1 John 1\2 (twice), 3\2, 3\5, 3\8, 4\9.

set in apposition to the phrase, "in spirit". So the resurrection body is flesh, but it is incapable of sin. Jesus was born flesh, resurrected flesh and bones (Luke 24\39, Ezekiel 37\4-13), and received the resurrection "spiritual body" (1 Corinthians 15\42-46). The "spiritual *was* not first, but the natural. The spiritual *came* afterwards".

So centuries of debates about some mystical incarnation were an irrelevance.

✶

ed20B

Select Bibliography

Alford, Henry, *The Greek Testament*, Vols. I-IV, Deighton, Bell, And Co., 3rd Edition (1866)
Alter, Robert, *The Art of Bible Translation*, Princeton University Press, 2019
Bagster, Samuel, *The Analytical Greek Lexicon*, Samuel Bagster & Sons Limited, London W1 (1973, originally published 1870)
Bagster, Samuel *The Englishman's Greek New Testament*, Samuel Bagster & Sons Limited, London W1 (1896, originally published 1877)
Bagster, Samuel, *The Interlinear Greek-English New Testament*, Samuel Bagster & Sons Limited, London W1 (1958)
Benson, Reed, *The Anglo-Israel Thesis*, Watchman Outreach Ministries, Missouri (2013)
Berry, George Ricker, *Interlinear Greek-English New Testament*, Baker Book House, Michigan (1991, originally published 1897Bullinger, EW, *A Critical Lexicon and Concordance of the English and Greek New Testament*, Zondervan Publishing House, Grand Rapids, Michigan 49530 (1975, first published 1887)
Bluer, Dr. Peter, *The Conspiracy. Why is μέλλω missing 32 times ...?*, www.biblemaths.com
Bluer, Dr. Peter, *The Truth about Eternal Hell Fire*, www.biblemaths.com
Elliger K and Rudolph W, *Biblia Hebraica Stuttgartensia*, תורה נביים וכתובים (= Torah, Nevi'im, ve Kethuvim, Law, Prophets, and Psalms), a Hebrew text, 2nd edition, ed. W Rudolph and HP Rüger, Deutsche Bibelgesellschaft, 70567 Stuttgart (1984, first published 1967)
Bullinger, EW, *Also: A Biblical Study of the Usage of This Word in the Gospels and New Testament*, American Christian Press, New Knoxville, Ohio 45871 (no date)
Bullinger, EW, *Figures of Speech Used in the Bible Explained and Illustrated*, Baker Book House, Grand Rapids, Michigan (1968, originally published 1898)
Bullinger, EW, *How to Enjoy the Bible*, Kregel Publications, Grand Rapids, Michigan 49501 (1990, originally published 1907)
EW Bullinger, *Number in Scripture: Its Supernatural Design and Spiritual Significance*, Kregel Publications, Grand Rapids, Michigan (1967)
Bullinger, EW, *The Book of Job*, Kregel Publications, Grand Rapids, Michigan 49501 (1990, originally published ?)
Bullinger, EW, *The Companion Bible*, Kregel Publications, Grand Rapids, Michigan 49501 (1990, 1st part 1909, complete volume 1922)
Bullinger, EW, *The Divine Names and Titles*, Truth for Today Bible Fellowship, P.O. Box 6358, Lafayette, IN 47903 (1983, originally published ?)
Bullinger, EW, *The Rich Man and Lazarus: the intermediate state*, The Open Bible Trust (1992, originally published 1902)
Bullinger, EW, *The Witness of the Stars*, Kregel Publications, Grand Rapids, Michigan 49501 (1993, originally published 1893)
Bullinger, EW, *Word Studies on the Holy Spirit*, Kregel Publications, Grand Rapids, Michigan 49501 (1979, originally published 1905)
Burgon, John, *The Revision Revised: a Refutation of Westcott and Hort's False Greek Text and Theory*, distributed by Penfold Book & Bible House, Bicester, Oxon, OX6 8PB (no date, originally published 1883)
Burgon, John, *The Last Twelve Verses of the Gospel According to Mark*, The Sovereign Grace Book Club, Michigan, (1959, originally published 1871)
Capt, E Raymond, *Stonehenge and Druidism*, Dolores Press (1983)
Capt, E Raymond, *The Lost Chapter of the Acts of the Apostles*, Artisan Publishers, PO Box 1529, Muskogee, Oklahoma, 74402 (1982)
Capt, E Raymond, *The Traditions of Glastonbury*, Artisan Sales (1983)
Capt, E Raymond, 'What Happened To The 12 Tribes Of Israel', https://www.youtube.com/watch?v=xAMRvGWnybI, YouTube (2011)
Daniell, David (ed.), *William Tyndale's New Testament*, ©1995 by Yale University. Originally published by Yale University Press
Daniell, David (ed.), *Tyndale's Old Testament: A modern-spelling edition*, ©1992 by Yale University. Originally published by Yale University Press

Davidson, Benjamin, *The Analytical Hebrew and Chaldee Lexicon*, Hendrickson Publishers, Peabody, Michigan, 01961-3473 (1981, originally published 1848)
Dodson, John Jeffrey, *The Greek New Testament for Beginning Readers: Byzantine Textform*, VTR Publications, Nürnberg, Germany (no date)
Fowler, Alan and Margaret, *Exploring Bible Language*, Ortho Books, High View, Litchard Rise, Bridgend, CF31 1QJ (1998)
Gesenius, HWF, *Hebrew and Chaldee Lexicon to the Old Testament Scriptures*, Baker Books, Grand Rapids, Michigan 49516 (1996, originally published 1847)
Green, Jay P Sr., *Interlinear Bible: Greek-English*, Baker Books, Grand Rapids, Michigan 49516, 4th edition (1996, first published 1980)
Green, Jay P Sr., *Interlinear Bible: Hebrew-Greek-English*, Sovereign Grace Publishers, Lafayette, Indiana (1986)
Hislop, Alexander, *The Two Babylons*, SW Partridge & Co, London (1916)
Hoffman, Nathan, https://www.youtube.com/watch?v=VI1yRTC6kGE, titled "Were the pyramids built before the flood?", YouTube channel NathanH83 (2017)
Johnson, James, *Reconciling Isaiah 65:20*, http://allpowertothelamb.com/2016/04/reconciling-isaiah/ (2016)
Josephus, *The Works of Flavius Josephus*, translated by William Whiston, Nimmo, Hay, & Mitchell, Edinburgh (no date)
Jowett, George F, *The Drama of the Lost Disciples*, Covenant Publishing (2011)
Keller, Werner *The Bible as History (Revised): Archaeology confirms the Book of Books*, Hodder and Stoughton (1980)
Knoch, AE, *The Concordant Literal Version*, Concordant Publishing Concern, 15570 Knochaven Road, Santa Clarita, CA 91387 (first published 1926)
La Sainte Bible, Trinitarian Bible Society, London (1995)
Liddell and Scott, *An Intermediate Greek-English Lexicon*, Oxford (1889)
Literal Idiomatic Translation, Hal Dekker, http://www.believershomepage.com/index.html
Marshall, Alfred, *The Interlinear Greek-English New Testament: the Nestle Greek Text*, Samuel Bagster and Sons Ltd, Second Edition (1966)
Martin, Ernst L, *Restoring the Original Bible*, Associates for Scriptural Knowledge, askelm.com
Mitchell, Jonathan, *The New Testament, Expanded, Amplified, Multiple Renderings*, Harper Brown Publishing, USA (2009), www.johnsonmitchellnewtestament.com
Nicolson, Adam, *Power and Glory: Jacobean England and the Making of the King James Bible*, HarperCollins (2003)
Novum Testamentum Latine (New Testament in Latin), Wordsworth *& White, Simon Wallenberg Press (2007, originally published 1889)
Petri, William, *The Universal Version Bible: The Greek Scriptures*, Beacon-Ministries Publishing, 7 Losson Garden Dr. #3, Cheektowaga, NY 14227 (2016); www.beacon-ministries.org
Roberts, Robert, *Christendom Astray*, C Walker, Birmingham England (1937, originally published 1884)
Robinson, Maurice A, and Pierpont, William G, *The New Testament in the Original Greek, Byzantine Textform 2005*, Chilton Book Publishing, MA 01772-0606 (2005) ISBN 0-7598-0077-4 (2005) (and available online at http://www.byztxt.com/GreekNT/RP2005.htm)
Robinson, MA, and Pierpont, WG, *Byzantine Parsed Text*, 2000, http://www.byztxt.com/download
Rogers, John, *New Testament (1537) Tindale's Triumph, John Rogers' Monument: The Newe Testament of the Matthew's Bible*, The Martyrs Bible Series, John Wesley Sawyer, PO Box 12964, Houston, 77217-2964 (1989)
Salemi, Peter, *The Throne of David in Prophecy*, BICOG, www.british-israel.ca (2019?)
Scrivener, FH, *Novum Testamentum (New Testament in Greek)*, Cambridge (1877)
Sellers, Otis Q, *Seed & Bread, Volumes 1 & 2*, The Word of Truth Ministry, Los Angeles (c1980)
Sellers, Otis Q, *The Challenge Stands*, The Word of Truth Ministry (1960)
Sellers, Otis Q, *The Earth, not Heaven, is the Future Home of God's Redeemed*, The Word of Truth Ministry (1955)
Sellers, Otis Q, *The Foundation of the World*, The Word of Truth Ministry (c1958)
Southgate, Peter J, and Wharton, Clifford J., *Revelation Explained* (2013), The Dawn Book Supply, 5 Station Road, Carlton, Nottingham, NG4 3AT, England
Sparkes, Christopher, "The Israelites in Dispersion. John 7/35". YouTube video, https://www.youtube.com/watch?v=68s2miq42-A&t=19s
Sparkes, Christopher, "John's Gospel, the Prologue. Translating verse 3"

https://www.youtube.com/watch?v=BW3vMTlByK4&t=107s
Sparkes, Christopher, "Who is the "satan" in Job? Job, Part 2 of 3",
  https://www.youtube.com/watch?v=vN4zQVC2rI8&t=389s
Sparkes, Christopher, "Would Paul have been with Christ in death? Philippians 1/23."
  https://www.youtube.com/watch?v=xXiutptv__E
Sweet, Colin, *Hell & Judgment in the Book of Revelation*, The Open Bible Trust (1992)
Tanakh: The Holy Scriptures, The Jewish Publication Society, Philadelphia (1985)
Thayer, Joseph H, *Thayer's Greek-English Lexicon of the New Testament*, Baker Book House,
  Grand Rapids, Michigan (1977, originally published 1901)
"thelivingword" YouTube, *Hidden code in Genesis 1:1*,
  www.youtube.com/watch?v=vyvqqkGP_kg (2015);
The New Bible Commentary Revised, ed. D. Guthrie et al, Inter-Varsity Press (1970)
The New Bible Dictionary, ed. JD Douglas et al, Inter-Varsity Press (1978)
The New King James Version, Thomas Nelson Publishers, Nashville (1985)
The Revised Version, Oxford University Press, Oxford (1895)
The Two Preachers, YouTube, *2018 update! Shroud of Turin reveals secrets. Strange
  End Times Signs*, www.youtube.com/watch?v=KBycQZug8Fo
Thomason, Graham, *Far Above All Translation of the New Testament*, www.FarAboveAll.com (2020)
Thomason, Graham, *Greek Prepositions and Conjunctions*, www.FarAboveAll.com
Thomason, Graham, *Scripture, Authentic and Fabricated*, www.FarAboveAll.com
Thomason, Graham, *Translation Issues in the New Testament*, www.FarAboveAll.com
Thriepland, LJ, *Did Jesus Die on a Cross?*, www.FollowInTruth,
  https://www.youtube.com/watch?v=0pTBlCSTDdo&feature=youtu.be (2019)
Tolstoy, Leo, *My Religion: What I Believe*, White Crow Books (2009, originally 1894)
Vine, WE, *Expository Dictionary of Bible Words*, Marshall Morgan & Scott, London (1981)
Vulgate – Novum Testamentum Latine, Simon Wallberg 1889, reprinted by Simon Wallberg Press (2007)
Westcott, BF, *The Bible in the Church*, Macmillan and Co (1866)
Westcott, BF, *The Gospel of John*, John Murray, London (1882)
Whitehouse, TH, *Ezekiel's Temple and Sacrifices*, Covenant Publishing, Co. Durham, DL14 0HA (2009)
Wigram, George V, *The Englishman's Greek Concordance of the New Testament*, Hendrickson Publishers, Inc.,
  PO Box 3473, Peabody, Massachusetts 01961-3473 (1999, originally published 1839)
Wigram, George V, *The Englishman's Hebrew Concordance of the Old Testament*, Hendrickson Publishers, Inc.,
  PO Box 3473, Peabody, Massachusetts 01961-3473 (1999, originally published 1874)
Williams, George, *The Student's Commentary On The Holy Scriptures*, Chas. J. Thynne & Jarvis, Ltd.,
  2nd ed. (no date)
Woodward, S Douglas, *The Witness of Ancient Scholars Verifies the Septuagint's Longer Chronology Is What the
  Original Hebrew Revealed*, https://faith-happens.com (2019)
Wilson, Benjamin, *The Emphatic Diaglott*, International Bible Students Association, Brooklyn (1864)
Young, Robert, *Analytical Concordance To The Holy Bible*, Lutterworth Press (1879)
Young, Robert, *Young's Literal Translation*, Greater Truth Publishers, PO Box 4332, Lafayette, IN 47903
  (2005, originally published 1862)

~ ✶✶ ~

Honours and Acknowledgments

No work such as this can be undertaken without its author benefitting ten thousand-fold from the multitude of the golden-rich fruits of others' labours. I am indescribably indebted to the following scholars and friends whose works have been a guide and inspiration, whose majestic lexical works have not been surpassed, and without whom this work would be impoverished and would have taken twice as long:

John Wycliffe, and William Tyndale (assassinated 1536), who both worked outside the city gates to make the God-authorized Books available in English;
George V Wigram, for his Hebrew and Greek concordances;
HWF Gesenius, for his Hebrew and Chaldee lexicon;
Benjamin Davidson, for his Analytical Hebrew and Chaldee lexicon;
Samuel Bagster, for his analytical Greek lexicon, and his Greek interlinear;
Robert Young, for his Analytical Concordance;
Dr Henry Alford, for the depth of his commentary, and initiating an emphasis on philology (rather than traditional homiletic commentary);
John Burgon, for his *Revision Revised*, and his other textual masterpieces, and who defended the Majority Greek texts from illogical and ill-founded attack;
Dr Ethelbert William Bullinger for his *Companion Bible* and other works, and who began the superior enhancements to translation and understanding, and who worked outside the city gate;
James Strong, for his Concordance, and for his inspired numbering system, a magnificent moment in Biblical history;
George Ricker Berry, for his Greek interlinear;
Joseph H Thayer, for his Greek-English lexicon, which is the most impressive book I've ever seen;
Otis Q Sellers, for his 200 *Seed & Bread* studies, and other works, and who furthered the quest for superior enhancements to translation and understanding, and who worked outside the city gate;
Jay P Green Sr., for his Hebrew and Greek interlinears, the most important books of the twentieth century;
Errol Palmer, whose conversations in the summer of 1997 in Berwick-on-Tweed helped to get this work started;
Maurice A Robinson and William G Pierpont, for their Byzantine Textform 2005, to date the most important book of the twenty-first century, representing probably the closest we have to the writings of the apostles;
Dr Graham Thomason, for his outstanding textual work, translation work, and countless advices;
Professor David Daniell, for his brilliant and inspiring work on William Tyndale;
Darren Nesbit for diligent editing and proofreading and copious suggestions;
another editor and proofreader who helped me with many understandings and who wishes to remain anonymous;
William Petri for his explanations of the NT order in his *Universal Version Bible*; and my friend and brother Wayne Sturgeon for introducing me to much superb research and work I would not otherwise have known;
Peter Southgate and Clifford J Wharton for their masterpiece concerning the Apocalypse, *Revelation Explained* (2013);
my late friends Rowland Wickes (author of *The Path to Immortality*) and Errol Palmer whose conversations in Berwick-on-Tweed and Llandudno set me on this course in 1997; Grzegorz Kaszyński, for diligent research on translation variations in international versions; Paul Ferdinand, for high quality editing and proofreading of early drafts, and for his own careful studies; Chris Wildtham for his inspiring teaching; Gordon Price, Sarah Lucas, Solomon Rodriguez and many diligent friends for encouragement, insights, suggestions and corrections along the way, and for enduring enthusiastic advice and helps; authors of countless other books and studies that have helped in understanding words and themes and wider concepts concerning this work; my son for questions leading to sharper clarifications; Chris Day of Filament Publishing for countless and tireless helps, advices, and support.

Christopher Sparkes was born in Birmingham in 1951, and lives in Hampshire, England. After lecturing in Higher and Further Education, he is now a free-lance editor and educator. He has run writing groups, a folk and poetry club, and managed a trout fishery. As well as being co-author of textbooks on writing and grammar, he has published poetry, short fiction, academic essays on poetry and stylistics, reviews and artworks. His other interests are cricket, trout fishing, cycling, oil painting, birdwatching, and playing the guitar and harmonica.

www.ingramcontent.com/pod-product-compliance
Lightning Source LLC
Chambersburg PA
CBHW041316110526
44591CB00021B/2802